Ghost Faces

Metropolitan College of NY
Library - 7th Floor
60 West Street
New York, NY 10006

THE SUNY SERIES

MURRAY POMERANCE | EDITOR

Also in the series

William Rothman, editor, *Cavell on Film*

J. David Slocum, editor, *Rebel Without a Cause*

Joe McElhaney, *The Death of Classical Cinema*

Kirsten Moana Thompson, *Apocalyptic Dread*

Frances Gateward, editor, *Seoul Searching*

Michael Atkinson, editor, *Exile Cinema*

Bert Cardullo, *Soundings on Cinema*

Paul S. Moore, *Now Playing*

Robin L. Murray and Joseph K. Heumann, *Ecology and Popular Film*

William Rothman, editor, *Three Documentary Filmmakers*

Sean Griffin, editor, *Hetero*

Jean-Michel Frodon, editor, *Cinema and the Shoah*

Carolyn Jess-Cooke and Constantine Verevis, editors, *Second Takes*

Matthew Solomon, editor, *Fantastic Voyages of the Cinematic Imagination*

R. Barton Palmer and David Boyd, editors, *Hitchcock at the Source*

William Rothman, *Hitchcock, Second Edition*

Joanna Hearne, *Native Recognition*

Marc Raymond, *Hollywood's New Yorker*

Steven Rybin and Will Scheibel, editors, *Lonely Places, Dangerous Ground*

Claire Perkins and Constantine Verevis, editors, *B Is for Bad Cinema*

Dominic Lennard, *Bad Seeds and Holy Terrors*

Rosie Thomas, *Bombay before Bollywood*

Sudhir Mahadevan, *A Very Old Machine*

PN
1995.9
.M46
G73
2016

Ghost Faces

Hollywood and Post-Millennial Masculinity

DAVID GREVEN

Metropolitan College of NY
Library - 7th Floor
60 West Street
New York, NY 10006

Published by State University of New York Press, Albany

© 2016 State University of New York

All rights reserved

Printed in the United States of America

No part of this book may be used or reproduced in any manner whatsoever without written permission. No part of this book may be stored in a retrieval system or transmitted in any form or by any means including electronic, electrostatic, magnetic tape, mechanical, photocopying, recording, or otherwise without the prior permission in writing of the publisher.

For information, contact State University of New York Press, Albany, NY
www.sunypress.edu

Production, Eileen Nizer
Marketing, Fran Keneston

Library of Congress Cataloging-in-Publication Data

Greven, David.
   Ghost faces : Hollywood and post-millennial masculinity / David Greven.
      pages cm
   Includes bibliographical references and index.
   ISBN 978-1-4384-6007-9 (hc : alk. paper)—978-1-4384-6006-2 (pb : alk. paper)
   ISBN 978-1-4384-6008-6 (e-book)
   1. Masculinity in motion pictures. 2. Homosexuality in motion pictures.
3. Motion pictures—United States—History and criticism. I. Title.

   PN1995.9.M46G73 2015
   791.43'65211—dc23
                                                     2015015566

10 9 8 7 6 5 4 3 2 1

Contents

List of Illustrations		vii
Acknowledgments		ix
Introduction: Disrecognitions		1
Chapter 1	Ghost Faces, Genre Bodies	45
Chapter 2	The Murderous Origins of Bromance: Genre, Queer Killers, and *Scream*	71
Chapter 3	"I Love You, Brom Bones": Beta Male Comedies, Bromances, and American Culture	105
Chapter 4	Apparitional Men: Masculinity and the Psychoanalytic Scene	135
Chapter 5	Trick-or-Treating Alone: Rob Zombie's *Halloween*	169
Chapter 6	Torture/Porn: *Hostel*, Homophobia, and Gay Male Internet Pornography	197
Coda		239
Notes		241
Bibliography		279
Index		295

Illustrations

Figure I.1	A secondary mirror stage: Bateman as Reynolds stares at himself in the mirror.	23
Figure I.2	Homoerotic doubling: The "changed-up" Bateman and Reynolds stare at themselves and each other in the mirror.	24
Figure I.3	Carell's character stares up at Gosling's amply displayed body.	28
Figure I.4	Gosling looms above Carell, his phallus signified by its absence.	29
Figure I.5	Gosling remains standing, visually dominant and demanding to be admired.	29
Figure 2.1	Edvard Munch, *The Scream*.	77
Figure 2.2	Homoerotic menace: Stu traces a line with his finger across Randy's ear.	87
Figure 2.3	Ghostface both proclaims and obscures an opposition to heterosexual desire.	89
Figure 2.4	Billy, the beautiful boy as destroyer.	98
Figure 3.1	*I Love You, Man* begins with a proposal and ends with marriage between the heterosexual couple.	122
Figure 3.2	Homosocial comfort and intimacy in *I Love You, Man*.	133
Figure 4.1	Monty and the mirror stage.	157
Figure 5.1	Trick-or-treating alone.	181
Figure 5.2	Portrait of the artist as a child monster: Michael's masks.	193

Figure 6.1	Theatrical poster for *Hostel* (2005).	207
Figure 6.2	Theatrical poster for *Hellbent* (2005).	208
Figure 6.3	The three backpackers, hardly innocents and on the verge of a nightmare.	210
Figure 6.4	Paxton, the Hispanic-American as the Ugly American.	216
Figure 6.5	Josh and the Dutch Businessman are paired and doubled.	217
Figure 6.6	"And what is *your* nature?"	217

Acknowledgments

Previously published versions of two of the chapters exist. I want to thank Taylor and Francis for giving me permission to reprint "I Love You, Brom Bones: Beta Male Comedies and American Culture," which was published in *Quarterly Review of Film and Video*, Issue 30.3, May 2013, and Wayne State University Press for the permission to reprint "Fears of a Millennial Masculinity: *Scream*'s Queer Killers," *Reading the Bromance: Homosocial Relationships in Film and Television*, ed. Michael DeAngelis (Detroit, MI: Wayne State University Press, 2014), 79–108. These articles have been revised and expanded for this book. This book has its conceptual origins in a paper that I delivered at the *Society for Cinema and Media Studies* annual conference of March 2011, "I Love You, Brom Bones": Beta Male Comedies, Homophobia, and the History of American Masculinity." I was invited to be on this panel by Amanda Lotz and Brenda Weber, and it included another panelist, Anna Froula. To be on a panel with such distinguished and insightful scholars was an honor, and to have the chance to learn from their provocative work a privilege. I also had the chance to work with Brenda Weber and contribute to her collection of essays, *Reality Gendervision* (Duke University Press, 2014), much to my delight and gratitude. I am also most grateful to Michael DeAngelis, a truly insightful critic who is also an exceptionally generous and warm mentor. I am honored to have been able to work with him and contribute an essay to *Reading the Bromance*. I extend my thanks to Timothy Shary for inviting me to contribute to *Millennial Masculinity* (Wayne State University Press, 2012) and to Jennifer Greiman and Paul Stasi for having done so with their reader on *Deadwood, The Last Western* (Continuum, 2012). These editors and fellow scholars have taught me an inestimable amount about good writing and the inspiring potentialities of collaboration. I want to thank my SUNY Press editor Beth Bouloukos immensely for her support of the project, and the SUNY team for their excellent work. I also thank Tony McLawhorn, my department's Computer

Support Manager, for his tireless and expert help with the images for this book. I have learned so much over the years from the great critic Tania Modleski, and I am grateful to have had the chance to learn from her work on bromances as well. I have many dear friends to thank, but a special note of gratitude to James Bogdanski, not only for getting me to give *Man of Steel* (Zack Snyder, 2013) another chance, and therefore benefit from the love I discovered for the film, but for his loyalty, kindness, and love of movies, television, and the popular culture gamut. As ever, I thank my family for their love and support, my friends for being the embodiment of these values, and, most of all, my partner Alexander Beecroft, whose love and support gives my life its sustaining joy.

Introduction

Disrecognitions

Ghost Faces argues that the representation of masculinity in mainstream films of the twenty-first century is both marked by an awareness of queer visibility and reflective of the irreducibly difficult problem that queerness poses to United States culture, however much progress has been made for LGBTQI rights in the past two decades. Even as the traditional cinematic model of straight, white masculinity buckles under the pressure of an ever-more-visible queer presence, mainstream films continue to maintain this model as the standard. What has resulted is a straight, white, male image reflective of queer potentialities and closed off from them. The divided nature of normative screen masculinity—striving to be current in its acknowledgment of queer desire, on the one hand, but maintaining its resistance to queerness in order to remain a coherent version of itself, on the other hand—has lent itself to suggestive levels of scrutiny with some disturbing implications. As I outline in chapter 1, my contention is that this period's filmmaking is sadomasochistic in its treatment of male characters. Through a queer reframing of Laura Mulvey's and Gilles Deleuze's paradigms, among others, I argue that this sadomasochism and its relationship to queerness find expression through a voyeuristic fascination with male bodies and a fetishistic one with the male face. A preoccupation with Deleuzian "faciality" intersects with Mulvey's theories of gendered cinematic representation when applied to the male forms offered for spectatorial consumption. The focus of this book is on genre film, comedy and horror especially, because of genre's close ties to the representation of masculinity, a historical trend that has become only more apparent in contemporary moviemaking, devoted in the main to franchise films, sequels, and action epics that all proceed from the basis of genre classification.

My close readings of films begin with Wes Craven's *Scream* (1996), which I establish as a crucial text both for the horror genre that it innovated and for its early exploration of the kind of ambiguous male-bonding that would come to be called the bromance in the post-millennial years. I then turn to a discussion of the new, interrelated styles of comedy in the '00s that foreground masculinity, such as the bromance and the "beta male" comedy pioneered by the director, screenwriter, and producer Judd Apatow. Subsequent chapters consider films such as *Donnie Darko* (Richard Kelly, 2001), *25th Hour* (Spike Lee, 2002), *Halloween* (Rob Zombie, 2007), and *Hostel* (Eli Roth, 2005) as representative of the post-millennial era's mutually reinforcing fascinations with male bodies and male faces, which emerge as allegorical zones as well as literal sites of cinematic interest for the depiction of male subjectivity, sexuality, and physicality in a post-queer moment. I pair gay male Internet pornography with my discussion of *Hostel*, tracing the disquieting lines of connection between both.

I want to establish at the outset that, while I attempt to locate my argument and choice of films in a specific historical period, this is not an analysis situated in reception studies or production history. Rather, it is an attempt to combine approaches from queer theory and psychoanalysis in the interpretation of contemporary images of masculinity that resonate with themes and motifs in antebellum American literature, the Gothic in particular, as I will expand in chapter 1. My effort is to demonstrate that the meanings of difficult, diffuse topics like the insidious nature of homophobia within texts that promote their own homo-tolerance and/or offer ostensibly less conventional portraits of masculinity, even those that appear to destabilize the male hegemon, can only be drawn out through close reading and interpretation. There is an entirely related and distinct book on these topics to be written about in terms of television of the same post-millennial period; indeed, I initially had hoped to write a book about both film and television. While many of the dynamics that inform portrayals of masculinity in film of the period can be found in post-millennial television works, and I will make frequent reference to them, the latter demand a discrete study.[1]

Narcissism, Masochism, and Contemporary Hollywood Masculinity: That Was Then, This Is Now

In some ways, the present study is a sequel of sorts to my 2009 book *Manhood in Hollywood from Bush to Bush*. There, I argued that certain works made within the Hollywood machine, or despite it, right before, during, and after the rise of queer identity in the early 1990s provided real, even heady alternatives to masculinist power as well as genuine opportunities for queer fantasy and appropriation, opportunities that in some cases were actively pursued by the films and/or filmmakers themselves. My contention was that narcissistic displays of beauty were potentially more subversive sites for queer desire than the masochism that was frequently framed in critical writing as a subversive "ruination of masculinity." I critiqued the valorization of masochism as a resistant mode of male gender performance in the writings of critics such as Kaja Silverman (1992), Leo Bersani (1995), and Gaylyn Studlar (1993) and the anti-social thesis, as it has been called, in the works of Bersani (1995) and Lee Edelman (2005).[2] Despite my deep admiration for all of these critics, I felt that it was important to register two key points: first, that masochism need not necessarily be a subversive mode of male gender performance but could, instead, reflect reactionary fantasies of the suffering and essential pitiability of the very males who wielded power in dominant culture, in other words a sentimental fantasy that benefitted these males; and second, that gay male masochism, embodied in Bersani's influential but problematic theory of passive gay male sexuality and "self-shattering," was less than a radical construct, not necessarily the profound resistance to normative modes of sexuality that Bersani artfully suggested it might be. Principally, what I critiqued was the associations made between queer male sexuality and the death drive, both as theorized within psychoanalysis and as made evident in cultural practice. Inspired by Robin Wood's discussion of a battle between life drive and death drive forces in his *Sexual Politics and Narrative Film*, I explored Freud's less-discussed theory of the life drive as an alternative to what, it seemed to me at the time, was the enshrinement of the death drive in High Queer Theory.

Writing as a critical queer viewer, I found moments to appropriate and to celebrate in films from the 1990s and the early 2000s that provocatively pushed the envelope or afforded the queer viewer ample opportunities for contemplation. Narcissism, it seemed to me, emerged in the period as a newly valuable rubric for the interpretation of queer-inflected representation—male beauty and self-regard now indicated a borderline-teasing fascination with the increasing openness and visibility of queer desire, a kind of mutual gaze between the narcissistically self-fascinated heterosexual male and the appraising, emboldened queer male subject. Masochism, in my view, had come to seem a hallmark of the fading, frustrated, hypocritical masculinities of the past—the Rambos of the Reagan '80s, to begin with, and their furious cries of reactionary pain, but also Kevin Costner's John J. Dunbar, a Union Army First Lieutenant, arms outstretched and waiting to be riddled with Confederate bullets as he rides on a horse, in the opening moments of *Dances with Wolves* (1990), the lumbering Civil War-era epic

Western that Costner directed and in which the sensitive, white male hero aligns himself with noble Native Americans (here the Sioux) against white male tyranny[3]; Mel Gibson playing William Wallace, a thirteenth-century Scottish rebel against British rule, in *Braveheart*, another masochistic epic directed by the star of the film (1995); Michael Douglas in umpteen movies in which his apparently irresistible charms incite volcanic passions in unstable women, much to his characters' dismay; *Gladiator* (Ridley Scott, 2000), with Russell Crowe's titular figure mourning for his lost wife and son in ancient Rome, all of his ferocious physical feats laced with burning emotional pain, and whose chief adversary is the cruel and sexually ambiguous Commodus (Joaquin Phoenix), prone to exclaiming in queenly fashion "I'm vexed—I'm terribly vexed"; and so forth. Masochism seemed less than subversive when associated with straight, white men, downright infuriating when ennobled as gay male resistance to the normative sexual order—infuriating because this was a resistance that reified the usual associations of gay masculinity with passivity and that was predicated on the annihilation of the gay male subject. In sum, I imagined that we were entering a heady new era of polymorphous-perverse sexual openness in the Bush-to-Bush era even as its murderous and annihilating agendas continued to intensify; perhaps this new sexual openness might be a means of resistance (however limited in the larger context of this geopolitical crisis).

I stand by the arguments that I made in *Manhood in Hollywood from Bush to Bush*. But such perspectives do not animate the current book. The films of the '00s have largely committed themselves to re-entrenching the male status quo and shoring up its ruins; to producing, precisely through assault, destruction, and a seeming consignment to obsolescence that actually functions as a project of renewal, a revivified and newly resilient version of the traditional male model.

The representation of masculinity has certainly become more diverse. Traditional modes of masculinity have come to seem like parodistic put-ons, forms of male drag. Forms of maleness that run athwart the normative model—the queer heterosexual, the trans male—seem less like disruptive alternatives to this model and more like prognostications of the male future. Yet the development of a non-misogynist, non-racist, non-homophobic, non-hegemonic form of masculinity still seems to be an elusive goal, much less the formation of an oppositional cinema that was the hope of so many in previous decades. As I will show, the films of the '00s have largely been an attempt to put the queer genie back in the bottle of straight masculinity. The re-entrenchment of hegemonic manhood, the remasculinization of wayward men, has been a wide-ranging, urgent project.

A startling new interest in exposing and exploring the secret depths of manhood—at times contained within the private homosocial spaces of men, sometimes shown to be housed in the male body itself—characterizes post-millennial film. The strategies for the containment and remasculinization of wayward masculinities include a decisive exposure of male bodies, one that is at times sexually tinged but is more often about states of bodily extremity that exceed or demonstrate little interest in questions and experiences of sexuality. For example, male-centered comedies routinely feature male bodies that are physically exposed to a certain degree, but the emphasis is often on public humiliation and/or scatological humor taken to extremes, not on suggestive eroticism. Similarly, horror films subject the male body to violations on screen, but without an overriding interest in producing erotic effects, overall. While outsize masculinities have proliferated on the screen since the 1980s, the films of the '00s emphasize depictions of male bodies in states of physical and emotional torment. I will further elaborate on the issue of the relationship between the male body and the body genres of contemporary film in a later section.

Linked analogies, to wax Melvillean, can be found in the twenty-first-century American cinema between the male body on display and another striking preoccupation: the male face. The almost obsessive interest with male faces that runs rife through films (and television) works of the '00s in some ways counterbalances the interest in male bodies, but is more accurately described as complementary to it. Male faces in contemporary film metaphorize the recurrence of previous images of American masculinity in the post-9/11 moment, as I will explain further. Chapter 1 theorizes these uses of male bodies and faces.

Aftershock: Straight Masculinity after Queer

To whatever extent masculinity remains the embodiment of national power, queerness threatens the cultural stability of hegemonic manhood. As R. W. Connell writes in *Masculinities*, "The patriarchal order prohibits forms of emotion, attachment and pleasure that patriarchal society itself produces. Tensions develop around sexual inequality and men's rights in marriage, around the prohibition on homosexual affection (given that patriarchy constantly produces homo-social institutions), and around the threat to social order symbolized by sexual freedoms."[4]

The threat that queerness poses lies in its perceived challenge to the integrity, resolve, and coherence of a masculinity that understands itself as white and heterosexual, not feminine, not gay, not queer, not other. Masculinity is defined, as Richard Dyer writes in his essay "The White Man's Muscles," by "hardness and contour." These defining qualities "protect the male body . . . from the threat posed by the possibility of being mistaken for female or drawn into the state of femininity, both of which constitute a loss of male power."[5] We can argue that gayness, queerness, and non-whiteness pose analogous threats. As I will show, the imperative to maintain identity and conformity to it—the lockdown of masculine identity and the strict control over the markers of this identity—in the face of ever-increasing queer visibility has rendered the maintenance and successful embodiment of twenty-first-century masculinities particularly vexed as national, cultural, social, and aesthetic projects. Assaults against the hardness and contour of male bodies repeatedly occur in twenty-first-century film, bodies that have been put on display in the first place. The films then work to restore these besieged, damaged bodies and the psyches attached to them.

It will help this argument to provide some brief historical contextualization of the term and the analytical category "queer." The early 1990s was marked by the emergence of queer as a catch-all term for myriad forms of nonnormative sexuality. These early years produced the New Queer Cinema, as B. Ruby Rich lastingly named it.[6] Mainstream hits, whatever their individual qualities, also trafficked in surprising and often quite controversial queer content.[7] While the post-Reagan-era New Man, as Susan Jeffords (1994) described the type—a sensitive masculinity that eschewed not only the hypermasculine muscle-bound cartoonishness of 1980s icons such as Arnold Schwarzenegger and Sylvester Stallone but also the perceived milquetoast qualities of feminized males in the 1970s—was emerging, queerness was calling not just gender but sexual norms into question. The gay rights movement would give birth to the quests for gay marriage equality while the development of "queer" would facilitate the later push for transgender rights.[8] Pioneered by theorists such as Eve Kosofsky Sedgwick, Judith Butler, D. A. Miller, David Halperin, Jeffrey Weeks, Michael Moon, Lee Edelman, Teresa de Lauretis, Terry Castle, and many others, queer theory, as de Lauretis has been credited with naming it, also first flourished during this period. The rubric of "queer" has been crucial to the critical de-centering of normative masculinity in both critical theory and the mainstream; my work proceeds from the basis of queer theory even if I am not in agreement with some of its positions at times.[9]

The early use of the word queer was alternately combative, politically in-your-face, and joyous. It was also a memorial, a testament to longstanding cultural wounds. As Heather Love writes, "The word 'queer,' like 'fag' or 'dyke' but unlike the more positive 'gay' or 'lesbian,' is a slur. When queer was adopted in the late 1980s it was chosen because it evoked a long history of insult and abuse—you could hear the hurt in it."[10]

By the '00s, however, queer had transmogrified into a cheerful mainstream moniker, as exemplified by the popular Bravo channel television series *Queer Eye for the Straight Guy* (2003–2007). Queerness has in many ways become anodyne, the stuff of teen-angst romance (a representative example being the same-sex relationships on the Fox series *Glee*, 2009–2015). It is the very comforting blandness of cultural products like *Queer Eye*, *Glee* (especially in its later, less subversive seasons) and the exceedingly popular ABC sitcom *Modern Family* (2009–present), which features a white gay male couple raising an adopted Vietnamese girl they have named Lily, that is most suggestive. Queerness has arrived, become normalized, even as it is demonized by politicians such as Rick Santorum, religious leaders, and Reality TV stars like Phil Robertson, the patriarchal center of the A&E series's *Duck Dynasty*. Important for cinematic and television representation, the image of the gay consumer (metonymic of mainstream queerness) has also played a role in popular culture's current saturation in gay/queer images in works ranging from the ABC legal drama *How to Get Away with Murder* (2014–), starring the great Viola Davis, to the HBO series *Looking* (2013–2016) to movies like *The Interview* (Seth Rogen, Evan Goldberg, 2014), starring the bromantic duo par excellence Seth Rogen and James Franco. With its endless series of gay-baiting jokes (such as Franco offering to help Rogen extract a mini-missile from his anus), films such as *The Interview* seem to be targeted at anyone but a gay/queer consumer. Nevertheless, the presence of the buying power of queer spectators accounts, at least in part, for the need to "represent," as mainstream works signal their awareness of an avid LGBTQI audience. The dark side of consumerism and specifically the dark side of a queer consumerism that is tied to nationalist policy and exported images of U.S. cultural superiority, as Jasbir K. Puar has argued, cannot be overlooked and makes any uncritical celebration of queer representation in mainstream practice impossible.[11]

The complete title of Linda Hirshman's 2012 book: *Victory: The Triumphant Gay Revolution* makes an important point: the quest for gay rights has been successful, if not exactly victorious, despite the enduring reality of entrenched homophobia and however ambivalently some may regard the increasing normalization of LGBTQI people. The dominant culture has accommodated and in some cases helped to further the political urgency of queer visibility. At the same time, it has found a variety of means to stall, deflect, delimit, preempt, avoid, and thwart it. These methods of combative deferment characterize homophobia, but manifest homophobia does not fully account for the need to keep queerness at bay.[12]

Timothy Shary observes that the "crisis theme has been quite popular since at least the 1990s, perhaps due to the softer presidency of Bill Clinton and the increasing feminization of men in the American home."[13] The latest male crisis narrative, which stems not only from the traumatic events of September 11, 2001, but also from the ways in which these events have been transformed into a national myth about the state of American masculinity, promulgates fears that men and boys are being left behind, superseded by a newly purposeful and well-equipped female class. (The emergent forms of national heroism are not male-driven but rather the "dystopia girls" of YA post-apocalyptic fiction, Katniss Everdeen in *The Hunger Games* books and films and her ilk.) The crisis narrative that has been used to frame both the United States and American men of the post-9/11 moment has been an expedient one. In national terms, this narrative of a crisis is one that is "continuously repeated across the media and other social institutions by the nation's most powerfully symbolic actors. . . . Given that the narrative was in every newspaper, on every radio and television station, as well as in novels, films, sermons, and the Internet, continuously for several years, it is unsurprising that it became the dominant interpretation."[14] However hypocritical, self-serving, and alarmist such male crisis narratives are, it nevertheless does seem to appear that masculinity is slipping, unable to maintain its stronghold as the dominant gender for much longer. Hence the intensifying levels of panic and the proliferation of defensive countermeasures.

In tandem with the crisis narrative, studies bemoaning the hapless state of American manhood and offering plans for its salvation have exploded in the past decade. Once the gender that saved, men now need saving. In her 2010 book *Save the Males: Why Men Matter, Why Women Should Care*, Kathleen Parker observes that in "the dangerous world in which we really live, it might be nice to have a few guys around who aren't trying to juggle pedicures and highlights."[15] Clearly, part of what ails men and manhood and imperils the nation is the threat of effeminacy, as men develop their own beauty culture and are implicitly turned into women.[16] If bombastic accounts of the perceived crisis in masculinity abound, even responsible and persuasive theorists have perceived a meltdown in male subjectivities. The real-life young men interviewed by the sociologist Michael Kimmel for his 2008 book *Guyland* live, work, and play in a special all-male world in which pornography reigns supreme and women are both the enemy and the desired object of sexual conquest. Films of the '00s both reflect these new social realities, even indulge in their antisocial possibilities, while also serving as cautionary tales about them, as I will show in my chapter on the comedies of the bromance and the beta male schools.

Amanda Lotz, one of the most insightful critics working on representations of masculinity today, notes that "Analysis must begin somewhere other than the assumption that crisis narratives are symptomatic of a mourning of entitlement thwarted, and, instead, the type of holistic contextualized analysis that has characterized thirty years of feminist media scholarship examining female character is needed to better understand changing norms among males." Progress in terms of these norms occur not through "flashpoints" but rather "over decades of steady erosion." There is at least, for Lotz, a "dim beacon suggesting a way forward" in contemporary texts (her focus is on television dramas, specifically what she terms "cable's male-centered serials").[17] I agree with Lotz in many ways, but I also feel that many of the series she values, as well as the films of this period, are not only overwhelmingly heterosexist in nature but also in narrative aim. Queerness may be registered, even positively affirmed, but it exists as a simultaneously irresistible and frightening netherworld that must be avoided or escaped after tentative entry. Where I believe my work dovetails with Lotz's is that I believe that close readings, the steady, careful attention to the specific details and nuances of works, is crucial to the development of an understanding of what's going on in these works, politically, socially, emotionally, and aesthetically.[8]

Magic Mike: The Ambiguous Impact of Queer and Postfeminist Spectatorship

One of the effects of queer visibility on mainstream representation is the acknowledgment of queer spectatorship. While still in many respects *dis*-acknowledged, the awareness of queer audiences makes an impact on the way films are made, distributed, and received. Concomitant with the queer audience and its imagined expectations, postfeminist female sexual consumership and anticipations of the kinds of images of sexualized masculinity that will appeal to it affect the representation of masculinity. Exemplified by the trend-setting HBO series *Sex and the City* (1998–2004) and more uneasily by Lena Dunham's HBO series *Girls* (2012–) and the novel *Fifty Shades of Grey* by E. L. James, its sequels and its 2015 film adaptation, postfeminist narratives frequently depict males as erotic provisions for their female protagonists (while at the same time often punishing the women for their sexual gamesmanship). Hollywood's attempts to anticipate and satisfy the presumed needs of queer and postfeminist audiences have produced images of screen masculinity that reflect a new interest in the sexual objectification of males. But it is far from the case that this emergent awareness that males are sexually desirable means that progressive, feminist, queer attitudes will be inherent in the films that get made (perhaps an obvious point). Indeed, the growing awareness that males can be ripe fodder for objectification seems to lead to greater levels of defensiveness.

For example, Steven Soderbergh's 2012 male stripper movie *Magic Mike* (given a 2015 sequel) is geared toward a female audience with buying power, perceived to be out there waiting for displays of male flesh, just like the screaming female fans in the diegetic world of the film. Yet the film, made by a director often considered a resistant voice in Hollywood, offers very little in the way of feminist critique and nothing in the way of queer male representation despite the subject matter, which at least nods to the gay male population as a potential audience for the film.[18] (Soderbergh also made *Behind the Candelabra*, 2013 HBO television film about the gay pianist Liberace and his lover Scott Thorson; this film may offer an alternative to my criticisms of *Magic Mike* for some viewers; I believe that it only compounds the problem.[19])

Magic Mike's hero, Mike Lane (Channing Tatum), has been a male stripper for six years at the Xquisite Strip Club, which is owned by the middle-aged but still physically fit Dallas (Matthew McConaughey), who teaches the young men who strip in his club how to perform most effectively on stage and who still strips on occasion himself. Mike longs to start his own business and assiduously saves money to do so. When Mike spots the 19-year-old Adam (Adam Pettyfer), who seems adrift and is looking for a construction job, he brings him to Xquisite to meet Dallas, the first stage in his mentoring of the young man. Mike meets Adam's sister Brooke (Cody Horn), a strong and resilient young woman who becomes Mike's love interest. The film evokes earlier classics such as *On the Waterfront* (Elia Kazan, 1954) and especially *Rocky* (John G. Avildsen, 1976) in its idealization of its incorruptible underdog hero, Mike. Like Marlon Brando's Terry Malloy in Kazan's film, Mike fights against corruption (in this case, Dallas's cynical exploitation of his strippers); like Rocky, Mike is transformed by the love of a good woman and finds the courage to pursue his dreams. *Magic Mike* substitutes stripping for boxing, the sport that defines and allegorizes the struggles of the male protagonists of these earlier films, an indication of the more central role that displays of male sexual desirability play in contemporary film.

Magic Mike amply demonstrates that the "opening-up" of masculinity—foregrounded here by our access to the secret behind-the-scenes world of the male strippers in their dressing-room—does not necessarily signal a critical or revealing analysis of it. Indeed, the seeming openness here camouflages a larger resistance to penetrating the veil of masculinity. The male stripper world of the film is not its chief subject but, rather, provides an unconventional, and therefore seemingly fresh, background for the film's highly conventional heterosexual love plot. Normative heterosexuality is steadfastly affirmed as the sensible, sound Brooke transforms Mike's wayward ambitions, both erotic and economic, into properly directed ones. (Mike initially has a dark-haired, duplicitous girlfriend whose siren spell he escapes thanks to the golden-haired Brooke's tough-love intervention.) The strip-club setting is a nod to the greater visibility afforded the desirable male body, but in no way does the film explore the peculiar and idiosyncratic elements of this milieu in any depth, or what the experience of being sexually commodified, and of actively pursuing and enabling this commodification, might mean for ostensibly straight men. Moreover, there is no diegetic indication made in the film whatsoever that gay male desire might be an element in the success of male strip clubs, which are usually known to have at least one gay night a week.

The stripper milieu ultimately serves to intensify the sense that the admirable but vulnerable hero is truly endangered, and in a way that is not his fault—his economic need has forced him to be "nude-for-pay." In the famous aphorism of John Berger, "To be naked is to be oneself. To be nude is to be seen naked by others and yet not recognised for oneself."[20] Herein lies Mike's problem—his nudity prevents him from being recognized for himself—and what lies in this recognition is the logic of heterosexual working-class masculinity, associated with sacrifice, endeavor, striving, and sexual normalcy. His physical denuding on the nightly stage allegorizes his economic and social privation. Mike's willingness to be a commodified sexual object—his own exploitation of his hunky desirability, not just Dallas's—is an untraditional masculine marker and therefore a problem that film will work diligently to resolve.

The salvational power of the good woman comes through with even more force here, for she saves him not only from waywardness but from, potentially, a descent into sexual unclassifiability and perversity. Mike's initial contact with Adam evokes a gay procuring theme—Mike must on some level find Adam sexually attractive, hence his decision to bring him to Dallas; it's a form of straight male cruising.[21] While Adam, as played by Pettyfer, with his troubled eyes, tousled hair, and overripe lips, has a winsome, 1950s-style young matinee idol prettiness, the suggestions of underlying homoerotic appreciation in their initial rapport degenerates into ugly scenes of rancor between the two. Indeed, one of the few moments in the film that can be described as genuinely erotic features Adam but not Mike. At a drug-and-booze-filled party for the strippers, Adam walks into a bedroom in which one of his fellow strippers, Ken (played by *White Collar*'s Matt Bomer) lies rather suggestively and shirtlessly on the bed. Ken's blond, buxom girlfriend kneels upright on the bed; noticing Adam's interest in his girlfriend's exposed and ample breasts, Ken encourages Adam to touch them, which he does avidly. As Harry M. Benshoff and Sean Griffin observe in their study *Queer Images*, the term "heterosexual orgy is something of an oxymoron, as it is part of the design of such an arrangement for sexual desire and pleasure to flow from person to person without regard to gender. Group sex is queer sex."[22] This scene is clearly meant to show us Adam's susceptibility to moral corruption, but it also serves to remind us of the homoerotic potentiality in non-strictly homosexual tableau. The look that passes between Ken—especially as played by the exquisitely handsome, dark-haired Bomer, who had recently come out as a gay man, adding to the frisson of his appearance in a film about male strippers—and Adam has an erotic intensity missing from the rest of the film.

Emerging as a different kind of siren threat, louche Adam effectively depletes stolid Mike, strangely devoted to helping Adam, of his savings. The physical contrasts between the actors—the brawn and height of Channing Tatum, the winsomeness of Pettyfer—come to signify the moral contrasts between the characters, with Tatum's Mike eventually reconciling his physical might and his moral stature as Pettyfer's more sexually ambiguous Adam sinks into perdition.

This may be overstating the case—Adam ends up aligning himself with corrupt Dallas after Mike leaves stripping behind. Dallas makes Adam the front man for his dancers; Mike and Brooke realize their love for one another. Everybody wins, really. It's an intensely schematic movie. As Peter Foster writes, "the meaning and purpose of the bromantic comedy," of which *Magic Mike*, for all of its anxious, fretful moments, is an example, "reside in the unseating of any queerness from the narrative resolution only to insist, finally, unequivocally, upon traditional masculinity and the ongoing—but culturally endorsed—tribulations of heterosexuality."[23]

Genre Film and Post-Millennial Masculinities

This book focuses on post-millennial genre films. The relationship between masculinity and genre film is a well-established one by now. Critics such as

Frank Krutnik (1991), Steven Cohan and Ina Rae Hark (1993), Steve Neale (1993 and numerous other works), Susan Jeffords (1993), Yvonne Tasker (1993), Constance Penley and Sharon Willis (1993), Peter Lehman (1993, 2001, 2007, 2008), Barry Keith Grant (2007, 2010), John Alberti (2013), Robert Lang (2002), Susanne Kord and Elisabeth Krimmer (2011), Kylo-Patrick Hart (2013), and numerous others have explored these linkages. Moreover, a great deal of analogous work has been done on the relationships between femininity and genre film by critics such as Mary Ann Doane, Linda Williams, Christine Gledhill, Tania Modleski, E. Ann Kaplan, and others. As Gledhill (2012) writes,

> Given the feminist lead in gender studies, it may not surprise that "gender" for many means "women." But if gender is a performance in answer of a discursive call, not all calls require we function in gender. Too long feminist criticism has assumed that "men" in movies and as audiences function like—men. But if we understand gender as generic, and "woman" as a symbolic as well as referential figure, and if we dissolve gender-to-gender identification, then exploration of the aesthetic effects, affective appeals, and significations of gentrified masculinity become possible.[24]

Gledhill's words are exact and inspiring. I have attempted to show, in my work on femininity and queer audiences in film especially, that gender-to-gender identification is deeply inadequate as a paradigm for spectatorship. At the same time, I have a great deal of sympathy for the view held by feminist criticism, if it does indeed constitute a consistent trend, of seeing men as "men" in mainstream film insofar as this typing of male screen entities is so crucial to the very meaning of mainstream film itself, its appeal to the broadest swath of audiences lying in recognizable and (that dread term) relatable personae. Laura Mulvey's work proceeds from the basis of a gender/sex essentialism that may be dated, as I will show, yet nevertheless continues to be relevant to screen depictions of gender and sex. But it is nevertheless a frustrating aspect of Mulvey's work—a critic I greatly admire and remain influenced by—that queer issues never come up in her treatment of gender and sexual orthodoxies in the traditional film text. Now more than ever the presence of queerness transforms the issues of screen spectatorship as well as what is placed on the screen. If masculinity has been foregrounded as a cinematic concern in twenty-first-century film, it is with genre film that masculinity has maintained its most intricate and intimate relationship. I will discuss what, reworking Linda Williams's theory, I call the new *male body genre* films below.

"Among their conventions," writes Barry Keith Grant, "genre movies feature standard ways of representing gender, race, class, and ethnicity. Into the 1980s, genres and genre movies remained almost exclusively the cultural property of a white male consciousness . . . women and visible minorities assumed subsidiary and stereotyped roles" as a result.[25] The white iconography that dominated mainstream narrative film into the 1980s was challenged in the later years of this decade and in the 1990s by films that put women and visible minorities at the center of previously male-dominated genres, e.g., *Thelma and Louise* (Ridley Scott, 1991), a female-centered version of the buddy film; the black Western, *Posse* (Mario Van Peebles, 1993). But, as Grant notes, many of these films reversed conventional expectations only to "fall into the trap of repeating the same objectionable values."[26] There are significant non-white characters in films such as the *Fast and the Furious* franchise headlined by the mixed-race star Vin Diesel, which features Hispanic, Asian, and African-American characters. As Mary C. Beltrán has discussed, however, the franchise foregrounds what she calls "racelessness." The AMC zombie television series *The Walking Dead* (2010–present) features an Asian-American character, Glenn, among its main cast, who fully participates in the scenes of zombie mayhem and violence. Stars such as Will Smith routinely bring in audiences (though was unable to do so in the Oedipal science-fiction film *After Earth* [M. Night Shyamalan, 2013], also starring his son Jaden Smith), and Denzel Washington still gets leading-man roles; emergent performers such as Kevin Hart hold promise as breakout movie stars. But it is clear that white masculinity remains the mainstay, as a survey of the comic-book franchise film-explosion of the past decade clearly evinces, but also horror film and straight dramas. What is especially interesting, and the focus of this book, is the manner in which this white cinematic masculinity remains the standard while consistently shown to be besieged, at the breaking point. Nearly taken to a level of total structural collapse, masculinity is then, even if in the eleventh hour, reassembled and restored. The various assaults to and destabilization of male identities and bodies attest to the enormous difficulties inherent in maintaining white heterosexual masculinity as a defining norm, but movies (and television works) maintain this norm even as they acknowledge the fissures within the project.

Rick Altman, in his much-discussed book *Film/Genre*, has alerted our attention to the contingent nature of genre, how much what we understand of genre has been the result of competing uses made of the term by critics and those working in the film industry. Altman provides a comprehensive breakdown of the history and attendant presumptions of genre theory. While such an approach is valuable, my focus in this book is less on genre per se than it is on the remarkable affinity the post-millennial representation of masculinity has had for the genres of comedy and horror, especially, and, as I will discuss in the last chapter, pornography. I am in agreement with Barry Keith Grant about the relationship between the male crisis narrative that has routinely popped up within American history and the relationship of genre film to it. As he writes, "to understand the history of American cinema as a series of masculine crises—perhaps even to think of any particular period in the history of American film, much less individual films . . . is both inappropriate hyperbole and a serious misunderstanding of Hollywood cinema." Grant steers us away from the understanding that "particular genre films and cycles" reflect "a series of representational crisis." Rather, certain kinds of genre films and cycles may be better seen as offering "part of an ongoing dialogue with audiences about the ceaseless challenges to and valorization of heteronormative ideals—what I call 'negotiation'—in a constantly changing society at specific points in time."[27] While I agree with Grant, I maintain here that genre films, comedy and horror especially, have been reflective of the *perceived* crisis in American masculinity in the '00s, and in this regard they come to be indissociable from the crisis itself. At their best, they do provide an opportunity for the "ongoing dialogue" about heteronormative ideals, but they are, as I will show, far more invested in maintaining the heteronormative status quo; indeed, depicting challenges to it which are then amply "met" by narrative closure and other "lockdown" strategies is a key element of their program and success.

The comedy and horror genres, in particular, have been heavily grounded in the dynamics of masculinity in the '00s and will be my focus in this book, though I will also discuss some key straight dramas.[28] Comedies often focus on male group dynamics, exemplified by titles such as *Horrible Bosses* (Seth Gordon, 2011), *The Change-Up* (David Dobkin, 2011), Todd Philips's *The Hangover* (2009) and its 2012 and 2013 sequels, *Pineapple Express* (David Gordon Green, 2007); "beta male" comedies, as they have been called, of the Judd Apatow variety, such as *Superbad* (Greg Mottola, 2007; co-produced by Apatow); the related phenomenon of the "bromance," exemplified by *I Love You, Man* (John Hamburg, 2009) and *Superbad* as well; and much discussed independent films such as *Humpday* (Lynne Shelton, 2009) and less discussed indies such as *Jeff, Who Lives at Home* (2011), directed by Jay Duplass and Mark Duplass (the latter co-starred in *Humpday*).

Straight dramas like *Magic Mike*, as we have discussed, put masculinity on lavish and languorous display for sexual consumption; horror movies figure men as zombie meat (*Zombieland*, Ruben Fleischer, 2009; *Shaun of the Dead,* Edgar Wright, 2004; *Dawn of the Dead*, Zach Synder's 2004 remake of George A. Romero's 1978 masterpiece; the AMC television series *The Walking Dead* follows suit). Zombie-themed movies and TV series of the '00s threaten to topple the hierarchies of horror representation by making male bodies as vulnerable as the female bodies so crucial to the genre and by foregrounding males as, principally, bodies. But movies like *World War Z* (Marc Forster, 2013) have begun to demonstrate that the project of male re-entrenchment and remasculinization is being incorporated into the logic of the genre. The protagonist, played by Brad Pitt, has a climactic encounter with a male zombie whose appearance evokes images of gay men afflicted with AIDS and its telltale symptoms such as Kaposi's sarcoma. Both *The Walking Dead* and *World War Z* make the preservation of the heterosexual nuclear family a central concern, a reactionary revision of the progressive social vision of George A. Romero's zombie classics.

Horror often treats masculinity itself as the source of horror. Following Alfred Hitchcock's 1960 *Psycho,* horror films frequently revolve around a male villain and routinely take the view that masculinity is a frightening and unsolvable psychological and social problem, as in *Insidious* (James Wan, 2011) and *We Need to Talk about Kevin* (Lynne Ramsay, 2011). Rob Zombie's *Halloween* (2007) and *Halloween II* (2009)—his remakes of John Carpenter's original *Halloween* (1978) and its sequel (Rick Rosenthal, 1981), respectively—are the auteurist pinnacle of the spate of remakes of horror films from the 1970s and especially the 1980s that have infiltrated post-millennial cinema, culminating, as of this writing, with the 2013 3-D reboot-sequel to the original *The Texas Chainsaw Massacre*.[29] As I will show, Zombie's films allegorize an increasing preoccupation with linking representations of American masculinity to a fascination with the American cultural and historical past. This American past has its chief location in the scene of nineteenth-century America, to which '00s film and television representation frequently returns. Indeed, a defining aspect of the '00s, perhaps the chief aesthetic implication of 9/11, is the framing of all earlier periods of American life as equally "historical." Movies of the '00s such as *Donnie Darko* (Richard Kelly, 2001) also look back at the 1980s of Ronald Reagan's presidency, a period that has emerged as another highly significant location for "historical" America, which, as I will show, has particularly powerful implications for masculinity.

Subjected to a similarly endless series of sequels, remakes, and reboots, science-fiction, broadly understood, intersecting with horror and the rise of the comic-book action film, must also be counted as a body genre. Post-millennial sci-fi films are similarly grounded in male-oriented themes and foreground assaults to the male body. Science-fiction films like *Chronicle* (Josh Trank, 2012) and genre television shows like NBC's comic-book-style *Heroes* (2006–2010), which focused in its first season on a young man with the force of nuclear reactor, extend horror's pattern of viewing masculinity as a force of chaos liable to explode at any point and with any provocation. Comic-book films alternately encase the male body in metal flesh (the *Iron Man* films of 2008, 2010, and 2013, the first two of which were directed by John Favreau, the third by Shane Black) and present it as genetically enhanced (*Captain America: The First Avenger*, Joe Johnston, 2011) or endowed with extraordinary powers (the various *X-Men* films; *Chronicle*; *Man of Steel*, Zach Snyder's 2013 *Superman* reboot). In whatever manner, their key component is that the male body is put on display, a preoccupation enhanced by the near-inability to create a successful female superhero franchise.

Beyond Mulvey? Straight Movie Males and the Sexual Gaze

Before turning to a discussion of male body genres, I want to revisit the important issue of gaze theory, since it relates to active and passing forms of looking in film texts and to shifts in patterns of spectatorship that have an impact on how films get made and marketed.

Laura Mulvey famously argued in her landmark 1975 *Screen* essay "Visual Pleasure and Narrative Cinema" that the male gaze dominated mainstream film and that the audience joined in with the onscreen male protagonist in a shared fantasy of narcissistic omnipotence. Her discussion concerned classical Hollywood, but her paradigms were broadly applied, for many years, to mainstream film practice generally. The desire to look was indistinguishable from the absolute right to look. Such an account of male visual authority remains, as I have noted, valuable. But it is not sufficient to theorize cinematic representation of the present. Males have become not just the wielders but the objects of the gaze, and, indeed, fodder for its some of its violent mutations. The hetero-male body now also connotes "to-be-looked-at-ness." This in no way implies that the female body has been superseded by the male body as the zone of scopophilic fascination, even frenzy. Mulvey's paradigms of voyeurism (investigating the woman, penetrating her mystery) and fetishism (breaking up the visual field of the woman's body into components) still apply to the representation and relentless sexual objectification of women. What is novel is that the male body is now subjected with equal measure to these techniques of looking, sexual appraisal, and consumption associated with cinematic femininity, though not necessarily in the same way or with the same effects.

Mulvey's 1975 essay, the influence of which spread with wildfire intensity in the late 1970s and the 1980s, has been systematically reappraised and also challenged in the past two decades. Susan White has examined the "almost hypnotically powerful effect on feminist film theorists" of Mulvey's work, noting that later treatments of the gaze hold that female desire, so elusive in "Visual Pleasure," can erupt in the "gaps" and fissures" of dominant texts, and that, moreover, the image of universalized white, middle- or upper-class woman Mulvey deploys itself needs to be painstakingly problematized.[30] In *The Real Gaze* (2007), Todd McGowan critiques Mulvey for her insufficiently Lacanian rigor and provides a more accurate version of Lacanian views of such crucial concepts as the gaze. One of the most consistent ways that critics have rebutted Mulvey's construction of cinematic viewing as narcissistic complicity has been to turn positively to an economy of masochism, a turn that I have discussed and critiqued elsewhere.[31] Gaylyn Studlar's *In the Realm of Pleasure* is exemplary in this regard; she argues that film returns the spectator to the pre-Oedipal realm of oneness between infant and mother and from there discusses the mother's central role in masochistic fantasy.

For our purposes, the challenges to Mulvey that reinsert queer issues into gaze theory are of most relevance. Steve Neale argues in his essay "Masculinity as Spectacle" that "there can be no simple and unproblematic identification on the part of the spectator, male or female, with Mulvey's 'ideal ego' on the screen."[32] Neale cites D. N. Rodowick's observation that Mulvey "discusses the male star as an object of the look but denies him the function of an erotic object. Because Mulvey conceives the look to be essentially active in its aims, identification with the male protagonist is only considered from a point of view which associates it with a sense of omnipotence, of assuming control of the narrative."[33] Neale conjectures that "it is not surprising that 'male' genres and films constantly involve sadomasochistic themes, scenes, and phantasies, or that male heroes can at times be marked as the object of an erotic gaze." Neale theorizes, drawing on Paul Willemen's article "Anthony Mann: Looking at the Male," that the pleasures of looking at male bodies in heterosexist patriarchal society are founded on "repressed homosexual voyeurism," which produces considerable anxiety. The implication would appear to be, in Neale's words, "that in a heterosexual and patriarchal society the male body cannot be marked explicitly as the erotic object of another male look; that look must be motivated some other way, its erotic component repressed."[34] As Jack [Judith] Halberstam argued in *Skin Shows*, "recent discussions of gay and lesbian cinema assume that the gaze is queer or multidimensional." I concur with critics such as White, Neale, Rodowick, Robert J. Corber, and Halberstam that Mulvey's theories of the gaze are inadequate when it comes to understanding both female and queer desire within structures of film spectatorship. But the main point that I wish to make here is the enduring relevance of Mulvey's paradigms, which now shed light on the sexual objectification of the male body in film.[35] The kinds of voyeuristic and fetishistic looking that Mulvey describes in terms of female bodies proves to be newly relevant to both the representation of male bodies in twenty-first-century cinema and the ongoing representation of female bodies. Critics such as Steve Neale and Yvonne Tasker and others have long since made the point that the representation of masculinity has been informed by these techniques; my contention is that post-millennial masculinity on the screen is *consistently* informed by them and that they are employed in mainstream filmmaking. The problems inherent in treating the new cinematic preoccupations with male bodies dates back at least to the early 1990s (studies such as Tasker's *Spectacular Bodies*).[36] Female bodies have long been subjected to fetishistic fragmentation at the level of form—close-ups of individual body parts, the face especially—and to voyeuristic investigation, on a formal basis as well as on the level of film content. Entire plots are devoted to the penetration of the woman's mystery in works ranging from Hitchcock's *Vertigo* (1958, a key text for Mulvey) to Paul Verhoeven's *Basic Instinct* (1992) to William Friedkin's 1995 film *Jade*.

That male bodies and male protagonists in contemporary cinema are subjected to forms of voyeuristic investigation and fetishistic fascination that have historically attended the depiction of femininity is not to suggest that these approaches yield the same results and effects as those approaches have and continue to do in terms of femininity. Nevertheless, the extension of such objectifying techniques to male bodies and psyches onscreen deserves analysis. As I will show, a project of physical and emotional disassembly occurs in the representation of males at the level of film content, e.g., the narrative and the plot. This violence gets replicated, at times, at the level of form, e.g., editing and/or cinematography. Voyeurism informs the current cinematic interest in investigating and solving the enigma of masculinity, presented precisely *as* an enigma, while the obsession with male faces evinces a fetishistic aim. Fragmented away from the male body and therefore revealed as a fixture of a recurring formal design, the male face emerges as a key element in a general fragmentation of the male body.

If the gaze is now properly understood as diverse and multiple, a concomitant understanding of the dynamics and implications of putting the white heterosexual male subject under scrutiny also needs to be developed. Hence the project undertaken in this book. Now as often, perhaps even more often, the object of the sexual gaze as they are the wielders of it, white straight men remain the chief, while not the exclusive, economy of the gaze. Watching or being watched, they remain the subject of principle fascination across media forms. In any particular genre manifestation, the male body exists as a sign of masculinity itself, overdetermined as "the phallus." If iconic stars from earlier eras like John Wayne and Clint Eastwood represented the image of masculinity as the phallus, their bodies were rarely as brazenly displayed—revealed—and presented as sexualized bodies to be consumed by the multiform desiring gaze as contemporary male bodies are. While Chris Holmlund makes the important point that cinema of the past thirty years or so has been marked by its depictions of, and refusals to depict, "impossible bodies," the cinema of the '00s, in terms of masculinity, has upheld the ideal of an impossibly perfect, indestructible body, which is usually a chiseled, perfected, white body as well.[37] The comedy genre has offered alternatives to this body in the beta male comedy subgenre. Stars such as Seth Rogen actively challenge as they eschew models of "perfection," yet, as I will discuss in chapter 3, while beta male comedies do not exclusively present males who conform to ideals of bodily perfection, they nevertheless find numerous means of re-bolstering disenfranchised and disaffected male characters and compensating for perceived lack.

Male Body Genres

One of my chief arguments in this book is that the re-entrenchment of masculinist power in Hollywood film has taken the form of and has its foundation in a desire *to flay open* males, specifically straight white males, on both somatic and psychic levels. The cutting and opening up of male bodies and psyches informs film across the genres and media representation generally, including gay male Internet porn, now democratized as material that can be accessed by any user, free of charge. This cutting and opening up of masculinity occurs both on the level of film content and of film form, in a process that I call *dismantling*. This should not be taken to imply that, somehow, the dominators have become the dominated, straight men the victims of an oppressive multi-directional gaze. Rather, the dismantling of the straight male body has emerged as an alternative route to dominance and centrality, and, as such, is an offshoot of the self-congratulatory masochism that has been at the center of male representation of the past two decades at least. Moreover, this dismantling is made possible only through the entirely inevitable process of restoring the male body and psyche to a state of coherence and emotional and somatic integrity by the end of the narrative. Nevertheless, the dismantling exerts its own fascination.

The desire to take straight masculinity apart emerges as a defining theme through what, in the paradigm Linda Williams provided in her essay "Film Bodies: Gender, Genre, and Excess," have come to be known as the "body genres" in their manifestations in twenty-first-century film. As Williams theorized, melodrama, horror, and pornography all have the central overlap of being genres that have a physical effect on the spectator's body. These genres all count as lowbrow in terms of cultural status. The spectator of these films is thought to be "caught up in an almost involuntary mimicry of the emotion or sensation of the body on the screen," a body that is usually a female one.[38]

Why doesn't Williams include comedy with her three principle body genres? Williams directly addresses this, establishing that while comedies do have some body genre elements, they are not equivalent to melodrama, horror, or pornography. As Williams writes, "Physical clown comedy is another 'body' genre concerned with all manner of gross activities and body functions . . . Nonetheless, it has not been deemed gratuitously excessive, probably because the reaction of the audience does not mimic the sensations experienced by the central clown. Indeed, it is almost a rule that the audience's physical reaction of laughter does not coincide with the often deadpan reactions of the clown."[39] The issue of comedy falls between Williams' discussion of the effects of body genres and her analysis of highbrow versus lowbrow culture—melodrama, horror, and pornography count as "especially low," and comedy does not.[40]

In my retooling of Williams's theory, the issue of mimesis is less important than the issue of the body itself. (The question of highbrow versus lowbrow are distinctions worth considering further, especially in terms of the possibilities afforded lowbrow genres for "extreme" states of screen subjectitity. But, as I will show, extreme is not synonymous with subversive.) In twenty-first-century genre forms, male bodies have taken center stage with the purpose of subjecting these bodies to an unprecedented scrutiny that culminates in the taking apart of these bodies to varying degrees of disassembly. Male body genres foreground the male body as the chief site of dramatic intensity and the chief site of spectatorial fascination. This applies to the science-fiction genre as well, which emerges as a male-body genre in its fascination with the disassembly, indeed the ruination, of the male body, albeit a body that will be magically restored by the end. Again, while audience responses to science fiction are not necessarily mimetic, the science-fiction genre has become what I am calling a male-body genre in its focus on bodies that are rendered visible onscreen and on the acts perpetrated on these bodies. The emergent '00s subgenres of beta male comedies, bromances, torture porn horror, horror comedies (such as *Zombieland,* Ruben Fleischer, 2009; *Shaun of the Dead,* Edgar Wright, 2004), and serial killer films, along with the distinctive stamp the period has put on science fiction, comic-book films, action films, crime dramas, et al., and the ubiquitous realm of Internet pornography can all be classified as *male-body genres.* As genre films and television shows have proliferated in the '00s, the male-body genres of comedy, horror, and pornography have made an especially strong, decade-defining showing and will be my focus in this book.[41]

Donnie Darko provides us with a salient moment for a consideration of male-body genres (true of this entire film, as I will show in chapter 4). In this film, set in Middlesex, Virginia, in 1988, the titular teen protagonist (Jake Gyllenhaal) struggles with an impending sense of disaster after an airplane engine crashes through his bedroom roof. A disaffected teen of the 1980s, Donnie chafes against his suburban surroundings and the conformity of his high school, which he attempts to blow up, flood, and otherwise destroy at various points. His malaise and apocalyptic dread intersect with his growing obsession with time-travel. At one point—in a scene saliently set in a darkened, flickering movie theater (Sam Raimi's 1987 *Evil Dead II* plays on the screen)—Donnie asks a rabbit-faced man (the figure that haunts, torments, and beguiles Donnie throughout), "Why do you wear that stupid bunny suit?" Not missing a beat, the rabbit-faced man takes off his mask and responds, "Why are you wearing that stupid man suit?" The line speaks to the representation of males in movies of the post-millennial moment. Masculinity in the '00s is a *genre* suit. One of the chief dimensions of the emphasis on body genres in this period (and more broadly in media forms generally, considering the hegemony of pornography in this past decade in its Internet manifestations alone) has been the emphasis on men and masculinities as, principally, bodies. This emphasis signals a major reconfiguration of American masculinity. Masculinity, once framed as *mind,* the seat of reason, has been reframed as *the body.* Movies are fixated on the male body, newly available as a site of screen inquiry and at times all-out assault. Movies are also fixated on the male *brain,* as opposed to mind—how that brain works, what makes men tick, what makes a man. And they demonstrate that males are chief among the inquiring minds who want to know more about masculinity, now figured, as femininity had once been, as the ultimate mystery. These dynamics are exemplified in the "Kissing my own dick" scene of *The Change-Up*, which I will discuss in in chapter 3. In this film, the two male protagonists—a sad-sack lawyer and beleaguered family man played by Jason Bateman and his best friend, a randy, ne'er-do-well bachelor played by Ryan Reynolds—switch bodies after they drunkenly urinate in a pond with a statue of a female deity in it. The deity is far from dormant: she mischievously grants the men their intoxicated wish to have the other's life. The scene in which the two men confront one another after their personalities and bodies have been switched metonymically expresses core themes in films of this period, in the bromance and beyond.

As I discuss in the chapter on the psychoanalytic scene, films of this period frequently feature a man confronting his own image in the mirror, a secondary mirror stage. When the Bateman character wakes up in Reynolds's body, he stares at himself in awe in the mirror. Then Reynolds in Bateman's body comes to the door, and as the two yell at one another in confusion they appear to be reaching out to one another intimately, only to wrestle, Bateman in Reynolds's body even jabbing his fingers into his friend's eyes, believing him responsible for the titular mishap. An insupportable emotional and physical intimacy transmutes into physical violence. As if to reinforce the homoerotic and doubling aspects of the mirror stage motif, the two men then each stare into their mirror images together.

FIGURE I.1. A secondary mirror stage: Bateman as Reynolds stares at himself in the mirror.

Figure I.2. Homoerotic doubling: The "changed-up" Bateman and Reynolds stare at themselves and each other in the mirror.

Later in the film, the Bateman character, now the randy bachelor on the inside, teaches the Reynolds's character, now the sadsack on the inside, how to shave his balls before going out on a date. As Bateman crouches before Reynolds at crotch-level, he muses that he is now in the position to "Kiss my own dick." As one man teaches another how to perform the proper, genitals-shaving pre-date toilette, masculinity is transformed into an economy of knowledge and mentorship that is undergirded by an explicit homoeroticism that has been rendered harmless by this explicit register—or that has been reconceived as an understandable narcissistic desire on the part of men, who cannot help but be fascinated by the prospect of self-fellatio. Self-fellatio substitutes for, and safeguards against the suggestion of, the act of one man performing oral sex on another man. That what is being referenced is a potential scene of homosexual sex is made anodyne through the strategies of (a) announcing this act as a humorous but unexplored possibility, and (b) claiming that it would indeed only be an act of one man kissing his *own* dick. Narcissism appears to trump homoeroticism even as both inhere in the other.

In film after film, the male body occupies center stage. This does not imply a radical dimension to the male body, but rather a consistent focus on it with myriad implications, chief among them the sense that this male body-focus will be of interest to mainstream audiences. This tendency is easy to track in the comedy genres, which have come to focus on male travails. These travails may be presented as a three-ring circus of potential mishaps and messy situations, as in Ben Stiller comedies, such as *There's Something About Mary* (Bobby Farrelly and Peter Farrelly, 1998) and *Meet the Parents* (Jay Roach, 2000) and its various sequels, which emphasize assaults to the male body and represent these assaults as humorous. Stiller films, while in comedic mode most of the time, foreground some of the issues involved in the representation of masculinity in the post-millennial era. On the one hand, his films are resolutely heterosexist in nature; queerness is neither an imagined nor a pursued quality in them. Nevertheless, they present the male body as vulnerable, under siege, in a way that is suggestive for queer readings. It is precisely the availability of the body of the Stiller character to scenarios of both physical and emotional mayhem—dismantling—that makes his body a queer body, despite the heterosexism of his body of work (including *Zoolander*, a 2001 film that Stiller directed and in which he casts himself as a high-fashion model; the film has its followers, but it trades in sophomoric homophobic stereotypes).

Peter Lehman, the critic who has most thoroughly examined the history and the implications of the representation of the male penis in film, identified in a 2007 essay a new kind of cinematic rendering of the male sexual organ: the melodramatic penis, which relates to and emerges within moments of melodramatic excess, spectacle, and shock. Lehman's examples of this trope include, significantly, *The Crying Game* (Neil Jordan, 1992), in which the revelation that the protagonist (Stephen Rea)'s possible female love interest, a hairdresser named Dil (Jaye Davidson), is actually male comes in the form of a shot of his penis, delivered as a shock effect; and *Boogie Nights* (Paul Thomas Anderson, 1997), about the American porn industry in the '70s and '80s, starring Mark Wahlberg as a porn star named Dirk Diggler, whose legendary endowment is finally shown at the end of the film. The comedies of Ben Stiller occupy—as does the male body of the present—a shifting middle ground between comedy and melodrama, which parallels the potent and precarious middle ground between comedy and horror that, arguably, even more centrally informs contemporary representations of masculinity. Most accurately, what we have here is a shaky continuum incorporating comedy, horror, and melodrama as modes through which to represent as well as define masculinity.

Lehman draws on the work of Richard Dyer, himself inspired by Lacanian theory. Of most relevance here is Lacan's essay "The Signification of the Phallus." As Lehman writes, "In Richard Dyer's memorable words, 'the penis isn't a patch on the phallus.' The privileged signifier of the phallus most easily retains its awe and mystique when the penis is hidden."[42] On the one hand, the penis is hopelessly inadequate to the phallus, the ideal of plenitude in signification. On the other hand, the phallus is also paradoxically a symbol for lack as Lacan theorized it. Therefore, images of the penis must be impressive, in size, length, and other characteristics, lest the visualized penis remind the audience of male lack. This duality reflects the larger one Lehman finds to be operative in representation, a male version of the Madonna/Whore dichotomy: masculinity is simultaneously or alternately presented as an invulnerable hard body or as deeply vulnerable, capable of being grievously wounded. The melodramatic penis eschews both "phallic spectacle" and "pitiable/comic collapse," and therefore is potentially a resistant cinematic figure; yet it still marks the penis as being of "monumental" significance: "The discourse of a melodramatic penis still seeks to block the penis from being merely a penis." The penis has replaced the vagina as the sexual organ that breeds castration anxieties, in that the representation of female genitals disrupts the notion of "the female body as complete without being fully sexed." At present, it is the representation of the male body as well as the penis that provokes the most anxiety because the "dominant drive to maintain the awe and mystique surrounding the penis is crumbling before the journalistic and artistic drive to break down the final taboo" of showing the penis. "The melodramatic penis is the result."[43] The penis remains a flashpoint for cinema, especially in the United States, and most often falls, when shown, into the comedic collapse-mode that Lehman outlines as a possibility.

I want to suggest that the bodies of men generally have undergone this melodramatic transformation, even as the penis is—largely though not entirely—kept at bay as a cinematic spectacle. The male body bears the brunt of this multipronged assault on all of the old standards regarding what can be represented of male physicalities—indeed, of what can be represented generally. Both the comedy and the horror genres have historically specialized in extremes, but the relentless push to shock and awe, to titillate, to push the envelope even further, to violate all standards of propriety, have had their impact on that most sacrosanct of domains, the male body. Again, this is in no way to diminish the crucial importance of, and the impact on, this new level of extremity on femininity and the female body onscreen; rather, it is to suggest that masculinity and male bodies have emerged as particularly interesting sites precisely because of this relentless push towards extremity for shock value and a concomitant (and arguably more important) result, commercial success.

Often, the male body itself serves as a fleshly template for the confusions and trials of the protagonist. For example, in the quintessential beta male comedy, Judd Apatow's *The 40-Year-Old Virgin* (2005), Steve Carell's titular beleaguered virgin Andy, goaded by his newfound friends at the electronics store where they all work to "do the deed" and lose his virginity at last, has his hirsute body waxed at their behest, all in an effort to make him more sexually desirable. His hairy body comes to represent not his access to conventional masculinity but, rather, his hermetically sealed inadequacy. This inadequacy stems, so it is suggested, from the sheltered life that has led him to collect retro superhero toys and other geek-centric items, to create an onanistic realm of arrested development in the private domain of his home, instead of dating women. Andy's friends both have arranged his waxing and are assembled around Andy as he is waxed. The homosocial group, presented as both racially mixed and unimpeachably heterosexual—indeed, their shared heterosexual identity is what unites this motley crew, played by Seth Rogen, Paul Rudd, and the West Indian-American actor Romany Malco—strives collectively to correct the mistakes Andy has made by leading a sexually inviolate, solitary life. Shirtless, lying supine and vulnerable, as the Asian "waxtress"—who seems to be placed within the scene to complement its racially tinged humor—strips off his hair in jaggedly uneven patches, Andy shrieks in pain and curses an incoherent blue streak that is peppered with "ethnic" phrases such as "¿Como se llama?" Somehow, "manscaping," endorsed—enforced—by the homosocial group, leads to the promised fulfillment of heterosexual male normalcy, sexual functionality, and desirability, just as the shaving of one's genitals, depicted as a male-male act for the purposes of being a comedic set piece, does in *The Change-Up*.

To forecast an aspect of the films that I will discuss at length in chapter 1, echoes of the American historical and cultural past, especially the Gothic literature of antebellum America, sound throughout contemporary Hollywood masculinity. This scene in *Virgin* intersects with themes in Edgar Allan Poe's 1845 story "The Facts in the Case of M. Valdemar," another work in which a "diseased" man lies on a bed while observed by a male group.[44] As I will show, the valences between works like *Virgin* and nineteenth-century texts are not incidental but an ongoing aspect of '00s movies. Any analysis of American masculinity is perforce a syncretic history of panic over male sexual failure. This failure never exists in isolation or without remedy, which comes in the forms of homosocial intervention and heterosexual sex.

For example, in another Carell comedy, *Crazy, Stupid, Love*, a 2011 film directed by Glenn Ficarra and John Requa, and written by Dan Fogelman, bromance cures heterosexual male failure and in reciprocal ways.

Carell's Cal Weaver, a staid middle-aged man who learns that his wife Emily (Julianne Moore) has cheated on him with a coworker, reluctantly and haplessly enters the dating scene once they have separated. To the rescue comes Jacob Palmer (Ryan Gosling), a studly and suave womanizer who notices Carell's Cal and oddly takes pity on him. Jacob is a kind of Henry Higgins of male heterosexuality to Cal's Eliza Doolittle of sexual cluelessness. Through Jacob's ministrations, Cal transforms both physically and personally into a successful ladies' man, able to have several successful sexual encounters with women. Meanwhile, Jacob, who has sex with a different woman every night, meets a young woman named Hannah (Emma Stone) who, despite his Lothario ways, enraptures him. He falls in love with her and decides he wants to marry her, but then he discovers that she is actually Cal and Emily's daughter, leading to a blow-up between the men despite Cal's gratitude to Jacob for having turned his life around. Ultimately, Cal gives Hannah and Jacob his blessing and the film leaves us with the sense that he and Emily may rekindle their relationship. Jacob restores Cal's manhood—or perhaps even bestows it upon him; Cal, in turn, helps Jacob to be a better, more moral, and monogamous person.

In one of the most telling sections of the film, Jacob trains the flabby Cal at the gym, claiming "Let's face it, the war between the sexes is over, and we won," claiming further that the fact that women pole-dance for exercise confirms this male victory. Then, in the locker room, Jacob stands, in godly Nautilized naked Gosling form, before Carell's Cal, seated on a bench. Jacob

Figure I.3. Carell's character stares up at Gosling's amply displayed body.

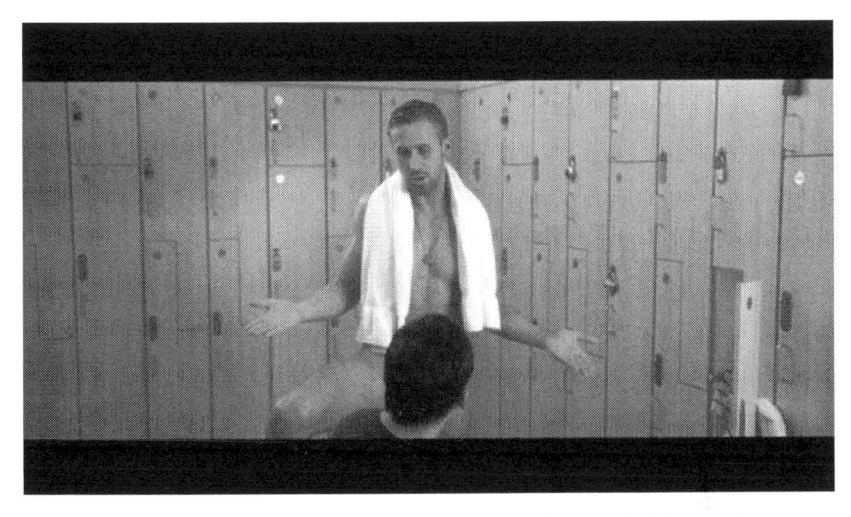

FIGURE I.4. Gosling looms above Carell, his phallus signified by its absence.

pontificates about being properly manly, which involves taking what one wants—Emily's coworker did that when he seduced her, Jacob taunts Cal. Cal looks visibly uncomfortable. Is it because he is being forced to stare at Jacob's apparently majestic penis, though it remains unseen on the screen?

FIGURE I.5. Gosling remains standing, visually dominant and demanding to be admired.

The visual framing here is significant—Jacob/Gosling is shown in full shot, with his right foot on the bench, knee bent and leg extended outward to the right and away from his body, emphasizing that his genitals are in the other direction and not being covered up, are indeed the visual center of the scene. His crotch is not shown. But Cal/Carell's head is positioned at crotch level, obscuring Jacob/Gosling's genitals but also *substituting* for this unseen area of the character's/actor's body. Jacob notices Cal *not* staring—a form of male-male looking emphasizing lack and impairment that I theorized in *Manhood in Hollywood from Bush to Bush* as *the masochistic gaze*— and challenges Cal for being uncomfortable about the exhibited spectacle of Jacob's naked body and impressive organ. "What, does this make you uncomfortable?" Jacob asks, gesturing to his penis. Initially saying no, Cal irritatedly admits, "Yes, it makes him uncomfortable. Would you please put some clothes on?" And then Jacob redirects his continuous diatribe: Cal *should* be irritated, Jacob explains: "If you're not uncomfortable, Cal, then we got a bigger problem." Then, later, Cal, as Jacob continues to pontificate, actually falls asleep, and his face crashes into the still-standing Jacob's crotch. Homoerotic desire in films of the present is pointedly referenced, foregrounded even, and at the same time repudiated, a process that I call *disrecognition*. That Cal may be drawn to, fixated with, sexually aroused by, or simply curious about the spectacle of Jacob as both body *and* penis/phallus are explicitly raised as possibilities. These possibilities are then submitted to the process of disrecognition, which takes the visualized form of Cal submitting to the nullity of slumber *in the face* of the homoerotic body/penis/phallus. Repressed homosexual voyeurism is taken to a new level of explicitness as such while being reinforced as such.

José Esteban Muñoz, in his much-discussed *Disidentifications: Queers of Color and the Performance of Politics*, showed us the ways in which non-white gay/queer/transgendered artists produce art that "disidentifies" with the dominant structures of power and the racist hierarchies they promulgate, the privileged whiteness they reflect. The white heteromasculine men on display in the films under consideration here reflect, instead, a simultaneous self-fascination and a refusal to see the self, certainly a refusal to see the self in the context of others and within social reality. This is the concept that I call disrecognition. Trapped in the mirror of self-disrecognition, the post-millennial male finds little challenge to this murderous solipsism in the realm of contemporary mainstream cinema.

The male body in horror, science-fiction, and comic-book films has emerged as a central figure in ways that exceed these genres' characteristic focus on the somatic. The exposure of male bodies, of which Steve Carell's waxing scene in *Virgin* is metonymic, matches, intensifies, extends, and allegorizes the deeper interest in exposing male *psyches* as well, a tendency that is indicative of what Mark Seltzer in *Serial Killers* has called American "wound culture." The wounding of men is graphically literalized in Eli Roth's *Hostel* (2005). Arguably the definitive horror film of the '00s, *Hostel* makes the ostensibly straight male body the chief location of trauma and violation, in this manner revising the entire splatter horror movie tradition (while also evoking the rape/revenge subgenre as it substitutes the male for the female protagonist of that subgenre). Roth's deeply troubling and pivotal work is indicative not only of post-millennial horror trends but of larger patterns in the period's cinema, which foreground male corporeality and its vulnerabilities, as I will show. At the same time, an obsession with faces distinctively characterizes the depictions of males in post-millennial film, and I will take this subject among others up in chapter 1.

9/11 and Historical Masculinity

In a review of Hari Kunzru's book *Gods Without Men* (Knopf, 2012), Douglas Coupland, famous as the creator of the concept "Generation X," writes of the strange temporal de-centeredness of the present moment, using 9/11 as a frame:

> One thing that struck me about the 9/11 footage shown during last year's anniversary was that in 2001, the people on New York City's sidewalks had no smartphones with which to record the events of the day. History may well look back on 9/11 as the world's last underdocumented mega-event. But aside from the absence of phone cameras, the people and streets of September 2001 looked pretty much identical to those of September 2011: the clothes, the hair, the cars. I mention this because it has been only in the past decade that we appear to have entered an aura-free universe in which all eras coexist at once—a state of possibly permanent atemporality given to us courtesy of the Internet. No particular era now dominates. We live in a post-era era without forms of its own powerful enough to brand the times. The zeitgeist of 2012 is that we have a lot of zeit but not much geist.[45]

The "state of possibly permanent atemporality" that Coupland diagnoses is crucial to an understanding of post-millennial Hollywood masculinity.

Images of a decentered American masculinity recur in Hollywood film and television texts of the '00s, which foreground fictive men who seem to be floating through time. This decentering frequently takes the form of a temporal and cultural dislocation, sometimes the literal blurring of time lines familiar to the science-fiction genre, but more often an eerie return to a different time, the eeriness of which lies in the allegorical significance of this earlier period for the contemporary moment.

One of the crucial aspects of the aftermath of 9/11 has been a preoccupation with American history, a preoccupation that has had the corollary of an equally sustained interest in what I call *historical masculinity*, a consistent view of masculinity as simultaneously rooted in time and timeless, of its moment and a continuous cultural identity with key precedents in the past. I call the larger set of fascinations with genre and the historical (the historical figured, as Kathleen Parker's diatribe in *Save the Males* indicates, as a longing for a return to the perceived vigor of earlier forms of American masculinity) *the retrospective impulse*. On the one hand, historical masculinity emerges from the valences between contemporary concerns and travails and those of earlier periods in American life. On the other hand, historical masculinity is a phenomenon that can be traced back to the Sexual Revolution period and the uneasy transformation of American masculinity that was wrought during and after the turbulent, transformative 1960s—after the Vietnam War, the push for civil, women's, and gay rights, and the economic collapse and uptick in national crime rates of the 1970s. At once, both the delimited genealogy of a post-Sexual Revolution American manhood and a manhood that derives from "historical" American culture—what we can refer to as the period from the Revolution to Reconstruction—informs post-millennial America and the historical masculinity it promulgates.

To break this concept down further, a preoccupation with the Reagan years give films of the '00s their peculiar flavor. The Reagan-era continues to make spectacular reappearances in numerous forms. Not only have action film genre franchises of the 1980s returned but also their original stars—Sylvester Stallone in *Rambo*, directed by Stallone, 2008; Bruce Willis in *A Good Day to Die Hard* (John Moore, 2013); Arnold Schwarzenegger in *Terminator: Genisys* (2015), notably battling the younger version of his killer-cyborg self, and so forth. *Donnie Darko* (Richard Kelly, 2001) exemplifies the retrospective impulse. The film, with its brooding *Tears For Fears*-infused soundtrack, resituates American teen male subjectivity in Reagan's America as it charts disaffected high school student Donnie Darko's descent into probable psychosis. In its early moments, images of Michael Dukakis, the 1988 Democratic presidential nominee, appear on the screen of the family television. Dukakis lost the election to George H. Bush, who had been Reagan's vice president. The film's palette of genre colors is broad, ranging from German Expressionism to Universal horror movies of the 1930s (both evoked in the images of the rabbit-faced man that Donnie sees in the mirror) to the teen comedies that were ubiquitous in the '80s. But perhaps most resonantly, the film recalls the American Gothic of the nineteenth century. The melancholy teen protagonist resembles Nathaniel Hawthorne's recurring figure of the young man on the verge of promise, such as Young Goodman Brown (the titular protagonist of Hawthorne's short story published in 1835), who becomes associated with a sense of blight, decay, and doom as well as an impending sense of evil. Young Goodman Brown leaves his pretty newlywed wife Faith behind to venture into the forest at night to keep his appointment with an old man who is most likely the Devil; there, he confronts his ancestors' history of violence, his Puritan forefathers' abuses of the vulnerable (women, Quakers, Indians). Or, more properly speaking, the Devil forces him to confront this history, an event that leaves him shattered, forever cut off from his wife and family and society. Brown's decision to venture out into the forest at night seeking Satanic company, leaving behind his young wife and his home, suggests a deep heterosexual ambivalence as well as an attraction to darkness. Donnie Darko's growing preoccupation with time-travel similarly uproots him, leaving him cut off from those around him. Time-travel here plays an analogous role to history in Hawthorne's tale, albeit in reverse: history is what Brown cannot cope with and must repress, whereas time-travel is what sets Donnie free from the constrictions of fate and conformity. Moreover, it allows him to save his family from the airplane-crash disaster that initially destroys them all and to restore his equally disaffected girlfriend back to life. *Donnie Darko's* themes reach much further back than the American Gothic: the scene in the movie theater in which the question of rabbit-suits and human-suits comes up includes a strikingly vivid Oedipus motif.

The scene of nineteenth-century America provides the setting for films as varied as *Django Unchained* (Quentin Tarantino, 2012), *Lincoln* (Steven Spielberg, 2012), *Meek's Cutoff* (Kelly Reichardt, 2010), *An American Haunting* (Courtney Solomon, 2005), *The Patriot* (Roland Emmerich, 2000) and cable series such as *Copper* (BBC America, 2012–2013), *Hell on Wheels* (AMC, 2011–) and *Deadwood* (HBO, 2004–2006). Series such as *Sleepy Hollow* (Fox, 2013–present) and *Turn* (AMC, 2014–present) return to the period of the American Revolution. Historical fascination extends to many other periods as well, as evinced by Paul Thomas Anderson's films *The Master* (2012), set in the postwar era, and *There Will Be Blood* (2007), set in the earlier twentieth century, and the trendsetting 1960s series *Mad Men* (AMC, 2007–2015).

As an example of the ways in which earlier historical periods impinge on present gender forms, we can consider a genre that is seemingly entirely divorced from the concerns of history. The beta males of Judd Apatow comedies would appear to reflect hyper-contemporary concerns with male sexuality, male bodies, and postfeminist challenges (and capitulations) to male rule. But the kinds of anxieties that they at times explore but more often symptomize have their roots in a longstanding American tradition of male disaffection, one that writers such as Washington Irving, James Fenimore Cooper, Nathaniel Hawthorne, Edgar Allan Poe, and Herman Melville were thematizing even as they were forging what has come to be known as classic American literature. One can readily imagine the Seth Rogen of *Knocked Up* (Judd Apatow, 2007) or the Jason Segel of *Forgetting Sarah Marshall* (Nicholas Stoller, 2008) sleeping off the traumas of American history and normative male identity in the manner of the title character of Washington Irving's short story "Rip Van Winkle" (1819). Beta male comedies evoke Rip's bewilderment in the face of gendered pressures (the ambivalence he demonstrates toward his household duties and his roles as husband and father) and his misogynistic opposition to strong women, like "Dame Van Winkle," his termagant wife. Apatow's and Stoller's films, and others like them, create, in their male stars and the predicaments they encounter, neo-Irving scenarios of male disaffection and bewilderment over heterosexual relationships. Similarly, the deep ambiguity that attends the depiction of young men in comedies as disparate as *American Pie* (Paul Weitz, 1999) and its sequels, *Superbad*, and, skewing a bit older in terms of their protagonists' ages, *Chuck & Buck* (Miguel Arteta, 2000), *Humpday*, *The Hangover* movies, and so forth, just as palpably recalls Irving's and Hawthorne's fiction as it does the days of *National Lampoon's Animal House* (John Landis, 1978) and *Porky's* (Bob Clark, 1981). In his work, Hawthorne treats masculinity as a symptom of national ills; his young men—troubled, dark, veiled—stumble through history as benighted and blighted harbingers of impending doom rather than figures that reflect the promise and bright prospects of the Edenic new nation. The more recent comedies share the sense of youthful male identity being under constant threat, in a state of siege.

Oedipal structures, or more aptly unresolved and failed versions of them, govern: contemporary young men are cast adrift in a world without fathers or in which fathers are hapless and helpless. Mothers continue to make little to no impact in masculinist scenarios of male development, as the absence of mother figures in father-fixated narratives such as *Star Trek* (J. J. Abrams, 2009) evince. What remains continuous is the emphasis on male sexuality as a battleground for the fate of the nation and a testing ground for its current state of health.

If all of this is true of comedies, it is infinitely truer of films in the Gothic/horror mode that directly continue the tradition of Irving, Hawthorne, Poe, and Melville. The varieties of the Gothic proliferate in the '00s; indeed, post-millennial masculinity can be accurately understood as a Gothic masculinity. Robert J. Corber, synthesizing the critical view of the cycle of "Female Gothics" of the 1940s, such as Hitchcock's *Rebecca* (1940), describes these films as works in which the heroine is terrorized by the institution of heterosexuality.[46] We can theorize that the Male Gothics of the '00s thematize the ways in which the heterosexual white male is terrorized by a culture defined by rapidly shifting gender and sexual roles, a culture that terrorizes the male subject out of any stable and sustained claim on or experience of a normative subject position. In other words, hegemonic masculinity perceives itself to be under constant threat. Many works of the post-millennial, post-9/11 moment attempt to remasculinize masculinity, make it more resilient and better able to withstand assaults against it. At the same time, acknowledging the besieged, vulnerable state of masculinity—in other words, the latest version of an ongoing male crisis narrative that has come to define the state of masculinity in the United States—emerges as not only important but necessary as a tactical strategy within this project of remasculinization. By incorporating an awareness of threats to the dominant forms and images of manhood, representation seeks to produce a more self-aware and self-reflexive but still recognizably coherent version of the standard model of masculinity. Lindsay Sternberg's assessment of the male subjects of Reality television seems apt on a broader level: "The targeted male spectator can play at a being hyper-masculine while congratulating himself for being a media-savvy postmodern media citizen who is on the show's jokes. Arguably, audiences can even turn those jokes against hegemonic masculinity by laughing at the absurdity inherent in the performance of hyper-masculinity."[47]

That the acknowledgement of postfeminist and queer spectatorships on the part of the heterosexual male cinematic subject is a key element in remasculinization may sound paradoxical and even bewildering, but, as I will show, it is nevertheless an indispensable maneuver in post-millennial Hollywood.

Timebends: Masculinities from the 1970s to *Seancody.com*

As a decade, the '00s have seemed to be, at once, preoccupied with the incipiently new and the enduringly old: an emerging technologically enhanced radical contemporariness, on the one hand, and, on the other hand, a newly urgent sense of the historical, exhibited in the demonstrable fascination with older forms of dress, speech, customs, in a word, style. This fascination takes the form of a preoccupation with earlier styles of masculinity, ranging from those of the action-movie stars of the 1980s to the suit-wearing sleek austerity of the 1960s man to the nineteenth-century, rangy frontier chic of the male characters on HBO's *Deadwood*, the Revolutionary War fashions of Fox's *Sleepy Hollow* and AMC's *Turn*. The new queer visibility has had the ripple effects of making the ostensibly straight male body the focus of the sexualizing gaze (for example, the brazen displays of male flesh in Reality-TV bulwarks such as *Jersey Shore* [2009–present], exemplified by its star, "The Situation," and his happily exposed abs; Jamie Dornan's body in *Fifty Shades of Grey*; the ongoing spectacle of Channing Tatum's hypermasculine form[48]; the media frenzy that ensues over the seeming exposure of the celebrity male penis, even as this anxiously protected organ is kept hidden from view, and so on and on).[49] These contemporary displays of male desirability that range from the thoughtful and nuanced to the egregiously silly all intersect with the ineluctably ominous aftermath of the events of 9/11 and the latest male crisis narrative that ensued in its wake, an uncomfortable mixture to say the least.

The disorienting blending of time periods and styles in the '00s attest to the haphazard atmosphere of contemporary Hollywood. Post-millennial film masculinity reflects the concerns of an era in which postmodernism as a concept seems inadequate, indeed quite dated, producing a constant need for new terms and even newer ways of discerning the cultural present; in which film as we knew it as a medium is all but dead, replaced by digital technology; in which, far from being repressed or sublimated, queer sexuality, long perceived as the ultimate threat to the straight male hegemon, is maximally visible, an endlessly present presence that must be forever negotiated, addressed, and incorporated into even the most normative schemes of gender identity.[50]

The complex genealogy of the decentered yet re-entrenched masculinity that I attempt to trace out in this book has its most immediate roots in the sexuality-redefining 1970s, the '80s reaction *against* these redefinitions, the '90s reactions to *both* the '70s and the '80s, and the post-millennial decade's quite distinct responses to the three previous decades *at once*. Which is to say, the tensions that define post-millennial masculinity derive from longstanding anxieties in American culture that pre-date 9/11.[51] At the same time, patterns evident in the literature of pre-Civil War America recur in depictions of post-millennial masculinities, namely the constant tension between a homosocialized and a more troubled, diffident, even endangered isolated male identity that recurs in the work of the great nineteenth-century American authors. What I have called historical masculinity emerges from an encompassing sense of all temporalities impinging upon representation at any given moment and also a blurring of several different temporalities. As my theory of "ghost faces," elaborated in chapter 1, suggests, the only means of understanding American masculinity in a particular period is a syncretic approach, one that acknowledges the living presence of prior gender manifestations in a particular "engendering" period. To treat American masculinity as a crisis in temporality is to link this study to the large-scale project in critical theory today to remap the issue of temporality. Chrono-studies of all kinds have emerged as a major genre of critical studies; what I am suggesting is that contemporary Hollywood masculinity is, at all points, a study in chrono-politics.[52]

The showcasing of male bodies that has been under development for quite some time might appear to be a recent phenomenon, but is more accurately interpreted as the fallout of the Sexual Revolution. The 1970s marked a new moment for cinematic masculinity in which male bodies became eroticized on the screen. The sexual objectification of men was hardly new to the 1970s—one has only to think of swoony male stars from the silent era, the new crop of femininely beautiful young men in the 1950s, the rocket-hard outlines of sleek 1960s men like Sean Connery's James Bond and Steve McQueen and the fetishized body of the TV-show Batman. The phenomenon of sexualized male bodies of the '70s, however, marked cinema's representation of masculinity in newly visible and direct ways. The mainstream emergence of pornographic films—such as *Deep Throat* (1972), shown in movie theaters in urban centers—amplified this new focus on male sexuality as a commodity.[53]

As Lynne Luciano observes in *Looking Good: Male Body Image in Modern America*, the blending of "gay and straight style began in the early 1970s, with the advent of the gay liberation movement in the wake of the Stonewall riots in Greenwich Village. Masculinization of gay culture, although it began in the 1940s, intensified after Stonewall."[54] Just as gay culture was emulating and parodying the straight male image repertoire, straight men were following gay fashion trends. "In 1975, Calvin Klein had premiered his new line of clothing at the Flamingo Club, a gay disco whose handsome young men inspired his print and TV ads—ads aimed not just at gay men but also at straight ones."[55] This hybrid gay and straight fascination with masculinity was a trend that continued to develop in the 1980s, albeit with significant shifts from the 1970s. As a quick study in contrasts, compare John Travolta's white-suit clad Tony Manero boogieing on the disco dance floor to Sylvester Stallone's cartoonishly hyper-masculinized Rambo. Both figures are Italian-American, "ethnic" masculinities put on sexual display. (The brilliant Chilean film *Tony Manero*, directed by Pablo Larraín, submits the psychic archetypes of male desirability and desire in films such as *Saturday Night Fever* to an unflinching scrutiny, turning these archetypes inside out.) The iconic images of ethnic masculinity in Travolta and Stallone from the linked but distinct eras of the '70s and '80s reflect demonstrably distinct qualities and produce quite distinct effects: one connotes a retro-elegance revitalized by the subaltern gay and black cultural influences that had exploded into such mainstream phenomenons as disco, the other a strenuous bodily homage to a perceived increase in imperialist might and vigor. Yet they are also part of a pattern, signs of a trend. The ethnicism they embody was reciprocally facilitated by the emergent visibility of male sexuality, the pageant of dark-haired, dark-featured, and often suffering and unstable male stars such as Al Pacino strutting outside the bank he is holding up in order to pay for his lover Leon's sex-change operation in *Dog Day Afternoon* (Sidney Lumet, 1975) or cruising, as an undercover detective, the gay leather scene in *Cruising* (Willam Friedkin, 1980); the parade of masculine styles in *Taxi Driver* (Martin Scorsese, 1976) and *Rocky* (John G. Avildsen, 1976); perhaps even Tony LoBianco in Larry Cohen's *God Told Me To* (1977). These ethnic masculinities appeared to signal an increasing interest in representing a *diverse* range of masculinities *marked as such*. Ethnicism was part of the carnivalesque public thrill of pop-culture forms of male display, analogous to the new sexualization of male bodies and an intrinsic aspect of the palpable, feral sexual charge of '70s masculinities. Blaxploitation similarly showcased male bodies: the films of the genre "portrayed a virile black male sexuality that had been missing in both mainstream and African-American cinema up to that point."[56] Stephanie Dunn observes that the "glorification of the stereotypical black male phallic reputation and of black male sexuality, along with the extreme sexual objectification of black women that pervaded blaxploitation movie culture, has found a kinship in rap music," further evidence of the ongoing impact of '70s popular culture on current pop forms.[57] The example of the protagonist Paxton's ethnicity in *Hostel* is revealing here. Except for the one moment when he makes use of his ethnicity to plead for his life, the Hispanic-American Paxton's racial identity is greatly deemphasized in favor of associating him with a rampant heterosexual all-American privilege and misogynistic sexual appetite. His American maleness trumps his ethnic-Americanness.

The famous "hard bodies" of the 1980s were cartoons of exaggerated manhood, as critics such as Susan Jeffords and Yvonne Tasker established two decades ago. They also strikingly opposed the garishly sexualized displays of the '70s, as noted. But the '80s hard bodies also opposed the brooding, pensive, pessimistic anomie of the men in many significant dramas of the '70s, especially its definitive surfeit of conspiracy films (*The Parallax View*, *The Conversation*, et al.). The Reagan era made a deliberate break with the styles, mores, and sensibilities of the 1970s, in flight from the perceived gender-bending excesses of that decade. But as it turned away from the previous era, the Reagan era was marked by what it rejected. Its anxieties about the alternative masculinities unleashed in the '70s defined the '80s as much as its efforts to oppose them; and the decade was a continuation of those alternatives even as it was a rejection of them.

The 1990s put forth a counter-image of the '80s hard body in the form of more sensitive and less physically outrageous specimens of manhood such as Kevin Costner's troubled Union soldier in *Dances with Wolves*; Daniel Day-Lewis as Natty Bumppo in Michael Mann's 1992 *The Last of the Mohicans* (playing an iconic American character almost superhumanly gifted at killing, but a recognizably human male in bodily terms); Denzel Washington and Mel Gibson, curly-haired and dopily affable, in their early star vehicles. These "New Man" types, as Jeffords called them, of the '90s knowingly recalled the unconventional male stars of the '70s—faltering, feminized men such as Woody Allen, Elliot Gould, and even Warren Beatty's dreamy Lothario in his fumbling aspects.[58] But the '90s New Man was not an attempt to return to '70s masculinity, with its male protagonists' agonized and adamant opposition to the system. Rather, the '90s New Man was a Clinton-era attempt, undergirded by a novel optimism, to devise a non-bleak, non-defeated, forward-looking form of American masculinity that drew from '70s male sensitivity but otherwise eschewed the perceived defeatism of that decade. At the same time, the New Man was a rejection of the bodily gargantuanism and comic-book irreality of the '80s. Presided over by the new Presidential style of Bill Clinton, one that emphasized empathy while foregrounding red-blooded American male sexual potency, the '90s strove to create a non-hyper-masculinized but also recognizably, reassuringly *masculine* male identity, a difficult set of goals and challenges, to be sure.

In the 1990s, the emergence of "queer" promised to offer a radical new category for an entire range of affects, styles, and manifestations of desire. The queer eroticization of the male body in films as diverse as *Batman and Robin* (Joel Schumacher, 1997), infamous for its decision to add nipples and enlarged codpieces to Batman's and Robin's suits, to *Fight Club* (David Fincher, 1999) and its tethering of homoerotic tableau to homosocial violence intersected with this developing and influential mode of sexual revolt, one that defied normative heterosexuality and its attendant social prohibitions and regulations.[59] As the 1990s gave way to the new millennium, fears of disparate kinds recast the innovations in not only the onscreen portrayal of masculinity but also sexual mores generally in ominous terms. The representation of masculinity in the 2000s has been an exploration of new forms of sexual interaction in this cultural moment. The perceived crisis in masculinity of this period has served as an allegorical indication of a perceived breakdown in the cultural meanings of sex, marriage, social relationships, and the body—a continuing decline in the sentiment of sex, to lift from Henry James.

The first film I explore at length in this book, Wes Craven's deliriously postmodernist *Scream* (1996), did more than update the fading, now-jokey slasher-horror genre with an approach that combined knowing meta-textual satire with authentic scares. It showcased, among other things, the millennial fears of a new sexual era. Masculinity seemed to be refusing its own privileges while opting for obscurer rewards, as evinced by the crypto-teen-male lovers of this film, concocting a scheme that takes them out of the teen world of their girlfriends and friends and into the harrowing and infinitely *hazier* world of psychopathology and gleeful violence. The new queerness informs *Scream*, but perhaps even more urgently the film is informed by the anxieties of its millennial moment that the American social order—much like the genre film—was grinding to a halt and hatching a strange new breed of beings who could only be described as post-sexual.

The domain of the sexual became the visible and consensual battleground for social trends, anxieties, conflicts, and shifts. This was a trend prognosticated by the new-style raunchy teen comedy of the late '90s exemplified by *American Pie* (1999) and *Dude, Where's My Car?* (Danny Leiner, 2000), which made the entire question of what role sex would play in and for the American future suitably nebulous. As if the entire social order were once again on Freud's couch, the sexual became re-entrenched as the key to the self on a large scale. A society suffering from sexual malaise was a society in danger of coming apart.

Fears of this kind gave millennial cinema—disparate titles like *Strange Days* (Kathryn Bigelow, 1995), *Scream, Scream 2* (Wes Craven, 1997*)*, *Chasing Amy* (Kevin Smith, 1997), *American Beauty* (Sam Mendes, 1999, written by Alan Ball), *The Blair Witch Project* (written and directed by Eduardo Sánchez and Daniel Myrick, 1999), *Boys Don't Cry* (1999), *Eyes Wide Shut* (Stanley Kubrick, 1999), *Fight Club* (1999), *Magnolia* (Paul Thomas Anderson, 1999), *Ravenous* (Antonia Bird, 1999), *The Talented Mr. Ripley* (1999), the new teen comedies, and *Memento* (Christopher Nolan, 2001)—its peculiar paranoid sensibility. What is striking about this group of films is how replete they are with homoeroticism as well as homophobia; with a sense of a breakdown in relations between the sexes as well as in sexual relations; with a languorous new focus on the potentialities of the male body itself. As *American Beauty*, written by the gay auteur Alan Ball, made clear, the unraveling but also euphoric defiance of the conventional white, suburban, straight man (played, improbably, by Kevin Spacey) could have odd queer implications. As the protagonist quits his high-paying corporate job, lounges around the house getting high with his brooding teen daughter's gadgeteer-stoner-rebel boyfriend, and defies his neo-Dame Van Winkle termagant wife (Annette Bening), he attracts the conflicted attentions of the military honcho next door, who is also a closet case. *American Beauty*, quite unlike Ball's subsequent work the HBO series *Six Feet Under* (2001–2005), is an extremely conventional and conservative work despite its louche trappings. It nevertheless amply evinced the emergent queerness within the millennial male anxieties of its era, while being a work that resolutely works to contain its subversive energies.

Queer representation, including gay porn, has now become so visible and pervasive as to be part of the dominant culture. *Hostel*'s overlaps with the genre of gay Internet porn, as I will discuss, reveals a great deal about the valences that exist between a newly visible, accessible, available contemporary queer archive and mainstream representational modes. While in many ways such an understanding of the hetero-male in gay porn is nothing new, what is novel is the nonscripted format innovated by such websites. Straight men who are willing to be "gay-for-pay," or who are, at the very least, performing as such, in gay porn have, in effect, begun to appear *as themselves*, frequently paired up with gay men who perform the role of the bottom who sexually services the straight male. This nonscripted, realist new porn aesthetic, featuring amateur performers, has radically innovated the porn genre by linking it to the Reality television aesthetic. We could call Internet porn today Reality Porn, porn that dispenses with scripted narrative and seemingly happens on the spot, right before our eyes. One of the most popular series in Reality Porn is the "man on the street" genres in which a solitary young guy—always classified as straight—is approached by a guy with a video recorder and his horny, young gay assistant, typed as the passive/submissive bottom. The point is to film a sexual act, fraught with the danger of exposure, between the straight guy and the gay guy who sexually services him in a public place. What was once simply a reality for gay men in a more homophobic era—furtively having sex with the constant threat of discovery, arrest, bashing, public humiliation, and harm—is now packaged as danger-porn, its excitement deriving from the staging of illicit pleasures that risk being caught by the public gaze, implying that now the only dangers posed by gay sex stem from this indecorous public performance of it.

In the last chapter, I will discuss gay male Internet pornography's surprising overlaps with torture-porn horror. If we take websites such as the popular *Seancody.com* or *Straight College Men* as examples, we can establish that this heterosexual male body is typically presented in three stages: first, as a stable construct, an impregnable fortress (signaled by the initial presentation of the man as fully clothed and altogether conventional in appearance and affect); second, as a stable construct that will be systematically *de*-constructed—taken apart, invaded, denatured, *ruined*—over the course of the gay-porn narrative (signaled first by the systematic removal of clothing, or removal of enough clothing, to facilitate sexual acts of which the straight man will be, in the most obvious sense, the beneficiary, and of course of the acts themselves); third, as a now-ruined body—or identity, or perhaps even spirit—that will be *reconstructed*. This ruination is signaled by the post-orgasmic collapse and weakness of the straight male top and the comparative buoyancy of the bottom, always shown still intact and ready for more. The reconstruction of the slack, limp post-orgasmic straight men often is most conveyed through a *bliss montage* of the men showering together ("washing off the sex") and then cuddling in fresh clothes.[60]

What is significant about the reconstruction portion of the porn video is its implicit suggestion that the men will now go back to their original roles. These original roles are as the straight white male and the gay male (also usually white in these videos) who will sexually service (ravish, ruin) the straight male. The post-climactic ablutions wash not only the sex away but also the momentary descent into male-male sexual intimacy that the porn film documented. The post-shower cuddling may signify a return to an infantilized state of innocence, but the instantaneous availability of the next porn video reassures the spectator that proper male roles have been restored. Moreover, the spectator is granted a limitless access to the spectacle of straight male ruination and reconstruction, the opportunity to watch one's favorite straight male porn star being put through the three stages of straight male re-entrenchment in an infinite series of videos available at one's fingertips via a scroll-down menu.

Such porn venues do many things, but, for our purposes, I want to argue that they primarily institutionalize homophobic and racist attitudes. The underlying premise of the *Seancody* porn film is that the hetero-male body is the only desirable sexual commodity available to gay men. The substitute body for gay males, the focus of spectatorial identification, is the gay man who performs sexual acts for the benefit of the central hetero-male. At the same time, these hetero-male bodies are also almost exclusively white bodies, with non-whites almost always cast—when they are cast at all; there is an absolutely shocking lack of racial diversity in gay porn websites—in the secondary, "gay" role.

If the desiring field has considerably widened, the subaltern desiring gaze—the transgressive gaze of women, queers, and non-whites—is nevertheless only part of the story; indeed, it may be a small part when considered in terms of the larger Hollywood picture. Many popular culture representations that I would consider essentially conservative in sensibility and aim—and that are, at least ostensibly, constitutionally uninterested in the sexual desirability of male figures—have also staked a claim on the representation of men and their bodies.[61] These venues also strive to expose the male body, to reveal it from the outside in and the inside out.

The trajectory of this book is as follows. In chapter 1, I offer a theory of representations of American masculinity in films from the late 1990s to the post-millennial moment. I develop the concept of *historical masculinity* that I discussed in the Introduction, and also discuss the analogous tendencies to focus on male bodies (voyeurism) and male faces (fetishism) in the cinema of the post-millennial period. Drawing on arguments by Deleuze, Freud, De Man, Laura Mulvey, José Esteban Muñoz, and others, I theorize post-millennial masculinity as the effect of a neo-Cartesian split between face and body, mind and material flesh, the basis for my theory of "ghost faces."

In chapter 2, I discuss Wes Craven's *Scream* (1996). I situate the film within its cultural context, arguing that it reflects the fears of a millennial masculinity that permeated the late 1990s. At the same time, I discuss the film's intersection with the spate of teen comedies that were emerging in the same period. The paired gay killers/lovers, I argue, provide an arresting template for the later "bromances" and beta male comedies of auteurs such as Judd Apatow, headlined by contemporary stars such as Seth Rogen, Paul Rudd, and Jason Segel. On the one hand, these films often depict men as cleaving—transgressively, in that to do so they defy marital bonds—to their male friends beyond marriage. On the other hand, some of the films also depict heterosexual men as being unable to form bonds with other straight men (*I Love You, Man* is exemplary in this regard). For all of their vaunted bromantic ardor, the films maintain an attitude of ambivalence towards male bonding. They are, in the main, marked by a relentless gay-baiting, which I tie to issues of race.

I turn to the question of filmmaking practice in the meta-textually oriented '00s in chapter 4. "The psychoanalytic scene," as I call it, is the near-explicit foregrounding of themes made famous by the "Screen" theory of the 1970s in contemporary mainstream film. Films such as *Donnie Darko* (2001) and *25th Hour* (Spike Lee, 2002) present masculinity in cinematic language that makes use of psychoanalytic tropes (the mirror stage, narcissism, and the gaze). These tropes as used do not challenge but rather fuel the re-entrenchment of hegemonic masculinity.

Chapter 5 focuses on Rob Zombie's remake of *Halloween* (2007). I consider the overlooked significance of the historical in the horror remake. One of the elegiac dimensions of the remake is a desire to re-inhabit past forms of male identity. Zombie's *Halloween* innovates Carpenter's original by much more extensively exploring the uncanny serial killer Michael Myers's childhood. The historical themes of the contemporary horror remake situate the genre within a larger cultural fascination with revising American history *through* horror, a tendency that links contemporary horror to the nineteenth-century American Gothic. This chapter concludes with a discussion of a concept I call "trick-or-treating alone": the use of the Gothic mode to reflect on and interpret male isolation.

In chapter 6, I turn our attention to the much-discussed "torture-porn" films—*Hostel*, *Saw*, et al.—that define the distinctive horror output of the '00s. By examining the valences between horror works like *Hostel* (2005) and gay male Internet pornography, which seeks to dismantle the straight, white male body while restoring it by video's end, I offer a theory of current representation's uses of the male body to "satisfy" the queer gaze while ultimately disciplining and repudiating this gaze altogether. I also examine the under-discussed racism in Roth's film, which I link to that in Quentin Tarantino's work.

1

Ghost Faces, Genre Bodies

Part 1: Bodies

The Enduring Reign of Masochism: Post-9/11 Hollywood and the Death Drive

The events of September 11, 2001, were the most significant act of terrorism on United States soil. Coming on the heels of the panic, now forgotten but then potent, over the new millennium and what it might bring forth, 9/11 seemed like a confirmation that society had entered into a horrifying new reality. Given the gravity and wide-reaching implications of 9/11, it is not surprising that post-millennial Hollywood masculinity is commonly read as a reaction to these events. If we consider certain films of the 1990s, such as Quentin Tarantino's *Reservoir Dogs* (1992), with its extended torture scene; Oliver Stone's *Natural Born Killers* (1994), in the connections it makes between a murderous, lawless society and the breakdown of the Oedipal family, signaled by father-daughter incest; and David Fincher's *Seven* (1995), with its grisly and unprecedentedly graphic images of violated bodies and its innovation of the serial killer aesthetic it helped to enshrine, the pessimism of popular culture was already well under way by the time 9/11 occurred. What changed after 9/11 was that this culture of exuberant grimness became newly validated along with a new representational mode of graphic literalism, especially in terms of violent content. Hence films such as Eli Roth's *Hostel* (2005), television programs such as *The Sopranos* (1999–2007), the zombie-apocalypse drama *The Walking Dead* (2010–present), and the endless glut of Reality TV shows that trade in on the public humiliation and suffering of their subjects.[1] What remains interesting in the post-millennial period and what requires further interpretation always are the ways in which films (and television programs) of this era continue to reflect what is at stake for American culture—and reveal that this "what" is forever staked on the image of masculinity.

The horrible and wrenching events of 9/11 made pessimism permissible as a popular culture mode.[2] "What was the long range impact of 9/11 on Hollywood?" asks Thomas Pollard. Filmmakers responded to these events—after an initial period in which it seemed that no real response would be offered (signified by the scramble to remove all images of the Twin Towers from films that were scheduled to be released shortly after 9/11)—"by producing some of the most pessimistic, violent, cynical movies of all time. 'Post-9/11' movies, not the peaceful, nonviolent fare desired by many, appear to be the norm."[3] The impact of 9/11 is most keenly felt in the rampant masochism on display in films of the '00s across the genres.[4]

As Freud argued, masochism, the desire to receive pain and the pleasurable experience of pain, is linked to the death drive.[5] Masochism, I argue, dominates the films of the '00s—not the politically subversive form of this sexual and affectional mode that theorists such as Steven Shaviro have extolled, but one that is tied to the combative and reactionary aspects of the broad pessimism of the era.[6] If, as I have argued, the period from the late 1980s to the early '00s can be interpreted as a struggle between narcissistic and masochistic modes of masculinity, masochism has emerged as the default mode of a normative masculinity that has adjusted itself to the contemporary and often incommensurate demands of feminism and queer sexuality. This retooled and innovated masculinity heralds a white, straight male privilege now founded on loss. Post-millennial films, in their rejection of beauty and embrace of savagery, ugliness, and pessimism, make the masochistic trends in the films of the 1990s the dominant mode of representation—make, in other words, the death drive central.

While the reality of torture and its myriad implications have characterized the post-9/11 moment, my focus here is not on torture as a legally sanctioned technique of law enforcement and anti-terrorism. A proper analysis of torture in post-9/11 works would require an exhaustive inquiry into the United States' political, social, and cultural complicity in a new era of human rights' abuses. My analysis of male sexuality in post-millennial Hollywood film must necessarily consider cinematic depictions of torture, which I argue are the most vivid indication of a gathering negativity in American film, one that suggests a willful embrace of the death drive. I have argued that the period of American film from the late '80s to the early 2000s (the Bush to Bush years) thematized a struggle between life drive and death drive forces, and I offered as an indication of the former a level of sexual playfulness that suggested a potentially exciting, novel transition from modes of staunchly hegemonic to more polymorphously perverse masculine styles.

We can say that the transition occurred, but without radicalism, without joy, without subversion. In other words, polymorphous-perverse styles of masculinity have become normalized, as the rise of beta male comedies and bromances most clearly, though not exclusively, reveal.[7]

A preoccupation with male bodies is nothing new in American cinema, which has since the 1980s at least been entrenched in this preoccupation. But this preoccupation has increasingly entered into masochistic and even more deeply sadomasochistic phases in the '00s. Masochism in this period reflects the "opening-up" theme that I argue characterizes depictions of masculinity at present. It also informs the process that I call *dismantling*, the cutting and opening up of masculinity, which occurs through both film content and formal technique, although not always both at once. Dismantling binds representations of masculinity across the genres. These assaults on the body and the psyche suggest, I am arguing, the desire to see masculinity laid open, laid *bare*. This was an underlying motivation of the films of the 1990s, which demonstrated an active curiosity about exploring the possibilities of putting male bodies at the center of screen scrutiny, as the distinct examples of Kathryn Bigelow's 1991 film *Point Break* and Tarantino's *Reservoir Dogs* evince.[8] It has become an ever-more literalized, brazen pursuit in post-millennial representation, indicative of post-millennial cinema's investment in and promulgation of graphic literalism.

The chief aspects of the masochistic sensibility of contemporary films, in terms of the parameters of this study, are the willingness of the male to suffer and the susceptibility of the male body to pain, torment, and ruination. *Hostel* became instantly infamous for subjecting young and largely, though not exclusively, white, straight American men and their bodies to sadistic and murderous violence at the hands of European clients (all of whom are male in this film, as opposed to the 2007 sequel, also directed by Eli Roth, which features female protagonists and female tormentors). Rather than innovating such an approach to masculinity, *Hostel* inherits an increasingly explicit pattern of cinematic male suffering, both in emotional terms and in terms of bodily assault. These bodily assaults are on prominent display in titles as disparate as *The Passion of the Christ* (Mel Gibson, 2004); the James Bond films starring Daniel Craig: *Casino Royale* (Martin Campbell, 2006), *Quantum of Solace* (Marc Forster, 2008), and *Skyfall* (Sam Mendes, 2012); *The Bourne Identity* (Doug Liman, 2002) and its many sequels; comic-book movies too innumerable to list; and the new sword-and-sandal-meets-classical mythology CGI epics such as *Immortals* (Tarsem Singh, 2011) and *300* (Zack Snyder, 2007). While grave wounds to the flesh seize our immediate attention, the more resonant wounds may be those invisible but no less onerous ones to the male psyche, as Mark Seltzer has argued in his analysis of what he calls "wound culture" in his book *Serial Killers*.

Casino Royale exemplifies the sadomasochistic tendencies of the '00s, as I will elaborate on below. This first Daniel Craig Bond film offers an exemplary representation of the pleasurable aspects of male physical pain, evincing its sadomasochistic sensibility. It also demonstrates the current cinema's characteristic maneuver of acknowledging queerness by foregrounding a homoeroticism that is then repudiated, a tactic that I call *disrecognition*. In one key scene, James Bond (Daniel Craig), the British secret agent also known as 007, is tortured by the villain, Le Chiffre (played by the Danish actor Mads Mikkelsen, who stars as the titular serial killer cannibal-psychiatrist on the NBC series *Hannibal*, which premiered in 2014). Tim Edwards analyzes the scene thusly:

> Removed of all tracking devices, a bruised and battered but still rather beautifully tuxed Bond is forcibly stripped and strapped stark naked on a chair with the seating removed. Le Chiffre then proceeds to torment him with a heavily weighted rope operating as implement for bodily punishment, [not conventional flagellation but rather] the whipping of Bond's genitals exposed through the open chair. . . . The blatant homoeroticism is also increased by the lighting of Craig's body which although bruised and bloody in places, literally gleams with phallic virility (the shirt ripping opening is the first of many mini-climaxes here), while his performance in the scene overall shows an extraordinary degree of both suffering *and* pleasure as if to ram home the sadomasochistic sexual thrill once and for all. Aside from the [question of the action cinema's role in] the increasing sexual objectification of the male body, what this scene would seem to highlight is the sense in which the true spectacle of male masochism within cinema depends quite literally upon the *simultaneous* display of suffering and triumph, weakness and endurance, pain and pleasure.[9]

As I will show, the sadomasochism on ample display here, which produces feelings of both pain and pleasure and derives its effects precisely from this mixture of affectional modes, is crucial to the cinematic rendering of male bodies in the contemporary era.

A New Sadomasochism

Cinematic masculinity in the '00s can most accurately be described as sadomasochistic, reveling in both the infliction of pain and in the experience of pain. This sadomasochism is distinctively rooted in this period in a playful performance of masculinity as ostensibly heterosexual but aware of its potentially homoerotic appeal. To clarify, I do not mean playful in a joyous or affirming sense; rather, I mean to imply levels of meta-awareness, of self-conscious performance, acting, role-*playing*. Cinematic masculinities revel in forms of sadomasochistic play.

As I will discuss, Gilles Deleuze and his collaborator Félix Guattari's *A Thousand Plateaus* is crucial to my theory of the uses of the face in representations of masculinity in the post-millennial period. Deleuze's work on masochism in his study *Coldness and Cruelty* is helpful to the consideration of male bodies in contemporary Hollywood. Deleuze famously deconstructed Freud's view of sadism and masochism as reversible concepts—the pleasure of inflicting pain versus the pleasure of receiving and experiencing pain—and persuasively demonstrated that each psychological process is distinct.[10] Deleuze argues that sadism is about negativity and negation, whereas masochism stems from disavowal and suspension.

In Deleuzian terms, we can theorize that the cinema's representation of the male body is sadistic, associated with negativity and negation, which, as I discussed in the Introduction and as examples from films such as *Casino Royale* clarify, takes the form of assaults to the male body that are linked to alternately defiant and sacrificial acceptances of the pain of these assaults. I argue that negativity and negation also takes the form of nullifying sexual freedom, a nullification that allows the male hegemon to maintain a coherent form of male sexuality that eschews any nonnormative associations and/or possibilities. This program of normalized sexuality has, of course, always been characteristic of the cinema generally, but what is novel in the post-millennial period is that a nod to—a pointed wink at—nonnormative sexualities (and genders) is now incorporated into male gender performance onscreen. The incorporation of the knowing sexual nod and wink does not impede or disrupt the overall program of sexual normalization, the strict maintenance of normative gender and sexual roles and affects—it simply, or not so simply, updates it. As I will show, the interest in male faces in film of this era complements while also being distinct from the fascination with male bodies.

In terms of sadomasochism as a compound structure, I am drawing on the work of Jessica Benjamin and Mark Edmundson. And as I will discuss in part 2 of this chapter, the sadomasochistic aspects of American cinema in the '00s relates to the prevalence of the Gothic mode, as Edmundson has established, across a wide range of genre and subgenre narratives and to the recurring interest in the historical aspects of American masculinity. Jessica Benjamin notes that sadomasochistic fantasy, "the most common form of erotic domination, replicates quite faithfully the themes of the master-slave relationship. Here subjugation takes the form of transgressing against the other's body, violating his physical boundaries. The act of violation of the body becomes a way of representing the struggle to the death for recognition. Ritual violation is a form of risking the psychological, if not the physical, self."[11] For our purposes, the desire for recognition in sadism—sadism as an attempt to know the other—is crucial.

> In intersubjective terms, violation is the attempt to push the other outside the self, to attack the other's separate reality in order finally to discover it. . . . The controlled practice of sadomasochism portrays a classic drama of destruction and survival. The thrill of transgression and the sense of complete freedom for the sadist depend on the masochist's survival. When the masochist endures his unremitting attack and remains intact, the sadist experiences this as love. By alleviating his fear (guilt) that his aggression will annihilate her, she creates for him the first condition of freedom. By the same token, the masochist experiences as love the sharing of psychic pain, the opportunity to give over to pain in the presence of a trusted other who comprehends the suffering he inflicts. Hence the love and gratitude that can accompany the ritual of domination when it is contained and limited.[12]

Benjamin, as many of even the most brilliant psychoanalytic critics do, is writing strictly in terms of dyadic heterosexual relationships, basing her theory on the French novel *The Story of O*, an S/M novel that focuses on a woman's submission to her sadistic lover's every sexual whim. (It was published in 1954 by French author Anne Desclos under the pen name Pauline Réage; *Fifty Shades of Grey* and its heterosexual S/M narrative clearly revisits the earlier work, thematically at least.) Without discounting the importance of this subject, or the complexities of the associations, quite conventional ones, between masculinity and sadism, on the one hand, and femininity and masochism, on the other hand, what I want to suggest here is that post-millennial film (and television, gamer, Reality, and myriad other media forms) versions of masculinity position the heterosexual male subject as both sadist *and* masochist. Males usually inflict the suffering, but males now also do the suffering, as *Hostel* and torture porn-horror most vividly indicate. The sadistic desire to know the other and the masochist's desire to have another person with whom to share the masochist's psychic pain find rather unusual treatments and reconfigurations in twenty-first-century representation. In the beta male comedies and bromances that I discuss in chapter 3, these patterns take the form of a recurring, even obsessive, gay-baiting, as males in dominant positions, in various ways, relentlessly probe the nonnormative male subject, usually about his sexuality.

We can return to *The 40-Year-Old Virgin* for instructive examples of the queer aspects of sadomasochistic desire, albeit from a perspective that is strictly within the heterosexual-homosocial realm and also heterosexist. Andy (Steve Carrell) is a shy, awkward fortysomething-year-old man who works in a big electronics store. He lives by himself in a home that is filled with his secret possessions: action figures and other telltale signs of his geek culture-obsessions occupy entire rooms, lining shelf after shelf. This geek *mise-en-scène* establishes Andy's sexuality as childlike and regressive. His big secret—that he is still a virgin—is discovered by his coworkers, who then actively work to help him to meet people of the opposite sex, grow confident about and within his own sexuality, and to have sexual intercourse at last with a woman. (He is eventually able to do all of these things when he meets a single mother named Trish, played by Catherine Keener, with whom he develops an ultimately fulfilling relationship after several roadblocks, some quite literal.)

"You gay, man?" one of his coworkers in the electronics store questions Andy. The question posed to the nonnormative, potentially queer male subject by the straight male interlocutor takes on the form of sadomasochistic ritual in the beta male film, albeit often in ways that can be described as variations on a theme; for example, in this same film, the sustained exchange between Seth Rogen's and Paul Rudd's characters organized around the question "Do you know how I know you're gay?." Gay-baiting is a core element in beta male comedies.

As I observed in the Introduction, Carrell's Andy is subjected to scenes of graphic physical violation, such as the body-waxing scene, which his male coworkers watch him receiving (and which he does in compliance with their commands). The laughs proceed from the procedure's having gone horribly awry and from Andy's ornate and often nonsensical verbal expressions of pain and suffering. Crucially, the scene of Andy's suffering is one that is witnessed by other men, which is the classic masochistic fantasy of having a witness for the event of one's prolonged suffering. At the same time, that

Andy's meddlesome, endlessly inquisitive coworkers are all standing around watching him getting waxed, great swaths of the hair on his hairy chest getting yanked off as he howls in multilingual pain, establishes this scene as sadistic, their own participation in the scene an expression of their desire to *know* Andy. That Andy is an enigmatic object of desire—that he must be violated, penetrated into decipherability—is further confirmed by the voyeuristic investigation of his inner realm, his house and secret possessions. The shelves full of action figures, comic books, and other geek-culture paraphernalia all confirm his regressive childhood state for the audience. This regressiveness is crucial, given that those who are sexually nonnormative are typically associated with arrested development, backwardness, even primitivism, as Valerie Rohy has shown.

Voyeurism and fetishism, the dual strategies that Laura Mulvey famously theorized were crucial for the representation of femininity in classical Hollywood film, strategies designed to alleviate male castration anxiety, take on a new life in contemporary treatments of masculinity on the screen. Mulvey's and Deleuze's theories usefully intersect. For the purposes of clarity, let me establish that I view the fixation on male bodies and on dismantling the male, on physical, emotional, and psychic levels, as voyeuristic. From the perspective of *Coldness and Cruelty*, we can establish that the interest in male faces is fetishistic, fetishism "belonging," as Deleuze puts it, to masochism and its modes of disavowal and suspension. Fetishism, however, exceeds the fascination with faces; it extends to the fascination with the parts of male bodies that have been broken down into components that have been, as I call it, dismantled. These new, male-focused forms of voyeurism and fetishism coalesce in movies like *The 40-Year-Old Virgin*. The desire to penetrate hapless Andy's bewildering mystery in *Virgin* is voyeuristic in nature. The inspection of his secret geeky possessions and the delectation over individual aspects of his exposed body in the waxing scene are fetishistic and voyeuristic at once.

Heterosexuality and heterosexual sexual intercourse play decisive roles in this film, as the entire point is to bring Andy not only into proximity but also normative alignment with these dispositions and experiences. But his relationship to the male group is equally significant, especially in its delineation of the sadomasochistic aspects of contemporary screen masculinities. Homosexuality and queerness, aspects of a continuum of nonnormative sexualities, play the important role in representation of being threats to the stability of the normative male. The male group desire to know the nonnormative male is, at least in part, a desire to know to what extent his sexuality is queer. The masochistic male desire to be seen, to be witnessed, stems, perhaps, from a longing for affirmation from the male group, which represents male heterosexual homosociality itself. It also indicates the ongoing effort to insinuate queerness in male characters, one that can be exposed but then ultimately transcended. Male heterosexuality is queered but ultimately safeguarded. The sadist is not just witness to masochistic male queerness but also sexual mentor to the masochist, hoisting him up to the upper rungs of normative male sexuality, the position from which the sadist's attentions flow. By implication, screen male masochists long not for the perpetuation of their own suffering but to become sadists themselves.

In *Manly Arts*, his ambitious and impressive study of masculinity's centrality to the transition, in the United States, from a white male-centered literary national culture to the early cinema and its similar fascinations with masculinity and pursuit of cinematic realism, David Gerstner notes that

> the repetition of discourse and practice that organizes the terms for American masculinism and nationalism by no means augurs a homogeneous ideological culture. Instead, it is the ironic failings, the peculiar twists and turns, and the over-determined polemical pronouncements that generate—with powerful affect—the uncanny resiliency of masculinist nationalism in the American cinematic arts.[13]

I agree with Gerstner that "a homogeneous ideological culture" does not exist, but, at the same time, I believe that twenty-first-century Hollywood movies *on balance* exhibit a strikingly similar series of conventions in terms of the depiction of masculinity.[14] The focus on bodies is, I argue, metonymic of the larger voyeuristic obsession with penetrating the mysteries of manhood, one that extends to the international cinema but can also take on more radical dimensions in films made outside of the United States.[15] This voyeurism is itself metonymic of a larger preoccupation with the image of masculinity, of which the fetishistic fixation on faces is the chief indication. Thinking about the disjunct between unruly bodies and uncanny faces allows us to develop deeper insights into the instabilities inherent within the representation of American masculinity. It also allows us to address a potent dimension of this representation, a split between a normative understanding of masculinity as stable, coherent, and rigidly contained and a queer understanding of masculinity as porous, fluid, open to interpretation, and always already destabilized.

Part 2: Faces

Ghost Faces in Film

In media representations of the '00s, the face emerges as the key to the male self, index of its conflicts, map of its overlaps with various others, code to its breaking point. The Ghost Face of post-millennial American films is a male character whose psychic and emotional conflicts, anxieties over his desires, potential for violence, or simply his inscrutability is made physically manifest in his face.

One particularly resonant image of masculinity recurs in the films of the '00s: a male face that has been rendered distorted or otherwise altered, that signifies either blank impenetrability or fiendish, mocking cruelty. The mask the killer known as Ghost Face wears in *Scream* (Wes Craven, 1996) and its several sequels provides the inspiration for my book's title. The mask both heralds a new kind of *male visual identity* and provides an apt allegorical depiction of the melding of genre modes (here, comedy and horror) in the genre-hybridic '00s, a tendency that *Scream* exemplifies. More literally, ghostly male faces abound on the Travel Channel series *Ghost Adventures* (2008–present), a prominent example of the popular and wide-ranging "ghost-hunter" genre of Reality television.[16] Self-promoted as "raw" and "extreme," *Ghost Adventures* is known for its combative tagline, "Can you handle the lockdown?" The lockdown refers to the ghost-hunter team's self-imposed incarceration in "haunted" buildings of various kinds over the course of an evening. The premise of the series is that its three male investigators, led by the host and creator of the series Zak Bagans, travel around the country and investigate its supposedly haunted sites. The series combines the travelogue and the Gothic genres, Americana, history lessons, and the male-bonding commonly associated with beta male comedies. During the nighttime lockdowns, the men film the interiors of the haunted institutions in which they have sequestered themselves; they also film themselves, images of their faces in the darkness captured in denatured, green-night-vision photography. With their eerie green faces and bodies and white eyes, the investigators gradually evoke the spirit forms they aggressively and theatrically hunt down.

The uncanny—strange, twisted, or denatured—male face emblazons such films as *Donnie Darko*, with its protagonist's encounter with both his own face in the mirror and that of a nightmarish, leering rabbit-man[17]; *25th Hour* (Spike Lee, 2002), with its protagonist's alternately triumphant and self-hectoring rant in the mirror, a sustained encounter between himself and his reflection; *The 40-Year-Old Virgin*, with its climactic close-up of its protagonist Andy, now triumphantly *post*-orgasmic after having sex for the first time and right before he bursts into song[18]; *Source Code* (Duncan Jones, 2011), with a revelation that its protagonist is, in actuality, little more than just a face; Rob Zombie's *Halloween* remakes, aforementioned; *Drive* (Nicolas Winding Refn, 2011), which focuses intently on Ryan Gosling's impassive and *intense* facial expressions and also tropes on the idea of masculinity as a mask (literally representing the criminal protagonist, a stunt double among other occupations, wearing a mask, and not just for diegetically justified reasons); and *Magic Mike*, discussed in the Introduction, which figures its protagonist's "turn" toward a moral and properly heterosexual life (i.e., a life in which he is no longer a male stripper for female audiences, and certainly not for gay male audiences, never shown in the film) through a sustained close-up of his face, his expression at once aghast and resolved. What's behind the face as a symbol for men? Especially when we consider that it is the woman's face that, throughout film history, has been not only the cinematic face, but the figural representation of the cinema itself?[19] (I will discuss the formal techniques for representing male faces in the last section of this chapter.)

Drive, starring Ryan Gosling as the unnamed "Driver," is a prime example of a film in which a meditation on the male face emerges with a focused intensity that exceeds the demands of the plot. *Drive* is not a successful work by any means, but it significantly indexes the possibilities of the male face and demonstrates the fertile possibilities of genre, here the crime drama, for the exploration of masculine styles as they are held in relief—as Deleuze would say, in suspension—in the contemporary cinematic moment, which is marked by a tendency to blur and blend not only genres but temporalities. In terms of the latter, *Drive* invites us to consider its relationship to classic film noir through its citation of noir tropes: the ambiguities and inscrutable motivations of the male protagonist, the evil mob boss, the good blonde woman versus the dark-haired gun moll, et al. Refn holds the camera on Gosling's smoothly even yet tautly held face, to the point that his intense, blank stare starts to suggest alternative possibilities, becoming not so much a mutable canvas as a canvas that mutates. The close-ups of Gosling held for such a lengthy duration invite us to consider the meanings of this expressionless/hyper-expressive face, the strange stillness of which is one of the major motifs of the film.

In addition to being a driver in the criminal underworld, Gosling is also a stunt double, using his driving prowess in this capacity as well. The film oddly intermixes the crime drama with the meta-filmmaking subgenre, which focuses on the behind-the-scenes world of making a movie. Gosling's brooding, impassive screen presence sutures these subgenres. The camera lingers, indeed loiters, on the image of his face. (Indeed, Gosling's cinematic works are obsessed with his facial image, making them one continuous story of a face.) As we contemplate this face, we are, I believe, invited to meditate on the stoical blankness of the male film noir protagonist, embodied by Humphrey Bogart in films such as John Huston's *The Maltese Falcon* (1941) (though not Nicholas Ray's *In a Lonely Place*, released a decade later, in which Bogart is increasingly unhinged and apoplectic). Gosling's impassive yet suggestive face—his skill at suggesting reserves of feeling beneath that impassivity—is here a frieze of filmmaking's fascination with traditional masculinity and its codes of silence and distance. Gosling's able embodiment of these codes updates them with the almost queer sense of wounded vulnerability in his persona—the quality that has, perhaps, allowed him to emerge as an unlikely feminist icon.[20] As Frank Krutnik writes from a Freudian perspective, the noir hero "can serve as an ideal ego, who, in the imaginary form of (fictional) fantasy, achieves the fulfilment of ambitious and erotic wishes. . . . [T]he hero can operate as an idealized figure of narcissistic identification who will ultimately unite authority, achievement and masculine-male sexuality." Among Krutnik's examples are Ian Fleming's James Bond and Mickey Spillane's Mike Hammer.[21]

I would argue that in contemporary film, the differences between a figure like James Bond and Gosling's Driver are telling. Bond is, in the first Daniel Craig film of the rebooted Bond films of the '00s, primarily a body, spectacularly displayed as such in the much-discussed moment in *Casino Royale* in which Bond rises up from the water at the beach and walks toward the camera, in gloriously bare-chested form, wearing nothing but a speedo. Interestingly, we are shown Bond in this objectified manner as Bond checks out a woman who is on a horse. Through his POV, we see the woman on the horse through a long shot. As she is put on a limited visual display, he is put on a more extensive visual display. In other words, in a sequence that ostensibly conforms to Laura Mulvey's paradigms of the male as the subject of the male gaze, Bond is the more emphatically object of the gaze. In contrast, Gosling's Driver is a face, almost decorporealized as such. As a face, he is a goad to dreamlike contemplation and fascination that dovetails with Deleuze's theories masochistic fetishism. In both cases, the male hero is the audience's ideal ego, but narcissistic identification is disrupted by the incitement of erotic desire (whether or not one actually experiences this feeling while looking at Craig; I do, but clearly not everyone in the audience does), on the one hand, and Deleuzian suspension of time and space, on the other hand. Which is to say, the meditation on the Driver's face disrupts desire and identification both, forcing us to contemplate the face as the *screen itself*.

When the Driver performs a car-chase stunt scene, he puts on an unusual, huge mask that makes him look like he has stepped off of an assembly-line of mass-produced musclemen. Gosling's mask, white and large and flat of feature, transforms the driver into a blank, inscrutable version of a hyper-masculine male. It suggests hyper-masculinity in that the face could only belong to someone of Titan stature. This motif has the effect of reifying the suggestions of blankness in the Gosling face-image, emphasizing the marbled, statue-like qualities of the impassive face on display. It also makes more salient the trope of impersonation (a feature of *prosopopoeia*, the impersonation of another through the wearing of a mask in a performance or by rhetorically representing a faceless other, as I will develop below) in the depictions of male identity in this era. At one point, the mask *explicitly* exceeds its diegetic function: Gosling puts it on when he confronts the mob boss (played with nasty aplomb by Albert Brooks in a surprisingly effective counter-intuitive casting) who wants him dead. The mask emerges as a metaphor both for killing-machine vengeance and for the play of masculine styles on ample display here. These styles emerge through the constant contrasting of the Driver against other kinds of men, defined by type: the violent but ultimately victimized Hispanic ex-husband (Oscar Isaac) of the "good woman" (the ubiquitous Carey Mulligan) that the Driver protects; the mob boss; his large, formidable, violent henchman (Ron Perlman); and Shannon, the sad, ruined friend, played by *Breaking Bad*'s Bryan Cranston, who runs an auto-repair shop and also works for the mob boss. The obsession with male faces finds, all too typically, misogynistic vent: witness the *Scanners*-like explosion of the surpassingly beautiful head of the redhead gun moll Blanche (Christina Hendricks) in the bathroom.[22] Adorned by lush Pre-Raphaelite crimson hair, Blanche's head, when shot by one of the mob men during a gunfight, splatters red everywhere; Gosling's character escapes unscathed.

Similar motifs inform other films of the same period. In *The Town* (Ben Affleck, 2010), based on real-life crimes, a ring of thieves from Boston's South Side dress up as nuns to rob banks. The nun outfits on the men do not feminize them, exactly; rather, they suggest elderly yet surprisingly musclebound men in drag crossed with otherworldly creatures. Affleck pauses on the shots of the men in their nun-drag, allowing the strangeness of their uniformly doleful expressions and appearances (a masculinized femininity) to dominate the image. The film prolongs our contemplation of these masked male faces so that we begin to view them as denatured, alien, baffling.

The masked Driver anticipates the looming, Titan-like centurions of Ridley Scott's *Prometheus* (2012), a prequel of sorts to the *Alien* film series (the first of which was indelibly directed by Scott). In this film's mythology, these hulking, looming, and exclusively masculine beings are responsible for seeding Earth with organic life. The centurions' mythic, musclebound bodies resemble works of classical sculpture come to life. An eerie, sumptuously visualized prologue sequence features aerial shots of the Earth before life appeared on it. One of the looming centurions, mysteriously hooded and dark-robed, stands on a precipice above a roaring chasm. An enormous mother-ship hovers portentously in the sky (a steal from Kenneth Johnson's 1980s NBC alien-invasion miniseries *V*). The centurion ingests some viscous concoction from a vial (it looks like raw, futuristic fish eggs). Then, his marble body begins to seethe with dark strands of newly engineered and activated DNA. As his body explodes, it plunges into the roaring water below and seeds the newly born planet Earth. It's a fantasy of male birth, life gushing forth from Adam's body with no Eve in sight. These DNA Centurions (as we can now call them) are the military personnel of an unseen alien race (called The Engineers by the characters in the film) that created humans but then decided to destroy the life they created. The DNA Centurions' faces and skin are a pale, pale white, their faces and bodies uniform in appearance.

The militarized male contours of the DNA centurion's body lend the film a surprisingly homoerotic dimension. The shapely, sleek contours of their bodies evoke marbled, godlike youth. The homoeroticism of the conception of these male figures is further amplified by the dandyish cyborg David (Michael Fassbender) and his obsession with the style of Peter O'Toole's masculinity in *Lawrence of Arabia* (David Lean, 1962), a homoerotic epic itself. The obsession with the male face reaches an apotheosis here, with the cyborg David endlessly rewatching *Lawrence* while styling himself physically after O'Toole in the film, dyeing his hair a similar shade of blond. The blond cyborg David explicitly evokes O'Toole's Lawrence of Arabia as it recalls the gender-bending young David Bowie and also Rutger Hauer's blond replicant-angel in Ridley Scott's earlier film *Blade Runner* (1982). Later, David will be decapitated by a reactivated Centurion, shown to be a killing-machine rather than a benevolent creator. This Centurion will *himself* be orally penetrated at the climax by the gigantic Alien-hybrid creature, which looks like one of H. P. Lovecraft's octopus-like alien monsters in his Cthulhu mythology. Discovering how murderous the Centurions—and, implicitly, the Engineers they serve—truly are, the scientist heroine Elizabeth Shaw (the great Noomi Rapace) utters the signature line of the film: "We were wrong. We were *so* wrong." She will carry around David's decapitated head, which continues to speak, unaltered, with Michael Fassbender's mellifluous British cadences. Reinforcing the visual scheme of the film, Meredith Vickers, the tough-as-nails woman commander played by Charlize Theron wearing short blonde hair, sports a queer fascist-masculine look. Vickers envies cyborg David's proximity to her old, wealthy, tyrannical, Citizen Kane-like father. Her metallic look and short blonde hair link her to her cyborg "brother" David. (Her underdeveloped character is the least successful element of the film, being a misogynistic cartoon of the female in power. Unsurprisingly, she is annihilated at the climax.)

Uncanny Men: Historical Masculinity and the American Gothic

While male protagonists of films of the '00s recall older versions of the male hero such as the Bogart noir protagonist or the John Wayne western lead, the specific obsession with faces in '00s film links this body of representation to deeper levels of American history, specifically, I argue, to the literature of the antebellum United States and its emphasis on the Gothic genre. Mark Edmundson in *Nightmare on Main Street* has posited that we live, today, in a culture of the Gothic, presided over by Edgar Allan Poe and Freud; moreover, this culture is sadomasochistic in nature.[23] Edmundson's thesis is more persuasive now than ever. This is an era steeped in the elements of the horror genre, in which most television programs feature grisly content, mayhem, and violated and mutilated bodies, images of violence so graphic one wonders how they made it past even the most lenient censor, and the movies follow suit.

I introduced the concept of historical masculinity in the Introduction. Historical masculinity evinces an understanding of masculinity as simultaneously rooted in time and timeless, of its moment and a continuous cultural identity with key precedents in the past. American Gothic works of the antebellum period provide such precedents and are explicitly evoked as such in contemporary representation (for example, a scene, set in the high school library, in Rob Zombie's *Halloween* in which the teen heroine and her female friends gossip about their romances, commences with a shot of various posters of great nineteenth-century American authors such as Poe and Whitman; the title and premise of the Fox network's Gothic-forensic television series *Sleepy Hollow* [2013–present] rework Washington Irving's famous 1820 short story "The Legend of Sleepy Hollow"). As I will demonstrate in the chapter on beta male films and bromances, Irving's tale haunts representations of masculinity, particularly its central relationship between the pedagogue Ichabod Crane and the ne'er-do-well Brom Bones and his homosocial gang—the conflict between isolate and group forms of male identity. But Irving's story is only one aspect of a complex lattice-work of cultural and historical allusions in the present. Current patterns of representation in terms of masculinity recall one of the most famous imperative sentences in classic American literature: "If man will strike, strike through the mask!" from Herman Melville's *Moby-Dick* (1851). As I will develop, the overlaps between a work like Melville's novel and films of the present can be seen in the shared preoccupation with the face as oblique, paradoxical, maddening, a mask. Melville's elaboration of the theme of a horrifyingly blank whiteness—what is, essentially, his invention of whiteness studies in chapter 42 in *Moby-Dick* called "The Whiteness of the Whale"—provides a crucial intertext for contemporary Hollywood's figuration of the mask-like nature of white masculinity.

As Christopher Lukasik has shown, an obsession with the face and with the truth it apparently makes visible has been a preoccupation of American life since the late eighteenth century. Within the visage lay, for the early American republic, "a permanent, essential, and involuntary sense of character . . . that no amount of individual performance could obscure." It was during this period that a now commonplace maxim began to dominate American social relations: "there is a face that you put on before the public, and there is a face that the public puts on you."[24] I argue that a sense of masculinity as an identity written on the face endures in images of masculinity in the '00s. These images strategically and indicatively make use of the face to hide "truth"—to register a fascination with the inscrutable nature of masculinity while forestalling inquiry and analysis. The Melvillean idea of a maddening inscrutability—an inscrutability that stems from malice or that concentrates the essence of malice—finds a continuous life in male representation.

The story of Melville's famous novel *Moby-Dick* is well-known, but to recapitulate, it concerns the obsessive quest on the part of Captain Ahab to hunt down and kill the White Whale, the titular Moby-Dick, who bit off his leg. The novel is narrated by the character Ishmael, whose famous first line "Call me Ishmael" commences the novel. Ishmael is a sailor who leaves Manhattan in search of adventure on a whaling ship, eventually making his way to New Bedford, Massachusetts, where he meets his newfound friend, Queequeg. An initially fearsome figure, the tattooed cannibal Queequeg is from a Polynesian island that has no geographical record. Ishmael's friendship with him is a model of interracial brotherhood, as Leslie Fiedler extolled in *Love and Death in the American Novel*. Both men make their way to Nantucket, Massachusetts; once there, they enlist in the *Pequod* whaling voyage, captained by Ahab. Ishmael recedes into the background after the first third of this epic novel, the remainder of which focuses on Ahab's vengeful quest.

Part of the greatness of Melville's conceptualization of the mad, defiant Ahab is that he possesses keen insight into everything except his own murderous obsession with the Whale. As Ahab says to Starbuck, the first mate of the *Pequod*, in chapter 36,

> All visible objects, man, are but as pasteboard masks. But in each event—in the living act, the undoubted deed—there, some unknown but still reasoning thing puts forth the mouldings of its features from behind the unreasoning mask. If man will strike, strike through the mask! How can the prisoner reach outside except by thrusting through the wall? To me, the white whale is that wall, shoved near to me. Sometimes I think there's naught beyond. But 'tis enough. He tasks me; he heaps me; I see in him outrageous strength, with an inscrutable malice sinewing it. That inscrutable thing is chiefly what I hate; and be the white whale agent, or be the white whale principal, I will wreak that hate upon him.[25]

The obsessive, tyrannical, monomaniacal, poetry-spouting Captain Ahab's view that everything we see before us is merely a series of "pasteboard masks" has proven a remarkably resonant one for American culture. Ahab's nebulous motivation for pursuing the white whale is a textbook example of the literary theme of vengeance. It also allegorizes the psychoanalytic concept of desire, the split between need and demand (Lacan) and a force that has neither aim nor object (Freud). The closest Ahab can come to explaining why the whale provokes him so is that he sees "sinewing" in the whale "an inscrutable malice." As Ahab declares, "That inscrutable thing is chiefly what I hate[.]" Nothing is more of a pasteboard mask than Ahab's own obsessive desire to destroy the whale. I posit that American masculinity is its own white whale, an inscrutable object, never more so than in the post-millennial moment. But what goads the pursuit?

There is more to say regarding connections between the White Whale and Ghost Faces, but let me add another crucial intertext for patterns of male representation in cinema of the present. Nathaniel Hawthorne's short story "The Minister's Black Veil," first published in the 1836, provides a template for the idea of masculinity as fundamentally masked, hidden, obscured, a surface behind which a mysterious other resides. The definitive Hawthorne story, "The Minister's Black Veil" typically concerns a young man on the verge of marriage, Mr. Hooper, the Minister of the title, who presides over a small Puritan village. Hooper mysteriously decides to don the titular black veil in order to remind others of the "secret sin" that the veil "obscurely typifies." The bachelor/marital anxieties that frequently mark Hawthorne's males are unmistakably linked to this young man's decision to wear the veil. He even asks his fiancée, Elizabeth, to bear with his decision never to take off the veil, not even for her. Unsurprisingly, they never marry.[26] The townspeople never lose their horrified dread of and fascination with the minister's veiled face, even when Hooper, now an old man, lies on his death-bed, still wearing the veil. The sheer blankness of Hooper's veiled face is suggestive for our reading of contemporary cinematic versions of masculinity—the ways in which this blankness defers and incites interpretation.

Freud's famous 1919 essay "The Uncanny" has been especially influential for theorizations of the horror genre.[27] Freud theorizes that the uncanny is the return of something familiar (*heimlich*) in a disturbingly unfamiliar form (*unheimlich*). Freud's concept of the "return of the repressed," as Rick Worland points out, has been broadened into a "sociopolitical critique" by recent horror critics, for whom the genre resonates with the return of any "number of [repressed] actions and desires."[28] This is certainly the view taken by Robin Wood in his influential writings on the horror film, in particular his essay "The American Nightmare," in which Wood popularized the notion of the uncanniness of horror and of the return of the repressed as its defining feature.[29]

Josh Cohen considers "The Minister's Black Veil" in terms of Freud's theory of the uncanny.[30] Cohen persuasively observes that it "is a narrative meditation on the uncanny otherness at the heart of every human being, on the stubborn inextricability of the uncanny and the human."[31]

> The veil is so awful because it reminds us, not unlike psychoanalysis, that even without a veil we're in perpetual disguise, as obscure and unrecognizable to ourselves as to others. . . . [What the minister's congregants] are seeing in the veil, then, is nothing more than their own possession of an unconscious, their haunting by what Freud calls a double of themselves: "the quality of uncanniness can only come from the fact of the 'double' being a creation dating back to a very early mental stage, long since surmounted' (SE 17: 236). . . . [T]he unconscious double is

itself double. The outward self or ego we present to the world enables us to pretend the double isn't there. My face, as I both know and don't want to know, is a black veil, disguising the uncanny other that 'I' is.[32]

Ghost Faces—masculinities defined by and that hide behind a face—evoke the black veil, disguising the uncanny other that the normative screen male protagonist "is." But what is this uncanny other? The answer, I posit, lies in the unknowledgeable (except in the limited and conditional ways I have discussed) presence of queerness. Given the preponderance of white faces onscreen, the male face is a *white* veil, obscuring all non-white identities. Ghost Faces point to a void at the center of white male screen subjectivity but also constitute this very void.

Theories of Prosopoeia: *De Man and Muñoz*

In his essay "Autobiography as De-Facement," Paul de Man discusses the ambiguous figure of *prosopopoeia* in several writings by the Romantic poet William Wordsworth. As de Man notes, prosopopoeia is "the fiction of an apostrophe to an absent, deceased, or voiceless entity, which posits the possibility of the latter's reply and confers upon it the power of speech. Voice assumes mouth, eye, and finally face [in Wordsworth's *Essays upon Epitaphs*], a chain that is manifest in the etymology of the trope's name, *prosopon poien*, to confer a mask or a face (*prosopon*). Prosopopoeia is the trope of autobiography, by which one's name . . . is made as intelligible and memorable as a face. Our topic deals with the giving and taking away of faces, with face and deface, *figure*, figuration and disfiguration." While I do not want to take us too far afield with a discussion of Romantic writings and de Manian theory, I want to establish that de Man points to a telling tension in Wordsworth's discussion of works by Shakespeare and Milton: prosopopoeia offers a crucial opportunity to give the dead a voice but must be used with caution and creates problems of its own. In terms of historical masculinity, de Man's location of a powerful ambivalence in Wordsworth's treatment of prosopopoeia is illuminating. Historical masculinity is a gendered prosopopoeia, an impersonation, a donning of various masks that indicate earlier forms of male identity but also uses them to deflect meaning and inquiry. This form of prosopopeia functions, on the one hand, as a citation of prior forms of masculinity; it functions, on the other hand, as disaffiliation with these earlier forms—a refusal to engage with the meanings of the historical masculinities being cited.

Judith Butler's early but still useful theory of performative gender identity as reiterative and citational is useful here. Butler distinguishes gender from sex, arguing that gender operates as "the social construction of sex."[33] The social construction of gender "is neither a subject nor its act, but a process of reiteration by which both 'subjects' and 'acts' come to appear at all." There "is no power that acts, but only a reiterated acting that is power in its persistence and instability."[34] Historical masculinity is just such a process of "reiterated acting"; Ghost Faces make clearer that such versions of masculinity are performances in which historical masculinities function as and are donned as if they were masks.

José Esteban Muñoz, reworking de Man's essay for the purposes of queer theory, discusses faces in the context of AIDS, gay men, memory, and the crucial concept of *prosopopoeia*:

> Prosopopoeia was understood by De Man as the trope of autobiography, the giving of names, the giving of face, "the fiction of an apostrophe to an absent, deceased, or voiceless entity, which posits the possibility of the latter's reply and confers upon it the power of speech." The autobiography and the portrait give voice to the face from beyond the grave; prosopopeia is also a way of remembering, holding onto, letting go of "the absent, the deceased, the voiceless." Thus, in the same way that she who writes in a biographical vein summons up the dead, by the deployment of prosopopeia, she who mourns a friend summons her up through elaborate ventriloquism. This contributes to an understanding of how the transhistorical call-and-response . . . might function. . . .[35]

Contemporary media's male faces signal the presence of and the preoccupation with history, as I have been suggesting. But, unlike the kinds of representation evoked by Muñoz, these faces frequently signal a conservative re-entrenchment rather than an attempt to memorialize. They *stem* from history, reflecting an ongoing set of problems as well as representations, as the examples from the antebellum American Gothic are meant to indicate. But they also deny history—the blankness of the male face forestalls attempts at historical inquiry and analysis. Male faces in contemporary media imply a *willed impassivity* on the part of contemporary masculinities; to the question of what men currently want, they offer a logic-defying, irresolvable, enigmatic response.

The ancient roots of *prosopopoeia* underlie this contemporary trend. According to the Oxford English Dictionary, the word has two meanings:

Noun:

1: a figure of speech in which an abstract thing is personified.

2: a figure of speech in which an imagined or absent person or thing is represented as speaking.

It is a Latin word that derives from the ancient Greek word *prosōpon*, which means "mask." Male Ghost Faces evoke the "pasteboard masks" that bedevil Ahab, who exhorts his audience to strike through them; post-millennial men have become their own masks.[36] These masks deflect the question of identity, carry the legacies of conservative re-entrenchments from the past, and embody similar attempts at re-entrenchment in the present. The male face is a figure for the effort to consolidate and compress all male identities throughout American history into one, seamless, coherent, blankly inscrutable image of stasis and stability. But as the fate of the mask worn by the killer Michael Myers in Zombie's *Halloween* makes clear, the mask itself is prey to the ravages of time. Michael's increasingly scarred, weathered mask embodies the disfiguration and scarring of male identities even within a massive movement to represent men as smooth, sleek, polished, blemishless surfaces freed from the taint of time, the scars of history, the marks of desire.

Making use of the metaphor of the mask, Murray Pomerance writes of the distinctions between the performances of gender in the 1950s and those in the 1990s. Gender performances in the '50s seemed much less aware of themselves as masquerades.

> But the masks of gender in the late 1990s may be less rooted in cultural practice, an expression of hope more than social fact; or a clever deception built and re-built to guide us away from the pathway to equality instead of toward it. Surely, much of the critique in this book [*Ladies and Gentlemen, Boys and Girls*, the collection Pomerance edited] seems perceptively to note a conservative, atavistic political abreaction beneath the surface of the apparently renovated society of sensitized men and empowered women we see laid before us on movie screen day after day. Liberation is everywhere, *but only as a garb*; and under it is the same old disenfranchisement, the same old inequality, perhaps even more brutal now than ever because painted as something else.... [For example] ... the dispersion of homosexual portraiture [in no way circumvents the continued placement of] gays in narrative compromise.[37]

Pomerance's observations offer a bleak vision of '90s progress, but I believe that he speaks insightfully to a series of conflicts that inform my own book. The masked nature of masculinity in the '00s, sometimes a literal mask, offers a strategic acknowledgement of normative masculinity's awareness of challenges to it; it also acknowledges what constitutes these challenges, namely the reality of the existence of nonnormative identities and alternatives to the rigid sexual stability and trajectory of normatively maintained sexual subjects. But these forms of acknowledgement do not represent an embrace of these possibilities or even a real recognition of them, much less an attempt at change. While 9/11 has been a powerful shaping influence for representations and understandings of masculinity in the '00s, the tensions within and that have shaped the most current forms of normative masculinity date back, as I have been arguing, at least to the '90s and the rise of queer visibility and the proliferation of queer and postfeminist perspectives. The masks of masculinity deflect the forces of change by suggesting that masculinity remains resolute, unchanging, in the face of them.

Deleuze: Fetishism and Faciality

The face is an especially salient metaphor for the myth of the subject, the subject being seen from Althusser and Foucault forward as central to power and its experiential and social effects. Along these lines, Deleuze and Guattari's crucial discussion of "faciality" in *A Thousand Plateaus* has been much discussed. "Primitives," they write, "have no face and need none." Why would this be so?

> The reason is simple. The face is not a universal. It is not even that of the white man; it is White Man himself, with his broad white cheeks and the black hole of his eyes. The face is the typical European, what Ezra Pound called the average sensual man, in short, the ordinary everyday Erotomaniac (nineteenth-century psychiatrists were right to say that erotomania, unlike nymphomania, often remains pure and chaste; this is because it operates through the face and facialization) . . . the face is by nature an entirely specific idea[.][38]

The post-millennial Hollywood face is a specific idea that flows from and depends on an ideal of whiteness that remains surprisingly consistent even in the work of Anglo-African and African-American directors such as Spike Lee as I will show in chapter 4. "Race is central to this system," notes

Amy Herzog, which places "Jesus Christ, superstar," the ultimate White Man, at its center, and that "overcodes, or facializes, not just subjects but the world."[39] Hollywood's Ghost Faces exemplify this overcoding. The awareness that white masculinity is also a raced masculinity, an awareness increasingly incorporated into discussions of both whiteness and maleness without an attendant spike in social justice, produces a racial blankness that analogically supports the sexual blankness inherent in post-millennial screen masculinities. This category of whiteness is no longer unself-consciousness, no longer unaware of itself as a privileged racial category, yet nevertheless endures as a stably maintained racial category. We are still brooding on the whiteness of the whale, and the whale is (remains?) white masculinity.

As I have suggested, Deleuze's theories of masochism and fetishism illuminate the thematization of faciality in the film era and works we are considering in this book. To review, Deleuze associates fetishism with masochism and sees fetishism as one of masochism's modes of disavowal and suspension. I want to suggest that to whatever extent faces are lingered over in Hollywood film, this momentary fascination suggests an interest in slowing down the relentless forward movement of screen masculinity, associated with phallic mastery of the diegetic film world, and to brood upon the image of masculinity itself. This lingering, brooding meditation, such as it can be described at times, fits in with at least one aspect of Deleuze's theories: suspension. This suspension of the male image, this freezing of masculinity as a face held on the screen, has genuine queer potentialities. But various strategies exist to delimit and forestall these potentialities, strategies that will be frequent topics for discussion in this book.

Ready for His Close-Up

A history of the cinematic rendering of the face, most closely associated with the formal technique of the close-up, far exceeds the scope of this book. Still, it behooves us to establish some of the formal terms for the focus on faces both in representation and in the present inquiry. The Hungarian-Jewish film critic Béla Balázs (1884–1949) was one of the most eloquent and incisive of early writers on film. He championed film's expressive qualities; in his view, techniques such as the close-up had the potential to express love and tenderness onscreen. For Balázs, film went beyond the "stereotypical distinctions" produced on the stage and could offer "the hidden expression" of an "*outlook*," such as one that might be called "supra-individual, class-determined." Film lets us see a "*disposition*." In a discussion of *October*, Sergei Eisenstein's 1928 film reconstruction of the Russian Revolution, Balázs notes that representatives of the competing classes of this film "all bear the marks of identity on their faces.... Face confronts face, and two world views collide." Moving on to a discussion of another film from 1928, Alexander Dovzhenko's *Arsenal* (the alternative title of which was *January Uprising in Kiev in 1918*), Balázs extends his praise: "The worker, the soldier, the ordinary craftsman, the small trader, the factory-owner and the rich merchant, the landowner, the peasant, the professional who works with his brain, the stay-at-home scholar, the déclassé Bohemian, the down-and-out . . . nothing but close-ups of all of their faces, and yet we know precisely that they are. A physiological cross-section of class stratification. Social distinctions and their attendant mentalities are clearly and unmistakably revealed in these faces. It is not just machine-guns and fists that wage war on each other here, but faces."[40] Contemporary Hollywood filmmaking is the antithesis of revolution. But it's nevertheless remarkable how much of what Balázs found to be true of these great Soviet filmmakers—their demonstration of the power of the cinema's expressive technique—and of film's ability to type entire categories of social identity through close-ups and other concise aesthetic techniques remains true for cinematic style and address today.

Even though I am not in agreement with her reading of the film, Diana Fuss offered a prescient analysis of several themes that would come to the fore in contemporary Hollywood masculinity in her essay on Jonathan Demme's *The Silence of the Lambs* (1991). Specifically, Fuss argues that Demme's use of extreme close-ups for the character of the serial killer Jame Gumb (Ted Levine), taken by many, Fuss included, to be a homophobic caricature of a gay man, crystallizes homophobic paradigms in Freudian psychoanalysis. *The Silence of the Lambs* involves another serial killer, the psychiatrist Hannibal Lecter (Anthony Hopkins), who killed and ate his victims, hence his moniker "Hannibal the Cannibal." A young FBI-agent-in-training, Clarice Starling (Jodie Foster), works with the duplicitous and dangerous but insightful Lecter, incarcerated in a Baltimore institution for the criminally insane, to hunt down the serial killer nicknamed Buffalo Bill for his penchant for skinning his female victims; Bill turns out to be Jame Gumb. As I argued in *Manhood in Hollywood from Bush to Bush*, while an indubitably disturbing film, *Silence of the Lambs* is not, on balance, a homophobic work but, rather, one that anticipates and analyzes the growing sense of dislocation and incoherence in white, straight, screen masculinity. (I would add, however, that, much as I admire it, *Silence* could with justification be called a transphobic film.) The film portrays Jame Gumb as an incoherent collage of various male styles, a welter of masculine signifiers that, in their confusion, attest to the impossible demands of maintaining a coherent gender identity.[41] I will have occasion to return to Fuss's argument in the next chapter; for now, let me establish that Fuss was right to focus on the face as the battleground for contending gendered and sexual forces in the film. If for Fuss Demme's treatment of Jame Gumb as a face to be broken down into components is resolutely homophobic, as are the associations made between his sexuality and a regressive orality, I would argue that the face, from *Silence* forward, continues to function stably as a metaphor for male sexual instability.

As I have been suggesting, representations of masculinity in contemporary Hollywood are organized around a body/face split. (Many other factors also help to shape the representation of post-millennial masculinity, as I will show, especially the conflict between isolate and homosocial forms of masculinity.) While films may make the divide that constitutes this split central, the body/face dichotomy nevertheless allows films to treat masculinity as a unified subject for concerned and at times hostile inquiry. In other words, the dual preoccupations with the body and with the face are complementary, each reinforcing the other as a potent symbol for masculinity under siege and in crisis. Such will be my understanding as I proceed to a series of close readings of certain key films in the chapters that follow.

2

The Murderous Origins of Bromance

Genre, Queer Killers, and *Scream*

Wes Craven's *Scream* (1996) took the moribund genre of the slasher-horror film, which had already descended into jokey self-parody, to a new level of deconstructive and satirical self-consciousness while also providing the terrors and scares endemic to the genre—indeed, reinserting terror into a genre that had become something of a genial, nostalgic pastime for audiences craving the "classic" period of American slasher horror in the 1970s and early 1980s.[1] The first two sequels to *Scream* were released, respectively, in the years 1997 and 2000; after a decade-long gap, the fourth film in the series was released in 2011. All four films have been directed by Craven, formerly an English professor; the first two films and also the fourth were scripted by Kevin Williamson (the creator of the hit CW network series *The Vampire Diaries* [2009–present] and the earlier WB touchstone *Dawson's Creek* [1998–2003]). Craven, mainly known prior to *Scream* for the first *Nightmare on Elm Street* (1984) film and its ensuing franchise, was praised by Robin Wood for his first film, the 1972 underground work *The Last House on the Left*. For Wood, *Last House* was a stinging Vietnam War allegory that critiqued the war and its pointless atrocities as well as bourgeois liberal culture.[2] While most critics would agree that Craven's films sustained neither their early promise nor their pointed political edginess, the first *Scream*, my focus in this chapter, is one of the defining films of the late 1990s. It anticipated while registering many of the fears that gathered around the event of the new millennium. The films of the series as a whole demand a sustained consideration, not just because they remain an index of the emergent fears of their era, and not just for their explicitly intertextual relationship to the history of horror, but because their thematization of issues of male sexual anxiety and racial panic anticipates many of the key strains in '00s films.

The *Scream* films synthesize both the shifts in masculinity that have occurred since the late '80s and, in their metatextual, genre-conscious manner, showcase the merging of modes of horror and comedy that have dominated the '00s. The body genres of horror, melodrama, and pornography, as Linda Williams has famously shown, have the central overlap of being genres that have a physical effect on the spectator's body.[3] As I discuss in the Introduction, I add comedy to the list of body genres (making a stronger case for its inclusion than Williams does). *Scream*, in its winking, deconstructive synthesis of the horror and comedy genres, places its focus on the male body, figured as the site of violation, homoerotic play, and homophobic rage.[4] The relationship between *Scream*'s two teenage male killers, in its coded homoerotic dimensions, anticipates the fusion of horror and comedy in the "bromance" and "beta male" films that have become such defining aspects of post-millennial filmmaking, a point that I will return to later in the chapter. At the same time, *Scream* evokes earlier movies that, explicitly or implicitly, foregrounded the figure of the homosexual killer. Tom Kalin's film *Swoon* (1992), based on the 1924 Leopold and Loeb case, and Alfred Hitchcock's *Rope* (1948), loosely inspired by the same case, are key precedents for *Scream*, as are Hitchcock's *Psycho* (1960) and Jonathan Demme's *The Silence of the Lambs* (1991). Further intertextual influences include William Friedkin's *The Exorcist* (1973), Brian De Palma's *Carrie* (1976), and John Carpenter's *Halloween* (1978), all of which *Scream* explicitly cites; Carpenter's film, literally incorporated into Craven's own, especially. *Scream* also grimly presaged the real-life events of the killings at Columbine High School in 1999; strangely enough, its pair of teen male killers have also been associated with a possible homosexual relationship.

With its mixture of sexual indeterminacy and metatextuality, *Scream* is not so much a "homosexual" as it is a queer murder mystery, and as such it is one of the pivotal texts for the transition from homosexual/gay to queer sexuality on the screen. The late '90s *Scream* trilogy was paranoid fantasy of the new millennium, a fearful prediction of the directions that American manhood might take. It prognosticated a new form of depraved masculinity, one in which queer and straight modes of masculinity intersect and become indistinguishable. *Scream* suggests that the core logic of fears of the new millennium was a paranoid anticipation of an imminent, increasingly visible, unstoppable queer identity.

Late '90s Teen Comedies and the Rise of Queer Visibility

As I discussed in the Introduction, the films and other media forms of the late 1990s and especially of the 2000s are marked by an inescapable awareness of queer desire.[5] This awareness stems from the much greater visibility of the LGBTQI community, a visibility with a complex genealogy that dates back to the late 1980s and early 1990s. This was a period marked, at once, by the distinct phenomena of the AIDS crisis, the transition from Ronald Reagan's two-term presidency to that of George H. Bush, who had been his vice president, the emergence of the term queer, and the flourishing of New Queer Cinema, as B. Ruby Rich lastingly called it.[6]

The comedies of the late '90s, in their distinct forms, vividly demonstrated the wide-ranging effects of the new queer visibility. First, a resurgence in the teen sex comedy genre in the late '90s, exemplified by *American Pie* (Paul Weitz, 1999), *Can't Hardly Wait* (Deborah Kaplan, 1998), and *Dude, Where's My Car?* (Danny Leiner, 2000), and, second, the emergence of more adult-oriented comedies, such as the Farrelly Brothers' *There's Something About Mary* (1998), which anticipated the beta male comedies of '00s auteur Judd Apatow, often made the threat of gay possibilities explicit and suggested that queerness was shaping the reimagined straight masculinities as well as heterosexual sexual situations of this crucial transitional moment.

American Pie features a scene in which one teen male drinks a beer in which another teen male has just ejaculated; *There's Something About Mary* features an infamous masturbation-gone-awry scene before Ben Stiller's character, Ted, goes out on a date with the titular Mary (Cameron Diaz). *American Pie* and its numerous sequels recalled the teen sex comedies of the 1980s, such as *Porky's* (Bob Clark, 1981), *The Last American Virgin (*Boaz Davidson, 1982), *My Tutor* (George Bowers, 1983), *Losin' It* (Curtis Hanson, 1983), et al., and spawned a mini-brood of like-minded sex farces such as *Road Trip* (Todd Phillips, 2000), *The Girl Next Door* (Luke Greenfield, 2004), *Euro Trip* (Jeff Schaffer, 2004), *Dirty Deeds* (David Kendall, 2005), and several others. *American Pie* put the male body on display, not a Nautilus-toned and hyper-masculined male body but the decidedly average body of a suburban high school male. In the first of the *Pie* films, the main character, the initially virginal teenager Jim Levenstein (Jason Biggs), attempts to get the alluring foreign-exchange student Nadia (Shannon Elizabeth) into bed. His efforts, unbeknownst to him, are broadcast via hidden webcam to the entire school, culminating—twice—in his premature orgasms.

Jim's public sexual humiliation provides a template for the similar kinds of publically witnessed agony in the film comedies of Ben Stiller, as exemplified by the scene in *Meet the Parents* (Jay Roach, 2000) in which Stiller's character, alone in the bathroom, finds his penis, or his testes, or both, ensnared in the zipper of his pants and must enlist the aid of his fiancée's family, presided over by her authoritarian father (Robert De Niro), adding further excruciatingly public embarrassment to Stiller's predicament. The masturbation scene in *There's Something About Mary* is also characteristic. Stiller's character, Ted, about to go out on his first date with Mary, is advised by his friend Dom (Chris Elliot) that he can't go out on the date without first "cleaning out the pipes," in others words masturbating in advance so as to relieve the apparently volcanic sexual pressure of a first date. Dutifully masturbating right before Mary arrives, Ted then cannot locate the semen his preventative measures have emitted. Mary notices a wad of fluid on Ted's head, and, mistaking it for hair gel, applies it to her own hair. What is significant about this scene is not just its misogynistic overtones, exemplified by the fact that Mary's implicit denigration—putting Ted's semen on and using it to style her own hair—is presented in a comedic manner, but that it stems from a scene of male-male sexual intimacy (the scene in which Dom instructs Ted to masturbate) that takes the form of the exchange of homosocial knowledge.

The focus on the male body—on display, in arousal, defaced, in a shambles—is the legacy of the early '90s that continues to inform postmillennial film and television representation. The male body had been on display in the action movies of the 1980s and in the decade's distinctive nighttime soaps like *Dynasty* (1981–1989), *Dallas* (1978–1991), and *Falcon Crest* (1981–1990). And then there was the definitive spectacle of teen male sexuality in Paul Brickman's 1983 movie *Risky Business*: shirted but pantsless, Joel Goodsen (Tom Cruise), a white-boy teenager from an affluent family, gyrates in his underwear when his parents are out of town to the thunderous sounds of Bob Seger's 1978 song "Old Time Rock and Roll." But, as Jim Levenstein's display of flesh and the semen-covered head of Ben Stiller's Ted evince, the focus now was on a "normal" American male body, exposed, humiliated, denuded or on some other level laid bare, made the visual spectacle of the mass audience. Tom Cruise's Joel danced in private narcissistic self-delectation, for himself alone; *American Pie's* Jim Levenstein, in a scenario that upends conventional structures of cinematic male voyeurism, becomes the site of sadistic visual pleasure for an avid audience, the object of the same surreptitious gaze he attempted to wield, and a public spectacle of humiliated masculinity. The voyeuristic Jim becomes himself the site of collective voyeurism.[7] As I discussed in chapter 1, the representation of the male body in the millennial and post-millennial period has been sadomasochistic in nature. Jim's humiliation in *American Pie*—the avid delight in his humiliation from the audience diegetically situated in the film (which stands in for the non-diegetic film audience presumably experiencing the same delight and certainly intended to do so) and his own suffering not only through the experience but during its social aftermath—exemplifies this tendency.

The Murderous Origins of Bromance

Comedies such as *American Pie* and *Dude, Where's My Car?* were forerunners to two later subgenres that have come to define the '00s: the "bromance" film, exemplified by *I Love You, Man* (John Hamburg, 2009) and the "beta male comedy" of the Judd Apatow school, which usually features stars like Jason Segel, Seth Rogen, Paul Rudd, Ben Stiller, Vince Vaughn, Owen Wilson, and Bradley Cooper and tend to skew older. These emergent '00s subgenres, the bromance especially, evince the effects of a newly visible queer desire while also confirming that secure strategies remain in place to contain whatever disruptive sexual energies may have been released. If queer desire is an inescapable dimension of the contemporary bromance, it behooves us to track the genealogy of this explicitness about the possibility of same-sex attraction in genre films especially. I am positioning the 1996 *Scream* at the start of this genealogy for the purposes of this discussion, but, to be sure, the origins of the bromance can be found much earlier—the "Road" comedies with Bob Hope and Bing Crosby (seven films, made between the years 1940 and 1962); the "buddy movie" from the '70s to the '80s, exemplified by *Thunderbolt and Lightfoot* (Michael Cimino, 1974), starring Clint Eastwood and Jeff Bridges; and the *Lethal Weapon* films starring Mel Gibson and Danny Glover (the first of which was released in 1987; *Lethal Weapon 4* was released in 1998; all were directed by Richard Donner). Even though the bromance usually takes a comedic approach to the issues that bedevil men of the moment, it represents a merger, a compromise, an attempt to paper the cracks in the façade of American male stability. In other words, masculinity is founded on instability and a repressive lockdown of all knowledge of this instability, patterns that *Scream*, in its own violent, menacing way, anticipated.

Both the bromance and the related subgenre of the beta male comedy take as their subject white heterosexual manhood as it has been refashioned, over recent decades, to meet challenges from feminism and a newly visible gay culture. In these terms, bromances and beta male comedies are particularly indicative of the shifts in the national construction of gender in the past two decades. For all of their antic humor, bromances and beta male comedies emphasize the masochistic suffering of the male characters. Yet, for all of the suffering on display, the films maintain a cool distance from their male characters, even as they present their emotional lives as the central narrative focus. What makes the films so interesting is the general attitude of ambivalence they maintain towards their subjects—an ambivalence that stems, in part, from fears over the increasing visibility of queer desire. In their anticipatory depiction of bonds between men that threaten to explode into terrifying homoerotic explicitness, the *Scream* films of the late 1990s emerge as a key forerunner to several recurring themes in the films of the post-millennium generally as they lay the groundwork for the bromance.

While treated with much greater explicitness today, queer desire nevertheless always remains an *undercurrent* in mainstream film and television texts, a site of repression that manifests itself in odd and discordant ways. As a result of the uneasy mixture of visibility and enduring repression, queer desire is most frequently registered through modes of defensiveness. The genres of horror and comedy become especially highly charged sites for the representation of male sexuality because both genres promote intensely *defensive* responses to sexuality generally—the one through physical violence and other kinds of bloodletting, the other through sidesplitting laughter. *Scream* emerged during the same period as the resurgence of teen/sex/gross-out comedies in the late '90s. These teen comedies were nostalgic paeans to male adolescence that figured adolescence as a state of acceptable male indulgence in polymorphously perverse pleasures. The pleasures, however, will have to be denied and repressed once young men pass into adulthood and its more coherent set of obligations, including, especially, heterosexual marriage.[8] *Scream*, as suggested by its killer Ghostface's distinctive mask, which seems to be a blend of the theatrical masks of classical comedy and tragedy, evokes the tragic dimension of horror. Unlike the teen comedies, horror films such as *Scream* are about the *end* of fertility, the *end* of pleasure, the *end* of sexuality. Nevertheless, what *Scream* shares with the anarchic teen comedies of its era is a view of adolescent masculinity as a last gasp before the normalization of adult masculinity sets in—hence the killers' hatred of father figures and hence, too, their indulgence in a state of polymorphously perverse, sexually open-ended, and violent pleasures.

Presumably, the mask of the killer "Ghostface" in the *Scream* films was inspired by the Norwegian painter Edvard Munch's series of late nineteenth-century paintings generally known as "The Scream." The wobbly, despairing figure in Munch's painting with a white ghostly face, wide-eyed and open-mouthed, stands shrieking on a bridge, his face in his hands, his flimsy body swirling along with the colors and the landscape in expressionistic despair. His cry of pain seems to stem from his recognition of man's condition in an unfeeling world and of his own terrifying aloneness in the face of the unceasing indifference of nature.

FIGURE 2.1. Edvard Munch, *The Scream*.

Tropes of expressionistic horror inform the representation of masculinity in films from *Scream* to the present, as evinced by the hideous rabbit-face man of *Donnie Darko* and the killer Ghostface, who provides a striking visual index of these tropes. It is fitting that Craven's indelible image of the killer evokes Munch's painting, given Munch's influence on

German Expressionism and its influential images of madness and horror. Such precedents inform my theory of ghost faces.

Scream's Ghostface subjects the suffering of Munch's screamer to parody, however, and this is a key point. His visage mocks his victims' incipient trauma, their imminent deaths at his hands. Wielding his trademark six-inch hunting knife, Ghostface is the killer who parodies his own monstrosity while insisting that it be recognized. The hideous zest with which he carries out his killings, forcing his victims to answer questions about horror movies, a deconstructive gesture that signals that these horror movies are in on their own grisly jokes; the speed with which he races after his victims, in stark distinction to the slow, inexorable pace of previous monsters, like George A. Romero's zombies and the original 1978 *Halloween*'s Michael Myers; the relentless mockery of his masked persona: all indicate a fiendishly knowing sensibility. Much like the murderous mastermind Jigsaw in *Saw* (James Wan, 2004) and its innumerable sequels, who invents elaborate torture contraptions for his victims, Ghostface stages his murders as elaborate, look-at-me games.[9] Perhaps chiefly, Ghostface's anarchic persona allegorizes the greater self-awareness with which men have come to inhabit their own maleness since the Reagan-Bush years. In *Manhood in Hollywood from Bush to Bush*, I described the years between the late 1980s to the early 2000s as the period in which "masculinity becomes self-aware." The films of the '00s reflect a masculinity coping with the burdens of and developing ingenious strategies against this self-awareness, one that is greatly intensified by the development of media technologies that make image and event instantaneously available to innumerable audiences.

The first *Scream* follows the classical rules of the slasher-horror genre, as Carol J. Clover expertly framed them, ending with a confrontation between the killer and the "Final Girl," who alone survives the bloodbath.[10] The film, as has been much discussed, is metatextual and self-referential, always maintaining an ironic, knowing relationship to its genre. It features not one, but two killers; not one, but two female survivors who together take down the killers. To evoke another important theory of the horror film, Barbara Creed has argued that a dread of being re-engulfed by the archaic mother powerfully informs the genre.[11] Building on its themes of narcissistic doubling, homosexual mother-son relationships, and the heroine's fraught relationship to her mother, the film reestablishes Freudian paradigms as the essential building blocks of horror while deploying them as a conservative blockade.

A savvy satire of the genre, *Scream* winks at the audience, putting all of its genre elements into relief, so that they can be enjoyed *as* genre elements. What is especially interesting about *Scream* is that, for all of its deconstructive hipness, it nevertheless perpetuates the same kind of reactionary offenses that characterized the genre at its least deconstructive and self-conscious. For all of its self-aware, deconstructive wit, *Scream* in no way updates, corrects, revises, or challenges the homophobic and, especially, misogynistic aspects of the classic slasher genre (its animus toward queer male figures, on the one hand, and female sexual agency, on the other hand). The heroine and chief Final Girl of *Scream* is the teenage Sidney Prescott (Neve Campbell). Her mother, Maureen, was raped and murdered a year before the action of the film begins; her apparent killer Cotton Weary (Liev Schreiber), whom Sidney testified against, is on death row. Sidney's nemesis is Gale Weathers (Courteney Cox), a brash, brazenly opportunistic television newswoman who has written a tell-all exposé of the case in which she claims that Weary is innocent on both counts and that, far from his victim, Maureen Prescott was an adulteress and Weary's lover. Weathers is convinced that Weary was framed for the murder. Moreover, she accuses Sidney of blaming Weary because Sidney cannot cope with the truth of her mother's town-tramp sexual exploits.

When Ghostface, a masked killer in a black gown, begins his killing spree, it becomes increasingly obvious that Sidney is his target. At first, she suspects her boyfriend, Billy Loomis (Skeet Ulrich) of being the killer. Yet Ghostface calls Sidney while Billy is in jail under suspicion, so it appears that Billy is innocent. At a party thrown by "Stu" Macher (Matthew Lillard), Billy's best friend and the boyfriend of Sidney's best friend Tatum (Rose McGowan), the incessantly knowledgeable horror aficionado Randy (Jamie Kennedy) pontificates about horror movie rules and genre conventions as the revelers watch John Carpenter's original *Halloween* (1978). The film, after the usual bloodletting, culminates with a showdown between Sidney and the killers. It turns out that Billy and Stu have *both* been doing the killings. Citing *Psycho*, Billy reveals himself by saying Norman Bates's immortal line, "We all go a little mad sometimes." The killers, who, in typical grandiose killer-style, want to recount the full extent of their nefarious deeds before murdering the heroine, also reveal it was they who murdered Sidney's mother a year earlier. As it turns out, Maureen Prescott was also having an affair with Billy's father, which apparently led Billy's mother to "abandon" him and his father. He and Stu framed Cotton Weary for the murder as well as the rape. The two killers stab each other, making it look like Sidney's father, whom they have gagged and bound and plan to frame for all of the murders, attacked them. Gale Weathers shows up and, in a reversal of her villainess role, actually aids Sidney in counterattacking the killers. Between the women, the killers are subdued and then killed. Sidney kills Stu, already mortally wounded by Billy's stabbing of him, by forcing a television set to come crashing down on his head; Gale shoots Billy; Sidney shoots Billy in the head when he, as predicted by the horror movie expert Randy, comes back to life.

Robin Wood famously argued that the horror film was an enactment of the Freudian theory of the "return of the repressed"—the energies and desires that culture has repudiated or otherwise deemed unspeakable inevitably come back to life, in monstrously violent form.[12] If we apply Wood's repressive hypothesis to *Scream*, we must ask what, exactly, is being repressed? The answer would appear to be, inescapably, the homoerotic bonds between Billy and Stu, which come into greater clarity along with the truth of their murderous exploits. To the extent that these bonds do come into greater clarity, no sense of anguished sympathy for them is produced in the audience. The homoerotics of their bond only add to the sense of their depravity, one that the film thematizes as being emblematic of their millennial generation. Indeed, that the millennium is producing a new generation of amoral, unfeeling young people is one of the major, consistently thematized preoccupations of the film.

Scream provides a foundational backstory to the often violent and haphazard relationships between males in bromantic and beta male comedies, in which men, while ostensibly friends or teammates or allies, routinely brutalize each other verbally and sometimes physically, as in *Pineapple Express* (David Gordon Green, 2007). Moreover, the first *Scream* brings into greater clarity what is at stake for movies in the representation of erotic feelings between males, especially those in pairs, which usually can only be conceived in terms of violence that can take many interrelated forms: abusive verbal play, emotional sadism, physical abuse.

Fears of a New Millennium

Discussing films being made at the *fin de millenaire/fin de siècle*, Joseph Natoli wrote in his 1998 book *Speeding to the Millennium* that "we find ourselves not on a well-charted main road to the new millennium but detoured, pathless. Despite Newt Gingrich's declaration that 'except for a generation spent in the counterculture . . . things were on the right track,' we are at this moment harboring a fear of being propelled toward our own destruction." As society attempts to link "present with future," it nevertheless remains gripped by the fear that we are "heading not into dream but into an abyss."[13] While millennial fears have been common throughout human history, it is worth noting that the profound impact of the events of September 11, 2001, was deepened by what had already been a period of dislocation and nameless-yet-named dread that stemmed from the imminent millennium. The Y2K scare, which derived from the possibility that the computers of the world would fail to recognize the number 2000 and would all, simultaneously, crash, envisioned a civilization in ruins, planes falling out of the sky, before 9/11. (The tagline for the 1999 television film *Y2K* was "Y2K: What if they're right?") Along with the new kinds of sex comedies in the late '90s, *Scream* reflected anxieties specific to the decade's gender and sexual shifts. These shifts intersected with fears of the new millennium that infiltrate *Scream* and relate, as I will show, to a larger sense of social disturbances produced by changing gender roles and sexual identities in the period.

One sequence in the film allegorically represents a sense of imminent and anxious change. Sidney, at home by herself while her father is away for a few days, waits for Tatum to come by in the evening. In one of the subtlest and most haunting visual effects of the film, Craven painstakingly depicts the passage of time from day to night as Sidney falls asleep in her house. In a deliberate stylistic choice, the film employs a series of three lap dissolves to depict this temporal transition. Through the transformation of a crepuscular sky into an ominously dark one, Craven conveys a dread of change that suggests a larger ambivalence related to the film's cultural moment, a time verging on a new age marked by greater levels of anticipatory fear than joy. As I will show, it is the killers who are most closely associated with millennial fears. They call Sidney right on cue when she awakes in the darkness. (The film constantly attempts to preempt our genre expectations. Teasingly, Tatum is the first one to make a call, which Sidney answers while still half-awake.)

In a telling exchange, the sheriff and the deputy, Dewey (David Arquette) consider the possibility of Billy's guilt as he sits in a locked office. (Dewey, in his mixture of awkwardness and sheepish charm, deserves a discrete analysis of his own, reflective as he is of a new-style male passivity that is presented as sexually appealing.) Looking over a packaged version of the Ghostface killer's outfit—marketed as "Father Death" and which, as Dewey says, can be purchased by any kid—the portly, middle-aged, world-weary sheriff remarks, "If you'd asked me twenty years ago, I would have said no way this kid was guilty. But now, this generation . . . I don't know." Though in a comedic mode much of the time, *Scream* strikes a note of seriousness here that echoes throughout the film. This generation of millennial males not only strikes fear in the hearts of older men but also leaves them fundamentally bewildered. Another key scene reinforces the theme of the older generation's uneasiness toward youth culture. The highschool principle, Mr. Himbrey (played by an uncredited Henry Winkler), aghast at the insensitivity of two male students who put on the Ghostface outfit to parody the hideous murders, threateningly jabs a pair of scissors in their faces and then uses the implement to cut the masks. As he does so, he rants, "I am sick of your entire havoc-inducing, thieving, whoring generation." In one of the genuinely eerie moments in the film, Himbrey, when alone in his office, puts a Ghostface mask on, and menaces *himself* in the mirror. The point seems to be that Ghostfaceness is contagious, and that men in positions of power envy the very amoral blankness they scorn in youthful psychos. Earlier, he had suggested that the only fit punishment for the pranksters was to be similarly gutted from stem to stern and publically displayed, a statement that links him to the killers and to their murder of the babysitter victim played by Drew Barrymore at the start of the film, who was similarly dispatched.

In terms both telling and phobic, *Scream* diagnosed an amorality in millennial youth, especially its male population. The homoeroticism of the Billy-Stu relationship, which the film develops into an all-but-explicit queer love affair, evinces both the unpredictable, anarchic, bewildering behavior of this "entire generation" and the shifts in male gender roles synonymous with it. *Scream* was first released in the December of 1996; in a horrible fulfillment of the film's paranoid fantasies, the Columbine High School massacre in Colorado occurred on Tuesday, April 20, 1999. In an eerie echo of *Scream*'s two teen-male killers, the teenage Columbine killers were two students, Eric Harris and Dylan Klebold, seniors in high school. They killed twelve students and one teacher, using sawed-off shotguns, pipe bombs, and other weapons. One of the most persistent "causes" offered for Harris and Klebold's actions was their apparent homosexuality, which, from my understanding, has never been confirmed. Paul Morrison has described homosexuality as "the explanation for everything": an explanation offered for every pernicious social problem, most notably the rise of fascism in Germany. The explanatory uses made of homosexuality in these ways are almost always homophobic. *Scream* sets into motion both new patterns of male relationships that will eventually cohere into the bromance of the '00s and illustrates why the bromance would be so useful as a response to these new patterns. As male gender roles began visibly transforming in the 1990s and early 2000s, one of the possibilities that emerged was that men would form new ways of interacting with one another, including open emotionalism, public displays of affection, and potential sexual contact. *Scream* might be said to register these fears and possibilities and to offer a paranoid response to them, matching anxieties over *fin de millenaire* American masculinity with a deeply anxious vision of American masculinity verging haphazardly on millennial change. The bromance would offer an ingenious means of registering shifts in male identities and interactions while effectively locking down and re-stabilizing both.

Lovers and Killers

Scream redeploys the longstanding American tradition of a homoerotic bond between a pair of young male killers. The foundation of the tradition is the infamous Leopold and Loeb case. These wealthy young men were University of Chicago students who murdered the fourteen-year-old Robert "Bobby" Franks in 1924, in an attempt to perpetrate the "perfect crime." (Both were sentenced to life imprisonment; one of the men was shortly thereafter murdered by another inmate.) This case has generated several fictional treatments, ranging from Hitchcock's significant 1948 film *Rope*, based on the 1929 British stage play by Patrick Hamilton (which was retitled *Rope's End* for its New York premiere) to the 1959 film *Compulsion*, directed by Richard Fleischer (based on the 1956 novel by Meyer Levin), to the 1992 *Swoon*, an independent film written and directed by Tom Kalin that has come to represent the New Queer Cinema of the era. Adding to the mystique of this paradigm is the real-life case that was famously turned into the 1966 "nonfiction novel" *In Cold Blood* by Truman Capote: the 1959 killing of the Clutter family in Holcomb, Kansas, by two young men. (Richard Brooks made a 1967 film of Capote's book.) Capote's tormented, erotically charged bond with one of the killers has been widely reported.

The killers in Hamilton's play and Hitchcock's film, as did the real-life Leopold and Loeb, consider themselves to be Nietzschean supermen, using their "superior" intellect as justification for their thrill-killing. The killers in *Scream*, in pointed contrast, have no lofty philosophical ambitions. Indeed, their motivations, which initially seem nebulously opaque, eventually become linked to personal vengeance, at least on Billy's part. Billy claims to be avenging himself on Sidney for her mother's crimes—her "whoring" ways that destroyed his family. Sidney's mother's affair with Billy's father caused Billy's mother to abandon him and their family, in Billy's view; intensifying their strangely twin-like pairing, both Sidney and Billy are bereft of a mother. Indeed, in an earlier scene in the high school when

Billy vents his frustration at Sidney for continuing to believe that he is the killer even after he was released by the police and is no longer a suspect, Billy explicitly compares the loss of his mother with Sidney's own loss. Her infuriated rebuttal to his comparison confirms that there is little empathy between them. Billy's frequent denunciations of Sidney as "Bitch!" during the climactic showdown between the heroine and the killers amplify the note of intense misogyny in his rage.

Stu, it would appear, is simply aiding and abetting Billy. If Stu's motives are left a blank, they are decisively marked *as* a blank. Sidney explicitly calls him on his lack of an apparent motive. In a bravura maneuver, Sidney turns the tables on the killers, procuring their cellphone for herself and calling them on the Macher family line. In one of the many moments of the climax that threatens to turn an unspoken homoerotic element in the killers' relationship into explicit reference, Sidney taunts Stu over the phone: "Stu, Stu, Stu, what are you going to tell the cops when they arrive?" "Peer pressure," he offers. "I'm too sensitive." Taunting Stu for his lack of clear-cut motive is one of Sidney's ways of undermining and retaliating against both murderers. Her own sense of their sexual nonnormativity as an area of weakness she can exploit in order to defeat them comes through explicitly in one moment. Having gained access to the killers' voice-altering device, which allowed them both to disguise their own voices and to torment their victims before killing them, Sidney now uses it to intimidate, confuse, and frighten *them* for a change. When she surprises the killers by calling them, Billy answers the Macher family phone, and she challenges him while speaking through the voice-altering device. This moment, as well as the one in which she surprises Billy by bursting out of a closet (which cannot be an incidental location) wearing the Ghostface mask and costume, suggest that she has absorbed their dark prankster wit and hints at a potential darkness in her as well. Significantly, however, it is in her *own* voice over the phone that Sidney taunts Stu and then calls Billy a "pansy-assed Mama's Boy." This shift back to Sidney's own voice confirms that this is her own apprehension of the killers as contemporary versions of homosexual thrill-killers—depraved but also pathetic—not a game that she is reciprocally playing on them.

The film thematizes a fusion between cinephilia (obsessive movie-love) and murderous queer sexuality. In the scene that leads to them finally having sex for the first time—Billy has complained about the lack of sexual activity and heat in their relationship—Billy tells Sidney that their lives *are* a movie: "It's all one great big movie, Sid. Only you can't pick a genre." Though film-geek Randy is the one directly associated with a failure to distinguish representation from real-life, Billy, especially, is obsessed with the movies, and specifically with horror. He compares, early on, his relationship with Sidney to *The Exorcist*. Understandably, she gives him a quizzical look in response. He explains that he had just been watching the "edited for television" version of Friedkin's film, leading him to realize that his sex-deprived relationship with his girlfriend could be described the same way, and further claiming that before her mother was killed, Sidney's relationship with him was more like an "R-rated" picture. Later, he cites *The Silence of the Lambs* and its heroine Clarice Starling's flashbacks of her dead father. Her flashbacks, according to Billy, help to explain Sidney's sustained grief over her mother's death. Finally seeing the cinematically enhanced truth of Billy's advice, Sidney declares that she will no longer wallow in her "grief process." To demonstrate that he has clarified things for her, she agrees to have sex with him at last.

The films of Alfred Hitchcock obviously loom large over this metatextual genre film with so obsessive an interest in making its relationship to other film works obvious if not altogether explicit. Though, given its pair of queer killers, *Rope* would have been more appropriate as a reference, Billy explicitly cites *Psycho*: "We all go a little mad sometimes," he says with a cunning glint in his eye as he reveals himself as one of the killers by shooting Randy (who survives for the sequel). This reference bears consideration. It is *Psycho*, after all, that most significantly and influentially creates the cinematic image of the overbearing mother and the mother-obsessed homosexual man—the Mama's Boy taken to homicidal extremes. (These images derive from a vulgar appropriation of Freudian theory; Freud's own treatment of the homosexual male's relationship to his mother and to his own narcissism is complex and intricate.) Appropriately enough, Billy's last name—*Loomis*—derives from one of *Psycho*'s main characters, Sam Loomis (John Gavin), the boyfriend of the eventually murdered heroine Marion Crane (Janet Leigh).

Psycho's representation of masculinity generally problematizes the oppositions between normative and nonnormative. The apparently straight male in the heroic mode, Sam Loomis is a surprisingly dark and increasingly off-putting character, while the villain, Norman Bates (Anthony Perkins) who murdered his mother and keeps her mummified corpse in the fruit cellar, is a site of sympathetic audience identification for most of the film. In one scene, Hitchcock films the two characters and actors in matching profile shots, emphasizing the physical resemblances between both while collapsing the distinctions that ostensibly separate them. Normative and queer-pathological masculinities cannot be easily distinguished in Hitchcock's challenging, unquiet film.[14]

Scream also offers contrasting portraits of masculinity, but only in order to intensify its vision of a gathering cultural depravity. Perhaps the first touch that links the killers to homosexuality is Ghostface's initial attack on Sidney. He tries to trick her into believing that he is on her front porch; "Well, I call your bluff," the intrepid, neo-Final Girl Sidney responds, walking out onto the porch. Ghostface then jumps out of her closet instead. In a scene in which Sidney, Billy, Stu, Tatum, and Randy discuss the possible identity of the killer (it seems at this point that there is only one), gender roles are discussed explicitly. "It takes a man to do something like that," Stu says, ostensibly referring to the physical strength needed to gut a victim and hoist her up on a tree. Tatum corrects him, chiding him for his sexism. When Sidney despondently muses, in this scene, "How do you gut someone?" Stu's matter-of-fact, coldly indifferent explanation of just how one does such a thing attests to his amoral disposition long before he is revealed as one of the killers. Billy chides Stu for his graphic descriptions, which visibly upset Sidney, of the violent acts that occurred within the murders. Interestingly, the epithet that Billy uses against Stu is "fuckrag," which sounds like a phrase that has tumbled out of the arsenal of misogynistic insults.

Skeet Ulrich's performance as Billy and, especially, Matthew Lillard's as Stu deepen the queer resonances of the characters, in this movie that poises forever on the knife edge of explication. Ulrich's teen anomie, brooding intensity, and perpetual white T-shirt clearly evoke James Dean in *Rebel without a Cause* (but without his trademark unzipped-up red jacket). The intent look in his eyes, either sad or cunning, keeps both Sidney and the audience off-balance as to his murderous identity. But when he does reveal his identity, the winsomeness dissolves entirely, and he becomes truly frightening, barking "Bitch!" at Sidney. Overall, the performance as delivered and directed evokes Anthony Perkins's sensitive yet secretly sinister murderer in *Psycho*, but with an effort made to show the dark side of his all-American geniality. Lillard's attention-getting performance is notable for its gender-bending potentialities. He uses his basketball-player height, rubbery face (sometimes it seems on the verge of melting), and excessive emotionalism to create a memorably frenetic character. Eschewing standard male stoicism, his ostensibly straight Stu would surprise no one by coming out in full drag regalia at some point.

In one scene, set in the video store where Randy works, Randy theorizes about Billy's possible identity as the killer after Randy has gone into hysterics about the ways in which victims in horror movies die because they remain stubbornly ignorant of genre conventions. (Randy astutely presages the fanboys who were to emerge in the new millennium, with their rigid attention to the rules, conventions, and the logic, or lack thereof, behind genre productions.) In perhaps the most daringly homoerotic moment in the film, Billy suddenly swings upon Randy, challenging him. "Maybe you're the killer, Randy," Billy taunts him. "Maybe your movie-freak mind got the better of you." As Billy gets in Randy's face, Stu comes up from behind him, holding him almost against Billy's body. (This gesture of physical intimacy will be exactly repeated during the bloody climactic face-off, when Stu puts his arms around Billy and holds him from behind as both explain their murderous plot to Sidney.) Stu even traces a line with his finger across Randy's ear.

Homoeroticism, in typical fashion, can only be expressed through violence between men, as in this tense scene in which Billy seems to verge on pummeling Randy. But the physical intimacy of the actors, and Lillard's teasing physicality especially, threaten to tip the balance of this scene from homosocial menace into homoerotic play.

The film toys with making the potentially radical suggestion that *all* forms of masculinity are pathologically queer. Ultimately, though, the film depicts its queer killers as the most exquisite embodiment of a widespread and deepening millennial pathology that its straight male characters vulnerably, clumsily, but heroically oppose. In opposition to the non-identification-forming killers' masculinities, characters such as the goofy Dewey, who

FIGURE 2.2. Homoerotic menace: Stu traces a line with his finger across Randy's ear.

develops a relationship with the hardheaded tabloid reporter Gale Weathers, softening her edges, and film-geek Randy are shown to be, respectively, appealing romantic prospects or essentially sweet-souled virgins. In contrast, the killers display not only a vicious misogyny but also an insufficient, faltering, confused understanding of their own masculinity. Indeed, their potential effeminacy may be more threatening to the general audience than their explicit hatred of women. What has been called "effeminophobia" intersects here with homophobia, as the killers' increasingly inept performance of gender mirrors their ultimately inept attempt to craft the perfect murder-plot.[15]

Craven makes the interesting choice to stage the big revelation scene at the climax in the kitchen—a particularly large, gleaming kitchen. Parodistically, the Mama's Boy-killers reveal their nefarious identities within the domestic space most closely associated with the mother and her private, familial, nurturing sphere. Clearly, Billy longs for return to the mother no less ardently than Sidney does. Indeed, he explicitly provides this as a motive, after echoing Randy's earlier line that "motives don't apply anymore" in the new millennium. Abandoned by *his* mother because of the "whoring" ways of the heroine's mother, Billy is doubly cathected to the mother, to her nurturing, which he all but claims to long for, on the one hand, and to her sexuality, which he rebukes but obviously obsesses over, on the other hand. His queer qualities, as the film would have it, appear to emanate from this confusion over mother's roles, and from unresolved Oedipal conflict. Freud is not dead.

A Negative Oedipus Complex

Billy and Sidney have sex after she announces that, if life *is* one big movie, the genre she will pick is porn. Ghostface suddenly appears right after they have had sex and seemingly stabs Billy to death. As we learn, this is only a ruse to distract Sidney from Billy's real identity as one of the killers. Billy staggers, it appears, back to life in his seemingly blood-drenched T-shirt, which ironically evokes James Dean's red jacket. Gaining possession of the gun Sidney now wields, Billy shoots Randy, cites Norman Bates's line about going mad from *Psycho*, dabs a finger in his seeming blood, and brings this sticky finger to his lips. "Corn syrup," he announces as he tastes his fake blood, "the same stuff they used for pigs' blood in *Carrie*." Through his gesture, the queer killer signals his onanistic delight in his own schemes; he literally tastes the mayhem he produces. This gesture also associates Billy

FIGURE 2.3. Ghostface both proclaims and obscures an opposition to heterosexual desire.

with a metaphorical female world of blood, suffering, and victimization; he explicitly links himself to blood-drenched Carrie and to the symbolic menstrual blood in which she is drenched at the prom. Lastly, through this gesture Billy links himself to a regressive orality.

The issue of a regressive return to orality and its associations with homosexuality link *Scream* once again to Hitchcock's *Rope*. In this film, the homosexual lover-killers, Brandon (John Dall) and Philip (Farley Granger), place the body of the young man they have murdered in a chest, which they will also use as a serving area for the perverse dinner party they host, one that includes the murdered man's aged father as a guest. These thematics are also linked to the influential paradigms of classical psychoanalytic theory. Freud established five stages of infantile psychosexual development: the oral, the anal, the phallic, the latency, and the genital stages. Orality is, importantly, the first of these stages, and orality and anality are "pregenital."[16] Freud's theories of male homosexuality remain controversial. In a footnote added in 1910 to his 1905 *Three Essays on the Theory of Sexuality*, Freud conjectures that homosexual identity emerges from an identification with the mother.[17] In sum, he theorizes that it is narcissistic in nature and related to the homosexual child's intimately close relationship to his mother, whose desire the child emulates, projecting the love she bestows on the child onto *another* male.

In response to these theories, Diana Fuss argues that Freud makes a linkage between a regressive return to orality and homosexuality.[18] In a discussion in which she argues that Jonathan Demme's film *The Silence of the Lambs* (1991) crystallizes Freud's homophobic paradigms, she argues that "male homosexuality is represented as fixated at the earliest stage of the libidinal organization—the oral-cannibalistic stage—in which the recalcitrant subject refuses to give up its first object (the maternal breast and all its phallic substitutes)." In this manner, the film acutely corresponds to Freudian theory, which would have it that "the male homosexual *ingests* the (m)other. . . . Oral-cannibalistic incorporation of the mother not only permits a homosexual object-choice but unleashes sadistic impulses."[19] *Scream* is, in my view, a much more homophobic interpretation of Freudian theory than that offered in Demme's film, which contains both homophobic and anti-homophobic elements, the latter deriving from the film's larger critique of hegemonic American masculinity.

Scream returns homosexual male subjectivity to the oral stage and to a central relationship with the pre-Oedipal mother. Craven crucially stages the climax in the maternal kitchen. The home, the mother's domestic realm, is embodied by the family kitchen where food is prepared and eaten, practical acts and symbolic rituals communicative of mother's love and nurture and familial intimacy. The kitchen stands in for the pre-Oedipal mother's breast, our first object of desire in the psychoanalytic scenario. *Scream* figures this return as indicative of the regressiveness of homoerotic desire and identity. It also stages this return as a showdown between the homosexual male, who refuses to be properly oedipalized, and the Oedipal woman, in league with the Father and with institutionalized heterosexuality (in the strictest psychoanalytic terms).

The Freudian and the later Lacanian accounts of children's psychosexual development, between them, posit the Oedipus complex as a rite of passage into the realm of patriarchy. This realm, to provide a brief summary of these accounts, is what Lacan calls the Symbolic. The Symbolic order is governed by the Law and the Name of the Father—his language and his law. It is in the father's realm or order that subjectivity is formed, through language and obeisance to patriarchal law. The father's order opposes the pre-Oedipal world of the mother, which is associated with sensations and the body, *not* with language or law. Both Freud and Lacan agree that individual subjectivity is won through the renunciation of the mother and an embrace of (or, perhaps, better put, acquiescence to) the father's order.

The normative Oedipus complex—in the son's case, desire for the mother, rivalry with and fear of the father—can only be successfully resolved in this way: the son must learn to *identify* with, rather than rivalrously to oppose, his father, and to recognize that the mother whom he desires is the father's possession. Heterosexual desire emerges from these two achievements: identification with the father, and the transformation of endogamous desire for the mother into exogamous desire for a woman who resembles her but is outside of the family.

But what of the so-called *negative Oedipus complex*, in which things go awry? Homosexuality is the chief amongst these. In *Three Essays*, Freud conjectures that, after the phase in their childhood in which they intensely identify with the mother rather than the father, homosexuals

> identify themselves with a woman and take *themselves* as their sexual object. That is to say, they proceed from a narcissistic basis, and look for a young man who resembles themselves and whom *they* may love as their mother loved *them*.[20]

For our purposes, what is especially interesting is the centrality of the mother to Freud's theory of male homosexual narcissism. Her role and her love and, most importantly, *her* desire become the models for the homosexual male's own version of all of these, as we have noted. While many have read Freud's theory as homophobic, in my view it fairer to say that it has been *put* to homophobic uses in American psychiatry, which historically used it to pathologize homosexuality as arrested development. Freud is describing the psychological experience of a male who identifies with mother rather than father, and while it would be naïve to say such an identification is true for all homosexual men, it certainly is true for some.

What works, as *Scream* make vividly clear, is the cultural *reception* of narcissistic, mother-identified desire. The killers in *Scream* are monstrous not only because they kill, but because their desire proceeds from identification with and, more urgently still, longing for the mother. What complicates, or is left quite deliberately unresolved by the filmmakers, is the specific nature of the boys' relationship to each other. Stu's desire is left especially unclear. But in some ways, it is his desire that more clearly has a basis in the homoerotic. Though he has a girlfriend, Tatum (she is dispatched via garage-door as the partygoers watch *Halloween*), Stu's chief affectional energies are directed toward Billy, to whom he is devoted. Billy's desire becomes *Stu's* desire. His emulation of his friend's desire emerges, perhaps, as a strategy for coping with his desire *for* Billy, an imitative substitute for sexual fulfilment.

That it is Stu who, in Ghostface garb, seemingly kills Billy after he has sex with Sidney (and one cannot help but noticing the masculine timbre of her name), even though an aspect of the killers' clever ruses, suggests Stu's jealous, possessive rage against Billy for his heterosexual relationship.

Narcissism seems very much at work, and in homophobic terms, in the depiction of Billy as mother-identified. As are so many horror-movie monster-males who cleave to their often equally monstrous mothers, Billy is presented as emotionally stunted precisely *because* of this maternal over-identification. Yet Stu's overly "sensitive" identification with *Billy* brings up a different psychosexual dynamic altogether. His Billy-fixation is a textbook definition of mimetic *desire*, a desire to resemble the other. Stu becomes the mirror reflection of Billy's narcissistic, mother-based desire. In psychoanalytic terms, mimetic desire is associated with *hysteria*, which often involves a wildly uncontrollable series of bodily ailments or phenomenon, instances in which the body itself seems to have gone awry. Hysteria often involves the copying of another person's illnesses. Stu, as a hysteric might, copies Billy's psychosis and makes it very much his own. That hysteria is also associated with bisexuality or some kind of gender role-confusion makes these connections doubly interesting, especially when we consider Matthew Lillard's acting style and what he brings to the role. With his pliant, rubbery body; intense and often comedic emotionalism; and his, at times, oddly theatrical and effeminate manner, he evokes both the somatic mayhem and the gender-bending of the classic hysteric. We can say, then, that between them Billy and Stu inhabit narcissistic and hysterical modes of queer desire.[21]

The Fury of the Final Girl

Carol Clover has influentially theorized that the Final Girl, who alone survives to confront and slay the slasher-movie monster, usually must face off against a sexually nonnormative male, such as Leatherface in *Texas Chainsaw Massacre*. As Clover herself points out, the Final Girl's function here does not fall within parameters that can be effortlessly recuperated for feminism. Making a point distinct from Clover's, I argue that to see the Final Girl as feminist icon is to ignore or to fail to perceive the homophobic basis of her triumph.[22] Like Athena at the climax of the Aeschylus's tragic trilogy *The Oresteia*, she appears in order to speak out on behalf of patriarchy and to establish its laws as binding.[23] Siding with the male rather than the female, Athena is the feminine face of the father's law, perhaps appropriate for a goddess who bursts forth fully armed not from her mother's womb but from her father Zeus's forehead. The Final Girl of horror sides not with her own mother but with the law of the father. In so doing, she spectacularly opposes the sexually nonnormative killer and his obsessive devotion to the mother.[24] (Confirming the validity of reading classical associations into the film and its characterization of Sidney, Craven's sequel *Scream 2* [1997] actually incorporates *The Oresteia* into its plot. Sidney performs the role of Cassandra in a college production. Kevin Williamson, *Scream 2*'s screenwriter as well, wrote a pastiche of the *Agamemnon* that makes Cassandra, the prophetic woman whose prophecies will be heeded by no one [the result of Apollo's curse], the leading character.)

Sidney is somewhat of an unusual slasher heroine because she maintains a loving devotion to her dead mother. Indeed, the film's only progressive politics lies in its interest in bonds between women—Sidney and her mother, Sidney and her cheeky, loyal friend Tatum, and even, and most surprising, between Sidney and Gale Weathers, initially presented as her nemesis (indeed, Sidney punches her in the face early on). That the two women work together to defeat the killers has an undeniable feminist charge. Yet it is an expensively produced one, depending, as it does, on the pathologization of the killers not for their killer proclivities as much as for their queer ones.

My reading of the *Scream* films' representation of femininity is quite distinct from that of Kathleen Rowe Karlyn. In her fine, measured analysis, she takes a view of the films as, ultimately, a reconciliation between mother and daughter figures. Karlyn does not address the significant costs of such a reconciliation, particularly for its queer personae, unmentioned in Karlyn's treatment.[25] Moreover, there is, in my view, no such intergenerational female reconciliation achieved in a film series that obsessively depicts, in thoroughgoing fashion from beginning to end, the mother as menace. Indeed, Sidney's loving loyalty to her mother in the first film is increasingly represented as something that holds her back, as a force as meddlesome as the murders that proliferate in her midst. The queer killers, the sexually adventurous mother, and the phallic career woman are all, alike, treated as monsters who must be slain.

Carpenter and Craven: Genre and Historical Masculinity

As I discussed in chapter 1 and further develop in chapter 5's treatment of post-millennial horror, the horror remakes so endemic to the period overwhelmingly figure horror as a return to the scene of history, an "American history" framed as the Gothic literary past. For example, in Rob Zombie's 2007 remake of John Carpenter's 1978 film *Halloween*, the section in which the child version of the killer, Michael Meyers, begins to wear the series of masks that prefigure his final, signature white mask (which more than anything else connotes facelessness) worn when he is the adult version of his killer identity, evokes the nineteenth-century Gothic, especially Nathaniel Hawthorne's short-story "The Minister's Black Veil." Reinforcing this motif, the scene set in the high school library in which young women bond over boys commences with a deliberate shot of great American literary archetypes—Benjamin Franklin, Poe, Whitman—shown hanging in portraits on the wall. The return to history in the films of the '00s is often rooted in two periods—the nineteenth-century (broadly figured as the site of American origins) and the Reagan 1980s (its reactionary dimensions best summed up by its defining political actor's line, "It's morning in America."). Horror film frequently returns to the latter while remaining heavily invested in the 1970s as well, with both the '70s and '80s emerging as the "classic" period of horror, to which, in a kind of extended genre origin myth, the post-millennial horror film endlessly returns. *Scream* is in many ways a template for the horror remake, being a synthesis of the "American Nightmare" of oppositional '70s horror and the tendency of conservative '80s horror to "paper the cracks," to use Robin Wood's terms.

Scream's citation of Carpenter's 1978 *Halloween*—which, if we stick with Robin Wood's paradigms, arguably represents a rejection of Craven's leftist horror films such as *The Last House on the Lake* (1972) and an embrace of Carpenter's reactionary politics— both evinces the self-consciously metatextual agenda of Craven's film and enacts a disorienting return to horror movie origins rooted in male sexual dysfunction with wholly murderous implications. I am not in agreement with Wood that *Halloween* or Carpenter's work generally should be described as politically reactionary; indeed, on balance, Carpenter's films constitute a leftist horror filmography. Nevertheless, the inherent problems of the slasher genre, such as misogyny, inescapably trouble *Halloween* and the citation-prone *Scream* as well (even though I would make the case that Carpenter's *Halloween*, in its assault on suburban complacency, is a much more politically resistant film than *Scream*).

Scream deploys a range of horror movie phalluses. On the one hand, the knives of its teen psychos clearly symbolize the male penis. (*Halloween*, exemplary of the *Psycho*-inspired slasher-horror film, takes the suggestion of *Psycho*'s infamous shower murder as a "rape" much further, and *Scream* goes further still in this regard.) On the other hand, given that *Scream* is a genre film made in the wake of queer theory, which calls into question not only the existence of authentic sexualities but also gender itself, knives, guns, and even umbrellas in this film function as phallic signifiers available to either gender. *Scream* situates itself in a disordered realm of shifting gender and sexual identities, not just the killers' but also the heroine's.

That Sidney and Billy have sex is partly Sidney's decision and also a part of the killers' plan. In their slavish devotion to horror conventions, they believe that Sidney can *only* be killed once she is no longer a virgin. In an interesting juxtaposition, Craven intercuts scenes of sex between Sidney and Billy with scenes of Randy, Stu, and the others all watching John Carpenter's *Halloween* and the various murders committed by the white-mask-wearing Michael Myers. Pointedly, the scene from *Halloween* that plays at this point is the one in which Michael kills Bob, the young guy with glasses who goes downstairs to get his girlfriend Lynda (P. J. Soles) a beer after they have had sex. As Michael impales lanky, wriggling Bob to the wall with a long phallic knife, Billy is shown to be sexually penetrating Sidney. It cannot be insignificant that in the scene from *Halloween* that plays during the moment of sexual consummation between Billy and Sidney, the particular victim in the cited text, Carpenter's film, is male. Adding to the complexities here, Michael Myers, in a bizarre parody, puts a sheet over his body, then impersonates Bob by putting his glasses on, creating the image of a bespectacled ghost. Michael then goes upstairs, initially tricks Lynda into believing that he is Bob playing a prank on her, and then kills Lynda by strangling her with the cord of the telephone on which she is gabbing with the heroine, Laurie Strode (Jamie Lee Curtis).

In killing off both the boyfriend and his girlfriend upstairs, Michael Myers provides a grisly foundation for the entire teen-slasher genre that would follow in the '80s and that *Scream* would eventually parody: the killing off of sexually active teens. When Michael kills Bob, he *nails him to the wall*, a grim parody of phallic penetration that suggests that the male victim has been put into a position of forced, helpless penetration. The crude as well as satirical implication made here is that, while Bob may have just penetrated his girlfriend during sexual intercourse, *he* has now been penetrated by Michael Myers. To whatever extent this was an implication being made in *Halloween*, *Scream*'s specific citation of the scene makes this implication an obvious one. If, on some level, Michael is parodying heterosexual male potency and would-be heroism by both killing and impersonating the boyfriend, *Scream* makes ironic use of *Halloween*'s own ironic stance. The penetration of the male victim by the male killer in *Halloween* is intertextually as well as aesthetically linked (through editing/

intercutting) to the scene of heterosexual intercourse in *Scream*, a confusing and provocative analogy, to say the least.

In a further and inescapable analogy, Stu's staged stabbing-murder of Billy *also* doubles the scene of heterosexual sex that has just occurred between Billy and Sidney. What emerges, then, is a portrait of homoerotic intimacy *as* violence, as possible only *through* violence. Further, this male-male violence-as-intimacy is a copy of heterosexuality, its perverse imitation. Homoerotic violence not only inadequately copies and substitutes for heterosexual sex, but is used to parody this normative relation. It is difficult to know what comes first for the filmmakers, but this sense of gendered and sexual originals and copies also has an aesthetic dimension. The video of *Halloween* becomes the film within the film, but also a copy of the film we are watching. Craven, in other words, forces '70s horror into the position of being a perverse mirror for '90s horror, for his deconstructive send-up of a genre in which his own legacy remains maddeningly ambiguous at best.

These associations find their most dramatic realization in the confession/revelation scene in which the killers tell Sidney who they are. As he did with Randy, Stu, from behind, wraps his arms around Billy as Billy tells their story of killing Sidney's mom, framing Cotton Weary, and killing the others. They then reveal their big surprise—they have tied and gagged Sidney's father, who plops out of a storage closet, immobilized and pleading with his eyes for Sidney's help. The killers' biggest coup will be to kill everyone, Sidney and her father very much included, and frame Sidney's *father* for it. To ensure the believability of their story, the two proceed to stab each, drawing dark, vivid blood, which contrasts rather beautifully against Billy's stark white T-shirt. As Billy stabs Stu, Stu keeps screaming "Get up"—the unmentionable "it" being the key word in the imperative sentence. As Billy commands, *directs*, Stu plunges his knife into Billy's side, a horrific parody of Christ on the Cross and John, the apostle Jesus loved, watching his suffering in anguished sympathy. Stu then complains that he's dying—Billy has cut too deep. The bonds between the boys, transmuted into violence, cannot be contained by this violence—even it goes awry, a little mad sometimes, along with the killers.

The delirious array of motifs of copying, doubling, and reflection in the film all suggest themes of narcissism while flaunting the metatextuality of Craven's cinema, its narcissistic relationship to the previous cinematic works it doubles and mirrors so aggressively and satirically. Confirming the centrality of the figure of a woman to narcissistic homosexuality, Billy holds on to Sidney as he and Stu stab each other. It's almost as if she anchors him to his own desire as well as to his and Stu's murder plot. Moreover, everything about the killers' plot revolves around Sidney and her mother. Is it possible that Billy projects the love he longed to receive from his mother onto Stu—loving him not as he had been loved but as he *wished* he had been loved? Any viewer of the film will know immediately that such a reading can only be speculative, since the film never shows us a Billy who has more than expedient feelings toward Stu; indeed, it is Stu who seems the more devoted to his friend and accomplice. Nevertheless, by strong implication, these young men share their deepest bond with each other, and serve as each other's double. Sidney seems to serve as a conduit for their desiring as well as rage-filled energies—as if she exists to take the sting of homoeroticism out of the murders they together perpetrate. If she is a heterosexual alibi, their actions deprive their alibi of much credence.

A potentially progressive theme keeps threatening to make *Scream* a more challenging film. Tatum strongly suggests that Sidney is unable to see that her mother was sexually active with other men in the town. But Tatum does not demean Sidney's mother. "Maybe your Mom was an unhappy woman," Tatum further and sympathetically suggests. Certainly, the smiling, earthy woman in the photographs we see at times, standing next to her daughter or in close-up, suggests a vital and intense presence whose death, especially such a horrible one, was a terrible loss. In its interest in strong women and female bonds, the film hints at a more radical sensibility. These hints, however, are overwhelmed by the phobic conservatism of its depiction of the queer killers.

We might more plausibly call Clover's Final Girl by another name: The Fury, or The Finalizing Woman, a female figure who comes into her own through her *own* bloodletting campaign. Through her retributive violence, she also ensures narrative closure. What I want to draw out here is the essential conservatism of the Final Girl's function: she exists not only to defeat the killer/male monster but also to correct his aberrant, nonnormative sexuality. In many ways, to read the Final Girl as a conservative figure is counterintuitive. How can one side with the *killer* against the heroine who finally defeats him? Every impulse of the viewer is to identify with the vulnerable and finally heroic woman who survives. The point here is not to side against the woman—and, personally, I am inclined to identify with the heroine of all films, especially genre films—but to develop an understanding of the ways in which her victory depends upon, is, indeed, constituted by, her destruction of queer energies. As a case in point, when Sidney learns that Billy is a killer, her reaction is telling. She experiences no apparent sense of betrayal or anguish, says nothing typical or expected along the lines of, "Billy, how could you do this to me, I thought you loved me," or even, "Why did you just have sex with me?" She makes a subtle but immediate shift from slightly uneasy girlfriend to slayer of queer—pansy-assed, Mama's boy—males.

The crucial touch in *Scream*'s climactic sequence is the appearance of the father within the scene of the Final Girl's revelation. Though bound and gagged, in a position of defeat, the father serves a vital function here. His presence confirms two important things at once. First, patriarchy—the father's realm, his law—is threatened, as suggested by the film's procession of wearied, bewildered, and concerned older male figures. Second, the father extends his blessing not to the degenerate new millennial sons of the post-patriarchal order, but to the emergent patriarchal *daughters*, the new Athenas who explode from the father's nearly defeated body and restore this body through retributive violence done in the father's name. In effectively destroying the queer, pathological sons of the new millennium, Sidney, as Fury, as Athena, restores the endangered but persistent patriarchal order.

In a bizarre parody of David Cronenberg's *Videodrome* (1983), in which the TV-screen itself reaches out to reaches out to media-obsessed Max Renn (the character played by James Woods), Sidney kills Stu by tipping

FIGURE 2.4. Billy, the beautiful boy as destroyer.

the television set over so that it lands, explosively, on his head, an acute parody of the movie-media obsessions of the meta-millennial generation. One of the few poetic shots in the film is the final image of beautiful, evil Billy, writhing on the ground in his death throes, his white T-shirt now drenched in blood from bullets successively shot by Gale and Sidney. In *Sexual Personae*, Camille Paglia discusses the figure of "the beautiful boy as destroyer," the male youth whose entrancing beauty and cruel indifference to those who desire him make him a male siren.[26]

Examples of the figure include the Narcissus of Greek mythology, Tadzio in Thomas Mann's *Death in Venice* as well as in the gay filmmaker Luchino Visconti's 1971 film version, Melville's Billy Budd (perhaps the inspiration for *Scream*'s killer Billy), Oscar Wilde's Dorian Gray. In the image of his slain, artfully blood-splattered body, Billy is now the beautiful boy destroyed. Twin Furies, Sidney and Gale Weathers, stand in phallic authority over his bloodied, dying, prostrated form. The death of the queer villain is the birth of a patriarchal feminine order that stands as the last bulwark against an impending millennial degeneracy.

From *Scream* to Bromance

Though far from immediately obvious, overlaps between the slasher-comedy *Scream* and the later genre of the bromance (which intersects at some points with the beta male comedy) exist precisely in terms of each genre's representation of femininity. I will discuss these later genres in chapter 3, but here I want to foreground the overlaps between them and *Scream*. *Humpday* (2009) is an especially interesting case because it not only foregrounds an interest in the homoerotic dimensions of male-male relationships but was also directed and written by a female auteur, Lynn Shelton. Though a surprisingly sensitive and at times affecting film, *I Love You, Man* (2009), squarely figures the woman as the culprit for the discord that develops between the male protagonist-friends of the movie. The main difference between slashers such as *Scream* and the bromances of the '00s is that, in the former, ardor between males has murderous dimensions. Yet what is oddly similar in both genres is that bromance emerges as a complex agenda that the woman must not only figure out but also find a way to defeat. In the bromance, the relationship between the men is not so onerous a threat to the woman as it is in *Scream*. Yet the homoerotic aspects of bromance prove to be quite threatening in their own way. *I Love You, Man* tells the story of Peter Klaven (Paul Rudd), a heterosexual man who has always felt bewildered by other men and has always had close female friends, and the new male best friend he finds, Sydney Fife (Jason Segel). His search for male companionship is instigated by the concerns of his fiancée Zooey (Rashida Jones) when she discovers that he has no male friends to throw him a bachelor party. While initially pleased that Peter has found a friend in Sydney, Zooey grows increasingly uncomfortable about the men's relationship. She is shown to be vividly disgusted by their antics when, in an imitation of their favorite band *Rush*, whose concert they attend with Zooey, Peter and Sydney flick their tongues at one another while wielding air guitars. Similarly, in *Humpday*, about two male friends, one married, the other a roving bachelor, the wife of the married friend is put off in numerous ways by the men's friendship. She is particularly alarmed at the admittedly over-the-top, absurd plot gimmick central to the film: the two heterosexual male friends' decision to film themselves having sex with each other so that they can enter this film into a local pornographic film contest (the titular "Humpday"). Across the genres, homoerotic bromance is threatening most especially to the woman—and the woman is shown, explicitly or otherwise, attempting to eradicate the threatening male bond, and almost always successful at doing so.[27]

I Love You, Man has emerged as the definitive cinematic bromance. The relationship between Peter Klaven and Sydney Fife demonstrates the evolution of the late '90s teen comedy into the adult-skewed bromance of the '00s, and also evinces the strange overlaps among the slasher and both forms of comedy. While Peter's initial and plot-motivating problem—that he has no friendships with other men—leads him to become obsessed with Sydney, in the end it is the initially charismatic Sydney who is shown to be the more desperate, need-driven friend. After secretly putting up a series of comic but also earnest billboards of Peter, a real-estate agent, in various James Bond-like poses, Sydney reveals his increasing desperation as Peter—at Zooey's behest—rejects him. Calling up his presumably endless number of other guy friends, becoming ever lonelier, the big, loping, intimidating Sydney becomes a mass of yearning, as Peter heads toward the comparatively stable and need-free stability of heterosexual marriage. There are weirdly resonant similarities between Matthew Lillard's Stu and Segel's Sydney—their height, their manic excessiveness, and also their seemingly aloof, detached, and sardonic distance from the proceedings. Just as Stu comes to seem desperate and even pitiable especially in his increasing separation from Billy, who seems willing to sacrifice him for his own ends, Sydney comes to seem like a spurned lover, cast adrift. That series of billboards suggests a homoerotic fixation with Peter on Sydney's part, fantasies of Peter in a series of male guises and personas.

The bromances, exemplified by *Pineapple Express*, *I, Love You Man*, and *Superbad* (the classic liminal work between the late '90s teen comedy and the later bromance), continue to indulge in the extreme states of bodily mayhem that marked both the earlier gross-out teen comedies and also Ben Stiller-humiliation comedies (really a genre unto themselves). But most of their content concerns their male protagonists' bewilderment over adult masculinity. What *Scream* most resonantly anticipates is the prolonged and sustained ambivalence at the heart of male relationships in the bromance. Being comedies, these films just about always effect reconciliations of some kind. For example, Sydney Fife shows up at Peter Klaven's wedding, and both utter versions of the film's title to each other. Yet the sense of an impasse between men remains equally inevitable. In the related genre of the beta male comedy, Seth Rogen in *Knocked Up* (Judd Apatow, 2007) as well as in Apatow's *Funny People* (2009) becomes disillusioned with his male friends, on the one hand, and comedian idol (Adam Sandler), on the other. In the more solidly bromantic *Pineapple Express* (David Gordon Green, 2007), Rogen and the happily pot-smoking and loyal James Franco inevitably come to emotional blows. Moreover, they do so after exchanging a set of arduous *physical* blows with Danny McBride. Indeed, the battle between the McBride character and the Rogen and Franco characters here is surprisingly bloody, mean, and violent in a manner that recalls the bloody climax of *Scream*, hinging as it does on irresolvable conflicts between males. This epic brawl begins in the kitchen, the climactic setting for *Scream*, and concludes in the bathroom, the site of Hitchcockian horror in *Psycho*. The teen guys on the verge of college in *Superbad* (Greg Mottola, 2007; co-produced by Apatow) are initially depicted as extremely close friends, but then they have a terrible falling out when one of them gets accepted into a much more prestigious college. While the friends do achieve a rapturous climactic reconciliation, their college-related conflict dominates the film.

The representation of women as "Woman," a monolithic figure of disappointment, judgment, and rectitude, is perhaps the chief connection amongst these genres. The Final Girl of *Scream* has a surprising amount in common with the desired woman of *Knocked Up*: as played by Katherine Heigl, she is aloof, glassy, and contemptuous of the slobby Seth Rogen's antics and inability to move on with his life. As does *Scream*, *Knocked Up* proceeds to chip away at the woman's stability and stature, rendering her finally a "body genre" all of her own—experiencing the pains of labor, uttering a string of expletives, and shown to be properly in love, at last, with Seth Rogen's character, depicted as having been in the moral right all along. I do not mean to suggest that the representation of a woman in labor is crude, only that *Knocked Up*'s representation of this experience is excessively, baroquely crude, highlighted by a series of laborious and borderline-racist jokes about Heigl being forced to be treated by a rude, abrasive Asian-American gynecologist played by beta-stalwart Ken Jeong. The eerie, almost frightening overlap that emerges through a comparative lens between slashers and *Knocked Up* is that both seem to engineer the apparently untouchable and invulnerable woman's confrontation with extremes of bodily pain, distress, humiliation, and vulnerability.

Ultimately, both *Scream* and the later bromances of the '00s continue to render male intimacy as an impossibility, or, more properly, as a possibility that must be defended against at all costs. The chief defense is almost always violence in its numerous forms—the wretched arguments between Michael Cera and Jonah Hill in *Superbad*, and the literal and even shocking violence in the brawl among Rogen, Franco, and McBride in *Pineapple Express*, as well as its melee of bodily harm during the film's climactic sequence. The violence that seethes beneath the antic surface of bromances recalls the violence the male duo perpetrates against its hated targets in *Scream*, but just as resonantly that which the male duo inflicts upon itself. Violence emerges as the economy of male relationships, what coordinates them and holds them in check, and what memorializes the central but unacknowledgeable loss at their center.

The great critic Tania Modleski, in her work on "male weepies," has argued that bromances thematize the psychic process that Freud called melancholia. In contrast to mourning, the normal grief process in which grief is fatigued out of the system through an exhaustive outpouring of tears and emotionalism that occurs in a delimited period, melancholia is an interminable mourning that seeks to preserve the lost object. Modleski's reading of melancholia in the bromance, informed by Juliana Schiesari's *The Gendering of Melancholia* and Judith Butler's work on "the melancholia of gender" in *The Psychic Life of Power*, seeks to navigate their levels of complexity while also establishing that male melancholia is culturally sanctioned, whereas female melancholia is either relegated to a lesser status or ignored altogether. As she observes,

> What I am hypothesizing about bromances is that they lend themselves particularly well to a reading in terms of the melancholia associated with (male) same-sex desire, desire that at times

comes close to the surface. While it is possible to argue that comedy as a genre allows for disavowal of the taboo subjects with which it sometimes flirts, it may be counterargued that precisely because disavowal is possible, comedy becomes a genre in which to explore subjects that are difficult to treat seriously. Subject matter treated as humorous may serve as a harbinger of things to come. Thus I do not wish to prematurely foreclose a discussion of feelings that, even as they are accompanied by misogyny and homophobia, may very well go beyond what Eve Kosofsky Sedgwick famously calls "homosocial desire." At the same time, of course, it is imperative in the euphoria of discovering elements that counter the heteronormative thrust of mainstream cinema not to ignore misogyny and homophobia where they exist.[28]

Scream exposes the melancholia at the heart of the bromance genre it anticipates.

In chapter 1, I established that post-millennial films oscillate between voyeuristic fixations on the male body and fetishistic contemplations of the male face. *Scream* incorporates these dual fascinations with the male body and the male face. The voyeuristic impulse to investigate the woman that Laura Mulvey argued in "Visual Pleasure and Narrative Cinema" was crucial, along with fetishism, to narrative film has now been extended to the screen male, a similar object of enigmatic fascination that must be investigated. As I will demonstrate in the next chapter, masculinity is now a mystery to be solved, especially in beta male comedies. *Scream* offers a treatment of white male youth as bewildering mysteries; only their own confessions shed light on their motiveless crimes. Treating masculinity as a beguiling mystery that demands to be solved, the cinema has devised certain techniques that fuse voyeurism and fetishism and that I call, overall, *dismantling*.

While the murderers of *Scream* penetrate and rend apart the bodies of their victims, they are themselves subjected to penetration, the stab wounds they inflict on one another as well as the retaliatory violence they receive at the hands of the film's avenging women. There is also a symbolic penetration as well, excmplified by the efforts on Sidney's part to goad Stu into self-analysis and self-awareness (the "Stu, Stu . . ." phone call). The teen killers must confess their crimes and explain their own motivations, but the assaults on their bodies and the camera's penchant for lingering over Billy's beautiful, bloodied body in death suggest a program of taking apart aberrant male subjectivity, in order to better understand it and also to possess it, if only in death, that happens at the level of the body. Corporeal embodiments of their own maddening mystery, Billy and Stu exist to be investigated, decoded, solved; Billy exists to be fetishized in death, the beautiful boy who kills most beautiful in artful death.

Along these lines, it is interesting that the first person the killers dispatch in the film is male—Steve (Kevin Patrick Walls), Casey's boyfriend. Casey, played by Drew Barrymore, is the blond girl making stovetop popcorn in her plush suburban house who is taunted and killed by Ghostface in the prologue. The prologue is a bravura tribute to *Psycho*, which kills off the character of its major female star, Janet Leigh, halfway through the film, a trick that *Scream* goes one better by killing off its one major star at the time in the prologue. Leigh plays Marion Crane, whose theft of $40,000 from her boss's client and mad attempt to flee with the money eventually lead her to the Bates Motel, where she meets a horrific death in the shower. Casey, desperately trying to scare off the killers over the phone, tells them that her football-player boyfriend is big and strong and will pulverize them. But, as they reveal, they have tied him to a chair, gagged him, and positioned him in Casey's patio so that she can see his bound and gagged, helpless form as soon as she turns, at the killers' behest, the patio lights on. Steve is then murdered in front of Casey when she fails to answer the killers' horror movie trivia question ("Who was the killer in *Friday the 13th*?" they ask; when she answers, "Jason," they mock her wrong answer, pointing out that in the original *Friday the 13th* the killer is Jason's mother, Mrs. Voorhees. This early moment nods to the killers' as well as the heroine's maternal obsessions.) While heterosexual males are routinely killed in slasher horror, rarely does a work in this genre commence by showing us the unimpeachably heterosexual male, a football player, being killed in this manner. *Scream* announces itself as a movie invested in the dismantling of the normative white male body—a tendency that it shares with a range of genre productions in the '00s.

3

"I Love You, Brom Bones"

Beta Male Comedies, Bromances, and American Culture

The titles of books from the post-millennial period that bemoan the child-man, regressive state of American masculinity are telling: *Manning Up*; *Save the Males*.[1] Inciting this glut of alarmist literature and embodying the male crisis at their core is the series of so-called "beta male" comedies, pioneered by the wildly successful director, producer, and screenwriter Judd Apatow, that have defined the American cinema of the '00s. Urban Dictionary.com's definition of beta male dovetails with many aspects of the cinematic representation of such figures.

beta male

An unremarkable, careful man who avoids risk and confrontation. Beta males lack the physical presence, charisma and confidence of the Alpha male.

Pete knew he was losing the girl he'd just met at the bar to the guy who bought her a drink, but he was too much of a beta male to do anything about it.

The beta male comedy focuses on men, usually of post-college age or older, who, at least initially, lack the Alpha Male's winning qualities and strengths, are "too much the beta male" to get the girl. Representative films include Todd Philips's *The Hangover* (2009), David Gordon Green's *Pineapple Express* (2008), Nicholas Stoller's *Forgetting Sarah Marshall* (2008), Apatow's *Knocked Up* (2007), Greg Mottola's *Superbad* (2007; co-produced by Apatow), and Apatow's *The 40-Year-Old Virgin* (2005). While most beta male comedies focus on male group dynamics, films such as John Hamburg's *I Love You, Man* (2009), David Wain's *Role Models* (2008), and David

Dobkin's *Wedding Crashers* (2005) reflect a larger trend of "double-protagonist" films.[2] In whatever form, the beta male film takes the traditional genre of the buddy film to an expansive new genre-crossing level.[3]

Many of these beta male comedies can also be called "bromances," a subgenre that came into definition later in the '00s. Michael De Angelis locates the origins of bromance in the surprising scandal that developed from the friendship of the actor Matthew McConaughey and the athlete Lance Armstrong, dating back to 2006. When spotted cycling or doing other activities together, the sexy male stars were said to be in a bromance, joined, in some accounts, by the actor Jake Gyllenhaal. As the term leapt into prominence, films and television programs self-consciously adopted and portrayed the newly vaunted male-male relationship. "It was not long before the term 'bromance' captured widespread public attention through its suggestion of an edgy and risky version of same-sex social intimacy, playing with sexual distinctions between 'is gay/is not gay' . . . With the friends-into-lovers model remaining such a familiar relationship dynamic . . . bromance sustains its identity from the anticipation of a sexual 'something' that will never happen, thereby becoming a phenomenon that depends upon the audience's acknowledgement and disavowal of sexual possibilities that the bromancers themselves never acknowledge," DeAngelis writes.[4]

In addition to being a beta male comedy, *I Love You, Man* is the definitive bromance, an index of cultural attitudes that informed the emergence of the term and the levels of longing and disavowal within it. What is simultaneously beta male and bromance about *I Love You, Man* is that its hero is, on some level, *a loser*—not in a socioeconomic sense, but in terms of forming social ties with other men. Indeed, if the beta male comedy often depicts its hapless protagonist as a member of a group of other hapless or wayward men, *I Love You, Man* presents an inverted mirror image of the same narrative, one in which the male lead has *no* male friends. *Superbad*, with its rapturous reconciliation between warring teenage friends at the climax, anticipated the bromance (as, in its dark manner, did Wes Craven's *Scream*), which achieved another decisive articulation as an emergent subgenre with *Humpday* (Lynn Shelton, 2009), the indie yin to *I Love You, Man*'s yang. Shelton's film submits a longstanding male friendship to a weirdly intense scrutiny that revolves around the gay porn movie the friends decide to make, one in which they will have sex. Their plan is to submit their movie to the amateur porn film-contest that gives the film its title, Seattle's infamous "Humpfest." The men meet in a hotel room to film themselves having sex but finally decide against both the sex and the porn film.

With the key exception of the horror genre, these comedies have become, in their recurring problems and themes, the primary means whereby the contemporary—read, the latest—crisis in masculinity can be explored.[5] Indeed, the exceedingly slight comedy *The Interview* (Seth Rogen, Evan Goldberg, 2014), starring the bromantic duo par excellence Seth Rogen and James Franco, gained instant notoriety when a cyber-hack of Sony Studios in December 2014 was allegedly perpetrated in retaliation for this film's depiction of North Korea's dictator Kim Jong Un (Randall Park). Suddenly, the seemingly inconsequential and lowbrow form of the bromance played a decisive role in United States foreign policy and international conflict; scores of patriotic moviegoers demanded that *The Interview* be shown in theaters and defied bans and threats of mayhem in order to see it when it was finally shown, as well the possibility of being personally hacked by seeing the film through streaming, VOD (video on demand), and similar methods.

Apart from its North Korea realpolitik and the depiction of a living political leader, the film is an index of attitudes, themes, predilections, and effects in the crossover subgenres of bromance-gross-out-beta male comedies. Dave Skylark (Franco) is the host of the tabloid-TV show "Skylark Tonight," produced by his friend Aaron Rapoport (Rogen), who informs Dave that the show is Kim Jong Un's favorite program. After the team successfully arrange an interview with him that will take place in North Korea, the CIA (embodied by Lizzy Kaplan's chic, bespectacled smartly sexy Agent Lacey) recruits them to assassinate the dictator. Rogen and Franco express their love to one another in a floridly mock-ardent moment that parodies the climactic declarations of love between the teen males in *Superbad*. But Franco, characteristically queering his persona, more interestingly shares an intense scene of bonding with the North Korean dictator, who, flush with the warm glows of their intimate conversation inside of a tank, asks, "Dave, do you think that margaritas are gay because they are so sweet?" The question springs from the leader's memories of his father's abusive condemnations of him for his effeminacy when a child. Franco's character resoundingly affirms Kim Jong Un's choice of beverage. "Margaritas are *awesome*, and if they are gay, who wants to be *straight*?" The two then bond over as they sing the song "Firework" by Katy Perry, especially its opening lines: "Do you ever feel like a plastic bag/Drifting through the wind, wanting to start again?/Do you ever feel, feel so paper thin/Like a house of cards, one blow from caving in?" As Dave learns, the dictator feels precisely along these lines about himself.

As with so many beta male comedies, the film concludes with a stunning montage of violence. The dictator, having discovered Dave's betrayal of him, transforms into an unhinged Rambo of retaliation attempting to obliterate the Americans from his machine-gun-toting perch on a helicopter. In contrast, Dave carries the puppy given to him by the dictator right before their fateful interview (in which Dave manages to expose the dictator as less than godly by getting him to cry over a reprise of "Firework") as he and Aaron flee, guided by Sook Yung Park (Diana Bang), a member of the dictator's administration who has an affair with Aaron and is actually working to overthrow the dictator's reign. (The film, to its credit, allows Sook to have an independent, politically oriented future apart from her assimilation into bromance as the fiery, tomboyish sidekick and love interest for Rogen's Aaron.) Kim Jong Un is himself annihilated through spectacular military pyrotechnics along with the undeniably palpable affection he briefly shared with Dave. The climactic violence is in direct proportion to the level of ardent homoaffectionalism on display earlier.

As Ron Becker argues, the biggest impasse between potential bromancers today is not the issue of homosexuality but rather that of effeminacy, the impassable deal-breaker.[6] While I do not fully agree with Becker—as I will show, films of this ilk obsessively foreground a paranoid awareness of potential homosexuality; further, the abjected males in these films are often conventionally straight and straight-acting, at least on balance—*The Interview*'s treatment of effeminacy certainly validates his claim. Indeed, effeminacy, precisely what Dave appears to affirm in his homoaffectional scene with the dictator, becomes the device he uses to smoke out the all-too-human vulnerability of the dictator whose PR claims that he is not human but rather a god (with no bodily functions or weaknesses). By getting the dictator to blubber uncontrollably on live television ("Fuck you, Dave," he says through tears), Dave effectively gets him to display the frightening effeminacy that lies at the core of his strategically denied humanity. But more than this, the revelation of his effeminacy is the inescapable, undeniable evidence that he is not only human but a failed man. Hence the grandiose display of militaristic carnage at the end of the film, a tableau of massive defensiveness against the public display of male emotion and desire. Like so many of the bromances, particularly those in which Rogen and Franco are involved, a cunning sleight-of-hand occurs in which homoaffectional affiliations are affirmed only to be used as the very evidence of a form of failed manhood that must be narratively repudiated and expunged.

Genre Matters

These films demand attention less for what they say about what ails postmillennial masculinity than for the ample evidence they offer that U.S. masculinity's historical penchants for misogyny, homophobia, and racism continue unabated. Physically unconventional looking, out of shape, out of work (though in this last regard they seem increasingly less unconventional), beta males defy leading man standards. Yet their physical and economic atypicality should not obscure their access to an enduring male privilege. Beta male comedies as well as the related, overlapping subgenre of the bromance represent one of the key cinematic strategies for the conservative re-entrenchment of normative masculinity that defines the '00s—the remasculinization of men.

In dialogue with the work of Tom Ryall and Rick Altman, Barry Langford notes that,

> Most theories of genre are based primarily on analysis of the Hollywood studio system. [Keeping in mind Ryall's argument about the importance of the audience and its expectations in genre theory, we can think of] the audience as the constituency to which the genre film addresses itself. The resulting model recognizes genre as an interactional process between producers—who develop generic templates to capitalize on the previously established popularity of particular kinds of film, always with a view to product rationalization and efficiency—and generically literate audiences who anticipate specific kinds of gratification arising from the genre text's fulfilment of their generic expectations.[7]

Beta male comedies and bromances enjoy a particular kind of relationship with their audience, based in part on the recurring use of the same group of stars—such as Seth Rogen, Jason Segel, Paul Rudd, and James Franco—and in part on the kinds of jokes that will be expected to characterize them. Repeated exposure to these subgenres reveals that the jokes most frequently devised center on penises and semen, and beyond that on the scatological, linking the '00s comedies to earlier sex-comedies of the '80s and gross-out teen comedies of the late '90s.

Hewing more closely to the realist tradition than horror and science fiction do, the comedy genre does not generally foreground the kinds of irreal, uncanny effects that, as I have been arguing, lead to the proliferation of ghost faces, images of masculinity that, in their denatured intensity, evoke the history-bound yet history-blurring, temporality-focused, contested, and deeply metaphorical nature of contemporary representations of male identity. So, the exploration of ghost faces per se will not be as germane to this chapter. That having been said, however, beta male comedies are very much haunted, and no less than other kinds of genre works, by historical images of American masculinity and traumatic wounds within this archive. And at times these comedic works also depict masculinity precisely in the intent and/or uncanny self-consciously visualized manner that informs other genre films, such as the apocalyptic comedy *This Is the End* (2013), directed by Evan Goldberg and Seth Rogen, who were also on the team of screenwriters. In one scene, a dark demon with Rastafarian dreadlocks rapes a sleeping Jonah Hill (playing, as do all of the stars in this movie, himself). The demon, endowed with a monstrous demonic penis, is shown in silhouette as he mounts Hill's bed and then the actor, but there is also a shot of the demon looking straight into the camera with its fiery eyes. The look suggests the film's own knowingness about its homophobic and racist iconography (Hill's character is depicted as the least manly of the bunch and therefore the obvious candidate for *Deliverance*-style male-male rape), its defiance in the face of its own offensiveness, which is also an appeal for indulgence.

Back to the Future: Teen Comedies and the Marriage of Males

As William Paul observes in a discussion of Freud's and Bakhtin's influential views, satire emerged in the twentieth century as a privileged form of comedy, one that emphasized wit rather than the scatological. Challenging this direction, Paul makes the case for the "repressed tradition of vulgar art."[8] As Ken Feil has discussed, vulgarity plays a crucial role in the bromance.[9] Vulgarity—its promise of a mode in which the social order can be disrupted, its demands kept at bay, which opens up possibilities for subversive male behavior—links the bromance to the late '90s spate of gross-out teen comedies. As I argued in chapter 2, the teen comedies were an innovative site for the exploration of new patterns in gender and sexuality emerging in the early twenty-first century. While these films had a radicalism in their excessiveness and depiction of a normative masculinity confronting its own potential dissolution, they were ultimately conservative and nostalgic paeans to a developmental (and therefore temporary) stage of masculinity, one that gives vent (or perhaps their last gasp) to polymorphously perverse energies, but inevitably leads to proper adult male socialization. The beta male and bromantic comedies similarly allow their male personae to indulge in vulgar behavior that ultimately leads to rehabilitation, usually in the form of heterosexual marriage. As in the psychoanalytic scenario, polymorphously perverse energies are left behind through proper oedipalization (socialization into the heterosexual sexual order).

In contrast to the late '90s teen-comedy genre, beta male comedies skew older, with male protagonists in their early twenties, or, in the case of the Steve Carell sleeper hit *Virgin*, their forties.[10] The films are often read as indicative of a new crisis in American masculinity—men who refuse to grow up, get jobs, get out of their parents' house, get wives, get lives. Yet they are also only the latest incarnation of the recurring theme of disaffected masculinity in American film. "What are you rebelling against?" someone asks black-leather-clad motorcycle pack-leader Marlon Brando in *The Wild One* (Laslo Benedek, 1954); his famous response, "Whaddya got?" alerts us both to the persistence of the American male need to protest against the status quo and the shifting, fill-in-the-blank openness of causes for this protest over the decades. From the motorcycle, rock-and-roll rebels and the Beats of the '50s to the draft-dodgers, stoners, surfers, and uneasy riders of the '60s and '70s, from the sex-obsessed pranksters of the '80s to Bill-and-Ted-style excellent adventurers of the '90s to the more recent gross-out teen comedians, and now the beta males, American movies are an ongoing portrait of male disaffection as acute as it is enigmatic. This national disaffection, as I have been arguing, goes much further back, being powerfully present in antebellum American literary texts, especially in the Gothic genre.

As did the teen comedies, the beta male comedies take as their subject white heterosexual manhood. And like the earlier teen comedies, the films are particularly indicative of the shifts in the national construction of gender—particularly in the post-Clinton era—and contemporary instabilities in cinematic constructions of heterosexual masculinity. These instabilities stem from the rise of queer visibility that can be dated back to the early '90s, which saw the emergence of New Queer Cinema as well as a new explicitness in mainstream representations of homosexuality. For all of their antic humor, beta male comedies emphasize the masochistic suffering of the male characters (*Forgetting Sarah Marshall* is a textbook example). This masochism is the thematic preoccupation that links the comedies to the horror genre, as I discussed in chapters 1 and 2.[11] Ultimately, the intersection of anguish, rage, and malevolent play within the murderous stratagems the queer killers of *Scream* (Wes Craven, 1996) devise, and their personal interactions, which oscillate between intimacy and violence, reflect this essentially masochistic disposition. One way to interpret this masochism is that it functions simultaneously as a vent for homoerotic desires that cannot be expressed in homophobic culture and as an ingenious defense against this venting. The masochistic suffering in *Scream* suffuses the more self-consciously antic, "humorous" domains of the later beta male comedy and the bromance, but always threatens to invert their genre paradigms, to turn comedy into violent action, and even horror. Yet, for all of the suffering on display, the films maintain a cool distance from the men in them, even as they present their emotional lives as the central narrative focus. As the collective lament for the state of contemporary American manhood that they are, they explore numerous difficulties in this model, although to say that they explore them is not at all to say that they do so critically. To begin with, they leave almost completely unexamined the gender and racial privilege that undergirds their dominant forms of masculinity.

The films demonstrate a pervasive interest in bonds between men. The figure of the male group (the homosocial, as Eve Kosofsky Sedgwick has influentially called it) in these films is alternately presented as an alternative to the family or as a regressive substitute for it.[12] The films revitalize the theories expounded by Leslie Fiedler in *Love and Death in the American Novel* about classic American literature; in Fiedler's view, male friendship provided a means of male escape from women, the home, and domestic duties.[13] But for Fiedler, the main element in these male friendships is that they involve white men and men from different races, such as Natty Bumppo, the white man living in the woods and among Indians, and his adoptive Mohican family in James Fenimore Cooper's novels such as the 1826 *The Last of the Mohicans*, Ishmael and Queequeg in *Moby-Dick*, and Huck Finn and the escaped slave Jim in Twain's novel. Fiedler called these interracial pairings "the pure marriage of males, sexless and holy, a kind of counter-matrimony, in which the white refugee from society and the dark-skinned primitive are joined till death do them part."[14] It should be added that Fiedler's theory implies a lesser status for the non-white male in the interracial pairing. The non-white male can therefore be effeminized into the more passive partner.

Unlike the poignant and prematurely cancelled TNT series *Men of a Certain Age* (2009–2011) starring Ray Romano, Andre Braugher, and Scott Bakula, the beta male and bromance films rarely show friendship between men across racial lines. In this regard, they also sharply contrast with the racial buddy-film exemplified by the jokey 1980s *Lethal Weapon* series starring Mel Gibson and Danny Glover, in other words, with the interracial bonding that was the one salutary aspect of that film series.[15] Perhaps the lack of interracial male relationships stems from the perceived crisis in white heterosexual masculinity—this is a time to consolidate and reinforce this enclave, not render it more diffuse and unsteady through confusions of color. Homosexuality presents enough threat of contamination.

What is especially novel in beta male films is that male bonds endure well into adulthood and present a genuine challenge to institutionalized marriage. As has been traditionally established in theories of marriage and in masculinity studies, marriage as a social institution exists in order to civilize men, who spend most of their time before marriage within the male group of their friends.[16] After marriage—because they are now presumably properly socialized—men largely leave other men behind. As it did in nineteenth-century America, even prolonged states of bachelorhood and brotherhood in beta male comedies almost always lead to marriage. The linkages between antebellum American literature and the beta male comedies demonstrate the endurance of certain archetypal patterns in American masculinity. While beta male comedies generally are "marriage comedies," ensuring the progression of their protagonists to a properly married state, they also provide some challenges to this enduring model of male development. On the one hand, several beta male films depict men as cleaving—transgressively, in that to do so they defy their wives—to their male friends beyond marriage. On the other hand, some of the films also depict heterosexual men as being unable to *form* bonds with other straight men (*I Love You, Man* is exemplary in this regard). For all of their vaunted bromantic ardor, the films maintain an attitude of ambivalence toward male bonding.

Reframing the Male Gaze

One of the truly striking aspects of '00s filmmaking practice is its fascination with the male body. To recapitulate some main points of our discussion thus far, this newfound interest in male bodies finds spectacular vent in the eroticized male spectacles of film and, perhaps especially, television. The contemporary erotics of the male body stem, to be sure, from the rise of queer visibility. As this visibility has given the queer gaze a new momentum and range, it has also had the effect of making straight, white men not just the wielder but the object of the gaze. Through both voyeuristic and fetishistic modes of representation, the male body is routinely put on display in film and on television narrative. Everywhere we turn, gleaming, chiseled male bodies pop out of our screens, an expanse of male forms. Most of these male bodies are white; the black—to say nothing of the Hispanic or Asian—male form is rarely ever displayed. Whereas women's bodies once constituted the essence of mass-audience visual display, male bodies are now just as readily and widely mass-circulated and mass-consumed. (The growing visibility of trans bodies further complicates these matters and demands a discrete study, as does the concept of female masculinity popularized by the gender theorist Jack Halberstam. The rampant denuding of masculinity in representation is motivated, perhaps, by a need to differentiate male masculinity from female and/or trans masculinity.) As I will show in the final chapter, pornography in its all-encompassing pervasiveness reifies these patterns. Popular sites for gay male Internet pornography such as *seancody.com* and *Straight College Men* are resolutely racist in their near-total exclusion of non-white subjects.

Fascinating though these erotic dynamics are, however, they are not the full story. To establish that masculinity can no longer be seen exclusively as the subject of the gaze, that it is often under desiring scrutiny itself in popular representations, and that male bodies are routinely offered for spectatorial pleasure and consumption, can only be the beginning of a critical inquiry into the dynamics of a post-millennial masculinity. The preoccupation with male bodies is not only symptomatic but also allegorical of a larger preoccupation. Related to but also distinct from the fascination with male bodies is one with *maleness itself*. Not only male bodies but the essential characteristics of masculinity must now be denuded. What used to characterize femininity—the mystery of "woman," the enigma of the female erotic arts, the secret goings on between women in groups—now extends to masculinity as well. As I discussed in the Introduction in the context of Steven Soderbergh's *Magic Mike* (2012), the "opening-up" theme dominates contemporary representations of masculinity. Now, it is masculinity that is framed as the ultimate mystery to be solved; men must be explored, investigated.

This sleuthing plays out in a number of ways, and is usually undertaken by the female characters. Consistently, the particulars of the male homosocial realm, the inner workings of male group mentality, are held up to the clinical light of the female perspective. This female observer is always figured as an outsider and her perspective as a detached, objective one, much like that, traditionally at least, of the anthropologist or the visitor to an exotic locale.[17] The female ethnographic observer figure is exemplified by *Knocked Up*'s Katherine Heigl and her outsider perspective on Seth Rogen's private homosocial realm. Adding to the tropes of exoticism and anthropological scrutiny, this male group world is represented as emblematic of arrested development—a primitive throwback disrupted by the presence of the modern woman.[18]

The most famous application of the anthropological metaphor to the apparently inherent mystery of "woman" remains Freud's phrase to describe femininity, the "dark continent." But whereas the woman and her mystery have been deemed and rendered erotic by a tradition that upholds "woman" as the mythological icon of sexual knowledge, men in the beta male tradition retain and exert little mysterious pull. The figure of woman became a site of perpetual clinical investigation yet forever a maddening, beguiling, unsolvable mystery; in contrast, contemporary film works posit that the mysteries of masculinity, when properly explored, can be easily solved. Moreover, the exposure of men's hidden ways and habitats serves to render the image of masculinity as denatured as possible, devoid of all illusion. No longer powerful nor mysterious, men are contemporary culture's chief anthropological specimens, to be studied or satirized, or perhaps even treated with sympathy, but never celebrated. This is not to suggest, however, that a certain reverence toward masculinity, especially in its straight, white cast, does not persist unabated. Rather, it is to suggest that the ways of *being* reverent have shifted along with transformations in the gendered public sphere. In a curious way, the discovery, exposure, and "solving" of the problem of manhood has only deepened the reverential attitude, enhancing the sense that "real" men, like the panda and other endangered species, are diminishing in number and need to be studied closely and treated with the utmost care.

Comedy, Horror, and Gothic American Literature

Perhaps most interesting of all, this emerging interest in the denuding of men socially and psychically—which stems, perhaps, from what Mark Seltzer has described as the "wound culture" of contemporary America, fixated on flaying open both bodies and psyches—has produced, simultaneously, the proliferation of seemingly distinct genres, comedy and horror.[19] The oddly blended tones of many significant films of the past fifteen years or so, resulting in movies that are tonally discordant (comedic and chilling, comedic and plangent, terrifying and tearjerking, and so forth)—ranging from David Fincher's *Fight Club* (1999) to Apatow's *Funny People* (2009), Fincher's *The Social Network* (2010) to Glenn Ficarra and John Requa's *I Love You, Philip Morris* (2009) to Ruben Fleischer's *Zombieland* (2009)—stem, I argue, from the larger, genre-hybridic mixture of the comedic and the horrific in contemporary cinema generally. As I argued in chapter 2, Wes Craven's satiric horror film *Scream* film provided a telling template for this genre intermixture. The mixture of tones in many films in the beta male category, as well as their obsessive interest in the forms of violence and the levels of shame and public humiliation to which their protagonists can be subjected, stem, I argue, from the fixation with Gothic themes that defined American literature in its first mature flowering in the early nineteenth century.[20] A template for this blending of genres and tones, on the one hand, and for certain enduring patterns of male interaction, on the other hand, is Washington Irving's 1820 tale "The Legend of Sleepy Hollow." Using this tale as a rubric, we can see the ways in which beta male films continue to narrate the struggle between an isolated, non-joiner male (the pedagogue Ichabod Crane) cut off from normative male identity and the cheerfully violent leader of a male group (Brom Bones), who simultaneously attempts to destroy the outsider and to assimilate him within his homosocial ranks.

In Irving's story, the schoolteacher Ichabod Crane, odd, unpopular, and prone to administer corporal punishment to his students (although only to the bullies), pursues the affections of the beautiful Katrina Van Tassel, daughter of a prosperous farmer and also the object of Brom Bones's desire. In stark contrast to the pedantic and humorless Ichabod, Brom Bones is a fiendishly likable practical joker much like the anarchic Stiffler (Seann William Scott) from the *American Pie* films. But the chief difference between them is that Brom is at the center of a group of male friends who revere him and join in with his sadistic games, his relentless campaign to oust Ichabod from Sleepy Hollow, whereas Stiffler is an outlier in his male group, too anarchic even for them ("I'll give you a spoon to eat my ass!" he gleefully responds to one of his friend's concerns in the first *American Pie* [Paul Weitz, 1999]). The pedagogue Crane is remarkably uninterested in competing against Brom or his gang; his main interests, as expressed in the story, range from exchanging stories with the old wives of the village, dancing with Katrina, and, most emphatically, fantasizing about the vast quantities and varieties of food that will be available to him at the Van Tassel farm should he win Katrina's hand; indeed, so lavish are these gustatory fantasies that one begins to suspect that the chief object of Ichabod's desire is that banquet table, Katrina merely the means of procuring access to it. The most ardent desire in the tale, however, is whatever impels Brom to fix so many of his energies upon Ichabod; reading the story, one gets the impression that it is Ichabod, far more than Katrina, who commands Brom's attention.[21] The fraternal pranks played on Ichabod by Brom and his gang have a violent edge, perhaps even a murderous one: when, it is strongly implied, Brom dons the guise of the Headless Horseman and flings the flaming pumpkin at Ichabod, Ichabod is knocked off his own horse, to the ground, and never seen in Sleepy Hollow again.[22]

John Hamburg's *I Love You, Man* (2009), depicts a remarkably Ichabod-like protagonist. An admirable and affecting work, it is one of the few beta male comedies that resists the male privilege at their core. Yet it, too, is riddled with the same frustrations that seem endemic to the emergent genre. Peter Klaven, played by Paul Rudd, is a real-estate agent who gets along extremely well with women, including his fiancée. What he lacks is the friendship of other men. Going out on a series of man-dates to find a best man for his upcoming wedding, Peter feels increasingly pessimistic about his best pal-prospects until, at a real-estate opening for his client Lou Ferrigno (of 1970s TV *Incredible Hulk* fame), he meets an investor, Sydney Fife (Jason Segel). Expansive, as big a personality as he is physically, and disarmingly nonchalant, Segel's Sydney appositely fills in the Brom Bones role to Rudd's Ichabod-like loner Peter. The difference between the film and Irving's tale is that this version of Brom Bones genuinely cares for the isolated protagonist. Going out for fish tacos; hanging out in Sydney's "man-cave" listening to their shared love, the band Rush; performing their songs together, in the cave and at a concert, which involves flicking their tongues out wildly at their guitars—Peter and Sydney share one of the most ardent emotional relationships between men since Ang Lee's 2005 *Brokeback Mountain*. The obvious difference, that that was a film about gay men, this about straight ones, is less important than what unites them: in both narratives, a cut-off male is awakened to new pleasures by a more daring, impudent male. Like Ang Lee's film, *I Love You, Man* presents this relationship as initially rapturous but increasingly troubled. While Lee's film is a melodrama with a tragic ending, and Hamburg's a comedy that ultimately ends in marriage—the happy resolution that is the proper one to the comedy genre, signaling union and procreative fertility—both films are interested in exploring the difficulties men face in forming bonds with each other, non-sexual and otherwise. The more emotionally direct and courageous Jack Twist (Jake Gyllenhaal) reaches out to and awakens Ennis Del Mar (the late Heath Ledger) both sexually and emotionally. Sydney, in a related way, awakens Peter, drawing him out emotionally in a manner that, while not explicitly sexual, does indeed have homoerotic overtones.

The overlaps between the films, intended for such distinct audiences, is the chief interest here. Both films explore the plangency of what Robert B. Putnam has described as "bowling alone," in his study by that name—the isolation of men in what had once been a culture that promoted the model of the group of male friends who all did things together, such as bowling.[23] The replacement of the bowling league with one stark, solitary bowler is Putnam's allegory for the collapse of social relations in the United States of the post-Vietnam era. Whereas the United States once made male bonds central, isolated masculinity has become the much more common experience, as Scorsese's great *Taxi Driver* (1976) elucidates. Yet, the idea that men are cut off from the world of male friendship, while at the same time expected to join in with it, is a longstanding theme in American culture, as Irving's story makes clear. Hamberg's film reveals the theme's continued relevance.

Peter Klaven is cut off even from the homosocial relationships in his own family. When he asks his dad (J. K. Simmons) who his best friend is, his dad unhesitatingly responds that he has two, his old war buddy Hank Mardukas ("Hank Mardukas has been my closest friend since our first year at IBM. Best man at our wedding.") and Peter's brother, Robbie (Andy Samberg, a *Saturday Night Live* regular known for his rap-parodies and, especially, the song he performed with Justin Timberlake, "Dick in a Box," and the star of the Fox sitcom, *Brooklyn Nine-Nine* [2012–2013]). Dad and Robbie—who is gay and a personal trainer—hit fists, in intergenerational as well straight-gay bonhomie. In a telling scene deleted from the film but included in the DVD, Dad is shown playing on Robbie's gay bowling team, the implication being that the divide between straight and gay has eroded, and only Peter—cut off from the fraternal order in either its straight or gay forms—bowls alone. Peter's series of man-dates only confirm his sense of disconnection from other men; in one of the most poignant scenes, he tries to invite himself along on a bachelor party vacation with the guys in his fencing club, who all regard him with bewildered, blank stares as they courteously rebuff him. ("Good luck with *that*," the groom-to-be, played by the Indian-American actor Aziz Ansara, tells Peter when he shares the news that he, too, is going to be married, as if he had just mentioned investing in a new business venture.) Yet, though a seeming maestro of male bonding, Sydney is also shown to be cut off from his bevy of buddies, all of whom ultimately reject him for their girlfriends or wives. Indeed, his loneliness comes to seem even more piercing than Peter's.

I Love You, Man plumbs depths of isolation rarely explored in contemporary Hollywood films; what is especially significant is the way in which it exposes the potential for isolation at the very heart of what is presumed to be the most natural, normative of relationships, the fraternal bonds between white, heterosexual men. The theme of gender-estrangement also has longstanding precedents in American culture, if nineteenth-century American literature is any indication. (The HBO series *Enlightened*, which ran for two seasons from [2012–2013] and starred Laura Dern, Diane Ladd, Luke Wilson, and Mike White, who also wrote and designed the series, is an exquisite study in the female side of American loneliness.) By the point at which it reveals Sydney's own isolation, however, the film's politics have become more suspect. The major failure of the film is its inability to take its theme of male isolation and gender-estrangement fully seriously. The film depicts Sydney's own isolation punitively, offering it as a sign that his bonhomie and anarchic personality are socially threatening—that, in other words, he, too, needs to be married. Much of the latter sections of the film are devoted to giving Sydney his comeuppance; indeed, in doing so, it facilitates the virilization of its hero, who becomes more of a typical "man" in his rejection of Sydney, urged by his fiancée. In other words, he finally "mans up." As an example of this, once he has rejected Sydney as a friend, seemingly for good, Peter also finds the masculine strength—in a word, the *cajones*—to tell off a deeply annoying and competitive male colleague who steals his clients and brags endlessly about doing so. Adding a surprisingly homoerotic edge to this virilization of Peter, Sydney (as I discussed in chapter 2) designs a series of billboards to promote his estranged friend's real-estate skills. These billboards, "starring" Peter in various action-movie poses (such as James Bond), make Peter a real-estate star, despite Peter's initial horror at them. They also reveal a surprisingly ardent fantasy life on Sydney's part—his own fantasy of what it would be like to see "Pistol Pete" ("Pistol" being one of Sydney's affectionate nicknames for Peter) in various forms of male gender-role play.

In contrast to *I Love You, Man*, most of the beta male comedies, whatever their level of skill and sensitivity, portray the homosocial as a given, an always already present facet of male experience. At the same time, these films almost always depict the homosocial negatively, a point that has been overlooked in criticism. That they register such a discomfort with fraternity yet also passionately embrace it makes them an exemplary reflection of American manhood at a particularly confusing point in its historical development. *Knocked Up's* never-ending male houseparty is populated by ghoulish, blank-eyed young men made so unappealing that the protagonist Ben Stone, played by beta male star par excellence Seth Rogen, comes to seem like an all-American Mr. Normal in comparison. Along these lines, his commitment to the mother of his child, Alison Scott (Katherine Heigl), comes to seem less like a testament to his maturation then it does an escape from a slough of male despond. *Superbad* is a paean to male friendship that culminates in an astonishingly passionate declaration of love between its young male protagonists (Michael Cera and Jonah Hill) while they lie beside each other at night, nestled in sleeping bags. The scene ends with Hill declaring words to the effect that he wants to proclaim his love for Cera from the rooftops. This expression of love is especially resonant, given that it arrives after some devastating arguments triggered by Cera's having gotten into Dartmouth. Attending differently ranked colleges produces a divisive rift between the best of friends that occupies most of the film's narrative attention.

Superbad makes male friendship and its urgency and travails central. Yet friendship between men is never depicted by the film as its *own* end, only a developmental stage toward properly heterosexual relationships. After this poignant, heady declaration of love between friends, the boys meet up with the female objects of their desire in a mall the next day. As each newly formed couple goes off in their own direction, we watch male friendship do its chief work: prepare the male for heterosexual love and, it is assumed, marriage. That the scene of heterosexual closure occurs in a mall reassures us that these four will be as properly consumerist as they are conventionally heterosexual. Male friendship leads, as it does in traditional theories of masculinity and the social function of marriage, to lasting bonds with women. But if the films follow this normative social trajectory that leads men to women, they in no way provide idealized portraits of the women with whom the men grope their way toward intimacy.

Women and the Beta Male

While many of the women in the beta male films, though granted more autonomy over their own social roles and sexual pleasures, remain aloof, icy goddesses, several more of them represent the new style "female chauvinist pig" who outdistances the films' often hapless men in conventionally masculine, raucous behavior.[24] The implication is that these female characters have been assimilated into the ever-expanding homosocial order, which may account for their lack of wit. These wit-deprived women are a come-down from the tradition of witty, verbal, energetically inventive women in film, in stark contrast to the "fast-talking dames" and "clever funny girls" of 1930s comedies.[25] As Richard Corliss writes in his review of *Superbad*, "Hollywood thinks girls aren't funny any more. Today, smart or sassy talk is something only the guys get to do. In *The 40-Year-Old Virgin* the main attraction of the female romantic interest played by Catherine Keener is that she laughs at Carell's jokes."[26] One has only to witness the witlessness of Allyson Hannigan in Jesse Dylan's *American Wedding* (2003), whose oddball character was so bracing in the first two films in the series, to chart the cinematic devolution of female aplomb. Female-centered ensemble comedies such as *Bridesmaids* (Paul Feig, 2011), self-consciously raucous and gross-out; comedies starring Anna Faris; Lena Dunham's work, particularly her HBO series *Girls*, which debuted in 2012 to controversial reception (which focused on the lack of non-white characters) but has gone on for additional seasons; and women-driven comedy series such Tina Fey's *30 Rock* (2006–2013) and Amy Poehler's *Parks and Recreation* (2009–2015), both of which were on NBC, and Comedy Central's *Broad City* (2014–present), created by its stars Abbi Jacobson and Ilana Glazer, mark a new moment of women-doing-comedy.[27]

If the beta male comedies register ambivalence over homosociality, they also portray males as fundamentally estranged from the world of women. In *Pineapple Express, Knocked Up*, and *Superbad* in particular, women and men seem to be two different species. Heterosexual romantic love seems almost entirely alien to the male drug-trafficking world of *Pineapple Express*; though Seth Rogen's twentysomething protagonist Dale Denton, who hands out court summonses to the unsuspecting, has a girlfriend, she is pointedly made to be a high school student, adding to the sense of arrested development in the film. Neither James Franco's sweet-souled pothead and pot-dealer Saul Silver or his rival, Red (Danny McBride), seem to have any contact with women whatsoever. The main female character in the film, Rosie Perez's crooked cop, allied with the evil drug lord whose murder of a henchman Dale Denton witnesses, is rabidly masculinized. Indeed, if anything she far exceeds his hapless other henchmen in virile gusto.

In *Knocked Up*, the relationship that Seth Rogen's Ben Stone pursues with Alison, an up-and-coming TV entertainment reporter, places him in stark contrast to the homosocial group he lives with, a collection of social misfits whose chief employment is trying to create a website that records every instance of female nudity in Hollywood film (after months of toil, they discover that an identical and far more profitable website already exists). Even though one of them has a girlfriend, she is made so pointedly odd that she becomes indistinguishable from this oddball male group's ranks, as opposed to the tense blonde goddess Alison (a contrast reinforced by the fact that this other girlfriend is an Asian woman). So aloof from them at first, Alison wants to join their ranks by the end. *Knocked Up* is yet another version of the hoary fantasy of the homely loser winning the unattainable woman. Though fashion-model beautiful in contrast to the cheerful slobbiness of Seth Rogen's onscreen persona, Alison appears to have more frustrations with Ben's lack of ambition or finances than with his appearance. Alison's sister, Debbie (Leslie Mann), regards Ben with so much contempt that she seems to be overcompensating for Alison's unconventional response to his charms. Again, the central problem in these films is not the men's non-standard physical appearance, or even their prolonged residence in the homosocial realm, but that decade-defining inability to "man up"; unconventional though beta males may look, what's important is the way they act, and that when they do act, they act like men, as we also see in *I Love You, Man*. When Ben finally stands up to Debbie in the delivery-room climax of the film, ordering her out as Alison prepares to give birth, Debbie, far from being taken aback by this vicious tongue-lashing, tells her husband (Paul Rudd) how much she now *likes* Ben. It is the integration of women into the fraternal sphere and their adoption of typically masculine attitudes that enables them to embrace these non-Adonises. So, rather than evincing a bracing new kind of receptivity to non-standard screen masculinities, the films emerge as programs for the development of conventional masculine attitudes for the female as well as male characters.

Like Ichabod Crane, Paul Rudd's real-estate agent Peter Klaven in *I Love You, Man* is, in marked contrast to his compatriots in other films, shown to be quite comfortable in female company. Indeed, his problem, insofar as the film is concerned, is that his emotional ties are exclusively maintained with women and not with other men. Yet in many ways the world of women is just as alien to Peter as it is to other beta men, another correspondence to the dynamics of the nineteenth-century social order. Peter's fiancée, Zooey (Rashida Jones), announces, while the couple drive home after Peter pops the question in a restaurant, their impending nuptials to her girlfriends.

When these women avidly discuss explicit details of the couple's sex life, or when Zooey and the girls sit around having a girl's night, Peter's solitude is juxtaposed against their rich, lively, loquacious women's world. This is a world he would be only too happy to enter, as his making dessert for girls' night suggests. Peter overhears, however, Zooey and her friends' expressions of concern over his lack of male friends. They prophesize that

FIGURE 3.1. *I Love You, Man* begins with a proposal and ends with marriage between the heterosexual couple.

lonely Peter will be forever clingy, never allowing Zooey any time for herself. Moreover, his having prepared all of them dessert, which he was about to surprise them with before overhearing their discussion of him, threatens to feminize him in the women's eyes—to confirm their fears of his lack of male attributes, having male friends chief among them. Women impose and maintain standards of heteromasculinity no less stringently than men do. Peter is adrift, cut off from the female company he might quite comfortably join while being acutely cut off from the world of men. As Robin Wood argued in *Hollywood from Vietnam to Reagan*, what chiefly characterized the buddy films of the 1970s was the theme of "homelessness"; this theme remains acutely relevant, as beta males search for a place to belong, singly and collectively.[28] Then again, his program of virilization in the latter sections of the film—defined by his ability to tell-off his obnoxious male coworker and to commit to Zooey without reservations—suggests that he has found not only a tongue but also a home at last.

In "Sleepy Hollow," the narrator laments over the effects that Katrina Van Tassel has on Ichabod; has she led him on only to spurn him, using a woman's witchlike methods? Woman is no longer witch, but warden, running the prisonlike institution of the home. This point informs *Knocked Up*, with scary Debbie ruling the roost (fascinatingly, adulterous transgression engaged in by her husband, also played by Paul Rudd, does not involve a woman but the male group of sports fans he sneaks off to hang out with); *I Love You, Man*, in which Zooey's friend Denise can get her burly, ill-tempered husband (played all too convincingly by Jon Favreau) to do whatever she wants, provided she agrees to perform various sexual favors; *Role Models*, in which Paul Rudd's frustrated girlfriend holds out on continuing their relationship unless he becomes a less uptight, looser person. Her warden-like behavior here is literally tied to the law, as she negotiates for Rudd's character to participate, along with a friend and fellow employee played by Sean William Scott, in a troubled kids' mentoring program after Rudd has a meltdown and totals several cars, including his own.

Perhaps the most telling film in terms of the representation of women is *Forgetting Sarah Marshall*, written by Jason Segel, who also stars. In its attentive devotion to its protagonist's suffering as well as the ways in which it resolves his nagging titular conundrum, the film is exemplary of the concerns of its ilk. In a much discussed scene that is one of the few examples of male full-frontal nudity in Hollywood film, the protagonist Peter Bretter, played by Segel, is naked when Sarah, his girlfriend (Kristen Bell, who starred in the series *Veronica Mars*) breaks up with him. (It should be noted that several European films of the early '00s, such as *Intimacy* [Patrice Chéreau, 2001] and *Fat Girl* [Catherine Breillat, 2001] showed not just male full-frontal nudity but also erect penises within graphic onscreen depictions of sexual intercourse.) Sarah is the star of a TV crime drama that Peter, a composer, scores. Devastated, Peter mopes around his apartment, alternately eating vast bowls of what look like Fruit Loops, poring over old photographs of happier days with Sarah, and weeping pitiably. His only friend would appear to be a family relation, his stepbrother, who is in a relationship with a placidly bland woman whom an angry Peter unfavorably compares to the high-fashion Sarah.

Notably, Peter's stepbrother repeatedly calls attention to the nonbiological aspect of their contentious sibling relationship. Such touches deepen the theme of disconnection in these films: these lonely men no longer have families to depend on, either. As another example, in *Knocked Up*, Seth Rogen's hapless hero has a father who tells him how much he loves him. Yet the father is ultimately revealed to be a bland cipher who offers little in the way of the support he promises. Rogen's character is shown to be disconnected not only from his male group but also the family. Interestingly, although he attempts to distance himself from the oddball friends with whom he shares a house, it is precisely these friends who show up at the hospital to support him during the birth of his child. Friends emerge as the family you make, especially if they are actually weirder than you are. I would argue that this thematic is a straight male version of a gay male commonplace—friendships that provide the succor and support of the family. Indeed, one of the chief strategies of beta male comedies is to reconfigure gay themes into new disaffected straight-male themes. (The feminized and female-identified outsiderness of Paul Rudd's character in *I Love You, Man* recalls the typical representation of gay men in every way save this particular character's sexual orientation.)

In an especially vivid post-breakup scene in *Forgetting Sarah Marshall*, Peter, at work, tries to provide music for a tense moment from the crime drama. The onscreen Sarah looming above him, Peter first adds jokey music that undercuts the onscreen action. But then, in a fury, he picks up an object and smashes it against the screen, ripping it apart, leaving Sarah's monolithic face in shreds. The entire scene indexes Western cultural attitudes toward women as it demonstrates that male defenses against the apparently archetypal power of women range from mockery to physical violence. Still despondent but trying to heal, Peter decides to go away to Hawaii, which he'd planned to visit with Sarah; no sooner does he try to check into a resort hotel than he discovers that Sarah is also a guest there, along with her current boyfriend, a faux-rebel British rocker. This character, Aldous Snow, is played by Russell Brand, and will become the "him" that Jonah Hill must "get to the Greek" in a later beta male comedy. Providing the only salve to Peter during this excruciating trip is the frontdesk clerk Rachel (Mila Kunis), with whom Peter eventually develops a genuine romance. Unlike his ex, she "gets" him: Rachel enjoys his spoofy Dracula musical, whereas it left Sarah deeply perplexed; goads him back to life; encourages him to take more risks; gets him to jump from a scary height into the water where she awaits, literalizing her symbolic function as the restorer of life.

Insofar as the film explores the Peter-Sarah relationship and the greater compatibility that exists between Peter and the cheeky, rowdier Rachel, it succeeds in exploring the difficulties of relationships between a successful woman and a guy still stuck in what the eminent sociologist and theorist of masculinity Michael Kimmel has called "Guyland" in his book of the same name. Guyland, as Kimmel theorizes, is a realm of retrogressive male behavior exhibited by males who refuse to grow up, as Peter's all-day-long kid's-cereal-eating marathons suggest. Yet, in its depiction of Sarah Marshall, the film reveals most clearly the misogynistic streak in the beta male films. Oddly, this misogyny emerges not from the narrowness of the film's representation of Sarah but precisely from its attempt, at points, to present matters from *her* perspective and with some depth. In one scene between her and Rachel, Sarah fights back tears as she encourages Rachel's developing romance with Peter, and Rachel responds sympathetically. This moment of feminine kinship is the most sensitive one in the film. Yet in one of the very next scenes, at a dinner the two couples share, the women revert to stereotypically competitive behavior: all sympathy gone, they claw at each other as catty rivals. Though Sarah is shown to be stuck in a miserable relationship with the vain, vacuously horny English rocker, and though she delivers a powerful speech in which she explains her motivations for breaking up with Peter to him—her repeated attempts to pull him out from Guyland—the film ultimately plays out as a male revenge fantasy against an aloof goddess. However tremulously emotional she appears to be—the film even adds a scene in which she desperately performs sexual charms on Peter only to be verbally rebuffed by him in the most violent verbal terms imaginable—Sarah must be both humiliated and vanquished. "You're the Devil!" Peter screams out at her as he storms off, taking his newfound masculine power and whatever interest the film had in exploring male-female relationships along with him. By the end, Sarah's TV show has been cancelled, Peter's comedic Dracula puppet-opera is a hit, and Rachel—who had cut off ties with Peter after learning that he had fooled around, however briefly, with Sarah—now returns to celebrate in the triumph that she alone had been able to foresee. Pointedly, at the close of the film, Peter is nude before a woman once again, but this time the woman is Rachel, and this time he stands nude before a woman at the *start* of a new relationship, rather than the humiliating end of one. With her warm appreciation for his talents, Rachel restores the phallus that Sarah had taken and thrown away. And, while it turns out that her cancelled TV series now has a new life, its title, "Animal Instincts," confirms that Sarah—playing a detective linked to a psychic dog—is not only the Devil but a real bitch.[29]

Without the melancholy, brooding quality that Jason Segel brings to his self-written role, *Forgetting Sarah Marshall* would be largely unwatchable. Yet it's undeniably a film that speaks to audiences, largely because of the ways in which it indulges the protagonist's masochistic excesses. His masochism is a kind of hypocritical narcissism, a wallowing in suffering that masks the investment in male power and privilege that characterizes this and several other beta male films. Of course, what ensures the acceptance of this masochism is that it's played for laughs; what most reviews comment on is the oddly funny quality of seeing Segel humiliated, in the naked-breakup scene, as he weeps despondently. ("Is that an old woman crying in your hotel room?" Rachel asks, over the phone. "We've been getting complaints.") Soliciting both bathetic empathy and laughs, these films repurpose the dreaded you'll-laugh-you'll-cry formula of the chick-flick as fodder for the farcical male melodrama.

Bromance and Its Discontents: Race and Homosexuality

The unconventional screen presence of beta males and their willingness to subject themselves to masochistic self-flagellation and physical assaults of all kinds (the shockingly realistic fight scene in *Pineapple Express* among Rogen, Danny McBride, and James Franco) can obscure the racial and gender privilege at the heart of the films. The films have been positively read as a new, non-neurotic tradition of Jewish masculinity, freed from the emotional burdens and the "kvetching" that marked previous generations of Jewish stars, exemplified by Woody Allen and Jerry Seinfeld. The films do indeed work to defy the stereotypes of the nonviolent and apparently passive American-Jewish male that have been discussed by such critics as Warren Rosenberg and Daniel Boyarin.[30] The star manhood of Seth Rogen, a central figure in the beta male comedy, is a striking rebuttal of Jewish stereotypes, beginning with his husky physicality and centering in the aggressivity of his screen persona. The bitter rivalry between Rogen's mall cop

Ronnie and Aziz Ansari's Iraqi mall shopkeeper Saddam in the unpleasant dark comedy *Observe and Report* (Jody Hill, 2009) exposes a pattern within beta male movies. Jewish masculinity is contrasted against a more visibly marked racial and cultural Other to reinforce the mainstream manhood (white-Christian-assimilationist) of the former and the foreign threat and difference of the latter.[31]

While issues of Jewish masculinity are an intriguing and by no means uncontroversial aspect of the films, what demands equal attention yet has not received it is their representation of non-white race. Non-white actors are almost never cast in significant parts; the parts they do play provide either absurdist comic relief (the oddly intense and impatient Asian obstetrician in *Knocked Up* or the weirdly energized Asian drug king in *Pineapple Express*, both played by Ken Jeong, to say nothing of his rabidly odd villain in *The Hangover*) or racial caricatures, such as the huge, formidable, yet infant-like Hawaiian local who takes pity on Jason Segel in *Forgetting* ("You look like a baby," Segel tells him). In Jeong's case, in particular, the effort to represent a non-stereotypical Asian masculinity eerily mirrors the similar effort made in the films on behalf of Jewish men. If, as Richard Fung eloquently argued, Asian males in the cinema are often represented as "castrated," when they are not being erased altogether, the characters Jeong plays emphasize their phallic aggressivity, as in the moment in *The Hangover* in which Jeong's character bursts out of the trunk maniacally brandishing a knife at the astonished white male group.[32] But Jeong's onscreen persona also radiates a disorienting queerness, making his threat as much about his enigmatic sexuality as it is about his predilection for violence. In the end, his characterizations, as deployed by the films, add up to a new racial caricature, the virilized, violent queer Asian male, a striking and disquieting variation on Fiedlerian themes.

The figure of the mammy, the black woman who represents the maternal and endless care of the white self, endures in current films, but now primarily in male form.[33] The immense Hawaiian man who takes Segel under his prodigious wing and the African-American male characters function as male mammy figures, providing straight-talk as they nurture addled white men back to psychic health. The fellow electronics store employee who avidly facilitates the hero's loss of his virginity in *The 40-Year-Old Virgin* and the bartender in *Forgetting* cut through the fat, as it were, articulating the hard facts that the white characters refuse to hear. (The bouncer in *Knocked Up*, played by the African-American actor Craig Robinson, an increasingly visible presence in beta male films, performs exactly the same role for white women when he explains why women beyond a certain age—which would appear to be 25 years old or so—cannot be allowed into the youth-market-focused club. "You old as fuck," he explains, adding to soften the blow, "for this club, not for the earth.") What the films can't seem to imagine is a person of color not marked by that status, whose race isn't used as a symbol of itself or in ironic counterpoint to the role being played (as with Jeong's characters).

The image of Segel and his immense Hawaiian mentor lying in bed together in *Forgetting* unmistakably recalls a famous scene in classic American literature that links race and homoeroticism: Ishmael and the Polynesian cannibal Queequeg in bed together at the Spouter Inn in the early chapters of Melville's *Moby-Dick*, which, as I theorized in chapter 1, is a seminal work that haunts contemporary representation, especially in terms of masculinity. This scene textualizes the link between race and queer sexuality in the films: that both are largely played for comic relief. Their incessant nods to the homoerotic allow the films to declare their comfort level with queerness while maintaining an ironic distance from it, a distance with phobic implications, as they consistently reinscribe the heterosexual binary.

A relentless gay-baiting informs beta male comedies. With a demonstrable obsessiveness, the films repeatedly evoke homoerotic tensions (two men in the man-cave or the sleeping-bag sleep-over in which declarations of unabashed love are made) or explicitly invoke questions about their characters' possible homosexuality ("You gay, man?" one of Steve Carell's electronics store coworkers, including a satyr-like Seth Rogen, asks of Carell's shy nebbish in *The 40-Year-Old Virgin*. "I touched a guy's balls in Hebrew school once," Rogen's character says during this homosocial roundtable discussion, as if to encourage Carell to out himself.). At other times, the homoerotic tension of a scene stems from a satirical verbal or visual gag, not only the well-known "You know how I know you're gay?" scene from *Virgin*, but also in moments such as the one in which Rogen attempts to help a despondent Paul Rudd, who is having a public meltdown in the electronics store over his girlfriend woes. Rudd's meltdown involves his pulling down his pants and underwear; to his extravagant horror, Rogen must pull Rudd's underwear over his exposed buttocks, while Rudd is lying across a seated Rogen's lap. The scene is played for laughs, and its depiction of male-male physical intimacy is leavened with Rogen's palpable disgust, but the physical intimacy is palpable as well. There are also innumerable sight gags like the men miming the varieties of sodomy as they ostensibly practice workout routines on the beach in *Forgetting*, or Jason Sudeikis staring, through binoculars, at a woman's sexy butt in a hardware store in *Horrible Bosses* (Seth Gordon, 2011), except that the woman turns out to be a young man with a sexy butt. For that matter, consider in this film as well as the highly odd, no doubt intended-for-laughs rivalry between Jason Sudeikis and Jason Bateman over who would be more "rapeable" in prison.[34] *This Is the End*, directed by Evan Goldberg and Seth Rogen, who were also on the team of screenwriters, is a veritable master class in homophobic humor and set-pieces, all under the guise of homosocial intimacy. While attending a party at James Franco's house (this is a meta-beta male movie in which all of the stars play themselves), Seth Rogen, Jonah Hill, Jay Baruchel, Craig Robinson, Danny McBride, Michael Cera, and many other celebrities are faced with the apocalypse. While there are some striking appearances by women stars, such Mindy Kaling and Emma Watson, this is a resolutely male-oriented movie. Gay-baiting takes on an inevitable, almost compulsory life of its own in these films, becoming indistinguishable from the representation of heterosexual masculinity.

In *The Change-Up* (David Dobkin, 2011), starring Jason Bateman and Ryan Reynolds as two wildly distinct men, the one an anxious buttoned-down corporate lawyer, husband, and father of twins (Bateman), the other a large, loping, crude ne'er-do-well (Reynolds), who switch personalities as well as bodies. The figure of Bateman's angry, neurotic, unsatisfied wife links this film to the others under discussion, especially since she is played by Leslie Mann, the real-life wife of Judd Apatow, who often casts his wife in just such roles.[35] Recalling the gross-out teen comedies of the late '90s, scatological jokes abound. Baby feces squirt into mouths; the men urinate together; Jason Bateman, as Ryan Reynolds, teaches Ryan Reynolds, as Jason Bateman, how to shave his balls before going out on a date. "It shows that you're *clean*," Bateman-Reynolds, responding to his friend's bewilderment, instructs Reynolds-Bateman as they discuss contemporary dating rituals at length. As he crouches down in a bathtub in which both men stand, his face at his double's exposed crotch, Bateman-Reynolds remarks that he's "tempted to kiss my own dick." Scenes like this one reflect the strange co-optation of dense concepts from psychoanalytic film theory by mainstream and often reactionary works, what I call *the psychoanalytic scene*, which I elaborate on in the next chapter. The "kissing my own dick" scene rehearses the tenets of the Lacanian mirror stage—when the incipient subject gazes upon his or her own reflection and becomes entranced by it, associating this illusory image of wholeness with an actual, authentic wholeness, an entrancement that then becomes the fragile, slippery basis for the ego—while exemplifying mainstream's cinema's emergent tendency to evoke the homoerotic while maintaining it as an unthinkable potentiality. Indeed, *The Change-Up* offers a crude secondary mirror stage in which what is "revealed" about male narcissism is that its fundamental obsession is with the image of the penis as self.[36]

The Change-Up indicates a general rule about these films. On the one hand, an obsessive gay-baiting, as noted, runs rife throughout them. On the other hand, they endlessly evoke homosexuality by refusing to do so. What I call an *explication/repression split* dominates in this regard. When Peter first visits Sydney in his man-cave, he notices a pack of condoms on the table next to Sydney's chair. In the discussion that follows, Sydney explains that his chair is the spot in which he masturbates, and the condoms are there to ensure "no messy cleanup." Usefully confirming that the filmmakers and stars were well aware of the homoerotic valences of this exchange, an outtake included on the DVD of the film depicts Peter watching and encouraging Sydney as he masturbates (the actors eventually crumple up in laughter). The film plays around repeatedly with the homoerotic tensions between the two, most dramatically in their shared tongue-flicking performance of *Rush* songs at the band's concert. To further confirm the potential unseemliness of their intimacy, Peter's fiancée Zooey stares at their antics at the concert in shock and even disgust, leading to a big fight with Peter in which the couple are briefly separated and their impending nuptials threatened. The woman, in a historically consistent role, still presides over male behavior in the social sphere: here, Zooey's horror at the men's antics, bordering on a specifically homophobic horror, alerts Peter to just how precariously he now verges on an unprecedented level of unmanliness. (His overly feminine comfort level with women and his love of making them dessert pale, as threats to his masculine integrity, next to his descent into fetishistic fandom with Sydney.)

The Brom Bones aspect of Sydney lies in his fascination with Peter's outsiderness, and the acute contrast between Sydney's physical largeness and vitality and Peter in his abashed, solitary vulnerability. If Irving in the story suggests that beneath Brom's tormenting of Ichabod lies an unacknowledgeable homoerotic fixation, the film suggests a similar, and similarly unacknowledgeable, fixation on Sydney's part, but one that the film itself maddeningly mirrors. Syndey's preoccupation with whether or not Zooey performs oral sex on Peter (leading to an excruciating "coded" wedding toast in which he urges her to do so, because Peter deserves it) and, more dramatically, the series of billboards that Sydney, unbeknownst to Peter, designs in which Peter is shown performing a range of styles of virile masculinity, all suggest Sydney's erotic fascination with his friend (in this regard, it must be said, aptly named). If the film revises Irving's tale so that Brom Bones is Ichabod's ally, not sadistic rival, it retains the tale's enigmatic depiction of the sexual tensions between the characters. Yet the differences between both works are more important. In Irving, this sexual enigma works to call attention to Brom's lack of self-knowledge and to the underlying motivations for his violence; in *I Love You, Man*, the explication/repression split in the depiction of Sydney's desires and self-presentation—the ways in which his behavior screams out and silences any mention of homoerotic threat—expresses an essential bafflement on the film's part over its own representation of masculinity.

As depicted in the much cruder *The 40-Year-Old Virgin* (buoyed principally by Steve Carell's affecting and funny performance in the lead), the homosocial group relentlessly questions the hapless hero about his sexuality while expressing their own comfort level should he happen to be gay. The films demonstrate disapproval of *closeted* homosexuality as their characters make concurrent claims of indifference to whether or not someone is gay. Or they demonstrate that gay male desire is acceptable as long as it is never made explicit. Summarizing both perspectives, *I Love You, Man* represents Peter as a straight man who has no trouble befriending gay men; the problem comes from their self-presentation as heterosexual, on the one hand, and the expression of their sexual desire for him, on the other hand. One of the men with whom Peter goes out on a friendship-hunting man-date presents himself as heterosexual—or, more accurately, does not explicitly present himself as gay. The two talk lavishly at dinner about food and fashion. When the other man gets the wrong idea and kisses Peter as they say their goodbyes, what offends Peter is not the man's desire but that this desire has been forcefully acted upon him. Gay male desire leaves an irremovable residue. This residue is literal as well as emotional, a taste Peter simply can't get out of his mouth, even after several furious mouthwashings, as he complains to his fiancée in bed, and that is instantly detectable by Zooey, who requests that he brushes his teeth yet again. Yet this gay man becomes part of Peter's eventual friendship circle, along with an extremely elderly man looking for friendship who deceptively posts a photo of a young man on his web profile and an embarrassingly squeaky-voiced man, a client of Peter's personal-trainer brother Robbie, who sets him up with Peter. The deaf muscleman actor Lou Ferringo, after Jason Segel's character enhances Peter's selling skills and Peter is finally able to sell the actor's house, also becomes an ally of sorts. Ferringo's deafness is relevant here because, when paired with the squeaky-voiced man, the gay man, and the elderly man, Ferringo contributes to the rogues' gallery of afflictions the film assembles and climactically presents as Peter's achieved circle of male camaraderie. All are present as groomsmen at Peter's and Zooey's wedding, with which the film, as do most beta male comedies, culminates.

With the exception of *I Love You, Man*, in almost none of these comedies, for all of their incessant nods to homosexuality, does the possibility of gay-straight, or, for that matter, intergenerational friendships ever emerge as a possibility. But even here, gay-straight friendship is a token gesture, as in the appearance at the wedding of friends whom we believed to have been discarded as unsuitable, or is overwritten as fraternal relations between biological brothers. For all of the film's sensitivity to the straight male experience of isolation and of being cut off from male identity and stereotypical male behavior—Peter winces when his obnoxious fellow real-estate agent makes derogatory comments about a coworker woman's weight and when he sends Peter a humiliating video of an elderly woman being sexually ridiculed—it cannot imagine a world in which homosexuality is not either foreign and troublesome, as with the man-date kiss, or strangely detached from human experience. As Samberg plays Robbie and the role is written, he is almost entirely affectless as he "trains" his brother in the ways of male friendship. Though an emotional blank, he also issues baroque pronouncements such as the one in which he claims that other gay men bore him as sexual prospects: too easy to catch, they pale in comparison to the straight men who make for more exciting, challenging opportunities for seduction. The film presents a homo-tolerant male homosocial order in which gay men like Robbie are shown to be successful at forming male friendships of all kinds. While no doubt all of this seems like progress, these elements also serve to homogenize gay and straight male experience, making gay social identity indistinguishable from a general heterosexual male one. No moment ever occurs in which Robbie discusses with Peter whatever inevitable challenges he might have faced in his development as an openly gay man, however confident in this identity he now is. The point seems to be that everyone, gay and straight, has moved on, that homophobia no longer exists, and that male friendship is so essential an aspect of masculinity, whatever one's sexual orientation, that to be without it is to be pathological. While this is not, in sum, an uninteresting idea—the idea that the problem is not sexual identity but social relations generally—as developed it has the unfortunate consequence of de-particularizing gay identity and experience while leaving the concept of compulsory fraternity unexamined. Let me add that I feel genuine love for *I Love You, Man*, despite these lapses; almost alone among these films, it attempts to explore the gender estrangement that can inform masculine identity even as masculinity is thoroughly situated within mythic models of homosocial comfort and intimacy. Paul Rudd's deeply affecting, nuanced performance, well matched by Segel's, adds depth to this film.

For all of their baroque hipness and willingness to go to extremes, the comedies scrupulously maintain a timorous attitude toward genuine

FIGURE 3.2. Homosocial comfort and intimacy in *I Love You, Man*.

intimacy between men, whatever their orientation. To return to an earlier point, the chief focus of their attention would appear to be the male body itself, upon which the films are utterly fixated, as the apparently transgressive displays of male full frontal nudity, erect phalluses barely contained by undergarments, waxed-off sections of hairy chests, uncontrollable volleys of semen, and other priapic imagery would appear to suggest. While homoerotic elements certainly inhere in this preoccupation with the male body, its potentialities, and dangers, more importantly, given the way the films pointedly eschew any homoerotic valences, the male body represents an attempt to return to basics—to an unvarnished, unblemished, clean male slate, a model of male purity that is antithetical to the "stain" of homosexuality. In this regard, the beta male comedies intersect with themes in many films in other genres that present us with men who, for whatever circumstances, usually having to do with amnesia, have been reborn, as exemplified by the *Bourne Identity* films. Moreover, the fixation with the male body and its dangers and comedic potentialities can be read as an attempt to recreate this physical form as a compelling site of fascinations that are *not* sexualized. Given the rampant display of sculpted male forms in film and television of the moment, the male bodies in beta male films pointedly eschew eroticism of any form, as exemplified by the male full-frontal nudity in *Forgetting Sarah Marshall*, which serves to intensify the man's humiliation while in no way his sex appeal.

A fuller consideration of Judd Apatow's influential oeuvre, issues of cinematic Jewish masculinity, and the beta male comedies' relationship not only to the earlier teen comedies of the '90s and '00s but also the 1980s precedents for these comedies, to say nothing of the histories of comedic masculinities in American film ranging from Harold Lloyd to Jerry Lewis, will have to be undertaken in order to grasp the full significance of the new genre. As I have attempted to demonstrate here, for all of the apparently deeply worrisome messages they convey about the current state of American manhood, unable to man up, leave home, develop lucrative careers, and start families of their own, beta male comedies offer a fairly cohesive portrait of an American masculinity comfortably inhabiting its privileges, privileges that include the right to be misogynistic, racist, and homophobic. The deep anxieties in them which can be traced back to classic American literature make them resonant, but not, for the most part, terribly illuminating. The anxieties that shape them only impel their ideological efforts to maintain, however fractured, an ultimately coherent and sustainable image of heteromasculine, white identity. For all of their metatextual, ironic self-consciousness, the films remain as fundamentally estranged from self-knowledge as the hapless but ultimately victorious men at their center.

While the teen comedies of the late 1990s and the early 2000s were ultimately conservative statements, they were also genuinely lively engagements with the emerging patterns of gender and sexuality of their shifting era. The beta male comedies are slicker, more cynical. They cannily survey the social scene, registering both the increasing though always controversial acceptance of queer people and the difficult struggles of the postfeminist era, with its conflicts over how to distinguish between retrogressive and radical roles for women. The beta male comedies do more, however, than reflect contemporary conflicts: they also provide solutions to the cultural crises they perceive. The solution they almost uniformly offer is a depressingly familiar one, Ichabod's choice all over again: act like a man, or get out of town, if not the world.

4

Apparitional Men

Masculinity and the Psychoanalytic Scene

A new emphasis on male bodies characterizes post-millennial cinema, in which the physical and emotional denuding of males has emerged as a central preoccupation and physical nudity allegorizes an emotional laying bare of a masculine subject now seen, to use Rey Chow's phrase in a different context, as "infinitely visualizable."[1] Films as disparate as *Forgetting Sarah Marshall* (Nicholas Stoller, 2008) and *Shame* (Steve McQueen, 2011) present their male characters through scenes of full-frontal nudity that occur early on (in the case of *Shame*, in the first scene of the film after the credits sequence, in *Forgetting* in the key early scene in which the hero's girlfriend, the titular Sarah, breaks up with him while he stands before her nude.). Movies like *Magic Mike* (Steven Soderbergh, 2012) showcase male bodies as desirable commodities, albeit strictly for the consumerist female gaze embodied by the enthusiastic women patrons of the male stripclub. The male body emerges as an economy of gender negotiations in these films. As I discussed in chapter 3, women are presented in bromances and beta male comedies as the brainy, savvy, hardheaded ones, males as commodified bodies. This is not to say that women are not frequently made to bare all in movies in a sexually gratuitous manner—one has only to think of Seth McFarlane's grotesquely misogynistic "We Saw Your Boobs" number when he hosted the 2013 Oscar telecast—or that male bodies have replaced female bodies as the emblems of cinematic sexual objectification. It is also certainly not to make the case that the depiction of femininity in these films—the women's successful corporate careers, business acumen, and general air of "togetherness"—indicate a feminist perspective: nothing could be farther from the truth, as evinced by the depiction of Katherine Heigl's "uptight," "prissy," "demanding," "humorless" character Alison Scott as the all-but-villain of *Knocked Up* (Judd Apatow, 2007), Seth Rogen's beta male slacker

Ben Stone as the hapless guy who "mans up" by the end, effected by two scenes in which he rails against powerful but hopelessly self-deluded and judgmental women, Alison and her sister Debbie (Leslie Mann), respectively.

Rather, the new emphasis on male corporeality suggests that a certain shift has occurred—one unclearly, unevenly reflective of current gendered social dynamics—that registers its effects through the once hallowed, verboten screen space, now one routinely visualized and inspected, of the male body. The male body emerges as a fleshly as well as symbolic domain that men must themselves confront—for example, in *The 40-Year-Old Virgin* (Judd Apatow, 2005), the palpable disgust that overtakes Cal (Seth Rogen) when, in attempting to corral David (Paul Rudd) into submission as he experiences a meltdown over his ex-girlfriend's rejection of him, Cal's hands find their way into David's underwear as David writhes on the floor of the electronics store, David's exposed buttocks literally in Cal's face as he sits beneath him. The disgust so palpably rendered by Rogen suggests that the male body has disrupted the male homosocial realm, has added the threat of homoeroticism through corporeal materiality.

As I have argued throughout this study, the emphasis on bodies, on men *as* bodies, finds a counterpoint in another post-millennial preoccupation: the male face. Something of a Cartesian split located in corporeality, a face/body dualism has emerged as one of the chief hallmarks of contemporary representations of masculinity. The male face emerges as a key symbol in works as disparate as *Donnie Darko* (Richard Kelly, 2001), *25th Hour* (Spike Lee, 2002), *The 40-Year-Old Virgin*, *Source Code* (Duncan Jones, 2011), and *Drive* (Nicolas Winding Refn, 2011). A visual extrusion of the bewildering impenetrability of men and an elaborate, shifting metaphor, the male face incites cinematic desire. Movies linger on faces, as if they will yield some secret knowledge of masculinity or as if to brood obsessively on a face is to possess the man to whom it belongs. At the same time, the face inspires and signals dread, especially when masked. The masked male face remains the central trope of male identity in the horror remake, to which we turn in the next chapter. Wes Craven's *Scream* (1996), as we have seen, presciently indicated the growing post-millennial importance of the face as male sign by transmuting the traditional masked or marked male face of the slasher-horror genre into its killer "Ghostface's" antic comedy-tragedy-satire mask. Ghostface's mask indicated that the killer male of slasher horror was now in on his own joke, in on the joke of masculinity, and perhaps mourning for the loss of male authority at the same time. Rob Zombie's *Halloween* remakes, however, reverently treat the mask of the killer Michael Myers as something akin to a horror-movie Shroud of Turin, making Michael's first donning of the mask a barbaric ritual of bloodletting that culminates in a fetishistic, ceremonial claiming of the mask as his own emblem (*Halloween*, 2007). The male face in horror is an economy that links this genre to its antecedents in the nineteenth-century American Gothic, especially works by Irving, Hawthorne, Poe, and Melville. Post-millennial horror, the remake in particularly, actively explores this linkage.

The strange sexual blankness of post-millennial movie males links them—in the syncretic approach that I take here—to the males of nineteenth-century fiction. By sexual blankness, I mean to evoke a sexuality that is referred to but remains crucially unavailable, there but not there, but also not "absent."[2] Male sexuality takes on a ghostly quality in post-millennial representation that is strangely analogous to the manner in which same-sex desire emerges within historical texts. As Terry Castle describes in *The Apparitional Lesbian* (to which the title of this chapter pays homage), the lesbian aspects of eighteenth-century fiction can be best understood through what she calls "the apparitional metaphor." Even in texts in which the "great unspoken theme" is lesbianism, "the sexual love for woman exists within the repressive framework of the fiction only as a haunting chimera, as that which, by definition, may be sensed but never *seen*."[3] It may seem counterintuitive to discuss post-millennial males in film through Castle's metaphor—after all, who could be more visible, more *apparent*, than the onscreen male in an era that makes males the visual focus as never before? If same-sex desire was occulted in the eighteenth and nineteenth centuries, it is no longer relegated to such enigmatic evanescence, to say the least. What I want to suggest here is that the visibility of queer desire and sexuality in the post-millennial moment has had the surprising, paradoxical ripple effect of "ghosting" straight men on the screen. Many other factors no doubt contribute to this, but queer sexuality's unprecedented openness has both opened up screen male heterosexualities and demanded that new ways of safeguarding them can be discovered and employed. The representation of males has been reoriented to include a sense that masculinity is in flux, a shifting set of paradigms, while always adhering to the demands of maintaining the veneer of authentic heterosexuality. The post-millennial male is "post-male." His gendered identity is always already destabilized by the forces of homoerotic and female desire, yet his sexuality must remain stably heterosexually oriented and typed.

I propose that the "psychoanalytic" has emerged as a cinematic register for the representation of a straight masculinity in flux, one that evokes queer desire while being opposed to it, that foregrounds the presence of the "gay" man while disavowing this presence. Straight men have become the true chimeras of the screen, not just objects of enigmatic contemplation but stand-ins for a future version of queerness that seems to be anticipated throughout culture and media but as yet cannot be articulated, represented, or acknowledged.[4] Which is to say, straight masculinity has emerged as the new gendered uncanny in cinema. Ghost Face masculinity is a Gothicized and psychoanalytically inflected form of male subjectivity. Psychoanalysis, which some might argue is a Gothic form itself (with its buried secrets, morbid preoccupations, penchant for sexual violence, and so forth) is well-suited to exploring this gendered uncanny; yet at the same time, "the psychoanalytic" is precisely what is being evoked and deployed in contemporary film to register this uncanniness in the first place.[5] The incorporation of psychoanalysis into the logic of mainstream representation—into the project of safeguarding heterosexual male authenticity through remasculinization—is a disquieting phenomenon, undermining the potentially radical power of psychoanalytic theory for the critical analysis of masculinity as well as representation and co-opting its insights for the promulgation of a newly self-aware yet enduringly status quo form of male subjectivity.

As I will demonstrate, the deployment of psychoanalytic tropes in post-millennial film is a reactionary version of a practice that can have radical effects in more progressive films. A cinematic masculinity understood in psychoanalytic terms—emphasizing fantasy states, a dream-like sensibility, the idea of an unconscious; foregrounding a self-conscious approach to gender identity as a performance, and so forth—can also be a queer masculinity. For example, in Anthony Minghella's brilliant *The Talented Mr. Ripley* (1999), his film adaptation of Patricia Highsmith's novel, the title character (Matt Damon) stares longingly at the beautiful, wealthy, charming, utterly unattainable Dickie Greenleaf (Jude Law) as he poses before a mirror after rising up dripping from a bath. What makes this moment "psychoanalytic" is that, for one, Ripley stares longingly, but never *directly*, at the object of his desire, desire in this case having broad meanings (class, sex, gender identity). Ripley's averted, balked, yet palpable desire is exquisitely figured in the averted, balked spatial and spectatorial position that he occupies on the screen, which paradoxically makes his unspeakable, unrealizable desire all the *more* palpable.[6] It is the figuration of desire here as an indirect, intangible line of vision that makes it psychoanalytic—which is to say, the anamorphic representation of desire as a form that can only be detected from an oblique angle, as the figure in the carpet, never directly seen but perhaps unconsciously registered.[7] Dickie, as ungraspable a phantom of desire as he is a maddening erotic provocation, turns back to look at the man who *looks at him precisely by not looking at him*.[8] While on the surface, as it were, Dickie would seem to be Tom's mesmerizing mirror self, his alluring ego ideal, the more perfect version of himself that he can only indirectly behold given the homoerotic ban that structures their conflictual desires, the film actually suggests that something closer to the opposite is at least equally true. Posed before a mirror, Dickie is the Ovidian Narcissus and a secondary version of Lacan's child before the mirror-stage, becoming entranced, captivated, by the illusory image of wholeness in the mirror that he misrecognizes for an authentic wholeness.[9] Even Dickie wishes he were Dickie. As I will show, the techniques and even the queer sensibility of Minghella's haunting film have seeped into commercial filmmaking practice, but with antithetical political results.

The Psychoanalytic Scene

As Deborah Linderman observes, many have noted the "auspicious connection between psychoanalysis and the cinema, their joint emergence around the turn of the century, their commensurate involvement in phantasmatic production, their mutual address to the unconscious, etc."[10] One of the most obvious citations of psychoanalysis in film is the image of someone looking at themselves in the mirror. A frequent instance in contemporary film, a man beholds a face, usually but not in every case his own, in the mirror. I call moments in which such encounters occur *the psychoanalytic scene*, restagings of the Narcissus myth as understood through the Lacanian mirror stage.[11] In his famous study *The Imaginary Signifier: Psychoanalysis and the Cinema*, Christian Metz uses Lacan's theory of the mirror stage as a crucial jumping-off place and analogue to his theories of film spectatorship. Lacan's theory is quite well known, but we can review it briefly. During the mirror stage, a key component of the imaginary order—"the formation of the ego by identification with a phantom, an image," in Metz's parsing[12]—the child first beholds his or her reflection in the mirror and, entranced, mistakes this image of wholeness for an actual, authentic wholeness, an encounter fraught with aggressivity and potential anguish. Contemporary cinema makes novel use of this archetypal psychoanalytic paradigm, and it is the basis for what I am calling the psychoanalytic scene. Through the psychoanalytic scene, post-millennial movies simultaneously acknowledge masculinity as a site of critical inquiry and defensively anticipate and counter this critique, the goal being to preserve masculine privilege while exhibiting a strategically useful awareness of this privilege as contested and uncertain. The psychoanalytic scene of current films could, of course, also represent femininity in this fashion; but, I would argue, current film seems much more invested in representing masculinity through this considered aesthetic. Of course, the depiction of masculinity as essentially narcissistic is both an "effeminating" maneuver and a male co-optation of the feminine "tradition" (a misogynistic one, obviously) of narcissistic self-regard.

The man's confrontation with his own mirror image, and variations to that effect, self-consciously evokes psychoanalysis, or, perhaps more precisely, psychoanalytically inflected film theory. Narcissism, the mirror stage, and Lacanian paradigms generally have been crucial to film theory since the 1970s—indeed, were most crucial *in* the '70s, associated with what has been termed "Grand Theory"—a critical approach to film that fuses Althusserian-Marxism with Lacanian psychoanalysis, or reframes Lacan through Nietzschean Foucauldianism.[13] The "Apparatus Critics"—so called because of their interest in the cinematic apparatus itself—such as Jean-Louis Baudry, Metz, and Laura Mulvey theorized about the narcissistic nature of film spectatorship and argued that film returns the spectator to early childhood and an imaginary narcissistic state. For Baudry and Metz, the film spectator primarily identifies with the camera itself. (Before Baudry, Walter Benjamin had made a similar argument.)[14] For Mulvey, the act of spectatorship is deeply and irreducibly gendered and gendering: we identify with the onscreen protagonist, who is most often male, and share in both his desire and the mastery of his violent, injurious gaze, the chief effect of which, for Mulvey, is to render the woman a sexual spectacle.

Lacan's theory of the mirror stage haunts Metz's *The Imaginary Signifier*, though he makes it clear that, however similar the child's encounter with the mirror and the act of watching a film are, film spectatorship is also crucially distinct from the mirror stage. Whereas the child perceives himself in the mirror, and identifies with this image—which becomes an idealized, illusory, unattainable image of wholeness and perfection that will haunt the subject—the film spectator does not look at himself on the screen. Absent from what he perceives, erased from the screen mirror, the film spectator is nevertheless "all-perceiving":

> At the cinema, it is always the other who is on the screen; as for me, I am there to look at him. I take no part in the perceived, on the contrary, I am *all-perceiving*. All-perceiving as one says all-powerful (this is the famous gift of "ubiquity" the film makes the spectator); all-perceiving, too, because I am entirely on the side of the perceiving instance: absent from the screen, but

certainly present in the auditorium, a great eye and ear without instance, in other words, which *constitutes* the cinema signifier (it is I who make the film).[15]

Later in the same section, however, Metz refines his meaning by asserting that, really, "the spectator *identifies with himself*, with himself as a pure act of perception (as wakefulness, alertness): as the condition of possibility of the perceived and hence as a kind of transcendental subject, anterior to every *there is*."[16] If Metz argues, as Baudry does, that the spectator identifies with the cinematic apparatus, there is another way in which Metz argues that the spectator chiefly identifies with an etherealized, metaphysical, floating, decorporealized, and therefore idealized version of himself. In Metz's account, an abstracted, ghostly spectatorial body—the all-perceiving phantom Metz evokes, recalling Emerson's famous "transparent eyeball"—safeguards against what he also suggests is a powerful aspect of spectatorial experience: a homoerotically charged narcissistic relation to one's own spectatorial position (an aspect of Metz's theory that has gone both undiscussed and possibly unnoticed).

What is particularly interesting about contemporary cinema's return to the scene of psychoanalysis is the juxtaposition between this return and Film Studies' own turn *away* from psychoanalysis, as exemplified by the Bordwell-Carroll "post-theory" position.[17] To speculate: the most logical reason for this is that filmmakers of the present have still been steeped in psychoanalytically-inflected film theory. One dimension of the knowing, self-aware, ironic and ironizing cultural atmosphere of the present is its familiarity with critical arguments directed against the strictures of the social order. For example, feminist theory is simultaneously acknowledged and disavowed through the critical mode of postfeminism. Indeed, putting the prefix *post* before any term lends it this paradoxical acknowledgment/disavowal effect (postgay, postrace, et al.). What lends the current representation of masculinity its *frisson* is the almost explicit sense that a critical standard like Laura Mulvey's "male gaze" is being overturned, with males now the objects rather than exclusively the wielders of this gaze.

The comfort level with a psychoanalytic, which is to say, an uncanny, view of masculinity in contemporary film reflects its awareness of males not as the invisible gender, invisible because male power need not be questioned but is always already securely in place, but as a gender that has become newly and unequivocally marked, subject to inspection. In other words, the film and television industry itself has followed Film Studies and queer theory in moving beyond the Mulveyan model of the gaze. As I noted in the Introduction, the gaze is now understood not just by critics and theorists but by representation itself as varied and multiple; male bodies are now the object of the gaze, not (only) its subject.[18]

Ann Kibbey, in her *Theory of the Image*, offers a salient elucidation of the fate of male bodies in Mulvey's theory. "The male body was invisible, in contrast to the marked visibility of the female body. The deflecting quality of metonymy cast visual attention away from the male body, made ideologically image-less by its metonymic power, and fastened on the female body as the vehicle of exhibition."[19] As Kibbey shows, Mulvey unwittingly re-inscribed the very binding gender ideologies she had hoped to critique. Certainly, contemporary representation always already figures the male body as a vehicle of exhibition. While there could be something salutary about this drawing out into the open of the "invisible male," the making visible of masculinity is relegated to the somatic domain; the workings of male power remain decisively invisible.

What might have been a radical maneuver as recently as the 1990s—a foregrounding of masculinity understood through a psychoanalytic or other form of theoretical framework—has become a self-conscious and deliberate style of representation that itself incorporates a theoretical understanding of masculinity into its depictions of gendered subjectivities, not waiting for the theoretical perspective to read such a critical understanding *into* the text. Which is to say, it has become much more difficult to claim certain texts as radical when their radicalism, such as it is, is itself a component of their conservative maneuvers. At the center of post-millennial representation is *a shrewd, self-reflexive conservatism* that ingeniously deploys the markers of resistance and radicalism—such as techniques for the destabilization of gender identity, especially male gender identity—for its own, not at all resistant ends. The re-entrenchment of masculine power does not subject itself to critique through its referencing and deployment of psychoanalytic tropes; rather, these tropes fuel the re-entrenchment, which acknowledges all challenges to the masculinist hegemon in order to incorporate these challenges into a sleeker, more streamlined, updated version of the original.[20] As Brian Baker puts it, the "increasing contemporary visibility of male bodies signals an appropriation of divergent and non-normative sexualities and subjectivities, a closing of dissent and resistance. Rather than the visible male body being any sign of the overturning of patriarchal imperatives of female objectification," this visible male body reflects the anxious state of the times.[21]

To be clear, the psychoanalytic scene may be a self-reflexive maneuver, but it is not inherently subversive or critical, certainly not *self*-critical, just as psychoanalytic theory itself is not *inherently* any of these things. The existence of the psychoanalytic scene—the comfort level with the uncanny, the mirror stage, the emphasis on the fragile underpinnings of the ego—primarily suggests that commercial film has assimilated the terms of psychoanalytically inflected film theory. Filmmaking practice proceeds from a metatextually self-aware basis that resembles that of contemporary forms of gender identity, in which everything is in scare quotes but remains strangely status quo. In the post-ironic, post-queer, post-feminist, Reality TV, Internet-dominated era of the present, the categories of "Men" and "Women," while maintaining sturdy provenance as concepts, have come to seem increasingly quaint. Gender identity is understood by fictional movie and TV characters and filmmakers, through an imprecise co-optation of the theories of Judith Butler, *strictly as a performance.*[22] The Driver's donning of a male mask in *Drive* indicates such an understanding—this male character dresses up as a heightened and conventional version of maleness itself. Clearly, I am not suggesting that mainstream film is offering gender theory of the caliber of Judith Butler's challenging, bracing, and innovative work about the social and psychic effects of hegemonic gender categories and compulsory achievements of gender identity—far from it. Yet there is more of a Butlerian approach to gender in movies of the present than one might expect.

Psychoanalytic tropes number among the many "haunting" techniques of resistant forms of media that have now been incorporated into contemporary film aesthetics.[23] *Donnie Darko* and *25th Hour* use the expressionistic device of a mirror image that talks back to the gazer to depict the internal struggles of their protagonists. In the work of filmmakers such as Jean Cocteau—*Le Sang d'un poète* (*The Blood of a Poet*) (1930); *Orphée* (*Orpheus*) (1950)—the tropes of narcissism, the mirror, and prosopopoeia have a subversive quality that adds to their destabilization of normative reality and also has queer resonances. But such techniques as cinematically deployed today no longer signify subversive stances or queer possibilities. As noted in chapter 1, José Esteban Muñoz, reworking the theory of Paul de Man, movingly discussed prosopopoeia in terms of AIDS and the memorialization of the dead: "the giving of names, the giving of face"; "prosopopeia is also a way of remembering, holding onto, letting go of "'the absent, the deceased, the voiceless.'"[24] Something is, most likely, being mourned in and through contemporary movies that deploy devices such as prosopopoeia to depict masculinity as an act of self-estrangement. But, as I will show, these seemingly resistant touches largely support the re-entrenchment of cinematic masculinity. Works such as *Donnie Darko* and *25th Hour,* my focus in this chapter, illuminate these ideological maneuvers.

Ghosts of the '80s: *Donnie Darko*

Initially and, given its imagery of planes crashing into houses, disastrously released during the month after the September 11th attacks, *Donnie Darko* eventually found fame when re-released the following year, transforming first-time director Richard Kelly[25] into a hot Hollywood property.[26] "Grossing a mere $600,000 in its mayfly initial run, *Donnie Darko* would become the millennium's first cult film," observes J. Hoberman.[27] Like *The Graduate* (Mike Nichols, 1967) and *Risky Business* (Paul Brickman, 1983), films that Kelly evokes, his movie is a touchstone-text of white suburban teen male anomie, "a huge cult hit that has been treated to a 2004 director's cut revamp."[28] With prescience, Kelly, setting his film in the late 1980s, helped to establish the Reagan years as one of the central preoccupations of post-millennial Hollywood. The 1988 Presidential debate between the Republican nominee George Bush, Senior, Ronald Reagan's vice president for two terms, and Michael Dukakis, who would be resoundingly defeated by Bush, hovers in the background of an early scene.

Donnie Darko (Jake Gyllenhaal) is the classic troubled male teenager. At the start of the film, Donnie wakes up in the middle of a winding road on a tree-lined hilltop in the early hours of the morning. After Donnie goes to sleep that evening, "Frank," a man-sized creature in a grotesque rabbit costume, warns Donnie of impending doom. A jet engine of unknown origin crashes into Donnie's bedroom; having been led outside by Frank, Donnie awakens in a golf course, seemingly spared a horrific demise. The subsequent narrative, laden with apocalyptic anxieties, will involve an increasing obsession with time-travel and Donnie's frequent encounters, often in a mirror, with Frank, "the man in the giant bunny-suit." While Frank dominates his scenes with Donnie, it should also be noted that Donnie must contend with Donnie's own reflection in the mirror at times as well. His concerned parents (played by Holmes Osborne and Mary McDonnell) send him to a psychiatrist, Dr. Thurman (played by Dustin Hoffman's *Graduate*-co-star Katharine Ross, in a fine, persuasive performance). Perhaps evoking Columbine, the film depicts Donnie as a budding high school terrorist. At one point, he deliberately damages a water main in order to flood his high school. At the same time, he begins to date a moody girl named Gretchen Ross (Jena Malone), who seems more mature than the usual run of students at his high school. (She has a dark backstory—her stepfather stabbed her mother in the chest and is still in hiding.) As Donnie's psychosis intensifies, terrible events occur, including the deaths of Gretchen and Donnie's mother, younger sister, and her dance troupe. In the end, we return to the morning of the initial plane crash. Using the principles of the book that obsesses him, *The Philosophy of Time Travel*, Donnie sacrifices himself to save those that he loves. The plane that crashes into his bedroom now kills him because he is in it, but everyone else is saved.

Endlessly brooding on the significance of the face as trope, *Donnie Darko* explores the varieties of the male image: its titular teen protagonist's face in the mirror, with an expression at once melancholy and aggressive; the face of Frank the bunny-suit man; the face of the young man *in* the bunny-suit, the "real" Frank. *Donnie Darko* provided a template for the mind/body dualism that will come to inform male representation of the post-millennial period. Split mirror images of faces allegorize this dualism and provide a metaphor for the mind of the protagonist, shown to be fundamentally divided. Kelly's film accords with the major principles of Lacanian psychoanalysis: all subjects are fundamentally split subjects (the result of the schism created when language created the subject as such); the basis of the ego is fragile and illusory (as exemplified by the mirror stage, the incipient subject identifies with an image, hardly therefore a solid basis for control, mastery, and certainty, and stability). By suggestively portraying Donnie's bouts with Frank as menacing secondary revisions of the mirror stage, and by making Donnie's sessions with his psychiatrist a crucial theme, the film foregrounds the psychoanalytic as a register of male identity.

Donnie Darko reflects the genre hybridity that marks post-millennial film, as exemplified by the horror-comedy. At the same time, its genre roots reach deeply into film history. With its misshapen rabbit ears, leering grin, and insect-like white eyes, Frank the bunny-suit man's face is a horror show that recalls German Expressionism and its emphasis on twisted, altered psychological states and figures and settings that appositely reflect them. "Horror," notes Angela Smith in *Hideous Progeny*, "has strong connections to the German expressionism that [Siegfried] Kracauer condemned for distracting viewers from a chaotic and sinister reality with abstract hallucination and psychological projections." As Smith describes, Kracauer's theories nevertheless open up horror film in interesting ways, one of these being that the cinema can "reveal the overlooked realities of our daily lives." In the case of horror film, images such as facial deformity, associated with criminality, can come to seem "familiar and nonthreatening."[29] *Donnie Darko*, however, makes strategic use of horror images like the bunny face to distance and alienate the viewer and to denature representation—and it does this denaturing, I argue, to preempt as well as to convey a sense of homoerotic threat. This threat perpetually verges on realization; once the bunny-suit man is revealed to be the attractive dark-haired teenager Frank, the crossover into sexual desire between male characters comes to seem a genuine, and therefore even more anxiety-inducing, possibility. Narcissistic desire flows from and also organizes homoerotic desire. The menacing bunny face is appositely matched by Donnie Darko's *own* face in the mirror, images of youthful male self-regard that evoke the autoeroticism of Cocteau's *The Blood of a Poet*, a film obsessed with the homoerotic spectacle of male narcissism and the mirror, which Cocteau imagines as an engulfing framed pool that swallows up and then just as quickly emits the male body. *Donnie Darko* creates a realm in which autoeroticism, narcissism, and homoeroticism uncomfortably, menacingly, and sensually coalesce.

Donnie's reflected image—Jake Gyllenhaal's dark hair, pale skin, his expertly distorted expressions—evokes the physical appearance of the dark-haired somnambulist played by the young Conrad Veidt in the classic German Expressionist film *The Cabinet of Dr. Caligari* (Robert Wiene, 1920). *Donnie Darko* studiously recalls the Expressionist cinema's use of stylized acting and sets and, as Thomas Elsaesser notes, "the *Kammerspiel* plot with its self-tormented characters [a kind of intimate psychological theater play in the mold of Ibsen and Strindberg] . . . the eloquent command of the character's hidden feeling[.]"[30]

As Susan Hayward notes, Expressionism drew on Freud, particularly his theory of hysteria. "Expressionism, in its attempts to display a metaphysics of the soul, mirrors to a degree the efforts in psychoanalysis to bring the workings of the unconscious to the fore, to the level of consciousness where the malaise or hysteria can be expressed."[31] The deadly encounter with the *doppelgänger*, or double, is one of the chief preoccupations of the Expressionist cinema, defined by an interest in the psychological, and is central to psychoanalysis as well. Donnie's encounters with Frank define the double. As Slavoj Žižek writes, " 'seeing oneself looking' . . . unmistakably stands for death . . . in the uncanny encounter of a double . . . what eludes our gaze are always his eyes: the double strangely seems always to look askew, never to return our gaze by looking straight into our eyes—the moment he were to do it, our life would be over. . . ."[32] Little wonder that Frank's bunny-insect eyes are white, blank, terrifyingly opaque, or that the real Frank's eye oozes blood from its gunshot wound, a further indication of the impossibility of connection, the impairment of visual exchange, between these brooding males, which suggests a crisis in cruising.

Gay cruising, a sexual economy classically typified by the covert exchange of looks and clandestine meetings, emerges as one of the chief allegorical implications of the scenes between Donnie and Frank, especially the early moment in which Frank in the bunny-suit leads sleepwalking (and lightly clad) young Donnie out into the night. Kelly's use of a jump-cut once Donnie, beckoned by Frank, has ventured out into the eerie nighttime frontyard further intensifies the sense of an all-too-fast, kindled homoeroticism—suddenly, the bunny-suit man is much closer than we thought he was, the jump-cut erasing the sense of distance between Donnie, our surrogate, and the bunny-suit man. On the one hand, the bunny-suit horror effect negates the idea of male-male intimacy—who would want to have sex with the leering, bent-antenna-waving bunny-suit man? Yet through this very negation, the idea of secret intimacy between youthful male characters, heightened by the series of surreptitious rendezvous between Donnie and Frank, is also made available. We are forever made to question why Frank is so interested in Donnie, why he beckons him so insistently—and why Donnie finds Frank so compelling. Moreover, the reveal that Frank the bunny-suit man is Frank, a dark-haired, broodingly handsome teenager—much like Donnie—retroactively charges their earlier scenes together with a more plausible homoerotic import that has not been explored in critical treatments of the film.

Once again, the psychoanalytic intersects with these cinematic depictions of male subjectivity and its queer dimensions. In his famous study of the double in psychology, folklore, and literature, Otto Rank argued that the double is a transformation of one's own narcissistic self-love into the *doppelgänger*, "the feared and loathed other of one's own desires."[33] Steven Bruhm, reading Rank through Eve Kosofsky Sedgwick, discovers the logic of homophobia within the paranoid terror that the double provokes.[34] Paranoia's relationship to homosexual panic, which, as I will discuss below, runs rife through *Donnie Darko*, inevitably brings to mind Freud and the tripartite schema he lays out in his essay "Some Neurotic Mechanisms in Jealousy, Paranoia and Homosexuality" (1922).[35] The interlocking mechanisms of jealousy, paranoia, and homosexuality inform Donnie's relationships with other males: Frank in both bunny-suit and human guises; Jim Cunningham, the self-help guru played by Patrick Swayze; and the mean boys, Seth Devlin (Alex Greenwald) and Ricky Danforth (Seth Rogen, making his screen debut), whose tormenting of Donnie and Gretchen ultimately leads to her calamitous death.

The play of horror film references and allusions in *Donnie Darko* link the film to the horror genre, intensifying the underlying view of masculinity as a spectral form of identity verging, even in this dreamy, hipster-absurdist film, on the monstrous. If we understand post-millennial American masculinity as a collage of previous masculine styles, *Donnie Darko* provides an early and resonant manifestation of this understanding. Poised, clenched in an expression that merges sadness, terror, and fear, Donnie Darko's mirror-face evokes Frankenstein's monster as so memorably embodied by Boris Karloff in James Whale's *Frankenstein* (1931). Indeed, there is a shot of Donnie carrying the dead body of Gretchen that evokes not only Whale's film but also the intertextual nod to Whale's film in John Carpenter's *Halloween* (1978), in which the killer Michael Myers ceremoniously carries one of his female victims in his arms.

Donnie Darko both extends the images of a Frankenstein's Monster-like American manhood that proliferate in Bill Condon's 1998 *Gods and Monsters* and creates a template for the ghostly male faces that will follow.[36] Kelly's film, in its citations of Whale/Karloff's Frankenstein, links its protagonist to the Universal horror movie of the 1930s, and in so doing suggests that freshly post-millennial American masculinity can be best understood not only through the lens of the classic horror past but also the horror genre generally. In recalling, by narratively situating itself in, the late '80s, Donnie Darko corresponds with another work of this era that also viewed masculinity through the lens of horror (and pornography), Bret Easton Ellis's 1991 novel *American Psycho*, a work as undeniably reflective of its era as it is aesthetically and morally execrable. Mary Harron's 2000 film of Ellis's novel, which at least attempts to fashion something suggestive out of Ellis's schematic schemes, also includes well-known shots of the serial killer and Wall Street executive Patrick Bateman examining his face in a mirror as he ceremoniously pulls a silken facial mask off—a signature ghost face.

The shot/reverse shot structure that defines the exchange of looks between Donnie and rabbit-faced Frank highlights their physical differences but also the similarities in their expressions. But then there are the shots of Donnie's *body*, acting as if autonomously possessed of a life of its own. As I noted, while some films emphasize one side of this split more than the other, a body/face dualism informs the post-millennial cinema. In one scene in Dr. Thurman's office, Donnie, who has been put under hypnosis by her during their session, begins to fondle his crotch and, smiling as he does it, attempts to masturbate. The film represents Donnie through pointedly matched contrasts. On the one hand, he inhabits a secondary mirror stage, occupying a spectral realm of longing and aggressivity in which he is captivated by both his own denatured image and that of his dark double Frank's. On the other hand, he is the masturbating teenager, and also a young man in a tentative, touching romance with an introspective girl who understands and appreciates him.[37] These contrasts work to accomplish two major thematic goals: to make Donnie's mental life a portent for apocalyptic doom; and to establish a decisive disconnect between this nightmarish fantasy life lived in the mirror and the active, pulsating teen body of the protagonist.

The "psychoanalytic" links the spectral mirror-Donnie and the masturbating Donnie—it cannot be incidental that this scene in which his sexuality is confirmed as both functional *and* heterosexual occurs in a psychiatrist's office while Donnie lies supine on the classic Freudian couch. We are relieved to learn—or meant to be relieved—that Donnie, who ventures out into the dark to hold court with another male, however grotesquely obfuscated his attractiveness may be at this point, has fantasies about "fucking girls" and can, moreover, bring himself to orgasmic fruition in the grip of these fantasies, at least before the authoritative clap of Dr. Thurman's hands dismisses her hypnotic master class. Donnie is a male version of Dora, substituting the hysteria of Freud's most famous analysand with a postmodern brew of narcissistic and apocalyptic obsessions, and substituting youthful male heterosexual potency for her wayward, stricken flight from the sexual.

The film consistently thematizes its dichotomous central concept of the male face as the zone of the uncanny and the body as the somatic site of the real, the real in this case being signified by the Symbolic structure of heterosexual desire, which depends on adherence to the Law and the Name of the Father and on conforming all experiences to language. The scene with Donnie unconsciously beginning to masturbate reminds us that *he is a primarily a body*, one that seeks to give (itself) pleasure. That he elaborates while under hypnosis about his fantasies of girls, begins masturbating before his *female* therapist, and says and does all of this while "under" and therefore authentically *himself*: all of these details reassure us that Donnie is normatively male. Donnie, for all of his troubles, emerges as a proper identification figure for the straight audience. Moreover, his session with his psychiatrist ensures that he is the properly Symbolic subject who transmutes his fantasies, desires, experiences, and sense of self into language.[38]

During the dreamlike scene in the movie theater, Donnie and Frank (James Duval) engage in their conversation while Donnie's girlfriend Gretchen (Jena Malone) pointedly *sleeps*. The sleeping body of the woman allows for the exchange between the male figures to occur. As Eve Kosofsky Sedgwick famously argued in her theory of triangulated desire, males express whatever desires they have for one another, including sexual desire if it exists, through the exchange of women.[39] Gretchen's structural position here dovetails exquisitely with Sedgwick's theory: the triangulated female, she is the battleground and point of exchange between men, the economy through which rivalrous men negotiate their often inexpressible desires. These are not necessarily sexual desires, though they can include the sexual. In the case of *Donnie Darko*, a strong suggestion of homoerotic desire between the males charges this scene with queer significance as well as homophobic panic. Gretchen is the most convenient version of the triangulated woman imaginable, placed within the scene to remove the sting of the homoerotic, yet passive and silent, no imposition to the desiring exchange between rivalrous males. The idea of the woman sleeping while powerful males engage in prophetic, ominous discourse is a longstanding one in Western culture.[40]

When Frank takes off his rabbit-mask, he reveals that one of his eyes has been gouged out, or, as we later learn, shot out. The bloody, gaping hole where his eye had been establishes Frank as an Oedipus figure of the film, one reinforced by his role in the film's hermeneutical paradigms (time-travel, portentous doom, and so forth). Frank-as-Oedipus bears the mark of future crime, an oracular Oedipus who warns the protagonist of an impending disaster, while also conveying in somatic terms the anguish of psychic turmoil. In other words, Frank's bloody eyeless eye is a physical manifestation of the psychic pain and conflict that undergirds male subjectivity as the film represents it.[41] The movie theater, as depicted here, returns us to ancient time, evoking not just Oedipus but also Plato's myth of the cave. Drawing on Kristeva's theory of the "chora," a womb/receptacle, Wheeler Winston Dixon argues that the camera is the dark womb, or chora, of film, the birthplace of imagery. In *Donnie Darko*, the movie theater scene metatextually figures the cinema as a chorastic zone for male-male relations.[42] Kelly reimagines the cinema-chora as a male zone of knowledge and intrigue that depends on the silent passivity of woman. Here, the cinema functions as a womb in which men are born into mythic, occult knowledge and tradition; the woman serves as décor and vessel. The bloody-eye motif also safeguards this scene in which Donnie and the real Frank could, conceivably, act on their intensifying homoerotic connection from depicting actual homoerotic genital and/or emotional contact. The bloody-eye renders Frank unthinkable as an erotic object for Donnie and cancels out the questions raised by Gretchen's sleeping form (that she is asleep means that she would not observe exchanges of any kind between them). The legendary capacities of the darkened movie theater to provide a space in which homosexual contact can clandestinely occur are acknowledged and repudiated, a process that, as noted, I call disrecognition. Yet the bloody-eye also signals penetration, violence, and the dread of the male body, thereby registering on some level the violent negotiations necessary to make this scene "work." If both queer male desire and female agency must be repressed here, the bloody-eye is the horror movie's signal contribution of the return of the repressed, as Robin Wood famously argued. (In his essay "The American Nightmare," Wood popularized the notion of the uncanniness of horror and of the return of the repressed as its defining feature.)[43] It evokes a bloody anus and a yonic symbol at once, a somatic sign of the repressed sexual energies of the film.

Kelly's film takes the teen comedy genre of the '80s and its late '90s *American Pie* resurgence and turns it upside down, letting its contents plummet to the ground. Donnie's parents are the familiar stereotypical parents of these films, the butt of the joke, but they are also given more depth and capacity for emotional responsiveness. Kelly recalls 1980s dramas like *Ordinary People* (Robert Redford, 1980) about a dysfunctional family. Calvin and Beth Jarrett (Donald Sutherland and Mary Tyler Moore) struggle over the travails of their depressed teenage son Conrad (Timothy Hutton), whose survivor guilt over having lived through a boating accident that killed his older brother Buck (Scott Doebler) has led to a suicide attempt. After being institutionalized, Conrad now sees a psychiatrist, and his sessions with Dr. Berger (Judd Hirsch) are amongst the most crucial scenes in the film.[44]

The sexual stagecraft in *Donnie Darko* appositely matches its aesthetic one; Kelly's expressionistic techniques allow for a range of sexual possibilities to be registered but kept at bay. Moreover, his film amply evinces the technique, which I have outlined elsewhere, of using the figure of the child molester/pedophile as bait-cover-sop in an era rapidly moving toward the widespread assimilation of gays and lesbians into the social order yet still dependent on the disciplinary function of homophobic retribution.[45] Patrick Swayze's self-help guru Jim Cunningham is widely embraced by the town, and his self-help videos are shown at the school by a rabidly conservative gym teacher Kitty Farmer (played memorably by the singular Beth Grant), who advocates the censorship of subversive books and also coaches the dance club, "Sparkle Motion," of which Donnie's younger sister is an avid member. (Some of the most memorable moments of the film include the adolescent girls of Sparkle Motion gyrating to the tunes of Tears for Fear's song "Head Over Heels" in languorous slow motion.) Donnie not only despises Jim Cunningham but exposes him as a pedophile. The self-help guru is not just an example of incipient New Age shallowness but also a sexual predator. When Donnie burns down his house, impelled by Frank to do so, not only does Donnie escape any punishment but also emerges as a secret hero for exposing Jim's kiddie-porn stash to the police. Cunningham's self-help videos seem blandly anodyne (they recall the weight-loss narratives of the 1980s icon, dance instructor Richard Simmons), but they are presented as totalitarian nightmares that further augment the apocalyptic portentousness of the atmosphere. The revelation of Cunningham's sexual menace camouflages and also expunges the threat of unlicensed and potentially queer sexuality in the film. Which is to say, the film gives narrative vent to its own homophobic attitudes through its demonization of the Cunningham character, the child molester being an incontrovertibly safer target for scorn than the homosexual male in the post-queer moment in which the film was released.

The conservatism of *Donnie Darko* is carefully hidden within its hipster logic.[46] Its conservatism is what makes *Donnie Darko* "weirdly consoling."[47] Kelly's film, for all of its affecting qualities, fails to understand that, as Todd McGowan puts it, "the elimination of the subject necessarily retains the subject as the source of the elimination."[48] Which is to say, *Donnie Darko* employs Lacan's myth of the mirror stage, but fails to grasp its critique of the subject as founded on an evanescent identification with evanescence itself.

The retrospective impulse of the '00s—the obsession with past forms of American *being,* expressed as a longing to experience other time periods, be they the 1980s or antebellum America—thoroughly motivates *Donnie Darko*, a film obsessed with temporality and specifically with time travel as a metaphor for the heroic intransigence of those who defy the social order, like Donnie and like the character of Roberta Sparrow, who wrote the book *The Philosophy of Time Travel* that so obsesses Donnie. The one progressive aspect of what is otherwise, despite its hipster guise, quite a conservative film is the hero's fascination with a female philosopher and Kelly's decision to make the author of this time-travel meditation a woman. Nicknamed "Grandma Death," the elderly Sparrow, her copious white hair wildly sticking out (she looks almost like an aged rocker making a triumphant comeback), stands in the middle of the road, constantly in danger of being run over, and periodically checks her mailbox for mail—celestial temporal intelligence—that never arrives.

Talking to the Man in the Mirror: *25th Hour*

Donnie Darko is not the only film of the '00s to feature a man's self-confrontation in the mirror, consciously or otherwise. For example, there is a decisive shot in *Brokeback Mountain* of Ennis Del Mar (Heath Ledger) in the bathroom mirror that ironizes both his closeted homosexuality and his inability to recognize the suffering he causes either his wife or his fervent male lover Jack Twist (Jake Gyllenhaal once more).[49] The most dramatic of such scenes occurs in Spike Lee's *25th Hour* (2002), adapted by David Benioff from his own novel. This film has attracted increasingly adulatory attention over the years; some critics cite it as not only the first but the one great "9/11" movie. To his credit, Lee was one of the first filmmakers to make explicit reference to 9/11 in an era when many were deleting any footage suggesting the event, any image that contained the real presence of the World Trade Center and other iconic symbols of the day. In my view, as my comments will no doubt evince, the film is a conservative work, conventional in its obvious efforts to shore up the ruins of American masculinity. Why an African-American filmmaker known for his critical disposition toward institutionalized whiteness would make a film that is so obviously a sentimental paean for an apparently lost white American male potency is one of many questions that hang over the film.[50]

Monty Brogan (Edward Norton) is an Irish-American drug dealer from Brooklyn on the verge of going to prison for seven years. The film focuses, for the most part, on Monty's last day before prison as he contemplates his life and reconnects with his father; his two best friends from childhood, Frank Slaughtery, "Slattery" in the novel, who works on Wall Street (Barry Pepper, a fine actor who never gets the recognition or the roles he deserves) and Jacob Elinsky, a sadsack high school English teacher (the late Philip Seymour Hoffman); the Russian mob boss, Nikolai, Monty worked for; and his girlfriend, Naturelle Riviera (Rosario Dawson). All the while, Monty attempts to figure out the identity of the person who ratted him out to the Drug Enforcement Agency (DEA). Was it the seemingly loyal Naturelle? Much of the movie pursues this theory. But the rat turns out to be Kostya, the huge, broken-English-spouting bodyguard assigned to Monty by the mob boss. Monty's last day includes a significant dinner scene at his father's bar/restaurant, where they have dinner and Monty rants at his own image in the bathroom mirror. Later that evening, Monty meets up with Frank and Jacob at the club where Naturelle works. At the club, Mary (played by Anna Paquin), a high school student that Jacob has a crush on, shows up and the two have a botched kiss that leaves Jacob feeling horribly rejected. Talking to Frank, Monty begins to hint at his plan for coping with his first days in prison that involves Frank. In the early morning, Monty reveals his plan to both Frank and Jacob—to avoid being raped in prison, Monty wants Frank to pulverize his face, to "ugly" him up. Initially refusing to do it, Frank—goaded by Monty, who begins beating Jacob to rile up Frank—eventually pummels Monty's face, weeping angrily as he does it. Monty goes back to their apartment to say goodbye to Naturelle, and his heartbroken father comes by to pick him up and drive him to the prison (Otisville Correctional Facility, a medium-security state prison located in Orange County, New York). In the car, Monty's father suggests a plan to avoid bringing Monty to his seven-year prison sentence: they will go west, and Monty will go into hiding. A protracted fantasy sequence of Monty's future in which he has avoided imprisonment, reunited with Naturelle, started a family with her, and they both grow old and preside over a large, affectionate brood, ensues. In the closing shots, we see Monty, with his telltale bruised face, still in the passenger's seat of his father's car. His father drives past the bridge that would have taken them west and is heading toward the prison as the film ends.

Mistaken for Russian but actually Ukrainian, Kostya provides comic relief in the opening scenes, a prologue, set on a highway, that occurs seven years earlier. Kostya attempts to dissuade Monty from rescuing a shot-up, wounded pit bull thrown out of a car and left to die on the highway by his former owners. Despite his grouchy complaints, Kostya grudgingly assists in the rescue of the pit bull, who becomes Monty's trusted companion "Doyle." Monty's rescue of the wounded dog, the first scene in both the novel and the film, alerts us to what a good guy Monty must really be. It is an early indication of *25th Hour*'s essentially sentimental take on the "good" criminal protagonist. The Russian drug boss gives Monty the chance to kill Kostya when the truth that he is the informant emerges, but Monty refuses, reinforcing the sense that he is a noble character, even something of a martyr. Nikolai dispatches the informant himself.

One of the key scenes in the film is set in the family restaurant and bar "Brogans," run by Monty's father, James Brogan (Brian Cox), an aged, guilt-ridden recovering alcoholic and the bartender at Brogans. A fixture of the Irish Brooklyn where Monty and his friends grew up, Brogans is a venue where everyone knows each other and the waitress promises to send Monty cookies ("Peanut butter, right?") every month. The homey familiarity of the place nevertheless conveys a sense of decay and loss, both of which are key tonal registers here, as I will show. During the dinner Monty has with his father (a last supper of sorts), James expresses deep sorrow about the mistakes he made in raising Monty after his mother died, self-pitying recriminations which make a resistant Monty both saddened and angry. (In the novel, Monty and his father have dinner at one of the few remaining decent Italian restaurants, according to the third-person narrator, in the Village in Manhattan.)

The scene at Brogans begins, pointedly, with a brief montage sequence in which framed photographs of firemen, regulars at Brogans who died during 9/11, flash across the screen, alternately seen individually in close-up and collectively in long shot. Benioff updates his novel, published in 2000, to include 9/11 as a defining feature of the narrative, and Lee's film links this fateful day to a larger, mournful sense of loss embodied by the working-class authenticity of Brogans and its poignant memorial to the firefighters amongst its clientele who died on 9/11. The array, or procession, of heroic male faces—faces of the nationally honored, locally celebrated, yet also anonymous, lost and forgotten, dead—crucially sets the tone for the dinner scene: elegiac, with a touch of anger, bitterness, and pessimism. A crucial distinction between novel and film is that Monty's father comes into much greater prominence in the latter.

The faces of the fallen firemen provide the "realia," a concrete reality, of the film, a blue-collar and therefore "authentic" group male identity. At the same time, Lee's ominously lyrical camera presents them as a pageant of *iconic* male faces, a procession of male styles and objects from the image repertoire of American masculinity. Rendered nostalgically in a dream-like montage sequence, the images of the firemen attest to the seemingly more authentic patriarchal and heroic masculinity of Monty's father, now a former fireman. This is a detail that is not present in the book, in which Mr. Brogan is identified as a bartender, as was his father before him. In the novel, the child Monty dreams of becoming a fireman, and proudly and poignantly wears a red plastic child's firefighter hat. In the film, Mr. Brogan himself is a fireman whom Monty wishes to emulate. Benioff in his screenplay and Lee literalize the fireman motif of the novel, a decision perhaps overdetermined by 9/11, the iconography of which figured the heroic, selfless fireman as central. Lee and Benioff, in his screenplay revision of his novel, emphasize the Oedipal dynamics of Monty's relationship to his father, and in doing so greatly de-emphasize two key dimensions of the novel: first, the importance of fantasy, especially as it relates to archetypal images of masculinity (the child Monty longs to be a "wonderful fireman" in the novel, a motif that informs his adult consciousness as well); second, Monty's devotion to his mother, and subsequent horror at her transformed appearance as a result of her illness (she dies when he is a child). In the film, the image of Monty as a boy wearing his father's fireman's cap nostalgically links him and his failed promise to the heroic masculinity of the memorialized 9/11 firemen as well as to the earlier version of his father and *his* lost former promise. During their dinner, Monty's father gives him an old photograph of the child-Monty to "keep," presumably to serve as an emotional balm during his prison term. The child-Monty in the photo wears his father's fireman cap and sits between his mother and father, all smiling happily; his father tells him that Monty slept in that cap every night as a child. The queerness of the child-Monty's free-floating fantasy of being a fireman, of being an iconic version of masculinity, in the novel is transmuted into the nostalgic and sentimental paean to a fading ideal of actual male heroism in the film.

In one particularly charged moment during the dinner, Monty goes to the bathroom and has a conversation with himself in the mirror. Or rather, Monty's mirror reflection launches into a monologue, a long and intricate rant to which Monty must helplessly submit. This mirror-monologue is the central sequence in *25th Hour* and for the obsessive trope of male faces that I argue recurs in post-millennial film. As I noted in chapter 1, Deleuze and Guattari's theory of faciality illuminates this troping of the male face, and nowhere more strikingly than in *25th Hour*. "The face is not a universal. It is not even that of the white man; it is White Man himself, with his broad white cheeks and the black hole of his eyes. The face is the typical European . . . the face is by nature an entirely specific idea[.]"[51] What most closely links this mirror moment to the theory of faciality Deleuze and Guattari lay out is its foregrounding of the white man's sense of himself as distinct from the racially and ethnically marked personae he fulminates against during his rant. At the same time, the rant is turned inward, and Monty ultimately castigates himself, complicating the racial/racist dynamics of the monologue.

A particularly intriguing distinction exists between the novel's and Lee's versions of the scene. In the novel, Monty does not speak to himself in a mirror, though his "Fuck You" rant also occurs privately in the space of a bathroom. Walking around pensively before meeting up with Frank and Jacob, Monty, passes by and then stares into a restaurant full of "white-clothed tables in buttery light, the people inside warm and comfortable" (96). He goes inside and flirts with the waitress, but his attempts fall somewhat flat when she tells him that she has a boyfriend. He asks if he can use the bathroom, and she responds, "You came in here to use the bathroom?" "No, I came in here to ask you out," Monty responds, but then ventures to the bathroom. Once inside, "Monty locks the door of the small bathroom and sits on the closed toilet seat. Someone has written Fuck you in silver marker above the roll of toilet paper. Sure, he thinks. And fuck you too. Fuck everyone. The French hostess, the diners drinking wine, the waiters taking orders. Fuck this city and everyone in it. The panhandlers, grinning on the street corners, begging for change. The turbaned Sikhs and unwashed Pakistanis racing their yellow cabs down the avenues. . . ." (97). And so it continues. It is only when Monty is leaving the bathroom as a patron pounds on the door that he looks in the mirror.

By setting this scene not in some random posh French restaurant but in Brogans and during the fraught exchange between guilt-ridden father and emotionally contained but angry son, Lee and Benioff emphasize its grounding in Oedipal dynamics that then transition into the secondary narcissism of a self-confrontation in a mirror. Lee transforms this mirror-self exchange into a self-consciously cinematic montage during which Monty (or his reflection) rails against the various denizens of New York City he loathes accompanied by images of these detested denizens of the city: Sikh and Pakistani cabdrivers, Korean greengrocers, Hasidic jewelers, Russian mobsters, basketball-playing blacks, Chelsea gays (they come and go, speaking of how long you can get your penis to grow), a Park Avenue harridan screaming shrilly for a "Taxi!," Wall Street brokers screaming into cellphones, corrupt white cops, and others, including, climactically, Jesus Christ himself. Monty utters a decisive "Fuck You" to each new detested group/type. (According to a poster at IMDB who counted, Edward Norton says the word "Fuck" forty times in about five minutes during his monologue in the bathroom. The phrase "Fuck you" is also irremovably written on the mirror in the bathroom. At the end of his rant, Monty tries to erase the phrase with a saliva-tipped finger, to no avail.) In the end, however, Monty reserves his ultimate "Fuck You" for himself, chastising himself for blowing his life to hell: "No, fuck you, Montgomery Brogan. You had it all and you threw it away. You dumb fuck." While there is much to interest us in so *explicit* a thematization of the male face as the key to male subjectivity—such overt use of the mirror, that most achingly obvious symbol of self-reflection in the Western tradition—what is actually even more interesting are the series of less explicit but more resonant meditations on the male face that emerge within the sequence.

Figure 4.1. Monty and the mirror stage.

Lee ties Monty's mirror-monologue to the visual meditation on iconic images of American masculinity—the fallen firefighters but also the aged, wearied, melancholy James Brogan. Monty may attempt to squelch emotional outpourings from his guilt-ridden and bereft father, but when he goes into the bathroom, he encounters an inescapably intense emotional atmosphere—figured as the eruption of his alter ego's pent-up rage. I suspect that this moment appealed to Lee—a filmmaker who focuses on New York City and whose films are deeply metatextual and intertextual at once—because of its obvious valences with Martin Scorsese's great *Taxi Driver* (1976), perhaps the ultimate paranoid New York City film, which thematizes the rage and the racism of its anti-hero, the titular taxi driver Travis Bickle (Robert De Niro), who talks to and looks at himself, with varying degrees of intensity, in a mirror (the famous "You talkin' to me?" sequence). Monty's monologue is both homage to *Taxi Driver* and the film's own version of the intense power of fantasy for the protagonist. The novel's depiction of "sway"—the quality that Monty possesses that allows him to get by so successfully in the world until he is ratted out and his luck runs out with it—has been much discussed. But a more carefully developed dimension of Benioff's text is Monty's narcissism: he is obsessed with his own image and his "prettiness."

> Monty cannot remember a time when women did not fuss over him. He has always been pretty. Growing up in Bensonhurst, Monty had to prove his toughness wherever he was unknown. His eyes were too green, his lashes too long, his nose too delicate. Boys did not trust him, not at first. When he was younger, Monty went out of his way to obscure his looks. He would wear baseball caps to hide his thick, dark hair. He never smiled because his teeth were perfect . . . Later, Monty realized his face could be useful. (92–93)

The mirror scene allows Lee's film to give vent to Monty's narcissistic-homoerotic self-fascination without having to name it as such through the cinematic figuration of the rhetorical device of the apostrophe, which makes for an interesting comparison to prosopopoeia.[52] The scene in the mirror symbolically prefigures—or showily obscures—the movie's real face-off, between Monty and his own handsome face.[53] When the "shocking" ending is revealed—that all this time what Monty has been planning is to have Frank pulverize him, specifically to pulverize his face, so that he will not look attractive to his fellow prisoners in jail—a great deal of its psychosexual logic, as depicted in the film, has been diminished. At the same time, the decision to make Monty's rant a moment set in a mirror signals that an implicit psychosexual logic—a potential psychic and emotional excessiveness, a need or desire in excess of the strict demands of the plot, and therefore an aspect of Monty's persona that exceeds heterosexual male typing—exists within his eventual decision to have one of his two best friends, Frank, "ugly him up" so traumatically. Moreover, the "Fuck You" scene in the film is surprising for its depiction of Monty as abashed, diminished, in the face of an ego ideal. The "real" Monty, looking at himself in the mirror, looks cowed, hunched-over; the mirror-Monty, however, is tough, aggressive, hectoring, relentless, *potent*. Both the mirror scene and the face-battering at the end suggest that Monty's sexuality is essentially not narcissistic but instead quite masochistic. As I argued in *Manhood in Hollywood from Bush to Bush*, contemporary cinema is much more comfortable with heterosexual male masochism than with displays of narcissistic hedonism: the former confirms that men penitently suffer in order to preserve their innate decency, whereas the latter threatens to spill over into homoerotic enticement. *25th Hour* the film's transformation of the novel's narcissistic Monty into a masochistic male figure accords with larger patterns in Hollywood moviemaking.

While it is tempting to read, as many critics have and as the film asks us to do, Monty's final self-recriminations in his monologue before the mirror as an indication that the entire rant has really been less about his racist (and homophobic) screeds and more about his own self-disgust, in the end the film offers this scene up as a sentimental paean to Monty's own transcendence through masochism. In other words, Monty demonstrates that his morality and sense of justice are admirable through his final self-critique—that he really holds himself responsible, not those whom he has ostensibly impugned. How does he *get* there, though? The various groups, types, and individuals that Monty rails against exist for this purpose, providing fodder for his projected self-loathing. Which is to say, a latent and more potent violence, opportunistic and dehumanizing, lies beneath the manifest violence of Monty's rant. The objects of his scorn provide multiple metaphors for his self-directed rage. Analogously, these same scorned personae metaphorize his transcendent self-reckoning at the end. They wave beatifically in slow motion at the bruised Monty while he is in his father's car on the way to prison; they are mirrors that capture his reflection, devoid of substance. Eve Kosofsky Sedgwick's reading of sentimentalism as a mode for the expression of straight male self-pity, concentrated in the display of the male body, takes on a new relevance here, especially since she also locates this sentimental self-display in modes such as the uncanny.[54] As

Sedgwick argues, heterosexual male self-pity is something of an open secret, with various strategies designed to keep it as such, such as the vicarious projection of one's own suffering onto others (as happens here) or the co-optation of another person's suffering as "really" one's own (such as the men's movements lamentation over its suffering in light of feminism, the rhetoric of which it has co-opted as its own without its political urgency about the effects of misogyny on female subjects). As I have been arguing, films of the '00s depict masculinity as an uncanny zone in which the male subject is decorporealized and rendered a primarily a face, as it is in Monty's bathroom-mirror monologue, or rendered a ravaged, suffering body that must then be reconstructed. Along Sedgwickian lines, these various strategies add to, emerge from, and work to maintain male self-pity as an open secret. Masochism, as I argued in *Manhood in Hollywood from Bush to Bush*, is a hypocritical narcissism. Monty's final "Fuck you, Monty Brogan" is a wallowing in self-inflicted pain that camouflages the ample uses he makes of non-white, non-male, and non-heterosexual subjects as fodder for his own masochistic ecstasy.

Portentously, Monty talks throughout the film about the "plan" he's developing, and at the climax he successfully goads the unwilling Frank to beat his face to a pulp. The multiple levels of discursive masculinity in the film all converge in this bitter, wildly anguished scene. Monty's status as a male face establishes him primarily as a visual subject and a desirable sexual commodity, perhaps especially for other men. While maintaining that Edward Norton is a man so desirable that any glimpse of him will set prison rapists wild may be a bit of an overstatement, it is not improbable that someone about to be sent to prison would be worried about the very real possibility of prison rape, one of the most mythologized facets of prison life, as well as a recurring male trope in '00s genre film, as films such as *Horrible Bosses* (Seth Gordon, 2011) and *This Is the End* (Evan Goldberg and Seth Rogen, 2013) evince.[55] Nevertheless, the urgency with which the film treats this issue exceeds the boundaries of narrative logic; Monty's desire to have his face beaten in is treated like the terrible secret that can only be revealed climactically, a traumatic knowledge akin to the real reason why the heroine Clarice Starling (Jodie Foster) longs for the titular "silence of the lambs" in Jonathan Demme's 1991 thriller.[56]

Monty, drawing a vivid picture of his impending violation, first begins to prep Frank for his role as his pulverizer while they are at the club where Naturelle works. (At this point, Frank still has no idea what Monty will be asking him to do at the climax.) Monty describes what will befall him during his first night in prison. The brutes will punch out all of his teeth—"not to hurt me," Monty explains but so that his teeth won't get in the way of the oral sex he will be forced to perform on the men during the night. The nuances in Monty's description are interesting. Why does he make such a point of the nonaggressive intentions of the prisoners who will so aggressively poke out his teeth? The phrase "not to hurt me" does not appear in the novel. In the novel, Monty's explanation to Slattery runs this way: "One guy starts smacking me in the face with a pipe. He knocks out my teeth; I'm choking on my own blood. They're kicking me in the ribs and I throw up, and there's teeth in there, I see my teeth in a puddle on the floor. They knock them out, they knock them all out. You know why? So I can give them head all night long and they won't have to worry about me biting. They'll make me a suck puppet for every yard queen in the house." This last line is not in the screenplay, and Monty's description of what will happen to him in prison is made considerably terser.

On some level, I believe, the film wants to cancel out the idea of enmity between Monty and the prisoners. It does so in order to emphasize that homosexual sex in prison is purely so-called situational homosexuality, driven by necessity, not desire. The prisoners will do their thing: violate Monty; Monty must do his thing: find a way to avoid playing the role of the violated. Nothing divides Monty from the future homosocial community of the prison save circumstance, status, and timing. Homosexuality therefore becomes part of the circumstantial mayhem of incarceration, further defanged—as it were—as a possible sexual identity and framed, instead, as yet one more aspect of the hellishness of being imprisoned. (The film offers the dramatic flipside to the endless jokiness of the topic of male prison rape in popular culture, which amounts to a refusal to address the traumatic nature of the issue, perhaps because male bodies and their vulnerability are such an irreducibly central aspect of it. *25th Hour* treats the issue of prison rape no less flippantly than do comedies such as *Horrible Bosses*, with its exchange among men about who is the most "rapeable," an exchange intended for laughs; the flippancy takes a different form in this drama, but derives from the same panicked source. Moreover, that female prisoners are also subjected to the endless threat of rape is similarly repressed.)[57]

In the face-beating scene, Monty goads—seduces, really—Frank into pulverizing him, as the nebbish Jacob, weeping, helplessly watches. (Monty has punched the non-pugilistic Jacob when he tried to intervene, clearly an effective ploy to get Frank to do his bidding.) This scene is the climax not only of the film but also of the film's deeply invested exploration of homosocial dynamics, not just those between Monty and his friends, but also between Frank and Jacob.

In perhaps the most tellingly "9/11" moment in the film, Jacob visits Frank in the evening at his apartment before they meet up with Monty for his last big night out on the town (Monty's seven-year prison term commences the next day). Frank, angrily pessimistic about Monty's prospects, tells the more outwardly neurotic, bespectacled Jacob (a Jewish high school English teacher, very much presented as a contrast to the more conventionally masculine Irish guys Monty and Frank, the one a drug dealer, the other a stockbroker) that not only Monty's life but also their friendship with him will be over once he goes to the "hoosegow."

Lee makes a telling stylistic choice, filming the bulk of their conversation in a tight two-shot image of the men in the window overlooking the clean-up of the Twin Towers far below Frank's Wall Street-area apartment building. Held entirely within the frame-within-the frame window in which their reflections cast an almost imperceptible shadow, these male friends are, like Monty, mirror men, images held within a window-mirror. They mirror one another in their concerns as they each provide distorted mirrors *for* the other. This window-mirror-screen hangs from a precarious height; below, the clean-up crews and lurching cranes and trucks look like tiny figures from a child's play-set come to jerky life. The eerie, bluish nighttime glow below lends the scene the additional genre resonance of sci-fi, a postapocalyptic gloom. (We could be looking down at a strange alien landscape, a nighttime world of rubble and tiny humanoids.) All of these shots of the aftermath of 9/11, the destruction and the efforts to clean up the area, viewed from such a high angle, God's-eye-view perspective, add to the sense of the sheer puniness of human lives and forces. The sinners-in-the-hands-of-an-angry-God tone is greatly reinforced by the operatic, swelling ominousness of frequent Lee-collaborator Terence Blanchard's score.

As Jeffrey Melnick puts it, 9/11 is the "answer to every question now." As Paul Morrison has written, homosexuality has long been presented as "the explanation for everything."[58] In an extremely odd way, 9/11 has replaced homosexuality as the answer to all current questions.[59] *25th Hour*, however, makes the slippages between the two "explanations" palpable. Ryan Gilbey has argued that Monty's intense fear of being sodomized in prison—treated with such depth as to emerge as the subplot of the film—is redolent of homosexual panic.[60] Given the notes of homosexual panic here as well as the film's obsession with beautiful male faces made gruesomely bloody and ugly, it is deeply interesting that Monty's name not only recalls but is also *diegetically* associated with the movie star Montgomery Clift, who was gay in real life and has become a gay icon.

As James Brogan tells his son during their dinner, his mother, in the face of James's protests, named Monty after the movie star, whom she worshipped as a result of his performance in *A Place in the Sun*, George Stevens's 1951 film version of Theodore Dreiser's novel *An American Tragedy*. (The film also stars Elizabeth Taylor as the aristocratic woman the impecunious hero played by Clift truly loves, and Shelley Winters as the unfortunate, overbearingly insecure woman he impregnates and then fantasizes about killing when she threatens to expose his relationship with her to Taylor's character. The Winters character dies when the boat Clift takes her out on one night, perhaps with murderous intentions, overturns. Her death may be an accident, in the end, but he is ultimately convicted and executed.) The film de-emphasizes the intensity of Monty's bond with his mother, which converges in her idolization of Montgomery Clift and the alluring Clift-like beauty she bequeaths to her son in Clift's honor.

In the novel, the narrator observes that,

> There was something fierce about the boy's love for his mother and her love for him. They were a beautiful pair. Later, when they marched down the street together, his hand clutching her, people turned to watch them, smiling. *What a darling boy.* She had insisted on naming her son after Montgomery Clift, her favorite actor, and she got her wish over her husband's objections. Back then, Mr. Brogan felt uneasy about the name . . . But Montgomery it was, and Mr. Brogan was glad to see that the boy looked like his mother: the same rich black hair; the same small, even teeth; the same straight nose; the same eyes, so green as to be unsettling. He was a beautiful boy and he grew into a beautiful man, and Mr. Brogan was always proud to have such a handsome son. Now, though, he wishes Monty were a little less handsome. (58–59)

This passage sounds rather closer to one in a gay coming-of-age novel written by Edmund White than it does to the crime novel genre Benioff is writing within; the mother-son bond, forged in male beauty, evokes Freud's theory of male homosexuality as an introjection of maternal desire, a desire for the loved male to love another male as his mother loved him, which we discussed in chapter 2. In Lee's film however, and in Benioff's secondary revision (i.e., his screenplay) of his more dream-like original, the emphasis has shifted to Monty's Oedipal emulation of his father, relegating mothers and maternal desire and mother-son relationships to the sidelines. The queer threat embodied by the star persona of Montgomery Clift uneasily remains, however, a trace of a volatile motif in the source material.

That no awareness of the post-classical Hollywood reception of Clift's stardom seeps into the film diegetically or otherwise is indicative of either silence toward the issue or simple unawareness of it.[61] For several decades, Clift's closeted homosexuality and tragic decline have been inextricable from his status as gay icon. Moreover, Clift's own real-life travails oddly dovetail with the fictional Monty's. A legendary addict, both of alcohol and pills, the young, astonishingly handsome movie-star Clift, drunk behind the wheel one night after a party, had a terrible car accident during the filming of *Raintree County* (Edward Dmytryk, 1957) that left him partially disfigured. While facial reconstructive surgery more or less repaired his face, Clift never looked the same again, his famously "perfect" nose a lumpy shadow of its former self. (Indeed, one of the famous tales about that terrible accident is that Elizabeth Taylor, who very much loved her friend Clift, reached into his mouth and prevented him from choking on his own tongue and broken teeth, an inescapable analogue to Monty's obsession with his smashed-in face and also smashed-out teeth.)

What could be the parallels between Clift's life and stardom and the fictional Monty? What I call the "retrospective impulse" informs *25th Hour* no less than any of the others films we have thus far discussed. Monty Brogan is a throwback to classic Hollywood masculinity, a kind of loner man's-man in the mold of Alan Ladd's Johnny Morrison, a retired Lieutenant Commander attempting to exonerate himself for the murder of his unfaithful wife in *The Blue Dahlia* (George Marshall, 1946), scripted by Raymond Chandler. The diegetic parallel between Monty Brogan and Monty Clift allows, on the one hand, the film to access the resonances of the classic Hollywood noir and its brooding male protagonist; one the other hand, it allows Monty/Norton to inhabit the beautiful, desirable, and also sexually ambiguous star masculinity of Clift.[62] *25th Hour* evinces the ability that contemporary Hollywood films, even Hollywood films as resolutely straight as this one, have found to "queer" masculinity while remaining staunchly and reassuringly heterosexual in sensibility. This is not to suggest that a film like *25th Hour* understands itself as queer, or is somehow queer despite itself, but that "queerness" has come to impinge so dramatically on post-millennial masculinity as to dramatically reshape it—and that queerness is an attractive mode that can be profitably evoked while being ultimately disavowed.

Perhaps most strangely of all, what is queer about manhood in films of the past decade is what is also psychoanalytically oriented about it. The uncanniness of the treatment of masculinity suggested by Monty's confrontation with the mirror is greatly reinforced by several passages that comprise the denouement. We have touched on these much-discussed passages. First, late in the narrative, the now "uglied-up" Monty, slumped in the passenger seat as his father drives him to prison, sees an apparitional stream of New Yorkers—among the very same New Yorkers he denigrated in the "Fuck You" monologue in the mirror—benevolently waving goodbye and beaming at him, a slow-motion tracking shot that conveys a dream-like lyricism. Second, the film dramatically visualizes the monologue, grammatically centered in the future tense and in the use of the second person, that James Brogan delivers in which he lays out Monty's fate if he decides to "go west" to the farm country of Pennsylvania, rather than go to prison, and where he will eventually send for Naturelle and they will have a big, happy (though, as shown, oddly listless-looking), multiracial family. In the novel, Monty himself fantasizes about his future, giving into the temptations of fantasy when his father suggests that he can drive Monty away from his seven year prison fate. "'Give me the word,' says Mr. Brogan, 'and I'll take a left turn.'"[63] The net effect of these passages is to make the representation of Monty's masculinity a hallucinatory, fantasy state and one that is also, in the film, crucially the father's fantasy of his son's alternative future.

James Brogan's long monologue at the end—shot in sepia tones that convey, in modern[12] visual practice, a distortion in the temporal arc of narrative, or, as in the case of Steven[13] Soderbergh's trend-setting *Traffic* (2000), locale—powerfully evokes *The Odyssey*, Homer's epic[14] about the Greek trickster-hero Odysseus, his wayward journey home after the Trojan War and[15] eventual homecoming. While a discussion of Homer far exceeds the scope of this chapter, let me establish for our purposes that James's monologue—a fantasy narrative of what will befall Monty should James stop driving north to the prison and take a turn west past Philadelphia and into the farm country of Pennsylvania ("it's beautiful there," says James, as paradisiacal images of verdant fields and happy fauna float by)—crucially evokes the final portion of *The Odyssey*; one epic about patriarchal power's reconsolidation mirrors the other.

In Book 24 of Homer's epic, Odysseus, finally returned from his ten-year journey back home to Ithaca after the ten-year Trojan War, once again displays his odd penchant for the cruelly sportive by tricking his aged father Laertes into believing that he is a traveler who once met Odysseus and served as his host. But then, seeing the old man's grief, Odysseus tells his father that he is alive, and, indeed, that he is Odysseus. To prove his identity, he tells Laertes about the fruit trees that the father planted for his son. The son's narrative of remembrance occurs in the past tense. Odysseus tells his father what he did for his long-absent son so that the father can know that his son is returned, that the man is truly Odysseus.

In *25th Hour*, it is the *father* who tells his son a story of what he *will* do to live a happy, fulfilled life full of marital and familial pleasures. In Homer, the son narrates the father's past actions in order to reestablish the father-son bond of the present and solder the heterosexual closure of Odysseus's reunion with his faithful, forever tested wife Penelope; in *25th Hour*, this Oedipal set-piece transforms into the father's narrative of the son's future actions in order to effect the same result of a satisfying heterosexual closure, one that has its foundation in a demonstrably ardent father-son bond. James Brogan's future vision includes the passionate, sustained reunion of Monty and the newly sanctified Naturelle, freed from her Salomé-like role. The suggestions of her perfidy have been intensified by her role as an erotic dancer and that Lee always films her in blueish, spectral, stylized light that emphasizes her archetypal status as the carnal woman. By the end, Naturelle has been established as the steadfast girlfriend. We see Monty settle into a pleasant, fully lived-in role as a bartender—emulating his father—and the couple becoming parents of a happy multiracial brood, over which they preside well into their senior years. James's tale even includes a moment when the aged Monty and Naturelle sit with their adult children and their children, and Monty finally tells them what really happened—how close it all came to never having happened at all (their sweet life as a big family). James's tale teems with enough realistic detail to seem and to feel not only eminently plausible but authentic, actual, not a tale but a vision of what will indeed happen.

Both the Homeric and cinematic works of narrative fiction insist on and effectively achieve patriarchal collaboration and heterosexual closure through the foregrounding of narrative itself in, respectively, Odysseus's recollection and James Brogan's future vision. But what is significant for the films of the '00s is that this collaborative masculinist closure can be achieved and have an equally healing, beneficial impact no less powerfully in fantasy than in reality. In other words, in the diegetic world of Homer, Odysseus truly *does* reunite with his father and his own son Telemachus, and all of the men together, an intergenerational triad of male power, defeat the troublesome suitors who constantly prey upon and test Penelope's marital fidelity and, implicitly, challenge Odysseus's manly stature. (It should be noted that Homer renders his resolutions ambiguous through a series of unsettling implications.)[64] In Lee's film, the triumphant, if low-key, shared life that Monty and Naturelle achieve if James Brogan doesn't take his son to prison occurs only in James's narrative—only, that is, in fantasy. Yet the power of this fantasy narrative to provide closure is indistinguishable from a diegetically "real" closure, an actual development that followed from James's words. Because James's words are so hypnotically visualized and complemented by Lee's own images, and because we in effect see his words being turned into real events (an authenticity bolstered by a wealth of realistic details, including the skillful aging of the actors), the movie successfully provides the audience with closure while also showing that all of this stuff is only happening in the minds of the men.

And in the end, that's really what matters most—the minds of men. Masculinity emerges as a shared fantasy state for the audience, a collective and reassuring hallucination that gives us virtual access to the apparently much desired fulfillment of heterosexual marriage and family—and masculine security and safety. Undergirding this reassuring oneiric vision is the fantasy of escape from prison sodomy, the hyperbolic version of the threat of homosexuality in this film. We inhabit James's fantasy of Monty's future life even as we are made aware of it as a fantasy, that James will be taking Monty to prison. Ending the film in a fantasy of rescued masculinity and heterosexual closure emerges as *good enough*, a feat that manages to transcend the devastations of reality.

The mirror scenes in *25th Hour*—to take the scenes of Frank and Jacob in the window and Monty before the mirror in the bathroom at Brogans as these—support rather than destabilize hegemonic masculinity. The scene between Frank and Jacob functions as visual expression of the film's view of straight American masculinity, post-9/11, as boxed-in, trapped within an increasingly constrictive culture that has no place for heroes. Neither the Wall Street world Frank represents and that his apartment window is poised above, nor the high-school-English-class world of literary knowledge that Jacob inhabits and embodies, provide possible alternatives to the truly closed-in world of Monty's drug-pushing, ties to criminality, and inescapable prison term. The haunting images of the fallen firefighters loom above such depictions of a tormented, trapped contemporary masculinity that can no longer move forward but can only retrospectively imagine a future state of imaginary bliss (chiefly represented by James Brogan's epic monologue at the end as he drives Monty to prison) or stand stock still in the mirror (as the friends do here and Monty does in the bathroom). The message conveyed through the psychoanalytic scene is that men are trapped within the narcissistic gaze of a nostalgic America longing for the restoration of its phallic omnipotence.

The eerie, distanced shots of the Ground Zero debris below Frank's window function less as an ironizing treatment of the destructive aftermath of 9/11 and more as a symbolic representation that American masculinity and its promise now exist in ruins only: all have been blasted to smithereens. American culture and its dream-big promise becomes a further symbol of masculinity and its power; the destruction of 9/11, ostensibly about the devastating blow to the American dream, becomes a further indication of American male malaise, its extruded essence and the evidence of male failure. Rather than a pointed critique of some kind that makes oblique as well as direct reference to 9/11, the scene of the men in the window-mirror above Ground Zero has very little to do with 9/11 as an actual event, but, rather, makes use of 9/11 as a suitably apocalyptic sign of American male decline. Similarly, the scene of Monty in the mirror works to establish Monty as a pitiable victim, the ultimate "Fuck You"-object precisely because he has reneged on his rightful male promise. The various phobically regarded types end up being *most* phobically regarded in terms of the final image of Monty confronting himself in the mirror, acknowledging his own failure. Which is to say, while *structurally* Monty occupies the same train of phobic images, images to be greeted with a "Fuck You" and a stream of epithets, tonally and visually he occupies a different space altogether. His crime is to have failed to realize his promise, as opposed to the *inherent* biological, social, and cultural inadequacies of his gallery of cited grotesques. Whereas these grotesques are presented visually as such—e.g., the rich harridan screaming for a taxi in garish close-up that allows us to see her ghastly, plastic-surgery-nightmare face—Monty's image in the mirror, in pointed contrast, is alternately sly, seductive, and, ultimately, deeply sympathetic, or meant to be. These mirror scenes work to restore masculinity to its former glory through the alternative route of negation. By mourning for a lost male ideal, encasing scenes of male gender performance in the amber of nostalgia, the film leads us back to an impossible, but no less ardently cherished for being that, state of straight-male grace.

5

Trick-or-Treating Alone

Rob Zombie's *Halloween*

Ghost Faces, as I call them, are male characters whose psychic and emotional conflicts, anxieties over their desires, and essential inscrutability are metaphorically represented through the figure of the male face. Returning to the symbolic and allegorical world of nineteenth-century American literature, as exemplified by Melville's *Moby-Dick* and its obsession with "pasteboard masks," contemporary film and television have made the male face a powerful and haunting symbol. In the horror genre this face is often masked. As I outlined in my theory of Ghost Faces in chapter 1, the meaning of the term personification derives from the ancient Greek word *prosōpon*, meaning face or mask. In classical Greek theatre, the actors onstage wore masks that symbolized the essential nature of the character being performed. Post-millennial masks extrude the non-essence of this period's hybridic and hyper-self-aware forms of masculinity. The scary-funny masculinity in the '00s, as reflected in the decade's defining investments in the genres of comedy and especially horror, find an apposite complement in a series of fusion-faces. The Joker (played by the late Heath Ledger) in Christopher Nolan's *The Dark Knight* (2008)—a film that demonstrates the horror genre's infiltration of all other genres, here the comic-book film—exemplifies the Ghost Face as sign of an unfathomable male identity. Much like the "Ghostface" mask of Wes Craven's *Scream* films, the Joker's face merges the classical masks of tragedy, comedy, and satire. The Joker's tagline, "Why so serious?" emerges as a rallying cry for the merging of comedy and horror: we are urged to laugh at mayhem, violence, cruelty, and despair.[1]

In the previous chapter, I discussed the return to the codes of Expressionist horror in Richard Kelly's *Donnie Darko* (2001). Kelly presciently anticipated the wide-ranging effects of this return, which are made manifest in contemporary horror. Distortions of the face and the mask as emblem for psychic and social turmoil, at once, stem from the Expressionistic aesthetic, as does the centrality of the horror genre. "Masks, madness, and shadows come together in the Expressionist horror film, where the threatening figure is often uncontrollably destructive, sexually aggressive, masked or in heavy makeup, and acting out some culturally repressed impulse," observes Bruce F. Kawin.[2] Horror films evoke the themes of German Expressionist cinema, especially the use of distorted images and sets (exemplary in this regard, Robert Weine's distorted, theatrical, two-dimensional sets in his Expressionist 1919 classic *The Cabinet of Dr. Caligari*, especially in its phallic but also twisted, bent buildings), the figure of the double, and the emphasis on horror as a psychological experience. In contemporary horror, the masked killer represents a return to Expressionist horror, and the mask a metaphor for the hidden and ultimately terrifying aspects of American masculinity in an era in which an endless culture of "openness" is the most telling indication of a fundamental enclosure. At the same time, the return to nineteenth-century literary preoccupations, especially within the American Gothic mode of the early republic and of the antebellum period suggests a view of male identity in the United States as a continuous Gothic subjectivity.

In addition to the much-discussed "torture-porn" films—*Hostel, Saw*, et al.—horror in the '00s has been defined by the ever-proliferating remakes of key horror movies from the 1970s and 1980s. One by one, definitive horror classics have been remade: *The Texas Chainsaw Massacre* (Tobe Hooper, 1974; Marcus Nispel, 2003), *Halloween* (John Carpenter, 1978; Rob Zombie, 2007), *The Hills Have Eyes* (Wes Craven, 1977; Alexandre Aja, 2006), *Last House on the Left* (Wes Craven, 1972; Dennis Iliadis, 2009), *Friday the 13th* (Sean S. Cunningham, 1980; Marcus Nispel, 2009),[3] *Nightmare on Elm Street* (Wes Craven, 1984; Samuel Bayer, 2010), and many others. (Craven's status as major horror auteur seems to be indicated by his prominence on this list.) The historical engagement evinced by the preoccupation with the late '70s and the '80s in these remakes has an elegiac dimension that stems, in part, from a desire to re-inhabit past forms of male identity.

Focusing on Rob Zombie's *Halloween* (2007), his remake of John Carpenter's original *Halloween* (1978), this chapter considers the thematization of what I call *historical masculinity*, a concept that I laid out in the Introduction, in the contemporary horror remake.[4] The remake itself is embedded within a meta-historical cinematic project, which holds true even for the inept genre fodder commonly associated with remakes (and sequels) but comes into much greater clarity in the work of filmmakers like Zombie, a heavy-metal musician turned filmmaker and former band member of the metal group White Zombie, and David Cronenberg in his superb 1986 remake of *The Fly* (Kurt Neumann, 1958). What interests me here are the implications for the representation of masculinity in the remake—how the remake establishes and explores tensions within masculine styles that have emerged at different historical points and then reflects contemporary attitudes about and contained within "remade" masculinities. Zombie's focus on the child version of the killer Michael Myers, only briefly seen in Carpenter's original, is a decisive decision that reveals a great deal about the moment in which Zombie's remake emerges.

The valences between contemporary horror remakes and the American Gothic of the antebellum period come to the fore as the child Michael Myers in Zombie's remake loses his soul to the various masks he creates, puts on, and hides behind. Nathaniel Hawthorne's acutely powerful short story "The Minister's Black Veil" (1836), which I discussed in chapter 1, emerges as the central intertext for Zombie's film; both works ponder the significance of the mask as symbolic of an essential unknowability within American masculinity. Another one of Hawthorne's most important tales, "The Gentle Boy" (written in 1829, first published the year after), makes for a striking comparison with Zombie's film as well, as I will show.

The ways in which horror seeps into a range of genres and continues to demand interest on its own terms demonstrate anew the validity of Mark Edmundson's thesis in his *Nightmare on Main Street*: the horror/supernatural Gothic mode has emerged as the dominant popular culture mode. The historical themes of the contemporary horror remake situate the genre within a larger cultural fascination with revising American history *through* horror.[5] History-mindedness is a trend that informs many post-millennial works in explicit ways, but also in much subtler ways. Post-millennial film and television frequently returns to the scene of early American history, which it treats as fodder for Gothic horror. Works like *The Raven* (James McTeigue, 2012), starring John Cusack as a crime-fighting Edgar Allan Poe, and *Abraham Lincoln: Vampire Hunter* (Timur Bekmambetov, 2012) make this return to history parodistically explicit; the Fox network serial-killer drama *The Following* (2013–present) pits star Kevin Bacon against a Poe-obsessed murderer—at one point, a naked young woman goes up to the Bacon character, and she has Poe's poem "The Raven" scrawled all over her body. Edgar Allan Poe comes to stand in for not only nineteenth-century America and history but also for the ways in which both have been consistently framed in the past decade—as besmirched, violent, gory, nihilistic, ruined.

The images of masculinity in a disarray that run rife throughout the '00s—ranging from the beta males of Judd Apatow comedies to the wayward, sexually ambivalent young men of horror movies like *Hostel*—eerily coincide with the similarly troubled depictions of male identity by writers such as Washington Irving and Hawthorne. Both Irving and Hawthorne (and other writers of the period such as James Fenimore Cooper in works such as his 1826 novel *The Last of the Mohicans*) were especially interested in diagnosing American culture as a traumatic response to history. In his tales, Irving explored the Dutch underpinnings of New York State, Tarrytown in particular, obscured in conventional historical accounts of the development of the United States; in his tales, Hawthorne explored the often violent and chaotic aspects of Puritan colonial America, reexamining the events that led up to and occurred during the Revolutionary War from a skeptical, even a bitterly sardonic, perspective. Both Irving and Hawthorne made masculinity their chief subject and satirical target, in ways that resonate throughout the '00s especially, perhaps because this decade emerges as a similarly decisive crucible of nation and history, as well as a kind of grotesque mirror-image of the Revolutionary War-era. We can call Irving's and Hawthorne's works a narrative of the un-founding of the nation. Filmmakers like Rob Zombie, as I will show, carry this tradition forward.

Zombie's *Halloween* innovates Carpenter's original by much more extensively exploring the serial killer Michael Myers's childhood; in the course of this biographical excavation, the film situates itself in the American cultural past, depicting the setting of Haddonfield, Illinois, as a repository of iconic American literary figures. The scene in the high school library that introduces the principle female characters, the heroine and her friends, begins with a brief montage of images that evoke this literary heritage: posters of Benjamin Franklin (looking younger than one might expect and with a particularly haunted, almost feral look in his eyes), Edgar Allan Poe (also looking younger than one might expect and with a surprisingly *un*haunted look), and Walt Whitman (in his old, "good gray poet" mode, but looking hale and forceful). The American past of the Revolutionary War era (Franklin) and the nineteenth century as a whole (Poe and American Romanticism; Whitman a figure who spans American Romanticism, the Civil War, and Reconstruction) inhabit the shifting temporal space of Zombie's remake. Unlike Carpenter's film, Zombie's film makes a deliberate point of not specifying time periods, though there are hints that come from the details. Zombie's remake invites comparisons with the historical American Gothic through its citation of themes current within this tradition in antebellum American literature. There is a great deal more to be said about Zombie's work, here and elsewhere. The intricate and ultimately incoherent *Halloween II* needs a careful examination that I am unable to provide here.[6] What is, for our purposes, especially interesting about his work (which I find to be wildly inconsistent, often quizzically underdeveloped, and occasionally piercingly brilliant) is that he offers a nearly explicit deconstruction of the Ghost Face aspects of post-millennial masculinity. His Michael is a Titan of masculine bodily strength and power, a strongman out of the nineteenth-century freakshow or the circus. At the same time, he is pitiably vulnerable and isolated in a manner that recalls the isolatoes of nineteenth-century fiction, bereft, cut-off from the social world, unthinkable in either a heterosexual or a homosocial context.

As David Sanjek notes, the fare at our multiplexes offers "a multitude of opportunities and a minimum of alternatives. The profusion of sequels, remakes, and narratives that amalgamate familiar elements into various forms of pastiche results perhaps not in contempt on the part of consumers but a weariness bred of sensory overload and intellectual understimulation."[7] While I both agree with Sanjek here and also always hold out hope for progressive and/or subversive cinema—and such works, however infrequently, are still being made—I also believe that he speaks to what would emerge as an ongoing sense of constriction, a lack of alternatives, and finally a weariness in film of the '00s. Indeed, the various bombastic forms that have developed in the post-millennial period, such as torture-porn horror (which does have its defenders), are brazen attempts to disrupt patterns of ennui that are themselves fully in keeping with Sanjek's pattern. In this chapter, however, I want to make a case that a seemingly moribund form—the horror remake—has provided, on occasion, one of the most dynamic opportunities for the critical analysis of mythologies of masculinity specific to the United States.

The horror remake bears an interesting relationship to both the historical preoccupations of the post-9/11 American present and to the historical masculinity of the nineteenth century. Zombie's films, especially, demonstrate that the Gothic mode that writers like Irving and Hawthorne deployed to undermine the presumptions and normative standards that underpinned American ideology can still be used to critique these presumptions and standards that exist in contemporary form and as they continue to relate to the promulgation of white heterosexual manhood as the image of American power. Moreover, Zombie, and, to a certain extent, Nispel in their remakes mine the deep reserve of male isolation in American literature for newly revelatory insights.

Marty Roth argues that part of the originality of Cronenberg's remake of *The Fly* is that "it does not lend itself to allegory."[8] While I do not agree with Roth about Cronenberg's film (and Roth himself seems to problematize his own argument by discussing, in his conclusion, the number of critics who have read the Cronenberg *Fly* as an AIDS-era allegory for the disease and its effects on human relationships), Zombie's film exemplifies Roth's argument in its de-allegorization of Michael Myers, offering the familial and psychosexual backstory of a serial killer, versus the emphasis on the metaphysics of evil in Carpenter's film. Roth argues of the remake that "the second is aware that it is looking again. The later films express their connection to earlier horror film as pastiche. . . . [R]emakes of horror film often return as comedy." Zombie pointedly eschews such a blending of genres. *Scream* blended horror and comedy: knowing, ironic metatextuality (the deconstruction of the slasher-horror genre) and self-parody. In its thoroughgoing seriousness, Zombie's work, much like the equally non-humorous "torture-porn" films of the '00s, is the antithesis of *Scream*. The remake is particularly relevant to studies of post-millennial masculinity if it is understood as itself a remake of earlier forms of American masculinity, the "second" version always "aware that it is looking again"—looking at *itself* again.

The Story of a Mask: Zombie's *Halloween*

In his essay "Twice-Told Tales: Disavowal and the Rhetoric of the Remake," Thomas Leitch has argued that four kinds of remake exist: readaptation, updates, homages, true remakes.[9] He quotes William Friedkin's reflections on his own *Sorcerer* (1977), his remake of Henri-Georges Clouzot's 1953 *The Wages of Fear* (*Le Salaire de la peur*): "there are remakes, and there are transformations. *Sorcerer* is a transformation which I want to stand up as the perfect example of the genre." For Leitch, Friedkin's claims to stand outside the genre of the remake "simply reinscribes the remake's dependence on disavowal for its definition."[10] Zombie's *Halloween* fits Leitch's definition of the *true remake*, which "combines a focus on a cinematic original with an accommodating stance which seeks to make the original relevant by updating it."[11]

Zombie's updating of Carpenter's film makes his original text "relevant" by associating its chief character, the killer Michael Myers, with two often interrelated obsessions that have come to define American popular culture since the early 1990s and well into the present: the serial killer and the dysfunctional family. In light of the sheer number of young men who have gone on a rampage and killed mass numbers of people at a single event in the past decade alone, Zombie's film emerges as an analysis of the creation of not just the serial killer but the mass killer, and the answer he provides is systemic familial abuse, domestic violence, and neglect. But there's more to it than these perhaps predictable factors in the development of a violent individual. Zombie primarily thematizes the young Michael Myers's loneliness in the context of highly charged symbols that resonate with those in American Gothic literature, the work of Irving, Poe, Hawthorne, and Melville in particular. Leitch's title aptly evokes Hawthorne's title for his first collection of short stories, *Twice-Told Tales*. Zombie remakes not just the Carpenter original but the slasher-horror genre in the tradition of the nineteenth-century American Gothic.

What is especially significant about the latter is how meticulously Zombie picks out the key elements in nineteenth-century American literature that relate to the ongoing deconstruction of American masculinity as haunted, ghostly, defined by a series of disturbances, in a word, uncanny. Moreover, Zombie's work explores, as do key nineteenth-century authors whose work Zombie's evokes, the potential for violence in male homosocial relationships that coexists with a seductive and also insistent demand for inclusion, partnership, belonging, fraternity, in short, "brotherhood," that has its roots in, on the one hand, a homosocial intimacy that depends on eschewal of any suggestion of homosexuality and, on the other hand, a misogynistic view of women as relegated to their roles as sexual fodder for men. Zombie's film has serious limitations, and I am not going to champion it as a masterwork. At the same time, it does contain, as does Zombie's later sequel to it, some extraordinary passages that represent some of the most exciting thinking going on in horror film at present.

The expansion of Michael's childhood backstory allows Zombie to come into his own as a horror auteur. Institutionalized for the murders he commits, the young boy Michael Myers begins creating and wearing masks incessantly. At times, he is shown to be capable of simple human feeling, as in the scenes with his tender, affectionate mother (initially either unaware of or in denial about his increasingly violent nature) and the one in which, lamenting his incarceration, he cries in his alternately kindly and clinically detached psychiatrist's arms. His psychiatrist Dr. Loomis (played here by Malcolm McDowell; Donald Pleasance played him in the original) is presented in Zombie's film as simultaneously more of a clinician and an opportunistic huckster (he writes exploitative bestsellers about his treatment of the young killer). The chill, spare section of the film in which Michael wears a succession of masks strongly suggests that Michael is turned *into* a monster, utterly depersonalized, his humanity emptied out, by both his institutionalization in a psychiatric facility and the immersion in a world of masks that becomes his one means of resistance. "It hides my ugliness," Michael explains to his mother in reference to one of his papier-mâché masks, made dutifully by him in his cell; eventually, the walls are covered with these masks, some of which are strikingly inventive and even beautiful. This is, once more, the portrait of the artist, this time as a young serial killer. Dr. Loomis's clinical voice-over narrative of his patient's deepening, mask-obsessed psychosis adds to the effect of depersonalization.

Masks in horror literalize its core themes of hooded, enigmatic psyches, especially in terms of masculinity. As Thomas M. Sipos observes, "Horror films often use eyehole masks to suggest a masked slasher's POV [point of view]. A POV is more unnerving when the POV's 'owner' wears a mask, because a mask implies that the wearer seeks anonymity, and hence, intends evil."[12] The masked nature of male identity and its disturbing implications runs throughout international horror movie traditions.[13]

In a wrenching later scene, the now adult Michael, massively tall and large, possessing and wielding the strength of a titan, pitilessly annihilates the Mexican-American janitor (the great Danny Trejo, in a rare genial role) who was kind to him when he was an institutionalized child. It's as if having worn the mask for so long makes Michael unable to distinguish any human being from any other. Or, perhaps even more harrowingly, the janitor—in the most telling nod to classic American literature, he is named Ishmael—must be destroyed precisely because, in his tenderness toward Michael, he represents an unsupportable tenderness that may yet exist in the killer. Indeed, it is this tenderness that ultimately comes to define the killer and proves his undoing (at least in this film).

As a further indication of valences between Zombie's work and the antebellum period's literature, the discussion of masks between child analysand and analyst is suggestive. In the Smith Grove Sanitarium, Michael displays his first mask, certainly his crudest—a white surface blackened by scribbled crayon, with two eyeholes—to Dr. Loomis during one of their psychoanalytic sessions. Loomis asks Michael why he created a black mask, and Michael responds that it is his favorite color. This leads to a rather surprisingly irrelevant, or pretentious, speech from Loomis about black not being a color, but the absence of all color, as opposed to white, which combines every color. This moment in the film indexes the development of allegorical themes in antebellum literature, moving from Hawthorne's brooding meditation on the meanings of the Minister's black veil to Melville's meditations, bordering on an obsessiveness that matches that of Ahab in his quest to hunt down the White Whale, on the "whiteness of the whale" in the famous chapter 42 of *Moby-Dick*.

Zombie wrote the screenplays for his remake of *Halloween* and its 2009 sequel, and his remakes transcend the confines of this category by exploring their own obsessions. Carpenter's brilliant, aesthetically considered film offers only a brief glimpse of the child Michael, albeit in a memorable prologue. It opens on Halloween night, 1963 (in this film, the periods are specified), in Haddonfield, Illinois. Michael Myers (Will Sandin), a six-year-old boy in a clown costume, goes into the kitchen and finds a big butcher knife. From his "I-camera" perspective, we sees through his eyes as he ventures upstairs and walks into his older teenage sister Judith Myers's bedroom. She has just had sex with her boyfriend; *Halloween*, though infinitely superior to most films made in the slasher-horror genre, establishes, as the *Friday the 13th* films and its ilk will do, that teenage sexuality leads to mayhem and murder. The child Michael stabs his sister multiple times with a butcher knife (to the accompaniment of awful, squishy sounds and Carpenter's chilling pre-electronica score). There is an unforgettable shot of the young Michael, as his parents come back home and discover him outside holding the knife, standing stock still on the nighttime lawn after the murder. When they remove his clown mask, he is shockingly innocent-looking, truly a mere child, yet with a million-miles-away expression. We then shift to fifteen years later, October 30, 1978. Dr. Loomis and his nurse assistant drive, during the infernal red, rainy, expressionistic night, to the mental asylum where Michael has been committed and treated by Dr. Loomis since the murder; Loomis is headed there to recommend that Michael be incarcerated for life, but they discover that he has escaped. He will return to Haddonfield ("The night that he came home" the famous tagline on the poster) and kill scores of teenagers, most of whom are sexually active and also friends of the heroine. The film concludes with the showdown between Michael and the heroine, Laurie Strode (Jaime Lee Curtis), a sensitive, bookish, tough-minded, and, crucially, virginal young woman who alone survives Michael's murderous campaign. (It is revealed in the sequel that Laurie was adopted and that she is really Michael's baby sister.)

Zombie takes the prologue in Carpenter's original and transforms it into the entire first act of his film, an extensive analysis of the child Michael and of the familial class dynamics that, as presented, play a decisive role in his development into a serial killer. "Serial killer" identity is the preoccupation of a great deal of contemporary popular culture, and Zombie squarely situates his Michael within this context, as opposed to the metaphysical, timeless "evil" of Michael in Carpenter's film. Zombie shows us how Michael was *made* into a killer, at least in part, by his surroundings and by the violence within his home; Carpenter seems to side with Dr. Loomis and his view of Michael. He has "the devil's eyes," the Dr. Loomis played by Pleasance says, describing Michael as the soulless embodiment of dark forces. At the terrifying end of the original film, Dr. Loomis bursts into the house in which Laurie has been babysitting and where she is now being attacked by Michael; he repeatedly shoots Michael, who falls from a balcony to the ground below. We see his crumpled body on the ground. "It *was* the boogeyman," Laurie whimpers. "Yes, as it matter of fact, it was," Dr. Loomis responds. But when he looks down again, Michael has disappeared. Then, in a masterly montage, Carpenter revisits all of the locations of Michael's previous mayhem, albeit absent of any life except for Michael's heavy breathing, which suffuses the soundtrack. The unknowable, mysterious evil Michael embodies now inhabits the world at large.

Zombie's Michael is a much more human presence. Both the child and adult versions of the character are shockingly "real." Blond, chubby, rather innocent-looking, as played by Daeg Faerch—his "angelic" appearance, as the Dr. Loomis describes him, completely at odds with his killer identity—the child Michael doesn't seem capable of the violence that will become synonymous with his identity. This is precisely Zombie's point. In Carpenter's film, the Myerses are an average-seeming middle-class suburban family, as are all of the subsequent families on display; in Zombie's film, the family is depicted as white trash, the home environment in which Michael is raised a chaotic and unstable place. Class issues emerge as a central preoccupation in Zombie's remakes of *Halloween,* and his signal contribution to the genre is his emphasis on these issues. Zombie's sequel *Halloween II* (2009), which ostensibly remakes the execrable *Halloween II* (Rick Rosenthal, 1981), frames Michael's inevitable rampage as an allegory for the deterministic failures of the survivors to escape their surroundings. Michael's uncanny and inevitable reappearance allegorizes systemic impoverishment, drug abuse, and a culture of gang violence. These resonances come especially to the fore in the sequel when Sheriff Lee Brackett (the great Brad Dourif) discovers his daughter Annie (Danielle Harris)—who survived Michael's bloodbath in the first film—now murdered by him in the shabby, deteriorating house in which they live along with fellow survivor Laurie (Scout Taylor-Compton), whose (adoptive) parents were murdered in the first film. Laurie's adoptive parents, Mason Strode (Pat Skipper) and Cynthia Strode (Dee Wallace, a horror movie veteran), are characters added to the Carpenter text by Zombie, and he goes out of his way to make them as recognizably middle-class suburban and "normal" as possible. When the escaped, adult Michael kills off Laurie's parents, his annihilation of the residents of the comfortably plush suburban home reflects the film's class politics pointedly. Laurie being Michael's sister, his murder of her new, much more socioeconomically advanced family is a particularly grisly form of class warfare.

In Zombie's *Halloween*, Michael's mother Deborah (Sheri Moon Zombie) works as a stripper; the abusive, foul-mouthed guy she lives with, Ronnie White (William Forsythe), his leg in a cast for unspecified reasons and unable to work ("Bitch, I'm all busted up over here, I can't work!"), derides her and treats Michael cruelly. Michael's behavior seems to reflect the cruelty he witnesses and experiences. In the first moments in which his character is introduced, Michael is obliquely shown torturing and killing a pet rat. While being brutalized by the school bully and his crony in the bathroom, Michael is confronted by the principle, who takes his schoolbag into his possession. When Principal Chambers (Richard Lynch) calls Deborah in after Michael's stash of dead animals—dogs, cats, and other creatures similarly killed by him—is discovered, she meets Dr. Loomis for the first time. He is there to investigate Michael as a budding young serial killer, his torturing and killing of animals an early warning sign. Back at home, Ronnie relentlessly goads Michael, referencing his animal killings. Zombie's dialogue is telling.

> RONNIE: Hey, clown. Hey. Psycho boy. Cat killer. Did you really torture and kill all them worthless animals, boy? Make you feel like a real bad-ass motherfucker killer, huh? That is some deep-ass, serious, faggoty-ass shit, man.
>
> MICHAEL: Judith, I'm gonna be late!
>
> RONNIE: "Judith, I'm gonna be late!" You really are a whiny little bitch, you know that?

Ronnie already made insinuations that Michael is "queer" and a "faggot" in the first scene in which this raggedly unhappy family in their unkempt home are introduced. Ronnie would appear to view "faggotry" as the most horrifying possibility suggested by Michael's disturbing behavior, viewing his "psycho boy" animal killings as indicative of it. Ronnie's misogynistic comments coalesce with his homophobia, as do his constant threats of inflicting violence on Deborah and his sexual salivation over Michael's teenage sister Judith (Hannah Hall). In a telling moment, the affectless Judith suddenly sparks to emotionally charged life when her boyfriend calls Ronnie her father, which point she angrily corrects, suggesting that she may have been abused in some fashion by Ronnie or fears that she will be.

A key point of the scene in which Ronnie verbally abuses Michael as "psycho boy" and physically abuses him as well, throwing cigarette butts at him, is his competitive mimicry of the boy. Ronnie mockingly repeats

"'Judith, I'm gonna be late!'" as Michael attempts to ignore him. The secondary Oedipal conflicts evoked here disorder the pattern of Oedipal resolution. If the boy, locked in rivalrous competition with the father, resolves the Oedipus conflict by identifying with his father, here Ronnie is an inferior father substitute with whom one can identify only at great peril. Here, the "father" competes with the "son" as if he were a fellow child, imitating Michael in a puerile manner.

In the woods, Michael stalks, ambushes, and violently beats the school bully who pushed him around in the bathroom and made extremely crude jokes about his stripper mom and his sister ("I heard they had to pump the come out of her stomach," and so forth). His violence and, especially, his palpable, howling rage, would seem to stem from his anger at his powerlessness, which the extended scene in which Michael beats the bully to death, with a thick wooden branch, harrowingly conveys. (Michael's killing of the boy is never mentioned afterwards in the film.) When, hiding behind a tree, he surprises the bully by seemingly leaping out from nowhere, wielding the branch, and whacking him with furious force, Michael utters a barbaric sound, a primitive war cry. Dr. Loomis will describe Michael's masks as "primitive," and in their evocations of non-Western art they establish a surprising discourse of primitivism in the film, as if to suggest that white male identity has "gone native," that savagism has, yet again, usurped civilization. These themes have recurred in our discussions.

Later that night, Michael restlessly waits for someone to take him out trick-or-treating; before Deborah leaves for work, she instructs his older sister Judith to accompany him. But after their mother leaves, Judith dismisses the idea with a retort—"Why don't you just go trick-or-treating by yourself?"—and instead goes upstairs to have sex with Steve Haley (Adam Weisman), her long-haired stoner boyfriend. (His attitude toward Michael is not terribly sensitive, either: "Sorry, squirt. But have fun!")

The abuse and rejections push Michael over the edge. Ronnie is sleeping off his drunkenness in a chair as old horror movies flicker on the TV (first, in a nod to Carpenter, Howard Hawks's science-fiction film *The Thing from Another World* [1951], which Carpenter remade as *The Thing* [1982]; then, a movie in which Bela Lugosi glares out from the ghostly screen). Michael wraps up Ronnie in thick layers of duct tape, one layer tautly stretched over Ronnie's mouth, as if to silence his venomous verbiage. Michael then cuts his throat, watching as he bleeds to death; with the taut control of a master, he stares down at the dying Ronnie and theatrically pulls off his clown mask so that Ronnie will look upward into his eyes, the last thing the dying man will see. Next, Michael kills Steve as he chomps

FIGURE 5.1. Trick-or-treating alone.

on a post-sex sandwich at the kitchen table. Then Michael goes upstairs and kills his sister, a complexly conceptualized and drawn-out sequence with significant thematic resonance.

After they've had sex and before he goes downstairs (unaware that Michael is following him and has just killed Ronnie), Judith's boyfriend puts on a mask, comically attempting (and failing) to startle her. This is the same mask that Michael will don to kill Judith and that becomes his signature emblem. Famously, to create Michael's mask in the original film, the producers used the Don Post Studios *Captain Kirk Star Trek Mask* that was first produced in 1977. By painting it white, they gave it a frighteningly blank and featureless quality, one oddly evoked in the Ryan Gosling film *Drive*. (As we discussed in chapter 1, Gosling's character the "Driver" wears a strangely featureless, "male" mask during his movie stunt work.) William Shatner's Captain Kirk is, among other things, an icon of American masculinity, a legendary Lothario who seduces the female guest star of every episode. With his brash optimistic adventurousness, Kirk embodies Americanness. That this iconic slasher-horror mask derives from the image of Shatner/Kirk is intriguing on many levels, suggesting an understanding of American masculinity as a performance for which one dons a mask, a striking example of *prosopopoeia*.

In Carpenter's *Halloween*, there is a moment in which Michael's mask slips off during his climactic battle with Laurie, the Final Girl. Anthony

Lane (not a critic I usually feel any kinship with, but whose observations here are useful) describes the moment this way:

> Laurie runs from one door to the next, trying to rouse sleepy householders with her howls; finally, she is alone with Michael in a single dark dwelling. When they grapple on the second floor and she pulls off his white rubber mask, the man underneath is more like a boy—a farmboy, almost, with broad, puffy features, who looks rather surprised to be exposed this way.[14]

If the real Michael Myers seems abashed when exposed, the mask fascinatingly bolsters his menacing manhood; once it is back on, his presence on the screen regains its terrifying stature.

Zombie's remake might be called The Story of a Mask. Much like Christopher Nolan's *Batman Begins* (2005), his film returns its (anti-)hero to origins. Zombie deconstructs Michael Myers as the anti-comic-book hero; when he dons his mask, he kills rather than protects. Zombie's extended analysis of Michael's acquisition of and donning of the mask and its multivalent meanings charge his work with an allegorical urgency, as I will discuss below.

Zombie is particularly attentive to the predicament faced by the child Michael when he seeks to kill, which appears to be retributively motivated. The child in his diminutive body must find a means of competing with teenage and adult bodies. Wearing a clown outfit (as Michael did in the prologue of the original film), Michael evokes the vengeful titular character of Edgar Allan Poe's short story "Hop-Frog," published in 1849. (Hop-Frog, a dwarf and the court jester to a cruel king and his cruel court, avenges himself and his friend and fellow dwarf, Trippetta, through violent means, dressing the king and his court as orangutans and setting them on fire.) In killing Steve, he is not only killing his sister's boyfriend but also his rival for her time if not her affections, since she refuses to take him out trick-or-treating. By donning Steve's mask, Michael is also attempting to co-opt his position within his sister's life. There is a telling shot of the young Michael tracing a line, with his bloody fingers, across Judith's legs as she lies on her stomach in bed, waiting for Steve. (At this point, Michael has already killed Steve and put his mask on). It's not clear if the child doing this is experiencing incestuous sexual desire or simply acting the role of the boyfriend, extending the sense of masculinity as a masquerade. Zombie's *Halloween* remakes make a point of eschewing sexuality from the picture, as the scene in the psychiatric institution in which coarse, hillbilly-typed guards unsuccessfully attempt to force Michael to have sex with a female inmate evinces (I will return to this scene). I interpret Michael's illicit touching of his sister's body as his attempt to impersonate her boyfriend—whose appearance marked the moment in which his sister fails and rejects him—and to demonstrate that he has victoriously eliminated Steve and usurped his position. The mask emerges as a key component of the male masquerade, associated by Michael with being older and therefore having autonomy, a theme that the film will explore further as it charts Michael's grief at being incarcerated. Most saliently, the mask figures male identity as a blank, a terrifyingly hollow non-identity. At the same time, that Steve puts it on in as a Halloween prank—he shakes his head, uttering variations of "bwhahahaha" at Judith lying on the bed beneath him—and then talks about "wanting to do it with the mask on," all indicate a parodistic attitude to this male masquerade that Michael's actions will extend, double, mock, and revise as a *true* adoption of a new identity. He offers a horrifying counter-parody by transmuting the comic threat into the genuine eruption of violence.

Judith responds to Michael's fingers on her flesh as if Steve is tickling her, but when she discovers her little brother in Steve's mask, she gets angry and smacks her sibling repeatedly. After a pause, he stabs her. Zombie then cuts to a shot outside of her bedroom, at the other end of the hallway, a long shot from a low angle, establishing a sense of distance on both physical and emotional levels. The shot aesthetically conveys the killer's state of total dissociation. As, in her white garments, blood running down her legs (a horrific parody of sexual deflowering), Judith staggers down the hallway, she evokes the sacrificial victim of ancient ritual. The entire sequence has a ritualistic, ceremonial solemnity; when Michael emerges from the bedroom, wearing the mask, his air suggests that of a high priest as he slowly makes his way, knife in hand, toward Judith. The grotesquely disproportionate contrast between his small child body and huge, outsize masked head makes the scene gruesomely comedic as well as horrific. The mask suggests a masquerade used in religious ritual, but without any notion of religious and social transcendence. The sequence and its particular configuration of the mask motif deepens the ongoing thematization of a racial contamination of white masculinity that is embedded within the sign of the primitive mask.[15]

This sequence can also be interpreted as a parodistic allegory for the conditions of the remake itself. In a way, the director of a remake is figurally a child wearing an adult head, the novice emulating the master, the initiate learning the rules of the game. Carpenter's original horror classic is a tough act to follow. With this in mind, we can interpret the child Michael's stiff gait as he makes his way down the hallway, but then also his slashing, relentless decisiveness as he cuts up his older, once more powerful, now subjugated victim, as aspects of an allegorical representation of the unwieldy attempt to move forward beneath the weight of a powerful predecessor. Zombie decapitates the original's head and bequeaths it to his child star. Of course, in keeping with the horror tradition's recourse to misogyny (which competes against its more politically radical dimensions, also present in the genre, such as the deconstruction of the traditional family), it is the murder of the woman that incites the most creative aestheticization and the most extended murder sequence.

The Predicament of the Perverse Child

Judith's name evokes the famous female Biblical avenger who cut off Holofernes' head. Far from an avenger, *Halloween*'s Judith is a murdered, unavenged young woman. The killing of Judith, emerging so deeply from within the heart of the sexually thwarted and thwarting family, is a different kind of "psychoanalytic scene." It merges violence and insight, ambivalence and reaction, probity and phobia.

The writings of Janine Chasseguet-Smirgel illuminate the sexual tensions within this sequence. Her analysis of the perverse child intriguingly corresponds to Zombie's vision of monstrous childhood. As she observes, "At the time of the Oedipus conflict, the neurotic, or normal subject, projects his Ego Ideal onto his father, thus making him his model, his identification aim, in order to become like him, i.e., like the mother's object, in the hope of replacing him at her side. The future pervert—usually encouraged in this by his mother who pampers and admires him and excludes the father—lives with the illusion that, with his pregenital sexuality, his immature and sterile penis, he is an adequate sexual partner for his mother and has nothing to envy in his father." As she continues, "Pregenitality, part objects, erotogenic zones, instincts: all must be idealized by the pervert so that he may be able to pretend to himself and to others that his pregenital sexuality is equal, if not superior, to genitality."[16]

Her discussion of the strategies of which the child "pervert" will avail himself is especially salient here:

> . . . the pervert will attempt to give himself and others the illusion that anal sexuality (which is accessible to the little boy) is equal and even superior to genital sexuality (accessible to the father), by erasing from the sexual scene all those elements that

might act as obstacles to his conviction. It is as if the equation penis = child = faeces, established by Freud (1917), should be taken literally. In reality, in order to have a genital penis and to procreate, it is necessary to grow up, to mature, to wait . . . The two differences—between the sexes and between generations—are abolished at the anal level. Time is wiped out.[17]

Clearly, discussing the Oedipal stage, the theorist refers to a much younger child than the one being depicted in Zombie's film. But reading, as I do, psychoanalytic theory as allegory akin to the Gothic literature we have also been referencing, I would posit that what we can glean from this discussion of the perverse child is that biology, gender, temporality, and other circumstances need not impede the ferociously challenged child subject from effecting a means of rising to challenges. In other words, Zombie carefully outlines and envisions the manner in which a child might murder adults in order to redress a state of imbalance in which he feels shunned, bereft, and powerless. His mother is definitely presented as doting and "pampering," but not in a manner that can make up for, alleviate, counterbalance, or simply provide an alternative to the other levels of abusiveness in the child's midst. Recalling Freud's theory, enduringly controversial, of male homosexuality as crucially tied to the son's relationship to the mother, whose desire he ingests and emulates, we can view the theory of the perverse child as complementary. The perverse child, like the homosexual child, represents a psychosexual development gone "awry."

What is especially relevant here is the perverse child's rampant rivalry with adult genitality and the Oedipal father. Instead of identifying with the father and thereby resolving his Oedipus complex successfully, the perverse child goes on competing with the father, refusing to acquiesce. Analogously, the homosexual child throws a monkey wrench into the Oedipal works by identifying with mother rather than father. It is significant in this regard that almost all of Michael's victims are males with power over him, the father-stand-in Ronnie ("castrated" by his broken leg, but virulently competitive with and unloving toward Michael), Steve, and the school bully.

The issue of anality raised by Chasseguet-Smirgel is a more complicated matter. Michael has clearly, and parodistically, entered the final "phallic" phase of psychosexual development, wielding the immense killing knife that grotesquely emblematizes and parodies the phallus (which term Freud used interchangeably with "penis," as opposed to Lacan, who distinguishes the biological penis from the phallus, an abstract symbol of genitality). The perverse child's creation and wielding of a "fecal penis," i.e., his stool, represents his ludicrous and strangely touching attempt to compete with the Oedipal father and adult genitality—to erase the differences wrought by time that have given an unfair advantage to the adult. Michael bypasses the fecal penis and goes right for the murder weapon as compensatory, competitive child-phallus.

Yet anality emerges as a symbolic register in Zombie's film as well. When the adult Michael, escaped from the psychiatric facility in which he has been housed for most of his life, returns to his old home, it is depicted as dark and chthonic. He rips up the dark, dank floorboards and retrieves his old murder knife and the moldering but still intact Michael-mask and dons it anew. This moment, along with various motifs of sunken depths in the climax (a huge, overrun swimming pool without any water in it), suggests anality as a temporal domain, the anus as the foundation and bedrock and core of the psycho boy/man and, moreover, of the destructive and destroyed family as well. It's as if Michael punches a hole within the masculine space of the house, retrieving his potent child identity for use in an even more savage adult world. In Zombie's designs, anality represents the triumphant eradication of time: the hole in the floorboards allows Michael to use his childhood serial killer trophies as markers of adult power and potency, for the child to be father to the man. Time is wiped out as the adult Michael fuses his newly gained adult strength with his child self's ambitious, unstoppable, intransigent rage.[18]

The perverse, anal Father of Enjoyment—enjoying his wicked pleasures with wicked relish—theorized by Lacan and frequently discussed by Žižek does not have a place in Zombie's world. As Chris Dumas parses Žižek in reference to Uncle Charlie (Joseph Cotten), the serial killer of rich older widows in Hitchcock's great *Shadow of a Doubt* (1943), the "anal Father" is "cultivated and savage, warm and yet ice-cold, impulsive but calculating, a social impostor and yet genuinely, coherently psychotic. A certain ambiguity and unfixedness is part and parcel of this social function. . . ."[19] Zombie's Michael—and for that matter Carpenter's—is unthinkable in such a capacity. The Dr. Loomis of this film is closer to such a model, though, in his earnest attempts to capture Michael and rescue Laurie, he is also not characteristic of it.[20]

The adult Michael is brooding and hulking, a monolithic and outsize presence inhabiting a darkened room as he stares impassively at an imminent victim. But this Michael is also an anguished, masochistic man, a monster who wants to be loved. Zombie's deepest innovation of the Carpenter text is to posit that Michael's murders are a furious attempt to recreate and recover family, to bond with his surviving sister. In this manner, Zombie's films update Carpenter and conform to the trends of contemporary cinematic masculinity by orienting his version of this killer archetype around structures of male masochism. When he has captured Laurie—after killing her parents and just about all of her friends—he nevertheless wants her loving benediction. He hands her the faded photo that was given to him in the sanitarium by their mother on her last visit. In the picture, Michael's smiling blond child-self holds Laurie when she was as an infant. He had spared her during the bloodbath, leaving her intact in her crib after he killed off Judith, Steve, and Ronnie; now, he wants her to spare him the grief of complete aloneness. The profound streak of masochism that runs throughout the cinematic depictions of masculinity from the 1990s to the '00s finds its culmination in the image of Zombie's Michael, as penitent and vulnerable as he is massive and murderous, begging for his sister's recognition, embrace, and love.

One of the recurring motifs of Zombie's depiction of the child Michael is his estrangement from the world of other boys. Sitting on his darkened, lonely front steps in his clown outfit, completely alone outside in the dark, "Love Hurts" sung by Nazareth playing on the soundtrack, with nothing waiting for him within the house, Michael watches as a group of boys in Halloween costumes walk in unison past him and his house. In an extraordinary moment that retroactively confirms this touch as significant, Michael, after he has bound and effectively gagged Ronnie, looks outside the window at two more boys in Halloween outfits out trick-or-treating—together. *Then* he kills Ronnie. I think the sequence of these events is significant; perhaps Michael might not have really killed Ronnie had his total isolation and estrangement from the social world of other boys not been clarified and confirmed once again and at precisely this moment. When he sat outside earlier, a little boy in an ungainly makeshift clown suit sitting in the barren, eerily glowing dark (the cinematography in *Halloween*, by Phil Parmet, who also shot *The Devil's Rejects* for Zombie, evokes the rich dark tones of New Hollywood cinematographers like Gordon Willis as well as Carpenter's rigorously designed films), the boys walking past him seem like wounding reminders of the living, active social world that has discarded Michael and left him bereft and behind. Zombie crosscuts shots of Michael's mother Deborah doing her stylized and slinky stripping in the lurid neon-lit strip club, and this conflation works to suggest an equivalence between his all-American isolation—the national motif suggested by the red, white, and blue color schemes of the clown mask—and her all-American subservience to the misogynistic demands of the porn and strip-club sex industries and their institutionalization of female sexual and labor exploitation. Social, sexual, and class critique brilliantly converge here, as Zombie offers a scorching portrayal of a peculiar form of American nihilism dependent on the abusive neglect of the wayward, the hapless, the perverse, the discarded (Michael), and the exploited (Deborah). The film draws a parallel between the experiences of the discarded, bereft child and the subjugated bodies and psyches of the female sex-workers, simultaneously worshipped and violated. Using parallel editing, Griffith's innovative technique and therefore a nod to the early days of cinema, Zombie juxtaposes Michael's position in which he is the ignored object of the gaze—a spectator facing in the wrong direction, as trick-or-treating children walk *behind* him, unnoticed as he sits though he notices the other children in costume—and Deborah's position as visual spectacle and the magnet for the gaze (though even here, her dazzling sexual show and limber grace attract the attention mainly of a grizzled man who appears to be verging on collapse). Both the outdoor world Michael inhabits—sitting outside his prison-like home—and the interiors of the gaudy strip-club world in which Deborah toils become different forms of enclosed spaces, different kinds of prisons, one an open air theater of social disconnection, the other a theatrical space designed to offer the salve of sex to the socially disconnected. Love not only hurts—it imprisons and isolates. In Michael's case, it kills. Deepening these associations, Zombie once again makes dazzling use of the montage to equate Michael's killing of Judith with Deborah's sexual exploitation in the strip club, as shots of both the denouement of his murders in the house and the denouement of Deborah's strip-club performance (shots of another woman dancing, suggesting the endless continuation of female sexual labor; shots of Deborah being walked out of her car, either by her boss or a john) are intermixed.

As I have been suggesting, Zombie's work, while this may or may not be happening on a conscious level, reimagines and intersects with that of powerful American literary predecessors, Hawthorne in particular. Another one of Hawthorne's most important tales, "The Gentle Boy" (written in 1829, first published the year after), is a powerful intertext for Zombie's film. Set in 1650s Puritan New England, the story examines the fate of the titular gentle boy, a Quaker child named Ilbrahim, whose father is hanged for being a Quaker and therefore a dissident member of the Puritan community and whose mother, left to die of exposure in the woods, leaves her son behind as she ventures out to foreign lands to proselytize. Over the course of the tale, the abandoned and orphaned Ilbrahim is adopted by a Puritan couple. While Ilbrahim, despite his adoptive mother's love in particular, never ceases to mourn for his lost mother, his spirits undergo a profound revivification when he nurses an older Puritan boy whose leg has been injured. This scene of childhood intimacy is shattered when this older boy, whose personality is mired in a cruelty that Ilbrahim's love cannot transform, joins in with a group of Puritan children who brutalize Ilbrahim, in one of the most striking depictions of childhood bullying in American literature. Ilbrahim is brutalized by the Puritan children of his community, but he is betrayed by the older boy he had cared for, who encourages Ilbrahim to come toward him for refuge, only to bash a stick against Ilbrahim's mouth, from which copious blood then flows. Ilbrahim's response to this betrayal is wholly Christ-like—he now acquiesces to all of the blows the children rain down on him. We can also establish that Ilbrahim's response is masochistic. Though Ilbrahim is (grudgingly) saved by some Puritan adults and taken back to his adoptive home to recuperate, he falls into an illness while lying in bed and from which he can never recover. Just before Ilbrahim dies, his wild, wayward mother returns to kiss him goodbye. This tale is one of Hawthorne's most affecting works and in keeping with his critique of masculinist forms of power and interest in the fate of nonnormative forms of masculinity.

Zombie's Michael is the un-gentle boy, raining down violence on those who persecute, abuse, and ignore him. Zombie's *Halloween* is a portrait of American masculinity as isolated, bereft, and abject, haunted even within its reserves of hyper-masculine strength and phallic brutality by the ghost of the unloved (or not loved enough), abandoned, powerless child. The scene in which the child Michael kills the bully "answers" the call to homosocial intimacy that is conveyed through the alternate route of negation in the scene of bullying in the bathroom. Implicitly, the bully and his friend are modeling what homosocial intimacy actually looks and sounds like for Michael, who, in protesting them, refuses inclusion: rampant abuse of and sexual appropriation of girls and women. In "The Gentle Boy," the details of the assault against Ilbrahim indicate gender and sexual anxiety. As Hawthorne describes the scene of mass-bullying—led by the Puritan boy ("the invalid") whom Ilbrahim had nursed back to health—and the gentle boy's response,

> The invalid, in the meanwhile, stood apart from the tumult, crying out with a loud voice, "Fear not, Ilbrahim, come hither and take my hand"; and his unhappy friend endeavored to obey him. . . . [T]he foul-hearted little villain lifted his staff, and struck Ilbrahim on the mouth, so forcibly that the blood issued in a stream. The poor child's arms had been raised to guard his head from the storm of blows; but now he dropped

them at once. His persecutors beat him down, trampled upon him, dragged him by his long, fair locks. . . .[21]

The blood that pours, at the boys' assaultive hands, from Ilbrahim's vaginal *mouth*; their animalistic violence contrasted against Ilbrahim's "long, fair locks"; and his submission to their brutal violence are unmistakable gender metaphors that almost literalize the associations between Ilbrahim and the feminine.

In Zombie's film, it is the *bully* from whose mouth blood gushes, forming an arresting visual and textural pattern of deeply dark gore on his mouth and face, that, along with his desperate whimpering and cries of "Please don't hurt me," in such striking contrast to his early displays of sadistic bravado, are suggestive of female sexuality and violation. In an unsettlingly lyrical depiction of bloody violence, Michael's beating to the death of the bully culminates in a startlingly aestheticized choice of an extreme long shot of the dead boy submerged within an autumnal ocean of fallen leaves and trees. Zombie returns the scene of homosocial violence and failed intimacy to nature, figured as beautiful, still, and void of life, no respite, alternative to, or refuge from the brutalities of the social order. "Part of what makes Zombie's films so weirdly compelling," writes Nathan Lee, "is the palpable, if decidedly problematic, compassion that runs through them." *Halloween*, he argues, is "best understood as a kind of perverse yet deeply felt biopic of Michael Myers himself. Its energies are all inward-turning, centripetal. The movie demands to be taken on its own terms, liberated from judgmental comparisons with the qualities and techniques of its source material . . . closer in spirit to Soderbergh's rethinking of Tarkovsky in his *Solaris* than an exercise in Marcus Nispel's 2003 version of *The Texas Chain Saw Massacre*."[22]

Trick-or-Treating Alone: Horror and Historical Masculinity

Scholars such as Linnie Blake have linked Zombie's work to the literature of the early republic.[23] I have been arguing that Zombie evokes themes central to the antebellum American Gothic. Zombie engages with and evokes, in particular, this literary period's uses of the Gothic mode to reflect on and interpret male isolation. The isolation of Washington Irving's protagonist Ichabod Crane in his short story "The Legend of Sleepy Hollow," the number of cut-off men in Hawthorne's work, who become the "Outcasts of the Universe," the isolatoes in Melville—these antecedents for American movie males form a continuum of deep loneliness. The affectional dimensions of this continuum include adriftness, disaffection, unsought solitariness, and, often and most disturbingly, rage, violence, and other forms of revolt against the demands of the social order. The compulsory myth of American brotherhood, the idea that men naturally form ties with other men and readily conform to male group identity, not only fails such men, allowing them no entrance into its promised land of connection, but becomes an active agent in their despair and rage, leaving them bereft while demanding that they come up to snuff, form social bonds, especially with other males, or else. What Robert B. Putnam has described as "bowling alone" in his study by that name takes on a new dimension in Zombie's *Halloween*. Putnam used the image of the solitary bowler as iconic of postwar despair: the isolation of men in what had once been a culture that promoted the model of the group of male friends who all did things together, such as bowling. Zombie matches Putnam's acute image with one of his own, the little boy in a Halloween outfit who must go trick-or-treating alone.

This image of the lonely boy Michael Myers sitting outside, alone, in the dark, with no one to take him trick-or-treating, is a newly iconic image of American life, one made possible through the filmmaker's visionary remaking of a "master" text. There is a great deal of interest in film and literary studies today in the "evil child" and the "monstrous child," but for Zombie the young Michael, however perverse and terrifying he may be, does not fit into either category, though he may fit into the category of the "queer child" that also generates considerable interest at present.[24] Neither the isolating social world teeming with the life of the properly socialized (those other children trick-or-treating together) nor the home full of neglect and verbal, emotional, and possibly sexual abuse offer refuge; indeed, they offer its antithesis. Putting on costumes and going door to door asking for candy allegorizes American social identity, to a certain extent: the desire to try on and try out new roles and identities and to display these experiments to the world at large, within the comforting community of fellow experimenters and revelers. It's the frontier myth in miniature. Zombie seizes on the ritual of trick-or-treating as a fundamental facet of American boyhood with allegorical implications for the experiential social and personal effects of living with others: maturing, developing, and forming a personhood that is both distinct and linked to the larger social world. (Zombie may be paying homage to the Halloween sequence in *Meet Me in St. Louis* [Vincente Minnelli, 1944]). The utter failure of the social and individual ritual, or rite, of trick-or-treating here foregrounds a sense of dissolution and despair in self and society without easy remedy—save the attempt at, in Richard

Slotkin's phrase, regeneration through violence that remains a terrifyingly inevitable recourse for the powerless.

Historical masculinity emerges in other genres, such as the beta male comedies and bromances that recall the codes and travails of males from earlier periods. Paul Rudd's Peter Klaven in *I Love You, Man* evokes the hapless Ichabod Crane, so comfortable with women and with the rituals of cooking and eating, so deeply uncomfortable with other men, just as Jason Segel in that film evokes the loping, grinning, potentially violent Brom Bones. The historical masculinity thematized in contemporary horror remakes do not only return us to the nineteenth-century American Gothic but suggest that its themes endure and continue to inform American culture. The Gothicization of masculinity in the horror film intersects with the psychoanalytic masculinity increasingly inflected in film that I discussed in the previous chapter: both the Gothic and psychoanalysis—in many ways a late-stage reimagining of the nineteenth-century Gothic—understand and figure masculinity as uncanny, subject to the terrors of the double, split off from itself, terrified by self-knowledge, devoted to ornate strategies that will block both the terror and the knowledge, mesmerized and horrified at once by its own image, a familiar construct that always comes back before itself in deeply unfamiliar form, forever a stranger to itself—and so forth.

Discussing Wes Craven's *The Last House on the Left* (1972), a remake of Ingmar Bergman's *The Virgin Spring* (1960), in which a roving band of louts kills a young farm woman in medieval Sweden, Adam Lowenstein writes,

> *Last House*'s insistence on the risky collision of public and private identifications as part of the audience's allegorical engagement with historical trauma concurs with Benjamin's claim that "to articulate the past historically does not mean to recognize it 'the way it really was.' . . . It means to seize hold of a memory as it flashes up, at a moment of danger." But in its own way, *Last House* also contends to portray 'the way things really are.'"[25]

Zombie's film does as well—it injects a powerful dose of socioeconomic realism into the stylized, allegorical, psychoanalytically charged horror genre, making its depictions of characters like the child Michael and his familial surroundings agonizingly real. Zombie establishes the horror cinema as a domain of social critique. His form of horror filmmaking, emphasizing socioeconomic realism, dovetails with the work of filmmakers such as Luis Buñuel in *Los Olvidados* (1950), a film about adolescents struggling in the crime-infested slums of Mexico City. This work is famous for its astonishingly lyrical and terrifying filmed nightmare in which the young Pedro's harshly unremitting mother gives him a piece of meat. Another work that Zombie's evokes is Víctor Erice's *El espíritu de la colmena/The Spirit of the Beehive* (1973), a quietly brutal film about a shy, sensitive little girl who lives in a tiny, rural village in 1940 Spain and is endlessly haunted by the specter of Boris Karloff's Frankenstein after seeing James Whale's 1931 film. Her descent into a lonely world of fantasy corresponds to Zombie's evocation of the child Michael's similar descent.

Lowenstein offers an important theory for the horror film in his concept of the "allegorical moment," "a shocking collision of film, spectator, and history where registers of bodily space and historical time are disrupted, confronted, and intertwined. These registers of space and time are distributed unevenly across the cinematic text, the film's audience, and the historical context[.]"[26] What is compelling about the horror remake at its sharpest is that it "remakes" history by updating and revising established notions of "reality." What Zombie offers to the influential genre world that Carpenter—himself, of course, an exemplary remake director of films, as evinced by *Halloween's* reformulations of Hitchcock's 1960 *Psycho* and his remake of Hawks's *The Thing from Another World*—created is that masculinity has a childhood, that Michael Myers is not simply The Shape but a person with a past.

FIGURE 5.2. Portrait of the artist as a child monster: Michael's masks.

This is not to suggest that Zombie in any way resists the overwhelmingly consistent cinematic tradition of treating the mentally ill as monstrous. It is to say that Zombie offers a sophisticated critique of the social order's investments in a culture of heteromasculinity and compulsory fraternity—Michael's chief conflicts would appear to stem from his fatherlessness and fearsome father substitute, who derides him for his gender failures, on the one hand, and from his utter exclusion from the social world, especially from the world of other males his own age, on the other hand.

The later scene with the prison guards extends these ideas. When the guards, shown to be racist, misogynistic, and homophobic all at once, abduct a female prisoner after hours, both molesting her themselves and then bringing her to Michael's cell in order for him to molest her as well, Michael sits stonily indifferent to the mayhem. It is not clear if a gang rape is what they have in mind, or watching the spectacle of the gigantic and silent Michael raping the woman. One of the guards, trying to rile Michael up by arousing him—or testing to see if he will be aroused—sticks his fingers into the woman's vagina, smells his fingers, and then offers them to Michael for *his* olfactory perusal. It's a sickeningly cruel scene, but I do not believe that Zombie's intentions here are misogynistically exploitative. As the boys in the school bathroom did when they taunted the young Michael, these prison guards model homosocial community for the resistant and remote behemoth whose only focus is on his own pleasures, here, his elaborate masks, on which he dutifully toils as the mayhem ensues around him. The guards' sexual abuse of the woman both "hails" Michael as a heterosexual male subject and challenges him to "prove" his sexuality (similar dynamics in Brian De Palma's great, underappreciated Vietnam War film, the 1989 *Casualties of War*). Gang rape sutures male bonds across the distinct forms and types of masculinity (not just physical and racial and ethnic but sexual and emotional) and allows males to be sexual with and before one another through the spectacle of *performed* heterosexual sex and the violation of a woman at once. Or, at least, this is the fantasy. Michael pulverizes the guards, not to save the woman, but because they violate his sanctuary—because they start messing around with his masks. The isolate, often murderously driven male of nineteenth-century American literature—James Fenimore Cooper's Natty Bumppo, the white man among Indians legendary for his skills as a killer, determined to remain inviolate in every way—has been stripped bare of his salvational aspects and reduced to his absolute commitment to individual integrity, to be defended by any means necessary, including the most violent.

Dr. Loomis remarks that the child Michael, obsessed with his masks and refusing to take them off, is a "ghost or shape of the child he once was." Of course, Loomis functions as an inextricable component of the psychiatric-incarceration machine that aids in Michael's dehumanization, even as Loomis can attempt to "reach" his increasingly remote patient. As the child Michael hides behind a series of primitive masks, he creates his own future as a killing machine who hides behind an air of spectral mystery, a mask of the uncanny. What is especially significant about Zombie's remakes of the classic slasher movie is that they figure masculinity as the hyper-masculine body, emphasizing the bulk of their monster males. His *Halloween* films send up the idea of a hyper-masculine male body as both desirable and an emblem for national gender standards as they pertain to males. Zombie, whose work has flashes of greatness, pursues a deconstructive project that seeks to take apart the mythologies of masculinity and examine their components with a critical eye. In the next chapter, I will discuss a work that foregrounds the taking apart of masculinity, but with much less potentially progressive results.

6

Torture/Porn

Hostel, Homophobia, and Gay Male Internet Pornography

Part of the conservative re-entrenchment of masculinity in the '00s results, as numerous scholars have shown, from the tremendous impact of the events of September 11, 2001. As Thomas Pollard writes, post-9/11 cinema seems to be "darker, more dystopic, and more paranoid."[1] As I have been arguing, however, while undeniably significant, 9/11 is only one of several factors that have shaped the onscreen representation of United States masculinity. To begin with, the financial crisis, called by some the Great Recession, which began in 2008 and may or may not have run its course as of this writing has certainly shaped the films of this period, such *Margin Call* (J. C. Chandor, 2011) and *The Wolf of Wall Street* (Martin Scorsese, 2013). Modes of heterosexual masculine privilege are linked to the reckless trading that brought about the financial crisis. No doubt these films and the financial crisis demand attention for the study of masculinity in this period. Nevertheless, my focus here is on the period most immediately affected and shaped by 9/11 and also on the impact that certain tensions in American culture were having on film before the events of 9/11. As I showed in the chapter on *Scream*, fears of the impending millennium as well as national shifts in gendered and sexual identity that were linked to millennial fears were important influences. Moreover, the expanding and ever-more visible development of a national queer identity and its attendant, though also not synonymous, relationship to the quest for gay civil rights (most clearly embodied by the gay-marriage cause), has also played a significant role in the shaping of contemporary forms of normative screen masculinity, producing a sense of destabilization that must then be met and countered, but through a variety of means, some of which resemble, though they do not constitute, progress. Straight masculinity must give the appearance of comfort level with the increasingly prominent range of sexualities in the culture while maintaining its inviolate and uncontaminated integrity.

While the ubiquity of queer at present shapes how we view male bodies onscreen and how they are presented to us, neither is extricable from new forms of homophobia that represent a backlash against this ubiquity. But the forms of homophobia have also evolved, and now remain cunningly implicit, if just as pervasive. This homophobia is laced with an equally implicit and unacknowledgable racism, both of which emerge through a fetishistic focus on the white, straight male body as *the* body of masculinity, *the* site of desire, *the* object for cultural fascination. (The films of James Franco evince this pervasive attitude while also complicating it.)[2] The male face that so captivates contemporary film (and television) emerges as a middle ground for fascinations with the male body, for strategic attempts to keep these fascinations hidden, unacknowledged—brooding on the male face signals erotic interest but defends against erotic abandon. While one could argue that such has always been the case, contemporary media forms reify the white male body in these ways by obsessively foregrounding it. Denuding, fatiguing, and then, crucially, *restoring* this body and the hegemonic purity it inevitably and always already signifies is the underlying narrative of media forms like torture-porn horror and the newer form of Internet gay male pornography—strange bedfellows, indeed, and even stranger components of an innovative new system of cultural re-entrenchment that situates itself in the maintenance of the white straight body.

The resurgence of the American military post 9/11—particularly its real-world images of destroyed and restored male bodies and the attendant mythologizations of these images, emphasizing the reclaiming of a mutilated manhood—demands a discrete study. As Jasbir K. Puar observes of the aftermath of September 11, "Heteronormativity is, as it always has been, indispensable to the promotion of an aggressive militarist, masculinist, race- and class-specific nationalism."[3] *Hostel* evokes the torture that the American military inflicted on its enemies during the war in Iraq that began in 2003 and that was notoriously documented in the leaked photographs of the treatment of detainees at the Abu Ghraib prison in Iraq. These grisly photographs showed male and female American soldiers smiling as they posed against the humiliated, abject prisoners. The human rights violations committed against the detainees ranged from torture, rape, and sodomy to murder. Once the abuses were leaked, reports were published at the end of 2003 by Amnesty International and the Associated Press. As critics such as Mark Bernard have argued, *Hostel*'s sleight-of-hand maneuver is to portray Americans as victimized and tortured by dark menacers, thereby erasing knowledge of the American military's inflictions of torture on its enemies. What I will explore in this chapter, in dialogue with Puar, is the heteronormative logic within this sleight-of-hand.

While tracking the full complexities of this period far exceeds the scope of this chapter, what I want to establish is that the 1990s are the period in which, as I put it in *Manhood in Hollywood from Bush to Bush*, "masculinity became self-aware"—aware of itself as a potential object of sexual contemplation and desire, and as such the site of visual fascination for those conventionally classified as the objects of the sexual gaze, not its wielders: women, queers, and the non-white. If, as Laura Mulvey famously argued in her 1975 essay "Visual Pleasure and Narrative Cinema," the screen protagonist and the screen spectator, both gendered male, share a fantasy of narcissistic omnipotence that depends precisely on this joint access to and wielding of the male gaze, what has begun to happen since the early 1990s is that the gaze, as critics like Jack Halberstam, José E Muñoz, and Susan White have shown, has itself become far wider and more complexly deployed in terms of who wields it and who falls beneath it.[4] As I will demonstrate, the principle fallout from this radical enlargement of the gaze has not only been greater self-awareness on the part of screen males of their sexual desirability to a range of spectators, but also the innovative development of strategies of resistance to and subversion of this susceptibility to visual and desiring fascination.

As I outlined in the introduction, horror and comedy have emerged as the two major genres of the '00s, exemplary body genres that focus on the male body itself, newly mapped and available as a site of multivalent sexual speculation and wonder, and on the dynamics of male gender identity, both in individual and group form, as they have been revised to meet the demands of the post-queer, post-feminist, post-identity present. Along with the horror remake in particular, which almost always focuses on a monstrous male figure, and which specializes in "Ghost Faces," as its masked murderers (Michael Myers, Jason Voorhees) attest, one emergent post-millennial genre especially demands attention, combining the body genres of horror and pornography. I refer, of course, to the much-discussed and so-called "torture-porn" horror film of the '00s.[5] The debates over such films—*Hostel* (Eli Roth, 2005), *Hostel II* (Eli Roth, 2007), *Saw* (James Wan, 2004), *The Devil's Rejects* (Rob Zombie, 2005), and several others—have dominated the discussion of post-millennial horror. *Hostel* is a crucial text not only for this emergent subgenre but also for any study of post-millennial masculinity. They join in with a wide range of films that foreground the forms of torture, including *The Passion of the Christ* (Mel Gibson, 2004), the Daniel

Craig James Bond films *Casino Royale* (Martin Campbell, 2006), *Quantum of Solace* (Marc Forster, 2008), and *Skyfall* (Sam Mendes, 2012), *The Bourne Identity* (Doug Liman, 2002), comic-book movies too innumerable to list, the new sword-and-sandal-meets-classical-mythology epic such as *Immortals* (Tarsem Singh, 2011) and *300* (Zack Snyder, 2007), and television series such as *24* (2001–2014) and *Homeland* (2011–present).

My focus in this chapter is less on the torture-porn horror genre itself, which has been the subject of intensive critical analysis, than it is on the ways in which films like Roth's illuminate certain trends in the representation of masculinity in the '00s. Adam Lowenstein has attempted to disabuse criticism of the term "torture-porn" in favor of what he calls "spectacle horror."[6]

As I will have occasion to note, I do not agree with Lowenstein's overall argument in this essay. But we can posit that the term spectacle is indeed apt for the uses of the heterosexual white male body in post-millennial horror and gay male Internet porn, respectively. What unites these seemingly antithetical genres, or subgenres, include the desire to denude (expose, flay open) men; to "ruin" them (psychically and/or physically mutilate them, to mar them, to force them to undergo heretofore unimagined trials, to render them transformed); and then to reconstruct them as weathered but strengthened, indeed, as better for the grueling effort. Torture-porn horror films and the variety of gay porn I am discussing here chart a passage from masochism to transcendence that indexes the reactionary but also ingeniously inventive efforts to re-entrench masculinity in this era. The brazen demonstration of a desire to disassemble and reconstruct straight masculinity in *Hostel* intersects with the new cyber-forms of gay porn, exemplified by websites such as *seancody.com* and *All-American Heroes*. *All-American Heroes* advertises that "All-American heroes are real rugged studs. These straight men have gay sex on this site." These "real rugged men" presented as unimpeachably heterosexual include those who have served in the military, firefighters, and police officers. The topos of *All-American Heroes* is, consistently, the scene of two men (or sometimes three, or a solo performer) identified as straight, watching a heterosexual porn film together, an experience that provides the basis for homosexual intercourse. The longstanding homosocial ritual of males watching pornography together—dating back to the 1950s and "stag parties" and films, as Thomas Waugh has discussed in *Hard to Imagine*, his crucial study of gay male photography and film—has been transformed into the scene of sexual stimulation itself; the spectacle of men *being* with other men, with sex added to it, in this post-identity era, has become newly eroticized for its seeming "realness."[7]

Both torture-porn horror and gay male Internet porn foreground a distinctive post-millennial mode of representation that I call "torture/porn." As I established in chapter 1, the representation of masculinity in the '00s is sadomasochistic, turning the infliction of suffering and the enjoyment of suffering on the part of screen males into spectacle. The approach taken to the depiction of masculinity in this period's filmmaking oscillates between the voyeuristic (the investigation of and the focus on the male body) and the fetishistic (the obsession with male faces). Torture/porn derives primarily from the voyeuristic dimensions of screen sadomasochism, though indubitably contains fetishistic elements as well. It foregrounds a fascination with the male body, figured as white, straight, and heterosexual, and reflects a new visual commodification and colonization of this body. This body has become the center of a new cinema of attractions that includes cyber media forms. Made to submit to a series of assaults, to withstand these assaults, and to emerge from them restored, unified, and purified by whatever means possible—in *Hostel*, murderous bloodletting; in gay cyber pornography, ablutions and smiles of relief *after* sexual intercourse, figured as an unrelenting episode in which the straight male is "tortured" into and through gay sex—the straight male body is both problem and solution, a new *pharmacon*, the poison and its own antidote. Or, more accurately, a body to be poisoned (ruined through torture and violence in horror films, or through gay sex as an alternative version of this ruination) and then "cured" by the restoration of straight male normalcy (the regaining of phallic male strength, the purification of the body).

While one does not wish to use the term *torture* lightly by any means, I seek to illuminate the odd ways in which torture informs the representation of masculinity in these emergent genre forms. Catherine Zimmer points out that "the contemporary appearance of so many films about the economies, bodily experiences, and technologies of torture must be viewed in conjunction with the politics of torture that has concurrently occupied the American and world stage."[8] If films such as *Hostel* not only make the awareness of torture palpable but also recreate its imagined *topos* in scenes of enclosure, entrapment, inescapable circumstances, total vulnerability, and sustained sadism and suffering, other media forms similarly evoke the trappings of torture, often more insidiously, as in the case of gay male Internet porn, which subjects its straight male subject to similar situations and conditions. Usually, the straight man, or several, is interviewed in a single room, made to strip bare, and then forced to undergo a series of "assaults" in the forms of the sexual services performed on him by the gay male, routinely presented as submissive "bottom" who sexually satisfies the straight male "top." Sometimes, the drama of such scenarios lie in the spectacle of two ostensibly straight men having sex, but one of these men is invariably cast in the role of the bottom, reproducing the more common straight top/gay bottom scenario. (The obsession with classifying sexual partners through these categories of dominance and passivity conforms queer sex acts to a straight binary.) These porn video narratives—and they are narratives, as I will show, not just filmed "events"—infrequently present the straight man as a willing participant in the sexual acts that follow his entrance into the scene of pornography. Rather, he is strictly "gay-for-pay" or presented as someone vaguely bewildered by what he's gotten himself into, an echo of the male hero of film noir and his predicaments as he becomes increasingly, and hopelessly, ensnared within the *femme fatale*'s stratagems. The chief effort made in the porn narratives is to exculpate the male from his willing participation in gay sex while making his presence in the narrative the focal point. If gay male Internet pornography would seem to be an unlikely source of cultural oppression, given the prevailing stigma against same-sex desire and sexuality in the nation, what I aim to demonstrate here is that a study of the way this genre works—to proceed from the basis of Linda Williams' recommendation that we see pornography as a genre, much like the musical[9]—reveals that subaltern forms of desire and representation can reflect attitudes prevalent in the dominant culture. (Analogously, the conservatism of a great deal of indie film belies the progressive, resistant stances commonly associated with this form of filmmaking—fodder for a different discussion.)

Many of the torture-porn horror films, such as *Hostel* and *Turistas* (John Stockwell, 2006), return to the longstanding theme in American culture of innocents abroad, helplessly seduced and preyed on by the cunning foreigner. As Zimmer discusses, "the emergence of these narratives of American youth, frequently men, going abroad and finding themselves immersed in what often amounts to an economy of torture must, I believe, be read as a tremendously projective fantasy—one in which American youth are figured as the victims rather than the perpetrators of this kind of violence."[10] I would add that these youthful males are not just white and upper-middle-class, as Zimmer notes, but also heterosexual. The assaults they endure prey not only on their national and class identities and status but also on the sexual normalcy they have ostensibly achieved and represent. *Hostel* recalculates the gender and sexual coordinates of the slasher film, which, along with *Saw*, it reinvents as torture porn, so that males are both the victims and the triumphant victors. Roth's earlier *Cabin Fever* (2002), however, established what is, in my view, one of the major themes of post-millennial horror, related to those outlined above: the tendency to turn the victim into the monster. The victim-monster emerges as monstrous precisely because, in her victimization, she—and it frequently is a "she"—emerges as a disquieting, maddening spectacle for the other characters in the film narrative, who then view her and her travails as the true source of oppression, more onerous, indeed, than the ostensibly real monster (in the case of *Cabin Fever*, a flesh-eating virus; in *Hostel*, the torturer-customer). The victim-monster strikingly contrasts against the reconstructed straight and, usually, white male, embodying his capacity for failure and the sheer horror of his descent into "feminine" victimization and passivity. The victim-monster in Roth's work derives from that of one of his major influences, Quentin Tarantino, who merits a brief discussion before we turn to *Hostel*.

The Tarantino Connection

Restaurant Dogs is the name of the student film Roth made as the culmination of his years at NYU film school (1993–1994), clearly an homage to Quentin Tarantino's *Reservoir Dogs* (1992). Tarantino was one of the executive producers of *Hostel*; Roth was one of the stars of Tarantino's film *Inglorious Basterds* (2009). *Basterds* is a notable intertext for *Hostel*. Starring Brad Pitt as the American First Lieutenant Aldo Raine, Christoph Waltz as the Nazi Colonel Hans Landa, and Mélanie Laurent as a Jewish woman named Shoshana who escapes Landa's massacre of her entire family at the start of the film, the film interweaves two (fictional) assassination plots against Adolph Hitler and Joseph Goebbels among other prominent Nazi villains. A motley crew of Jewish Allied soldiers led by Raine (Pitt), after dispatching a series of Nazi soldiers whom they ambush along the way, plan to kill the party's leaders at the cinema, now run by Shoshana, where the Nazis will attend a gala event of a propaganda film, *Nation's Pride*; in turn, Shoshana plans her own bravura revenge at the same event. During the climax set in Shoshana's movie theater, the titular "basterds" triumphantly gun down the nefarious Nazi leaders Hitler and Goebbels, among others. One of the most prominent basterds is the American soldier Donny Donowitz, known by the Germans as "The Bear Jew"; Donny Donowitz is played by Roth. Moreover, Roth directed the film-within-the-film *Nation's Pride*, a fitting gesture for the hyper-metatextual Tarantino. As I will show, Roth's cinema—in its tendency to turn the victim into the monster and its deeply phobic tendencies—extends and reinforces key components of Tarantino's sensibility.

Tarantino's work provides a crucial precedent for the later horror movies with an emphasis on graphic depictions of torture. The cop-torture-ear-mutilation scene in *Reservoir Dogs* anticipates and exemplifies work of filmmakers like Roth especially. This 1992 crime film about a botched diamond heist and the various criminals, all male characters, involved in the heist, was Tarantino's debut. What is and is not shown in this film, which in characteristic Tarantino fashion distorts and alters temporality and narrative, is crucial. For example, the director depicts the events before and after the heist, but does not show us the actual heist taking place. Tarantino carefully designs the scene in which one man tortures another man so that its *duration* will be as interminable and excruciating an experience as possible. Mr. Blonde, or Vic Vega (Michael Madsen), one of the group of criminals who attempt to perpetrate the heist, ambles out, in real time, of the big hangar in which a cop, bound to a chair, awaits Mr. Blonde's return with the proper tools for torture and mutilation. At a similar unhurried real-time pace, Mr. Blonde ambles back in, tools in hand. Exemplifying the Tarantino sensibility, the song "Stuck in the Middle with You" (written by Gerry Rafferty and Joe Egan and originally performed by their band Stealers Wheel) plays throughout this scene. As Tarantino demonstrates, the palpable horror of torture is as much about cinematic duration as it is about the act itself. What was especially notable about *Reservoir Dogs* at the time was its focus on the male body as a new domain of onscreen vulnerability. The male body is fascinating to the metatextual Tarantino precisely for the genre-bending opportunities it provides. The ravaging of the male body that Tarantino depicts here is a revision of the earlier forms of horror, 1980s slasher-horror especially, that focused on prolonged violations to the female body. Moreover, the male body in Tarantino is depicted as immobile and passive, indeed, powerless, as the body that lies ready and waiting, as it were, for another man. When the large, shambling thug Mr. Blonde returns, eager to inflict inventive kinds of pain on the seated, bound cop, and begins his sadistic adventure by cutting off the cop's ear, the entire scene begins to resemble the heterosexual pornographic film in which the woman, rendered helpless, must wait for and then allow the man to ravish her. Cutting off the cop's ear is an obvious castration metaphor; it is also an act of invagination, rendering his ear a site for penetration. In making the male ear an alternative vagina—or anus—Tarantino establishes that the male body is now deeply vulnerable to such assaults. The male ear emerges as a metonymic wound for the newly ravishable male body.

The novelty value of making the male the site of onscreen violence rather than merely its agent continues to arrest filmmakers like Roth. As

I have demonstrated, torture-horror films are not the only post-millennial genre that make the male body, marked as the white, straight male body, a focus. What is especially interesting in the post-millennial moment is that the goal seems to be not just to gaze upon the white, straight male body but to disassemble this body and make it available for consumption on multiple levels. As I have argued, this desire to take straight masculinity apart, a process that I call *dismantling*, emerges as a defining theme across the body genres, ranging from beta male comedies to torture-based horror.[11] The exposure of male bodies matches, intensifies, extends, and also allegorizes the deeper interest in male *psyches* and in exposing these as well, a thematic that has been rigorously explored by Mark Seltzer in *Serial Killers*.

This post-millennial development is a startling departure from the traditional view of masculinity as the seat of reason and femininity as the body. Luce Irigaray has influentially demonstrated the ways in which this dichotomy has underpinned the Western tradition.[12] To parse Irigaray's larger argument in *Speculum of the Other Woman*, great male minds, desiring to see their own reflection, attempt to reproduce their own stature through philosophical discourse, which puts them in contact with other great male minds, a culture of narcissism entirely situated within male homosocial relations. This fantasy of masculine autogenesis, a shared male world of spiritualized male desire and male beauty, is what Luce Irigaray critiques as *hommosexuality*, her neologism. As a result, women function as flawed copies of men, useful mirrors that reflect male glory. Women are reified as maternal and reproductive (the primary social roles of the mother and the girl, as if these were the only possible social/cultural roles for women), femininity as a sign of the body itself. Women have been historically, socially, and culturally constructed as bodies that produce much more elevated male forms, birthing machines that produce male greatness.

In the post-millennial moment, however, it is masculinity that is figured as the body, and one that exists to be manipulated, distorted, transformed, and reimagined. In turn, women are very often portrayed as the centers of control. It should be immediately noted, however, that there is little in the way of an attendant progressive, feminist sensibility in this maneuver. The women of beta male comedies appear to be shrewd and well-organized, but are almost always presented as, ultimately, failed, oppressive, aloof individuals. They put the shrew in shrewd, and badly need a comeuppance of sorts. (Seth Rogen's furious mock apology to Katharine Heigl in *Knocked Up* is a definitive example of this comeuppance, as is the speech in which he excoriates her sister [Leslie Mann] in the delivery room when she tells him to butt out of Heigl's delivery.) Similarly, there is little in the way of a progressive politics in making males the objects of torture and violence in the horror movie. This new development, though interpreted by some critics as a critique of structures of male power, actually only reinforces these structures, as I will show. While women can sometimes don distinct roles as a result, the women in contemporary horror films, much as they are in the beta male comedies, exist to be diminished, if not eradicated altogether. If the women in *Hostel* are certainly much more in charge than the males are, this female agency is a narrative problem that the film will redress in its climactic section.[13] While, again, some critics acknowledge Roth's misogyny, the larger effort made by several critics is to champion Roth's films as political critique of Western capitalism, imperialism, and the culture of repression. The difficulty presented by Roth's work is that it is highly self-conscious, self-aware, and in certain respects sophisticated. As I will demonstrate, Roth's cinema, while phobic and reactionary, is complexly designed, a complexity that needs to be interrogated—dismantled, as it were—in order for its constrictive political statements to be seen for what they are.

Poster Boys: *Hostel* and *Hellbent*

The ad campaign for *Hostel* reveals a great deal. The poster for the film can serve as the initial object of our analysis, allowing us to consider the images of masculinity that inform and are produced by this genre-making work.

The most immediately striking aspect of this poster—which was clearly commercially efficacious, given the immense box-office success of the first Roth-directed *Hostel* (unlike the second film, a box-office failure)—is its brazen evocation of a gay sadomasochistic porn film, which, I will show, the film also evokes at key points. Another, related work released in the same year as *Hostel* makes for a good point of comparison. The gay independent horror film *Hellbent* (2005) features a killer who dons the same kind of horned-devil-monster mask that the sadist-tormentor-killers (and later the hero) do in *Hostel*. Written and directed by Paul Etheredge-Ouzts and billed as the "first GAY slasher-movie!," *Hellbent* is set during the Halloween Parade in Hollywood's West End and also concerns a group of young male friends who are systematically picked off, slasher-movie-style, by the killer. Carol Clover has famously theorized that the slasher-horror film climactically concludes with a confrontation between the killer, almost always male (and sexually dysfunctional), and the "Final Girl," a sensible, not conventionally feminine, usually virginal young woman resourceful enough to stay alive,

Torture / Porn 207

FIGURE 6.1. Theatrical poster for *Hostel* (2005).

outwit the killer, and annihilate him by film's end. Adhering to slasher conventions as Clover parsed them but adding a gay slant, *Hellbent* ends with a confrontation between the killer and the Final *Boy*.

Much like Roth's work, Etheredge-Ouzts's film is extremely self-conscious and cinematically metatextual. And, again like Roth's film, it self-consciously evokes the tropes of not only the horror movie tradition but also gay porn. Unlike Roth's film, though, it is a film that attempts to

208   Ghost Faces

rework the slasher genre and its inherent conservatism to produce a more resistant genre vision. Indeed, vision and its relationship to masculinity is a thematic that *Hellbent* critically explores for its potential menace, as the poster for the film suggests.

The poster for *Hostel* emphasizes several aspects of the film's sensibility and the appeal it makes to its audience: its explicit investment in male phallic power, symbolized by the cartoonishly huge chainsaw wielded by the seated figure, who is presumably the killer or one of them; the onanistic quality of the violence in the film, conveyed by the seated posture of the killer, who evokes the classic pose of the Internet masturbator and who

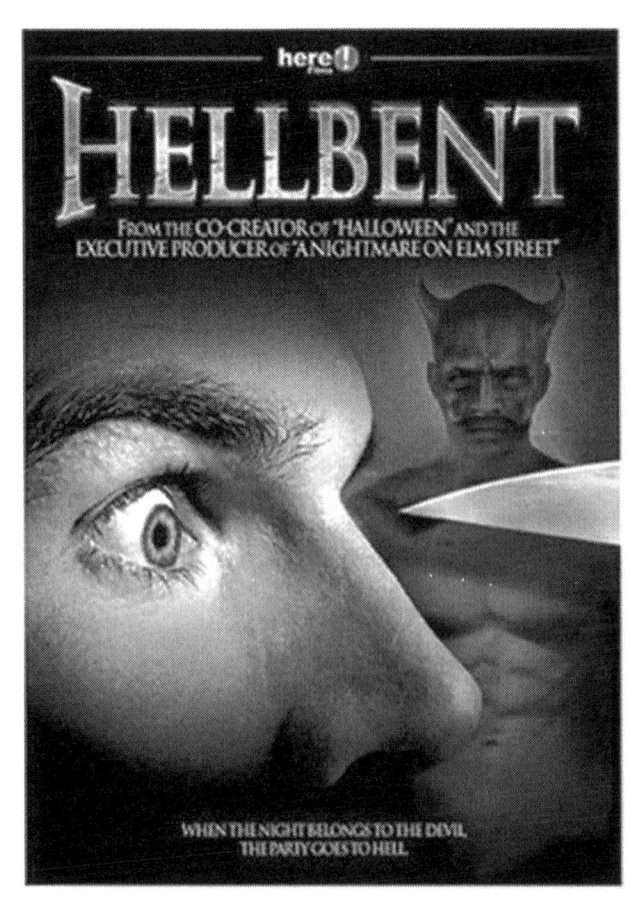

FIGURE 6.2. Theatrical poster for *Hellbent* (2005).

seems mesmerized by his own phallic gigantism and power; the opacity of the killer, symbolized by his masked, blank, inscrutable visage. Suggesting all of these qualities as well as gay and heterosexual varieties of S/M porn, the film commercially presents itself as an attempt to reach new heights of screen terror but also to explore the meanings and the menace of masculinity itself. We are invited, in other words, to contemplate the image as representative of the central subject matter of the film, a self-mesmerized masculinity run amok.

Male mayhem is informed by narcissism here, a libidinal mode with none of the liberatory potential it might have in a more resistant work, to say the least. Narcissism is suggested in the most conventionally phobic manner throughout *Hostel* as the core-conflict in not only the chief killer's psychological makeup but also that of his chief victim. Masculinity is synonymous, so the poster implies, with an unconstrained access to power, specifically the power to inflict violence. Indeed, the masturbatory, narcissistic, and homoerotic valences of the image intersect with and deepen the promise of *sadistic* desire, to inflict violence and revel in the *duration* of this act. As I will show, *Hostel* follows works such as *Scream* in perpetuating the most homophobic aspects of Freudian theory, as conventionally disseminated in culture and conservative forms of psychoanalysis. (Freud's work on the subject of homosexuality is difficult, often discordant, and still highly valuable; in contrast, the reception of Freud's ideas in the United States has tended, especially in terms of homosexuality, to reify their most conservative aspects.) We can posit that what the poster thematizes is phallic narcissism.[14] The chainsaw-phallus that bifurcates the screen not only equates the phallus with violence and death but also suggests tumescent male sexual arousal at these prospects. Indeed, it suggests a come-hither invitation to be wildly penetrated, if not torn asunder, by the seated figure and his upright chainsaw. We can posit, then, that this is an image of homoeroticized male violence that depends on a homophobic understanding of any concept of male-male penetration as inherently a form of the most savage violence imaginable. This thematic will be actively pursued within the film.

Not Another Teen Movie: Or, Americans Abroad

Significantly, *Hostel* emerges between the wane of the new-style teen comedy that flourished in the late 1990s, exemplified by *American Pie* (1999) and *Dude, Where's My Car?* (2000), and the rise of "beta male" comedies and the bromance. These latter subgenres focuses on hapless, disaffected, wayward men who usually either still live at home, by themselves, or with a circle of equally wayward, slovenly male friends, and who find heterosexual relationships deeply mystifying. They live in what the sociologist Michael Kimmel has called Guyland. The polymorphously perverse Dudes of the late '90s teen comedies displayed a new openness not only about male bodies but also their apparently sacrosanct sexual mysteries.[15] Between the teen and beta male comedies, male bodies and their emissions and mysteries have become acceptable and even common fodder for mainstream representation, along with the near-explicit homoerotic threat that imbue these representations. Indeed, the nonchalance with which this threat is foregrounded in contemporary film attests to the ubiquity of homoerotic threat as a factor in all homosocial relationships. *Hostel* intersects with these innovations in the comedy genre and takes them to graphic new levels of dread, phobic defensiveness, pain, violence, dismemberment, and mayhem.

In its depiction of three backpackers—two young American guys Josh (Derek Richardson) and Paxton (Jay Hernandez), and the older, mid-thirtyish Oli (Eythor Gudjonsson), from Iceland, whom Josh and Paxton have met on their travels—traveling across Europe, mainly in search of sexual conquests, *Hostel* reworks the familiar "innocents abroad" theme and its attendant sexual dangers.

Though very much presented as the avid, relentless sexual consumers, the males are shown to be the easily beguiled victims of the Seductive

Figure 6.3. The three backpackers, hardly innocents and on the verge of a nightmare.

European Other. The seduction of the American innocent by the attractive foreigner has been a common theme in American culture, present in such classic nineteenth-century works as Nathaniel Hawthorne's novel *The Marble Faun* (1860) and numerous Henry James novels. Fascinatingly, it has its most indelible cinematic realization in lonely-spinster-awakened-by-love woman's films such as *Now, Voyager* (1942) and *Summertime* (1955). Perhaps it is this feminine cinematic tradition that informs the representation of Josh as a somewhat non-standard male. With his tousled-sandy-ginger hair, gentle eyes, and unassuming look, Josh is an unusually vulnerable male screen presence. These traits are emphasized through contrast with his traveling companions' much more aggressive styles of masculinity. Dark-haired, olive-skinned, and Hispanic, Paxton is nevertheless much more emphatically depicted as the "ugly American." In his ravenous sexual tourism, Paxton oddly blends coarse consumerism and all-American cultural arrogance. Paxton is an oddly devised character; he never adds up. That he speaks fluent German is not presented as a marker of his interest in other cultures but as yet another incommensurate detail in his character makeup, though it will be a key plot point. In contrast to the wan and reserved Josh, Paxton and Oli share a misogynistic view of women as primarily "pussy," "clits," and so forth. Seeing the titillating displayed posteriors of curvaceous models exhibiting themselves as wares in the upper windows of a high-concept Amsterdam brothel, the interior of which resembles an S/M performance-art theater, Paxton howls, "I hope bestiality isn't illegal in Amsterdam, because these women are hogs!"

Josh wants to be a writer and encourages the group to do culturally improving things like going to a museum rather than getting stoned all day. Paxton and Oli forever taunt Josh for his naiveté, awkwardness, and lack of sexual rapacity. Oli, whose tagline is "Of course, my horse," is large and loping, a hearty screen presence energized by his indefatigable relish for sexual adventure. Josh frequently calls him a Viking, especially when Oli flashes his naked buttocks and genitalia in Josh's face ("Can't you keep your fucking Viking ass in your pants for two seconds?" Josh complains) as his compatriots chortle.

Paxton, in his relentless goading of Josh to engage in sexual romps, recalls the affable, smooth Kevin (Thomas Ian Nicholas) of *American Pie*, which focuses on a group of male high school students whose friendship revolves around their sexual appetites, fantasies, and hopes. While depicted as eager to have sex with his virginal girlfriend, Vicky (Tara Reid), Kevin's true obsession is with ensuring that all of the members of his high school group of male friends lose their virginities along with him. He forces them all take a pact with him that, by prom night, they will each have done so. Kevin loses his effortless charm and transforms into a cold, remote character by the end. The Josh of this film, its main character, Jim (Jason Biggs), is horny enough to have sexual intercourse with the all-American apple pie adumbrated in the title. But by the time the prom has become a reality, his frustrations with sexual matters reaches a breaking point. As he snaps at Kevin during the prom, "I haven't even had sex yet and I hate it!" In *Hostel*, no moral or social qualms impede Paxton and Oli from their relentless attempts to assimilate Josh into their ethos of endless sex and view of women as primarily orifices at their sexual disposal. Indeed, the only obstruction they encounter is the grisly torture-deaths they, respectively, escape and succumb to at the torture-lair operated by the "Elite Hunting" group. Elite Hunting provides a service to those who can afford it: victims to be tortured, brutalized at will, and killed with impunity. Strangely enough, in this film nearly all of the victims seem to be male (there is a fleeting shot of one female victim during the Elite Hunting section of the film, and the sequel focuses on female victims), with one important exception, the character Kana.

In their Amsterdam hostel, the backpackers meet Alex (Lubomír Bukový), a young Eastern European huckster who tells them to visit an undocumented hostel in Bratislava (the capital of Slovakia) "that isn't in any guidebook" and that teems with porn film-sexy, horny women who will have sex with any foreigner. "You just . . . take them," Alex promises, his eyes luridly aglow. Following his feverish recommendation, the friends all travel to Bratislava. Once there, the backpackers meet two women in a sauna who do indeed appear to match Alex's description: a lush, dark-haired seductress Natalya (Barbara Nedeljakova) and a tall blonde named Svetlana (Jana Kaderabkova). After constantly turning down opportunities to do so in Amsterdam, Josh, eventually does have sex, with Natalya. As Josh has sex with her, Paxton, in the adjacent bed, has sex with Svetlana. Unbeknownst to the friends, Natalya and Svetlana actually work for Elite Hunting, luring men into their lair. Ecstatic, Tangerine Dream-esque music, recalling the group's score for *Risky Business* (1983), engulfs Nathan Barr's score as Josh accedes to his own sexual ravishing from Natalya. (Adam Lowenstein notes that suggestive resonances of the score to a relevant intertext for *Hostel*, *The Wicker Man* [1973], also suffuse the soundtrack in this moment.)

Numerous valences exist between *Hostel* and the endless spate of teen-sex comedies from the late 1970s to the early '00s that make the male loss of virginity their chief narrative goal: *The Pom-Pom Girls* (1976), *Porky's* (1981), *My Tutor* (1983), *Losin' It* (1983), *Risky Business* (1983),

Class (1983), *Revenge of the Nerds* (1984), and the revisionist late '90s teen comedies. *Hostel* echoes these films' defining moment in its depiction of Josh finally achieving genital contact with a woman on the screen. Now, Josh has been properly and incontrovertibly heterosexualized, both in diegetic terms and *before Paxton's eyes*. Indeed, as they have sex with the women, the men assume the same physical positions, lying beneath the towering women astride them. The women's eyes lock, indicating their knowing dominance over their prey. As Josh is about to begin making love to Natalya, Oli comically mounts Josh, pretending to sodomize him. Though played for laughs, this moment once again reinforces the overall sense of Josh as penetrable, the passive partner or bottom in gay sex.

If the teen comedy leads up to the loss of male virginity, the slasher movie inverts the pattern by making the preservation of virginity a crucial stipulation. Usually, to rehearse the pattern laid out by Carol J. Clover, it is a young woman who faces off against the killer by the end, and she is also usually a virgin or at least not shown to be sexually active. For much of the movie, Josh seems headed towards a Final Girl-role and a confrontation with the killer or killers. Yet, while not the first one killed—which is Oli—Josh's death *feels* like the first because it results from the first graphic and extended scene of torture, violence, and killing that defines the film, primarily devoted to such depictions of sustained sadism and brutality. One question inevitably arises, then, in genre terms: Is Josh killed because he has become sexually active? Making Paxton rather than Josh the Final Boy and the way that Oli's death is depicted are equally telling decisions that reflect, as I will show, the *complexly* homophobic sensibility of the film.

What is *Your* Nature?

As noted, compared to Paxton and Oli, Josh is reserved, shy, nonaggressive—in a word, the image of the sensitive straight boy. While he does have some sporadic outbursts of violent reaction, these outbursts convey a sense of his insecurities over his gender as well as sexual identity. The film pursues an increasingly explicit thematic of repressed/closeted homosexuality that involves not only Josh but also his torturer and murderer. By implication, the unspeakable abuse that Josh undergoes at his torturer-killer's hands—and, as Adam Lowenstein persuasively demonstrates, hands are relentlessly emphasized in this film—is on some level an act of shared self-denial on the part of victim and villain, equally closeted but asymmetrically paired in this regard. The killer, the Dutch Businessman, as he is called, is a failed surgeon with shaky hands who *knows* that he is homosexual and has *chosen* to lead a closeted life as a married family man, as he strongly implies to Josh in a scene in a pub. In contrast, Josh either does not consciously realize that he is gay or is living a closeted life. Whatever the story may be, the young man's death is figured as a savage reprisal for Josh's self-denial and sexual uncertainty and sexual appeal to the Dutch Businessman, who, it would appear, kills Josh primarily because he is himself sexually drawn to the young man and also because Josh rejects him on the train.

Josh's rejection of the Businessman is both an affront to the Businessman's own desires and marks the older man as "queer." At the same time, however, Josh's grisly death at, literally, the Businessman's hands is figured as the inevitable outcome of the young man's own closeted homosexuality, his inability to "taste" his true desire, in a film obsessed with eating and other gustatory processes as metaphors for sexuality. If the homosexual theme of *Hostel* is a surprise in its nearly explicit readability, in the end it is used to reinforce the film's larger investment in a culture of male heterosexual dominance.

In the most cinematically inventive scene in the film—the one at the high-concept, performance-art brothel in Amsterdam, which occurs early in the narrative—the irrepressibly horny Paxton and Oli have wild sex with a prostitute while the withdrawn Josh wanders up and down the hallway, tentatively considering the various rooms and their possibilities behind closed doors.[16] Josh observes as Paxton and Oli have sex with one prostitute behind a closed white door, albeit only seeing the silhouettes all three cavorting bodies cast against the door. Heterosexuality is depicted in deeply stylized terms, as an act of shadow theater. (The scene of male-male rape in *This is the End* is also depicted in expressionistic silhouette.) Passing another room, Josh hears what sound like cries of pain; peering in, he finds a resplendently attired dominatrix beating a customer who has paid for this service, an obvious foreshadowing of the later torture scenes at Elite Hunting. "You watch, you pay!" she impatiently chastises. Then, the still unappeasably lascivious Paxton and Oli, after informing Josh that they have procured the services of a prostitute for him down the hall, go into the dominatrix's room, Oli grabbing Paxton to join him ("I pay—come on!"). Josh proceeds to the waiting prostitute's room, the décor of which suggests a 1960s erotic-sci-fi epic like Roger Vadim's *Barbarella* (1968) crossed with an icily austere Kubrick film. The high-tech ambiance of the room and the prostitute's space-shuttle-hostess demeanor and attire all convey the sense of heterosexual sex—at least for Josh—as a mysterious, mystifying, otherworldly, stylized ritual. This prostitute (unlike the brusque dominatrix) gives him encouraging instructions, telling him he can wash up and prepare for their lovemaking. From the prostitute's point of view, the camera then turns to the doorway where we expect to find Josh. But there is no one there. That absent figure in the doorway is a telling cinematic representation of a male sexuality that has absented itself—and that has relinquished the male heterosexual authority rampantly wielded by the other backpackers.

Yet their earlier silhouetted images also conveyed a sense that, even for Paxton and Oli, sex with women is on some level a shadowy, stylized event. This tonal register is intensified by the highly considered aesthetic design of this entire scene, which works to distance the viewer from the ample erotic activity being suggested. The ambiance here, in its chill, remote quality, desexualizes the entire set-piece and its fantasies of endless sexual freedom and opportunity. And the subsequent scene in Alex's bedroom in which a couple have sex while oblivious to all others around them—their sexual exertions continue unimpeded and uninterrupted as all of the men talk about them and with each other—further adds to this sense of sex as impersonal ritual. The couple is utterly self-absorbed, seemingly unaware that anyone else is present. Oli waves a hand over the face of the woman astride the man on the bed, and his gesture has no effect on her; Alex explains that they are too stoned to notice anyone else. Sex is either a museum piece, a piece of performance art, or a feat of stylized lyricism as imagined in this film. Sex emerges as the aesthetic complement to the equally stylized set-pieces in which the men are tortured, heightened acts of physical proximity between human beings that foreground intimacy and a harrowing disconnection at once.

Once on the train to the undocumented hostel near Bratislava that Alex recommended, the Dutch Businessman (Jan Vlasák) comes into their booth and sits next to Josh. This scene on the train opens with an image of a smirking Paxton drawing a happy face on Oli's naked buttocks positioned very close to a sleeping Josh; as Paxton takes a photograph of Josh's face next to Oli's exposed posterior, Josh wakes up and begins protesting, leading to peals of laughter from Paxton and Oli, and to Oli intensifying the comedic assault by then flashing his equally "Viking" genitals before Josh. While these fratty antics are presented as just that, the opening of this scene carefully prepares us for its chief purposes: first, to introduce us to the Businessman; second, to make much more explicit the theme of closeted homosexuality (here, this theme is comedically adumbrated by Josh's quasi-horror at Oli's exposed buttocks and "man-parts"); third, to establish that a phobic attraction-repulsion desire and kinship exists between Josh and the Businessman.

As the Businessman walks in, he is on his cellphone speaking with his daughter, which leads Oli to take out a photo of his own daughter. "You have a daughter?" Josh incredulously asks; apparently, Oli's anarchic sexual adventurousness does not connote the responsibilities of fatherhood. The Businessman proceeds to eat a grilled chicken salad with his hands, much to the dismay of his onlookers. "You need a fork there, Chief?" Paxton asks. The Businessman—bespectacled and beady-eyed, and played with an unsettling quiet intensity by Vlasák—proceeds to explain that "we humans" have lost touch with the food we eat.

An animal gave its life so that we might live, hence his attempt to recapture that primal connection through tactile contact. Paxton's use of the term "Chief" once again identifies him as the typical boorish American; but then again, his self-identification as a vegetarian associates him with the liberal educated classes. "It's human nature," the Businessman offers as a justification for his meat-eating. "Well, I'm human and it's not my nature," Paxton responds. Then the Businessman puts his hand on Josh's knee, and asks, "And what is *your* nature?"

This gesture and, it would seem, the question lead Josh to retaliate violently. "WHOA! Don't touch! Don't fucking touch me!" Josh yells, as the Businessman makes his apologies and a hasty exit. "Fucking freak!" Josh yells again. Paxton and Oli break out into laughter, Paxton noting, "Edward Saladhands just groped Josh!" Still chortling, Paxton further comments,

FIGURE 6.4. Paxton, the Hispanic-American as the Ugly American.

FIGURE 6.5. Josh and the Dutch Businessman are paired and doubled.

"Dude, you finally hooked up, that's awesome!" Obviously still upset, Josh responds, "Yeah, that's fucking hilarious." Having called Josh a "handsome American" earlier in the scene, the Businessman all but outs both himself and Josh, but putting his hand on the young man's knee while asking him about his nature crosses the line into an insupportable explicitness.[17]

FIGURE 6.6. "And what is *your* nature?"

This scene is paired up with the subsequent one in Slovakia, where the friends are now checked in to the fateful undocumented hostel. Josh wanders out of the bar where Paxton and Oli are once again zealously pursuing sexual conquests, and is besieged by a gang of impoverished, menacing street urchins who threaten him with their child-mob violence. Josh is rescued by the Businessman, who has strangely reappeared. "Hey, let me buy you a drink," Josh tells him, both gratefully and apologetically. While inside, the two men sit facing each other on bar stools as they have their drinks, and as Josh apologizes, he puts *his* hand on the Businessman's knee. Josh's reciprocal gesture is a reversal of the crucial earlier moment on the train in which the Businessman placed his hand on Josh's knee, triggering thereby his livid expression of gay panic.

In reference to Josh's response to him on the train, the Businessman, telling him that no apology is needed, says, "I would have done the same thing when I was your age"—and further explains that he found marriage to be a helpful solution. Clearly, the Businessman refers here to their shared homoerotic "tendencies"; Josh looks somewhat bewildered, but also does not act with his former anger. In contrast to himself, though, says the Businessman, Josh "can do anything." What Josh does do is to have sex that night with Natalya alongside Paxton having sex with her Czech accomplice Svetlana. That this scene precedes the one in which Oli mimes sodomizing Josh as he has sex with Natalya cannot be incidental.

As Mark Bernard writes,

> When the businessman later reappears as Josh's torturer and murderer, he resumes his "courtship" of Josh whilst torturing him, touching Josh's thigh again after he drills holes in his chest and legs with a power drill (penetrating him) and slicing through the tendons of his heels so he cannot walk (castrating him). Thus, Josh's body is made more heterosexual, more normative, and, by extension, more grievable when contrasted to the monstrosity of his "queer"- and foreign-killer.[18]

Bernard, drawing on Judith Butler's *Precarious Life*, makes an excellent point about the film's construction of a "hierarchy of grief." As Bernard interprets the film's politics, what seems to some like a radical maneuver—making the victims of torture white, American, and male—actually works to distract attention from the actual, real-world victims, the darker-skinned Iraqi/Arab peoples, of *American* torturers. Moreover, it designates as "less grievable" those who are not white American men. The character of Kana, a young

Japanese woman the guys meet at the hostel and who will be horribly tortured, is a case in point, as I will discuss below.

Victim-Monsters: The Varieties of Torture

One of the oddest intertextual linkages the cinema-obsessed Roth makes is that between his film and the 1958 play *Suddenly, Last Summer* by Tennessee Williams, made into a 1959 film directed by Joseph L. Mankiewicz with a screenplay by Gore Vidal (though Williams officially received credit). In the film, a young woman, Catherine Holly (Elizabeth Taylor), is threatened with lobotomization because of the strange stories she recounts about her travels with her now-dead cousin, a poet named Sebastian Venable. Violet Venable (Katharine Hepburn), outraged by Catherine's allegations, leads the effort to have Catherine lobotomized, appealing to the rather clueless psychiatrist played by Montgomery Clift for his approbation of the procedure. The film, following the play, never visually represents Sebastian except in the most oblique way, a point that Vito Russo made central to his well-known reading of the film as deeply homophobic.[19]

There is a great deal going on in Williams's play and in the Mankiewicz film.[20] For our purposes, I want to make note of some crucial valences between these works and Roth's film: the child-horde, cannibalism, women and the "procuring" theme, and, of course, the unrepresentable figure of the homosexual. The child-horde is one of many instances in which Roth presents the impoverished and/or socially abnegated denizens of Slovakia as monstrous. Though their very horde-mentality and criminal threat stem from their poverty, abandonment, lack of care, and hardscrabble street existence, these impecunious children are presented as demonic. Similarly, the cab driver who takes the friends from the train station to the hostel is depicted as grotesquely unkempt (his bad and missing teeth are emphasized in close-up) and unintelligible. As I will show, these denizens of a decrepit Slovakian world are examples of what I am calling the victim-monster. But then again, the shots of European grotesques are not a new development in the Slovakia sections of the film; the server in the hookah bar in the early scenes in Amsterdam is similarly depicted in these terms, as are, in their own way, the drug-stupor-possessed couple having mindless, endless sex in Alex's hostel room. Except for the women who exist to be sexually consumed, Europe stretches out before the friends as a barren wasteland of ugliness. Indeed, the women associated with the torture-hostel, Svetlana and Natalya, are initially presented as seductively tall, beautiful, and alluring, but are then shown without makeup, looking so deglamorized as to suggest that any semblance of beauty they possessed was part of the ruse to lure the males to the Elite Hunting hostel.

Still, Bratislava, on the friends' arrival there, is initially presented as quaintly charming. Bratislava stretches out before them like a quaint German village from a fairy tale, and the immediate environs around the undocumented hostel are stately and verdant at once, picturesquely arrayed with young European students reading books near handsome old monuments on the green. The film diligently works to reveal that all things in Bratislava/Slovakia merely conceal the ugly depths that will be finally revealed in the Elite Hunting torture-lair.

The first other visitors that the friends encounter in the undocumented hostel are a pair of young Japanese women, Yuki (Keiko Seiko) and Kana (Jennifer Lim). Significantly, these young women act in a sexually provocative manner with the three male friends, who, in turn, demonstrate no sexual interest in them, gravitating instead to the statuesque and European Svetlana and Natalya. Later, Kana reports to Paxton and Josh that she cannot find Yuki; in turn, they cannot find Oli. Eventually, they get an odd text message that includes a picture of Oli and Yuki with the word "Sayonara" beneath it, implying that they have left and are now traveling together. Later, Paxton and Josh get another text-image message supposedly from Oli, a close-up shot of his face with the sentence "I go home." But then, we cut to the scene that reveals the source of the photo: the torture-lair room in which Oli's decapitated head rests upright on a table.

Oli is a victim, the first we see, in fact—but he is not depicted as a victim-monster. First, there is no scene whatsoever of his torture or murder, only the shot of his severed head that reveals his fate. Second, his head—as much as a severed head can, of course—resembles him, indeed, can be serviceably employed as proof of his continued existence and as a clue to throw his friends off. In extremely sharp contrast, when Kana is tortured and nearly killed, she becomes an unrecognizable creature. Escaping the torture-lair and in disguise as one of its paying customers, Paxton, wearing a long, elegant black coat, speaks to a rabidly energized American customer (Rick Hoffman) right before he tortures Kana; about to make his escape, Paxton has a change of heart once he hears the screams of the victim, who turns out to be Kana. Paxton kills the American customer, who is holding a blowtorch up against the right side of Kana's face, leaving her hideously disfigured. In addition, her right eye now hangs by its optic nerve down the side of her burned face. Paxton, following Kana's instructions, cuts into the nerve to sever her dangling eye from it. Torrents of yellow fluid flow out of the cut nerve.

To call this scene offensive does not do it justice. Roth's imagery here blends an altogether transparent racism as well as misogyny. With all due respect for any biological verisimilitude the scene might possess, to make the fluid that gushes out of this now-monstrous-looking young Asian woman's face starkly yellow has obvious racist connotations—the yellow perils of victimization. Adding to the sense that Kana, the victimized woman, has become the monster, once she and Paxton have escaped and are about to board a train, she stops, arrested by her own reflection, to stare at her face, one of the many moments in the film that evoke narcissism and the mirror stage in sinister ways. The ultimate victim-monster, the horribly violated Kana herself becomes the violator of all social boundaries whose Medusan ugliness is too overwhelming even for her own eyes. Apparently overcome by the horror that she now represents, Kana commits suicide by throwing herself before the oncoming train. As the train crunches over her body, her blood sprays several passengers on the train platform, much to their horror. Their faces and bodies are drenched in waves of blood. Kana's self-immolation recalls the particulars of one of the retributive murders in David Fincher's *Seven* (1995). The serial killer (Kevin Spacey) boasts of cutting off the nose of a supermodel and giving her a choice to live in this condition or be killed by him. She opts for death at his hands. Her choice is apparently the true mark of her ugliness, and one that Spacey's killer offers as evidence of her pride, one of the seven deadly sins that necessitate his murderous biblical campaign. Kana's self-immolation handily relieves the film and its hero of the burdens of caring for the injured, the violated—and the female and the non-white.

The hideous castration image of Paxton cutting the long shaft of Kana's optic nerve brings the film's characterization of her full circle. When we first see her and her friend in the hostel, Kana makes a sexually provocative comment to the three backpackers, leading her friend to giggle as she grabs her arm and pulls her away. This hint of Kana's sexual agency—her lascivious gaze—informs the unmistakable phallic imagery of her monster-eye when Paxton rescues her. In cutting off her eye, then, which gushes out fluid in a manner reminiscent of the money-shot of pornographic film, Paxton seems to be cutting off the phallic quality of her desires as well. Now, the early images of Kana and Yuki's unlicensed sexual adventurousness and their identities as two young women on a search for adventure in a foreign country who are not chaperoned by men or even an older female figure all begin to make phobic sense. What undergirds the film's representation of Kana as a victim-monster is the implicit message that her victimization is, if not deserved, at the very least absolutely inevitable. (Kana's scorched eye recalls Frank's bloody gunshot eye socket in *Donnie Darko*. Both hideous ocular violations relate to some form of sexual threat and punishment, for homoerotic desire in *Donnie Darko*, for female sexual desire here.)

This entire episode plays out like a grotesque parody of Brian De Palma's *Casualties of War* (1989), based on a real-life case that occurred during the Vietnam War, in which a sensitive young man attempts to rescue a tortured, abused young Vietnamese woman. *Hostel*'s phobic imagery has its chief intertext in Tarantino's films. The gimp in *Pulp Fiction* (1994), the various women (killed or vengeful) in *Death Proof* (2007), and, especially, Shoshana in *Inglorious Basterds* are precedents for Roth's depiction of otherness. To take the character of Shoshana as an example, Tarantino presents her as a victim-monster, the Jewish woman as vengeful cinematic Medusa. The Medusa of classical myth was a beautiful young maiden raped by the god Poseidon in Athena's temple; Athena punishes not Poseidon but Medusa herself, making her the ultimate victim-monster, a creature with snakes for hair whose hideousness of visage turns spectators, usually men, into stone. Tarantino revises the Medusa myth by fusing it with that of the tragic Jewess, a longstanding trope from Walter Scott's historical novels and Victorian literature.

Though horribly victimized—she is the only member of her family to escape annihilation at the hands of the Nazis at the start of the film—Shoshana transforms into a monstrous female figure at the climax, her face projected on the immense cinema screen as she cackles in triumph at the successful achievement of her revenge plot. As the cinematic Shoshana, her face as wide and immense as the screen itself, leers at and taunts the Nazis, her actual body lies crumpled in death in the projection booth. In death, Shoshana is an even more powerful force. Even as the screen and her gargantuan image both go up in apocalyptic flames, Shoshana continues to erupt into demonic, victorious cackles. These effects recall other versions of the Medusa: the Gothic fatal woman, the film noir *femme fatale*, Barbara Creed's image of the monstrous-feminine, and also legends that Hitler was traumatized as a young man by some kind of Jewish succubus, hence his intense anti-Semitism. These images are not, to say the least, sensitive, empathetic, or historically sound accounts of the historical trauma being represented. In this manner, they are metonymic of the film's treatment of the Nazi persecution of Jews and other minorities during World War II. Indeed, Tarantino's treatment of the Holocaust, and that of American slavery in his 2012 *Django Unchained*—an even worse film that was also a box office hit—establish Tarantino as the contemporary cinema's chief revisionist historian, who combines the 1970s grindhouse pulpy revenge-fantasy film with treatments of historical atrocities. Roth's junior-league Tarantinoism contents itself with a slew of racist, misogynistic, homophobic images in pursuit of a tantalizing master narrative of the kind Tarantino—whose work makes a mockery of daring forebears like his much-touted, but obviously completely misunderstood, influence Brian De Palma—has amply discovered.

Dismantling the Male

That Josh is so languorously tortured in terms of duration and content makes the chaste, elliptical representation of Oli's death especially notable. Seated in a chair wearing only his black underwear, the nearly nude Josh occupies the conventional position of the woman in sadomasochistic porn and also of the "bottom" in the gay variety of this genre. We are invited to perceive his near-denuding as part of his violation and also part of the titillation it ostensibly offers. Indeed, the torturer, revealed to be the Dutch Businessman, punctures Josh with his power drill in ways both unspeakably violent and sexually suggestive; he penetrates Josh and creates multiple orifices for this penetration at once. Confirming that this torture scene extends the would-be scene of homosexual cruising on the train, the Dutch Businessman once again puts his hand on Josh's knee and squeezes it, all but saying that now Josh must submit to his wiles.

When Josh begs to be let go, the torturer seems to be assenting by loosening Josh's foot straps but, instead, severs his Achilles tendons instead. As Josh tumbles and falls during his escape, he recalls the teenage male victim being turned into Freddy Krueger's human marionette in *Nightmare on Elm Street 3: Dream Warriors* (Chuck Russell, 1987), his own flesh becoming outsize strings attached to his anguished body. The evil impish Freddy Krueger, who enters into teenagers' nightmares and wreaks havoc on them in this oneiric realm, sadistically tortures his victims with bravura relish. That marionette-male scene evokes nightmares; it's clearly in the realm of the dream-like, the symbolic, and the allegorical. In contrast, the scene of the Dutch Businessman torturing, maiming, and killing Josh is brutally realistic, emphasizing the actual penetration of a violated body by implements of mayhem, such as the power drill that bores holes into Josh's body. Moreover, this imagery has a clearly sexual resonance. The image of the torturer violating Josh from behind his body, along with Josh's howls of surprised agony, unmistakably suggests sodomitical rape.

In terms of the film's own representational logic, Josh's victimization can be lengthily and explicitly represented in a manner that Oli's cannot. The film preserves an older sense of heterosexual males as sacrosanct visual objects in its refusal to depict the scenes of Oli's degradation. But then again, there is a way in which Oli, the "Viking" from Iceland, is also depicted as being less than human because his violation need not be in any way recorded or, really, grieved over, as opposed to the young American Josh's. The film relegates the non-American male to obsolescence as it reifies the young Japanese woman as a yellow-peril monster whose physical ravages suggest nuclear-war horror films and Godzilla movies from the 1950s. (Indeed, the image of Kana's burnt face recalls the image of the disfigured, toxic-smog-begrimed scientist-father Dr. Yano's face in *Godzilla vs. Hedorah*, aka, *Godzilla vs. the Smog Monster* [Yoshimitu Banno, 1971]).

Adam Lowenstein reads *Hostel* as a more resistant work than commonly perceived, one that maintains something of a critical stance toward the Bush regime, the Iraq War, and the revelations of torture at Abu Ghraib. While I applaud an effort to read an interesting mainstream film as potentially resistant and do not believe that *Hostel* can be simply dismissed as "torture porn," I do not share Lowenstein's view of the film as resistant—far from it.

One of Lowenstein's more interesting observations is that the film makes novel use of the "I-Camera," most typically associated with the POV shot of the masked killer of slasher films. The scene in which Josh is tortured and then killed begins with I-Camera shots of Josh, desperately trying to make sense of his surroundings, looking through the eyeholes of the hood that has been placed on his head by the Businessman. Lowenstein reads Roth's choice of the I-camera here as a maneuver that eerily unites torturer and tortured—and therefore makes a crucial political point. "Through horror genre iconography, then, the I-camera provides a visual suggestion that Josh strands in not just for an American victim of torture, but also for an American torturer. The inverted use of the I-camera is one way (but not the only one, as I will explain below) that *Hostel* confronts the audience with responsibility of Abu Ghraib rather than dismissing it."[21] Lowenstein does make note of the "whiff of homophobia" in this scene, "a thinly transposed 'sexual' encounter between two 'deviant' characters." Yet, he further argues, this sexual anxiety cannot "completely explain away the unsettling sense of Josh as figurative American torturer as well as actual torture victim."[22]

Lowenstein draws parallels between the "cinema of attractions," as Tom Gunning has influentially described the early cinema and its foregrounding of unprecedented spectacle, and *Hostel*.[23] Given the overall thesis of this book, we can argue at this point that masculinity, specifically white heterosexual masculinity, has become the centerpiece of the new cinema of attractions, this cinema broadly understood as a genre-bending, hierarchy-defying, media-spanning conglomerate of produced images that extends from the art cinema to disreputable horror films like Roth's, from gross-out teen comedies to beta male comedies with older protagonists to the bromance, from scripted television to Reality shows, and indeed from film to television to YouTube and other free-floating media forms. The uncanny sense of Josh as both the torturer and the tortured that Lowenstein provocatively discovers has, in my view, a complexly conservative sexual logic within the film's design. The voyeuristically displayed form of Josh is another version of that white male heterosexual body that has proven so endlessly arresting to viewers and narratives alike in the '00s. As such, even within his lavishly detailed victimization, he is on some level always already the victimizer precisely because he represents white heterosexual privilege and the normative American subject who colonizes foreign locales, cultures, women, experience, and so forth. One can theorize that the giddy and queasy thrill for many of watching horror like *Hostel* lies in the subversive pleasures it provides to see this normative figure *and* face violated, in a word, defaced, in keeping with the sadomasochistic sensibility of the contemporary cinema.

What makes *Hostel* a cinematic work specific to its era and allows for the abuses inflicted on this body to be so ample are the continuously offered suggestions that Josh is not only the white straight body-subject *but also* the queer body-subject as well. Indeed, it is no accident that his torture is the most sustained and significant in the film, far exceeding that of Oli (whose torture is never shown) and overshadowing that of Paxton (which is disrupted by a triumphant set of maneuvers in which Paxton, the grindhouse revenger, doles out retributive abuse on not just his torturer but the guards, the clean-up man, the American customer who abuses Kana, the seductive Eastern European women as well as the trickster Alex, and finally the Dutch Businessman). Josh's torture can occur at length because he has been feminized by the homosexual valences of his characterization, and Kana can be tortured so graphically because she is both feminine and the racial Other.

Before he slits Josh's throat after duplicitously giving the brutalized young man a chance to escape, the Dutch Businessman holds up Josh's face to a mirror. This image will be repeated at the climax when the vengeful Paxton does the same to the Businessman in the bathroom stall (another coded, or not so coded, gay allusion of the "unusually wide stance" variety).[24] The shot of the Businessman holding Josh's head in his hands while he forces Josh to look at them both in the decrepit mirror that jaggedly reflects them is deeply significant because it so succinctly summarizes the thematic between these characters. To look at this from a queer-literary perspective, the Claggart-like Businessman holds up the beautiful, Billy Budd-like Josh up to his own gaze, so that Josh can see that it is his beauty, his desirability, his own conflicted sexual identity that is responsible for the abuses heaped upon him and that culminate in his murder.[25] Or, the Businessman is showing the young man that, try as he might to resist, the Businessman is the dominator, the victor who possesses the helplessly passive Josh. Freud's theories of homosexual narcissism (discussed in chapter 2) take on a particularly phobic cast here, in which homosexual desire can only exist as a murderous exchange between two mirror men. Moreover, the older man can most acutely be said to be projecting his own self-hatred onto the younger, forcing him to confront the grisly truth of their shared sexual secret.

The inability of the film to make the sensitive and, it is strongly implied, closeted Josh the Final Boy, the gender-variant version of Clover's Final Girl, is the chief indication of the film's homophobic sensibility. It can only imagine the much more demonstrably hetero-identified Paxton as the—Final Man? Final Boy does not seem the appropriate description for his character, whereas it would for Josh, reminding us that a sense of virginal innocence is not only endemic to the Final Girl but to images of youthful gay male sexuality. In his classic study *Monsters in the Closet*, Harry Benshoff exhaustively catalogued horror's history of homophobic portrayals as well as the particularly homophobic forms of violence that befall gay-coded characters. What is novel in *Hostel* is that the gay-coded character threatens to be not ancillary but the protagonist and the Final Boy.

It is impossible to imagine what this film would have been like if Paxton had been the victim shown to be brutalized by the Dutch Businessman, and Josh had come to the rescue at the end. Paxton undergoes a scene of terrifying torture and violence himself, but the kind of torture he undergoes is largely threatened against rather than inflicted on him. While voyeuristic and fetishistic aspects of the representation of masculinity in the '00s have impinged on screen images of masculinity, in the end, it is the queer and/or effeminate male body that will be depicted as violated, penetrated, ripped asunder. What *Hostel* does is to literalize the process of dismantling to the *nth* degree. Josh's body is penetrated and cut open by the Dutch Businessman, but then this would-be surgeon and killer is shown stitching Josh's body back up. The effort to take apart and then to reconstruct masculinity, which happens in alternating ways over the course of the period's films (sometimes physically, sometimes formally, sometimes on the level of film content, sometimes emotionally, sometimes by implication), literally occurs on the screen in *Hostel*.

When Paxton, having grown suspicious, interrogates Svetlana and Natalya about his friends' whereabouts, the latter tells him that Josh and Oli are visiting an art exhibit, to which venue she promises to take him. The art exhibit turns out to be the Elite Hunting lair where the rich pay to be able to torture and murder their captured victims. "I get a lot of money for you," Natalya brazenly tells Paxton after he discovers the Dutch Businessman sewing up Josh's gory, split-open body. "I guess that makes you *my* bitch." She adds this line in response to the series of furious epithets Paxton directs at her for her involvement in his friends' death and his imminent own. Clearly, the haunting power of Natalya's line—its proclamation that she has emasculated Paxton—was resonant for the filmmakers, since it is repeated at the very end of the end credits scroll, emphasizing Natalya's inescapable power over Paxton even after he has run over her body with his car, twice.

Paxton, bound to a chair, is "given" to a German client named Johann for torture/murder purposes. The guard puts a gun against Paxton's chest, commanding "Speak"; the client wants to be reassured that Paxton is American. "I am not American! Look at me," Paxton says in response, one of the few, but telling, moments in which Paxton's ethnic identity is explicitly noted. Paxton's skill with languages comes into play when he tries to plead with the Businessman in German, but the client calls in the guard to put a gag ball inside Paxton's mouth. Johann begins to torture Paxton, holding up an active chainsaw to his face; the terrified Paxton begins vomiting, leading Johann to take out the gag ball. Johann then severs two of Paxton's fingers with the chainsaw, but in the process he unintentionally saws through Paxton's restraints, and when he charges at his victim with the chainsaw, Johann slips on the gag ball and saws off his own leg in the process. Paxton finds a gun, shoots Johann in the head, and then also shoots the guard who enters the room. Paxton escapes the cell, and during his effort to get out of the dungeon finds himself in direct proximity to Josh's corpse. After he talks with an American man who is about to torture someone, Paxton nearly leaves the Elite Hunting lair, but the cries of the American's female victim, who turns out to be Kana, stop him. Paxton goes back to free Kana, killing the American torturer.

Hostel can imagine horrific violations to the male body, but what is key here is which body gets violated and how, what we are shown, and not shown, of violations to the body. Paxton's fingers are severed, but he remains fully clothed the entire time—there is no denuding of his flesh. Moreover, Paxton is able to survive the bloodbath, to rescue Kana and to escape the torture-lair along with her, and to annihilate Svetlana, Natalya, and their accomplice Alexi by running them over with the escape car he is driving. And he is the one who kills the Dutch Businessman. At the train station where Kana has just killed herself in self-disgust, Paxton takes a train on which the Dutch Businessman is also riding. When the train stops in Vienna, Austria, Paxton follows the Businessman to a public restroom. He places an Elite Hunting Club card under the Businessman's stall, and when he reaches for the card, Paxton grabs his hand and cuts off the same fingers that were cut off of Paxton's hand by Johann. Paxton then slams into the adjacent stall and pushes the Dutch Businessman's face in the toilet bowl, almost but not quite drowning him. Paxton allows the Businessman to realize who he is before he slits his throat and thereby kills him. As shot, from an overhead angle, Paxton's murder of the Dutch Businessman looks like an act of sodomy, which is reinforced by the cruisy bathroom stall-setting for this final act of vengeance. Paxton's murder of the Dutch Businessman echoes his sodomitical torturing and killing of Josh.

Hostel and Gay Male Internet Pornography

There is an unsettling effect within a larger terror-sequence in *Hostel*. Paxton, hiding within a cart laden with dismembered body parts in order to escape the Elite Hunting torture-lair, looks up at one point when wheeled into the room where Josh's body lies on a table above Paxton at the bottom of the cart. Paxton's first glimpse into Elite Hunting's nefarious activities was seeing the Dutch Businessman carefully sewing up Josh's torn flesh, reconstructing the ruined body of the young man. Looking up into his dead friend's eyes, which are wide open, Paxton and the dead Josh share a look, a shock of recognition. Eerily, Josh's expression seems as knowing as it is becalmed, as if he, too, were in on the macabre joke that Elite Hunting has now played on Paxton as well. The film clearly fetishizes the image of Josh's face, here finding an irresistible contrast between its beatific, oddly knowing expression and the grisly, gory contents in its midst.

The symbolic valences of the Businessman's sewing up of Josh's body cannot be ignored. The violated body of the beautiful young man becomes sacrosanct, purified, in death—reborn as a reconstructed form. Clearly, a parody of the Christian myth of Christ's Resurrection is at work here. As I have been arguing throughout this book, the ruination and reconstruction of American manhood emerges as a recurring trope of film in the '00s across the genres.

Strangely enough, gay male Internet pornography continues these trends. While a great deal more would need to be said about pornography generally to do the subject justice, what I want to suggest is that gay male Internet pornography specializes in the ruination and the reconstruction of the white straight body as well. Websites like *Sean Cody*, *All American Heroes*, *Straight College Men*, and many others consistently produce pornographic narratives with eerie similarities to that of *Hostel*, replacing violence between men with sex between men. The substitutions are themselves unstably maintained—it is very clear from *Hostel* that violence between men has an erotic dimension, and very clear in online gay porn that sex between men is charged with particular kinds of violence.

Each week or so, these websites produce two new "movies," usually one of a single performer, newly introduced, masturbating alone on camera, and another in which two men, or a group of men, have sex. In the latter, the main focus of attention is usually the newly introduced male "star" of the previous week, and this star is almost always presented as a heterosexual male who is performing in gay porn for monetary reasons. Given that the performers in these films are overwhelmingly white, we can say that the heterosexual star is also the white heterosexual star, performing with other white males. In the films centering on sex between men, the heterosexual male is most frequently paired up with a male who is identified, in contrast, as gay, bisexual, queer, or more "experimental." The overwhelmingly consistent premise of Internet gay male porn is that the white heterosexual male will be subjected to the sexual ministrations of the more demonstrably queer male. I use the term "subjected" advisedly, because the white male heterosexual subject of the online gay porn film is almost always presented as a resistant subject, one who must undergo a regimen of gay sexual attention, stimulation, worship, and subservience, all of which frequently take on the tone of abusive torment, albeit of a helplessly pleasurable kind. The premise of these weekly films—the solo ones but especially the pair or group ones—is that the white, heterosexual male subject will submit to this gay sexual attention until he experiences orgasm, which, in keeping with the standard protocols of pornography, occurs in "the money-shot" climax of the film. That the hetero-male subject experiences pain—distress, manifest ambivalence about the sexual attentions he is about to receive or the acts he is about to perform—as well as money-shot-confirmed pleasure all contribute to the sadomasochistic nature of these porn films, which they share with mainstream narrative films.

To be sure, the heterosexual male is often shown to be the sexually dominant one, penetrating the passive gay/queer partner. Yet before the act of anal penetration occurs, it is common for the heterosexual male to be shown to be receiving oral sex, which is presented as a heretofore never experienced form of sexual ecstasy. The off-screen interlocutor, the person who "warms up" the models by asking them about their personal histories (usually about how many women they have had sex with, if they currently have a girlfriend, and what kinds of sexual experiences they like to have with women and/or their girlfriends), creates a narrative in which the heterosexual male, whether or not he is the top or the bottom in the gay sexual experience to follow (and he is almost always the top, the one who sexually penetrates the other male), is effectively deflowered by the gay male bottom, his straight innocence stripped away by the cunning, knowing, sexually adept and more experienced gay male partner.

For the heterosexual male, sex is usually depicted in gay male Internet porn as a form of sustained torture, signaled as such by cries of what sound like pain even more than ecstasy as the straight male receives and performs sexual activity almost against his will. Receiving pleasure, worshipfully administered, the heterosexual male becomes the truly passive object of the Internet gay porn film, the gay/queer bottom emerging, surprisingly, as the more active subject.

This surprising dominance on the part of the seeming bottom, however, is anything but a subversive maneuver. Instead, the entire scenario in which these typical roles become strangely reversed works to reestablish, through the alternative route of negation, white male heterosexual dominance by establishing the heterosexual male subject as unquestionably the most significant figure on the screen, absolutely the central member of the sexual group. The homosexual sexual pleasure to which the heterosexual male must submit is a form of ruination, reducing him to a state of helplessness, chipping away at his steely masculine composure until he transforms into a pliant site of sexual satiation—ostensibly his own, but more emphatically that of the bottom and the paying viewing audience.

Of equal interest to our discussion, usually the porn-narrative does not end with the money-shot, however. There is very frequently a denouement. After the money-shot moment (the straight top's orgasm shown always, sometimes the gay male bottom's as well), the men are shown in the shower, performing ablutions in soapy water. And the shower is also not the concluding image. Post-shower, the men, usually clad in white bathrobes, sit on a bed or a sofa and are once again interviewed by their unseen, camera-wielding interlocutor. Faces beaming with relief, the men sit in their purifying white bathrobes and discuss what has just happened to them. These discussions recall the way that hostage victims who have now been rescued and restored to sanity recount their experiences and how wonderful it feels to have been rescued. The ablution of the shower and the ritualistic wearing of the robes are elements of a ritual of purification that restores the male to his position of unsullied dominance. The ritual absolves him of the on-screen crime of homosexual sex.

The reconstructed, relieved bodies of the white straight subject at the end of the online gay porn film are coeval with Josh's strangely reconstructed body—stitched back together, seeming to stare impassively back at Paxton—at the climax of *Hostel*. Moreover, in Paxton, heterosexual manhood is itself reconstructed, as he gets to perform the role of hero. (Had Josh been the hero at the end, it would have been conceivable to call him the Final Boy. Somehow, Paxton cannot be incorporated into this paradigm, his aggressive male sexuality transcending it despite his access to heroic vengeance by the end.) Through Paxton, the reconstructed homosexual-fetish body of Josh—the Businessman's tribute to own fantasies, such as they are presented—becomes the reconstructed body of white heterosexual manhood itself. Surviving the bloodbath, Paxton avenges Oli as well as Josh, and symbolically the order of white male heterosexual privilege all three friends together represent. If it is to be argued that Paxton is the raced, the ethnic, male subject rather than the white one, I would argue that he is overdetermined as the implicitly white male subject through his associations with ugly Americanism, rampant heterosexual appetite, and also by his eventually heroic, avenger role. (One remembers the original name given to George W. Bush's "Iraqi Freedom": "Infinite Justice.") Ghost Faces that roam throughout the expanse of the genres, the heterosexual male subjects of torture-horror and torture-porn—for this phrase most applicably defines the gay male Internet pornography of the present—are alike the subjects of their narratives. The horror of their ruination is always already relieved by the eventual promise of their reconstruction.

Torture/Porn

Eric Freedman, discussing the shifts in gay/queer sexual identity in the wake of the Internet, turns to the subject of gay dating sites and the "imagined community" (to use Benedict Anderson's perhaps overused phrase) of those seeking out such services. Freedman notes the ways in which such websites "promote a bond between producer and viewer" through "readily definable production techniques" among other methods.[26] The same can be said for porn websites. *Seancody.com*, *All-American Heroes*, *Straight College Men*, and others, each present distinctively designed and recognizable brand images for their audiences. *Seancody*'s men are almost always clean-cut, youthful, with shaven genital areas, and much the same can be said for *Straight College Men*. The hairless and lithe and smooth male bodies on display exemplify the overall sense of the males as pure before they are sullied by gay sex, and the purification rituals that follow the sex return the males to their prelapsarian state of heterosexual grace. The young men in these websites seem affluent, healthy, and placid. The men on *All-American Heroes*, on average, appear to be rougher around the edges—hairier, less manicured, less polished, less sunnily "Californian," and also seem to be more generally working-class/blue collar. Hence *this* site's distinctive appeal. Potential viewers of *All-American* videos are advised, in the language on the home page of the website, that

> All-American heroes are real rugged studs. These straight men have gay sex on this site. If you are offended by straight men having gay sex, gay facials, or seeing naked firemen, gay military sex, police sex, or even seeing men fucking men then don't come in. The amateur straight guys do things that are incredible.

All-American emphasizes the straightness of *all* of its models, whereas *Seancody*, on occasion, describes its bottoms as gay men, and usually, in the jovial descriptions that accompany the videos, further detail the joys the gay bottoms derive from getting to service the tops, suggesting that they would do it even without being paid for it. What all of the sites have in common are two nearly binding principles: that the actors/models, especially those who will be the "star" of the porn narrative, in other words, the top who receives sexual attention and then acts as the dominant partner in sexual intercourse, are straight; and that these actors/models are uniformly white. This is not to suggest that non-white performers never appear on these websites, but that their appearances are extremely rare. The absolute majority of the actor/models are white—very few are black, Hispanic, Asian, or any other non-white ethnicity or race. A regime of the visual undergirded by both racist and heterosexist standards, gay male Internet porn does not, for the most part, allow for the occasional creativity that some have found in earlier works of gay male pornography in the pre-digital era, such as Michael Ninn's *Shock* (1996).[27] Pre-Internet, scripted gay porn films have inevitably ceded to the Reality TV-like forms of gay Internet pornography, which emphasizes "realism," a maneuver that inevitably casts pre-Internet, scripted porn in a romantic light. *All-American*'s fetishization of "amateur straight guys" transparently frames the non-professional aspects of its models as the source of their appeal, one rooted in their non-artificiality. The equation of American men with non-artificiality and with "Nature" has longstanding roots in American culture, being a rhetoric that dates back to Andrew Jackson's presidential campaign against John Quincy Adams, the frontier hero and his "Nature-schooled" machismo versus the effete, European-educated aristocratic American.[28] While slick productions can be found at *Seancody* and *Straight College Men*, contemporary pornography, designed with the Internet rather than home video in mind, emphasizes the homemade, raw, "real" look they promulgate along with the fiction that the performers are "real rugged men," actual straight men, not gay actors simulating straight-acting realness. (It should be added that I am discussing commercially produced gay Internet porn. There are amateur sites online such as X-Tube that may provide alternatives to the patterns I am outlining here.)

The remainder of my analysis will focus on the online gay videos produced by the *All-American Heroes* website. The valences between the American-tourists-preyed-on-by-dark-foreigners horror films and *All-American Heroes*'s typical porn "plot" are immediately apparent in the setup for these videos. In a postmodernist "let the seams show" gesture, each video begins with shots outside the studio where the video's action will take place and be filmed. (Sometimes, the action takes place in a home or apartment as well.) The men are shown walking outside, during the daytime, to the studio destination; we then cut to the scene of the men being interviewed. This setup evokes the Gothic plot in which the unsuspecting innocent guilelessly enters a hidden world of depravity and potential mayhem. The sunny outdoor space presented at the start of the video, which the men are shown to inhabit, provides a striking contrast to the enclosed space of the studio, emphasizing that the men are "in nature" before they enter the studio and are subsequently processed into fodder for our delectation. This point is more emphatically made in the videos that take place inside a house, as this "pre-footage" often shows the men walking through leafy, tree-lined paths before getting to the house. A familiar nature/culture split organizes the before-and-after porn narrative, in which the natural man before gay sex transforms into the no-longer-natural man through both gay sex and the apparatus (the camera, lighting, editing, and so forth).

Once inside the studio, or home, the men are then interviewed, specifically about their military experiences if they have served, and often at length. The interviews—clearly a nod to the documentary format favored in sitcoms today, which signals the influence of Reality TV-techniques and sensibility on scripted television in both comedy and drama—focus not, as might be expected, on the male subject's past sexual experiences, which may have included sex with other men, as is the case with the extensive interviews conducted in the *Straight College Men* porn video. Instead, here, they focus on the men's experiences in the military and in battle, about which detailed questions follow from the unseen interviewer. The interviewees/performers go into a great deal of detail about their time in the military and in battle, and, given that it is usually two men being interviewed at once before their sexual performances begin, there is usually a sense that the males are also bonding over their experiences. As hard as it is to imagine, the gay porn video has emerged as something of a safe space for men who have returned from war to discuss their histories, consider the impact of what they saw and participated in (and, at times, perpetrated), and compare notes. Sometimes, a jokey competitive air takes over, as fighter pilots squabble with Marines, for example, over which served with a superior force.

While in the *Seancody* video the actor/model playing the bottom is much more clearly marked as such, identified *as* the gay man eager to pleasure the straight actor/model who plays the role of the top, in the *All-American Heroes* video these roles, while still in place, are also not as clearly marked. There is a more general sense in the *All-American* videos that both men are straight, and that therefore the drama as well as the presumed erotic appeal lies in seeing one straight man "go gay" live on camera and perform sexual services on another straight man. For the most part, the top in these videos remains impassive, not even uttering a sound as he receives sexual stimulation from the bottom (usually first through fellatio). The straight male performs his archetypal straightness—the affectional modes of rectitude, impassivity, blankness, stolidity, stoicism—even as he is being transitioned into the ecstatic state of libidinal pleasure that is usually associated with the loss of control and the involuntary expression of reactions to somatic and possibly emotional stimulation. Indeed, the point of this video is to track the seismic shifts in the straight male subject's somatic and bodily comportment, to stand witness to his responses, if they come at all, the suspense generated over his possible responses accounting for a considerable amount of the video's effect overall.

Typically, the video begins with the two male subjects, after they have been interviewed, sitting on a bed (or a sofa, if the video takes place in a home setting), each slowly beginning to masturbate as they watch a porn video. This video—the porn within the porn—is never shown in the frame of the video we watch; it is always relegated to off-screen space. The porn that the male subjects watch is also always heterosexual porn. We know this because (a) the male subjects of the video are always presented as unimpeachably straight, and would therefore only be watching hetero porn; moreover, the men comment on the porno's action, specifically the women in it, and the kinds of sexual experiences they would like to have with these women, and (b) because we *hear* the male and especially female performers of the porn film the men watch having sex. I say "especially" female, because, as the sounds of the unseen but quite audible porn-within-the-porn make clear, heterosexual porn enunciates itself, literally, through the representation of female pleasure that is conveyed through high decibel levels as well as "the frenzy of the visual," to echo Linda Williams.

Sound emerges as the multivalent medium through which numerous levels of heterosexual authenticity are established and maintained in the *All-American Heroes* video. The near-constant, and extremely audible, sexual soundscape foregrounds, especially, women's voices. Female cries of pleasure diegetically surround—indeed engulf—the scene of homosexual sex that occupies the frame. From a psychoanalytic sense, the video returns the straight male subject to the pre-Oedipal stage of physical and emotional closeness to the mother. Indeed, the entire enterprise of the porn video as designed at this website does away with the Oedipal father, focusing on the experiences of the "sons" who have gone to battle for the patriarchal father/nation and have returned to recount their histories together. The symbolic father—in the guise of Uncle Sam, who sent the men to war; the porno industry producer; the actor/model in the unseen but constantly heard video having sex with the ecstatically screaming woman—is relegated to off-screen space as well.

The engulfing sounds of women's sexual cries—what Natalie Purcell describes in *Pornography and Violence* as the "pornovoice" of the women performers of straight porn, their screams, wails, moans, and exclamations of encouragement—is worth considering here, given that women's screams of panic, fear, terror, and suffering are associated so thoroughly with the horror genre, and also given that the innovative novelty of a film such as *Hostel* is that it specifically replaces these cries with those of terrified, violated, murdered men. As Natalie Purcell notes in reference to women's numerous uttered sounds in porn,

> it strains the imagination to believe that they are either spontaneous or authentic (any regular porn viewer knows this and is not fooled). Using the ubiquitous "pornovoice"—a high-pitched, ultra-feminine wail—the women deliver lines like "I love that great big cock in my tiny little pussy." They are generally expected to make noise throughout the scene—to pant, moan, scream, and cheerlead constantly.[29]

Josh's screams in *Hostel* both simulate and substitute for the sounds of screaming women in horror, but they also—especially given the homoerotically tinged sexual intrigue of his being tortured by the Dutch Businessman—evoke the female pornovoice, especially in that so much of straight pornography revolves around the idea of female submission to masculine will. At the same time, Josh's oddly serene expression when dead, his body lying on a heap of broken bodies of other victims, intersects with one of the prevailing fantasies of straight porn. Just as Josh's expression, which Paxton stares up at, suggests that somehow he condones and has also been complicit in his violation and destruction, straight porn relies, as Laura Kipnis has argued persuasively, on the sense that women desire sex in the same impersonal way that men do, and that women either willingly join in with the scene of their own sexual subjugation or secretly want to do so despite their most vociferous protests. Josh, in his faulty performance of heterosexual masculinity, has basically wanted his own torture-laden demise.

In a discussion of Jack Deveau's film *Night at the Adonis* (1977), filmed primarily on location at the famous Adonis theater in Manhattan, "an early twentieth-century midtown movie palace somewhat typically turned porn theater," Rich Cante and Angelo Restivo consider the uses of sound in the film within the film in *this* film, a "documentary" that the filmed spectators at the Adonis watch. "By seizing spectators equally and indiscriminately, the sound of the movie creates the 'democratic' space for sexual possibility within *Night at the Adonis*. The sound of the pornographic film is (generally) posited as giving ultimate voice to the utopian sexual possibilities of pornogay prgraphic space."[30] In *All-American Heroes*'s videos, the incessant, intensifying sounds of women's voices do not signal utopian possibilities but, rather, metonymically signal the all-pervasiveness and inescapability of heterosexuality as the totalizing and binding sexual standard. They signal heterosexuality understood as the production of women's cries: in childbirth, in sexual suffering/ecstasy, during scenes of male violence, all of which experiences equally lend themselves to what I have called pornographication, especially the discussion of the concept of "pornographication" of the male consumer of pornography, the compulsory submission to pornographic sexuality that defines our long cultural moment from the 1960s to the present.[31] In an inadvertently parodistic fashion, the female pornovoice both signifies and supports the structures of male dominance that undergird conventional hetero porn (and homo porn as well, to be sure). The grisly semi-parody here lies in the fact that the woman seems to be cheering on her own subjugation. Similarly, in slasher-horror movies, the female "horrorvoice" on increasingly high-decibel display registers the suffering of *all* of the victims, the males (whose screams are quieter and less prolonged, usually) as well as the females, and also has the special burden of "atoning" for the sexual sins that provide the rationale for why the victims of these films are terrorized and killed in the first place.

Michel Chion's well-known study *The Voice in Cinema* is an obvious place to turn here. Chion discusses the relationship of the voice to the body in film, the processes whereby the voice without a body (such as the infamous Mrs. Bates) comes to acquire one. Surprisingly enough, Chion has very little to say about pornography despite this genre's fetishistic reliance on sound for its effects and its obvious reliance on the body for these as well. But what he does say, in many ways, says it all: "For showing everything, including the unshowable region of off-screen space, think of pornography and violence, which leave nothing to the imagination. They leave nothing to say, either. These are images to render the voice speechless."[32] In many ways, the women's voices that suffuse the aural world of the *All-American* video but are thoroughly relegated to off-screen space must do the work of representing gay sexual pleasure for the silent "straight" men on the screen whose taciturn anti-vocality not only signifies but provides the final bulwark against their onscreen degradation, as presented. The torturing of "straight" men has become porn fodder for an audience unwilling to acknowledge the realities of torture within a geopolitical context, certainly not the United States' investment in torture, and unwilling to believe that straight men could desire physical proximity to other men, much less sex with other men, without being tortured into doing it. Hence the valences between *Hostel* and gay male Internet pornography. While critics such as Michael Johnson, Jr., following Lauren Berlant and Michael Warner, have found radicalism in gay porn's deemphasization of conventional narratives of love and commitment, there is little radicalism on display in the venues we have considered in this chapter. Instead, these venues rampantly promulgate the heteromasculine and, frequently, white racial standard to the exclusion of any other potentiality. Another possible approach to pornography that I have not pursued in this chapter is the question of fantasy and its destabilizing potentialities. While theories of fantasy and mobile, polyvalent forms of identification, such as those eloquently limned by Elizabeth Cowie, are certainly germane to any study of pornography, my political reading of commercially produced Internet gay porn has emphasized the homophobic, limiting, indeed carceral aspects of the form.[33]

Thomas Waugh, in the midst of a consideration of Victorian-era gay pornography, speculates more generally that

> there is a continuity in the trajectory of gay eroticism beyond the pleasure of men looking at images of men: the codes of

subterfuge, sublimation, and shame with which we have had to mask and divert that pleasure from the beginning. The discourse of the Alibi becomes the determining framework for gay eroticism, even for those illicit and bohemian currents most liberated from social control.[34]

Waugh's words, as always, are so insightful to the genealogy of homosexual subjectivity from the Victorian era into the twentieth century. We are now living in an era in which—haven't they?—the masks have been discarded, the need to divert our pleasures has transmuted into the pursuit of endless queer diversions, and no Alibi need exist any longer.

The straight male of gay Internet pornographic narratives—these porn videos tell a story and should therefore be seen as narratives; the story they tell, an old one now revamped, center on the seduction of the innocent, the torture and terrorization of this innocent, and the rescue of the innocent, a narrative structure emblematic of the Gothic genre—is not used as the Alibi of gay porn. How can he be, when this media form's brazen public existence evinces the transcendence of the need for an Alibi? Rather, what had underpinned the Alibi has transformed into the story itself: the need to maintain a visible public heterosexual identity has now itself become the eroticized subject. The queer viewers have now become the torturers, placed in this role by a culture that can only understand sexual interest in the male body from other males as a pernicious form of violation.

Coda

I do not mean to suggest that good movies—in this context, challenging, not easily classified movies—are not being made. I have pointed out the genuine virtues of *I Love You, Man*, as well as of Zombie's *Halloween* remakes. The films of Derek Cianfrance that star Ryan Gosling—*Blue Valentine* (2010) and *The Place Beyond the Pines* (2012); Kelly Reichardt's enigmatic, frustrating, and beautiful films such as *Old Joy* (2006) and *Meek's Cutoff* (2010), starring Michelle Williams; Lynne Ramsay's *We Need to Talk About Kevin* (2011), driven by the brilliant performances of Ezra Miller as the titular troubled, and ultimately murderous, Kevin and Tilda Swinton as his mother: Ira Sachs's films about gay desire and American masculinity such as *Keep the Lights On* (2012) and, especially, *The Delta* (1996), come immediately to mind as challenging and provocative and also stimulatingly complex. *Elephant: A Film by Gus Van Sant* (2004) and Van Sant's *Gerry* (2002) along with Todd Haynes's corpus all inspire sustained reflection. I continue to love and cherish Ang Lee's *Brokeback Mountain*, his 2005 adaptation of E. Annie Proulx's short story, routinely treated today to a backlash by gay male critics, as well as Tom Ford's 2008 adaptation of Christopher Isherwood's *A Single Man*, similarly critiqued.[1] After being dismayed by the rampant male privilege on display in his study of sexual addiction and despair, *Shame* (2011), starring Michael Fassbender, I found myself overwhelmed by the beauty, rigor, and analytical depth of Steve McQueen's *12 Years a Slave* (2013), based on Solomon Northup's memoir. Overall, this has not been a great time for film, to say the least, much to television drama's benefit. I wish that I had the space here to discuss my admiration for post-millennial works such as *Six Feet Under* (HBO, 2001–05), *Mad Men* (AMC, 2007–15), *The Walking Dead* (2010–present), *The Fall* (BBC, 2013–present), *Top of the Lake* (Sundance, 2013), *Hannibal* (NBC, 2013–2015), and *Looking* (HBO, 2013–2015), all of which I would make a strong case for as both stimulating and resistant television, especially in terms of the multilayered depiction of masculinity (and in the case of *The Fall* and *Top of the Lake* career femininity). What happens next, as film itself vanishes into the digital age, is anyone's guess, but we can at least keep watching—and watching out. Michelle Williams's indelible line in *Meek's Cutoff*—a stunning deconstruction of the racist underpinnings of nineteenth-century America's cult of male supremacy—seems especially apt: "I'd be wary."

Notes

Introduction

1. Some of my arguments on television masculinities in *Dexter* (Showtime, 2006–2013), *The Walking Dead* (2010–present), and *Breaking Bad* (AMC, 2008–2013) have been offered in a series of essays in the online journal *Flow*, from 2012 through 2013. See also my essays "The Return of the Father," on the HBO series *Deadwood* (2004–06), and "Spectral Men," on the ghost-hunter Reality TV shows.

2. See Greven, chapter 1, *Manhood in Hollywood from Bush to Bush*.

3. Strikingly enough, Kevin Costner's Pa Kent in Zach Snyder's Superman epic *Man of Steel* (2013) actually immolates himself in just such a manner, offering himself up to the winds of a terrifying tornado and thereby sacrificing himself so that his son Clark (Henry Cavill), who will be Superman, will not be exposed as a superhuman being in a rescue attempt of his human father.

4. Connell, *Masculinities*, 85–86.

5. Richard Dyer, "The White Man's Muscles," in *Race and the Subject of Masculinities*, 301.

6. See Rich, "The New Queer Cinema: Director's Cut," *New Queer Cinema*, 16–33.

7. Daring and inspiring films constituting a new queer canon proliferated from the early 1990s to the mid-'00s (*My Own Private Idaho* [Gus Van Sant, 1991], *Mulholland Drive* [David Lynch, 2001], *Far from Heaven* [Todd Haynes, 2002], *Tarnation* [Jonathan Caouette, 2003], *Brokeback Mountain* [Ang Lee, 2005]). Difficult, controversial works have deserved reassessment, not just putting pain and suffering on display but exploring the genuine anguish and also the incoherence of national demands for normative gender as well as sexual identity (*The Silence of the Lambs* [Jonathan Demme, 1991]).

8. Analogously, a gay-rights movement that sought to demonstrate that gays and lesbians were indistinguishable from other Americans, that they cared about the same values and were raising families, that they deserved equal protection under the law, the right to serve in the military, and even the right to marry, also gained momentum at this time. The in-your-face politics of queer activists such as the

AIDS-agitation group ACT UP uneasily coincided with the rise of grassroots gay-rights groups. If ACT UP knocked communion wafers out of Archbishops' hands, grassroots gay-rights groups appropriated one of the major thematics of the era for its own purposes, as evinced by the slogan "Hate is not a family value." Family Values—family as a value, the value of families, the relationship between economic value and the family—is a core aspect of the rhetoric of gay rights today as organized around the effort to legalize gay marriage, successfully achieved in 2015.

    9. As David Lugowski writes, "In a society that reads sexuality in terms of gender, masculinity and heterosexuality are linked in hegemonic discourses; masculinity-in-film is 'ideally' white, male, bourgeois, Christian, and not physically challenged. Queer theory paralleled developments within critical race theory, cultural studies, postcolonial and film theory, and these discourses have informed each other compellingly. Analyses of film returned the favor, influencing these theories within their disciplines (literature, women's studies, area studies)" (95). See Lugowski, "Ginger Rogers and Gay Men?" See also Doty, *Making Things Perfectly Queer*.

    As I argued in *Manhood in Hollywood from Bush to Bush*, a peculiar osmosis occurred in the 1990s whereby mainstream representation began to reflect these innovations in critical theory and its understanding of sexual history and subjectivity in the new queer moment. Film, too, both independent and dominant-culture-based began to evince a queer awareness of the continuum of sexualities as well as genders, rather than the hard and fast categories of male/female, straight/queer, and, of course, black/white.

    10. Love, *Feeling Backward*, 2.

    11. Puar writes,

> Taking the position that heterosexuality is a necessary constitutive factor of national identity, the "outlaw" status of homosexual subjects in relation to the state has been a long-standing theoretical interest of feminist, postcolonial, and queer theorists. This outlaw status is mediated through the rise during the 1980s and 1990s of the gay consumer, pursued by marketers who claimed that childless homosexuals had enormous disposable incomes, as well as through legislative gains in civil rights . . . [such as the *Lawrence and Garner v. Texas* decision of 2003].

Puar, *Terrorist Assemblages*, 4. I do not want to suggest that exciting, idiosyncratic works like HBO's *Looking* should be lumped into a suspect consumerist aesthetic (i.e., a cable network simply churning out product for its affluent customers). But the pervasiveness of queer images in contemporary representation is less than comforting when analyses such as Puar's are taken into account.

    12. Queerness threatens dominant culture because it imagines alternative social arrangements that may be just as, if not more, satisfying than those offered by the existing social order and ways of feeling and being that exceed the social. The dominant culture has investments in deferring and delimiting the queer pres-

ence; even in these much more enlightened times, homophobia remains a persistent problem in the United States, to say nothing of other parts of the world.

13. Shary, "Introduction," *Millennial Masculinity*, 7.

14. Jackson, "The 9/11 Attacks and the Social Construction of a National Narrative," *The Impact of 9/11 on the Media, Arts, and Entertainment*, 29.

15. Parker, *Save the Males*, x.

16. Ron Becker makes a similar point in his essay "Straight Men, Gay Men, and Male Bonding," *Reading the Bromance*.

17. Lotz, *Cable Guys*, 192–23.

18. In addition to *Magic Mike*, Soderbergh films such as the 2009 *The Girlfriend Experience*, a wholly misogynistic work despite its purported critique of such attitudes, belie his status as a progressive filmmaker.

19. *Behind the Candelabra* perpetuates several gay stereotypes, being essentially the typical story of a predatory gay man who seduces and corrupts a more authentically masculine male innocent. That it is based on a true story—the turbulent six-year relationship between the famous musical performer Liberace (Michael Douglas) and his lover, Scott Thorson (Matt Damon), who was much younger—has led some critics to celebrate its odd mixture of glitz and Kubrickian coldness.

20. Berger, *Ways of Seeing*, 54.

21. There is a similar moment in *Boogie Nights* (Paul Thomas Anderson, 1997) when the maker of porn films played by Burt Reynolds, appraising porn star-in-the making Dirk Diggler (Mark Wahlberg), asks him to strip down, saying, "I think that there's something wonderful going on in those pants." The porn-producer role and porn milieu here, resolutely classified as heterosexual, allow this male-male sexual appreciation to occur without incurring the wrath, even in this seemingly racy, ribald film about the sex industry, of homophobic reaction.

22. Benshoff, *Queer Images*, 6.

23. Forster, "Rad Romance," *Reading the Bromance*, 210.

24. Gledhill, "Introduction," *Gender Meets Genre in Postwar Cinemas*, 6.

25. Grant, *Film Genre*, 4.

26. Grant, *Film Genre*, 82.

27. Grant, *Shadows of Doubt*, 6–7.

28. Some notable exceptions exist, such as the female-centered comedy *Bridesmaids* (Paul Feig, 2011) on the one hand, and horror movies like *Mama* (Andres Muschietti, 2013) and *The Descent* (Neil Marshall, 2005) on the other hand.

29. That infamous 1974 film was directed by Tobe Hooper and praised by Robin Wood as one of the great works in the horror genre of the 1970s, exemplary of what Wood called "The American Nightmare." That not only another reboot-remake of the original *Chainsaw* (Marcus Nispel, 2003) but also a prequel film (2006) were released within the '00s attests to the enduring power of not only this film but the stature that '70s and '80s horror works have gained. Indeed, the 2013 3-D version debuted with a bonanza box-office take. ("Never underestimate the Chainsaw," said one industry analyst.) As I will show in chapter 5, not all of these remakes—though alarming in what they suggest about the paucity of creative

imagination in the industry—can simply be dismissed as dull genre fodder, Rob Zombie's films especially.

30. See White, "Problems of Knowledge in Feminist Film Theory," 278–98.

31. See chapter 1 of *Manhood in Hollywood from Bush to Bush*.

32. Neale, "Masculinity," *Sexual Subject*, 280–81.

33. Rodowick, "The Difficulty of Difference," *Wide Angle*, 1982, vol. 5, no.1, quoted by Neale, 281.

34. Neale, "Masculinity," *Sexual Subject*, 281.

35. Mulvey herself has also written an immense body of scholarship well beyond her 1975 article, including "Afterthoughts to 'Visual Pleasure,'" in which she does address female desire but argues that the female spectator is essentially in a masochistic position due to her transvestic role, in that she can only inhabit the male-gendered spectatorial subject position. A discrete and worthwhile project would be to examine the Mulvey archive for shifting views on gaze theory and masculinity's relationship to it, but my own sense of her work is that queer issues rarely ever enter into her discussions.

36. Hence Tasker's introduction of the term "musculinity" in her analysis of the action cinema and the male body: "'Musculinity' indicates the extent to which a physical definition of masculinity in terms of a developed musculature is not limited to the male body in representation." Tasker goes on to examine the female action stars/heroines of the late 1980s and early-to-mid 1990s. Tasker, *Spectacular Bodies*, 3. I am, perhaps, offering the inverse of Tasker's theory, since I focus on what happens to male subjects and male bodies when subjected to the kinds of invasive narrative and cinematic techniques to which females of the cinema have historically been subjected.

37. Holmlund's impossible bodies include three basic types: outrageous (Schwarzenegger, Dolly Parton, Jennifer Lopez, and others offered as examples), constrained (interracial and lesbian desire offered as examples, but also the casting of Swedes as anything other than Swedes), and invisible (the presence of Asian-American actors in westerns, for example). See Holmlund, *Impossible Bodies*, 5.

38. Williams, "Film Bodies," 4.

39. Williams, "Film Bodies," 4.

40. The question of comedy and the body is an extensive one that has been addressed by several critics; see especially Bergson; Clayton. Williams's omission of comedy from body genres is especially strange since comedy is often considered a lowbrow form par excellence, especially in terms of frat-house, gross-out, teen, beta male, and bromantic comedies from the 1970s to the present. Of course, drawing room and manners comedy is on the highbrow end.

41. I would argue that the male side of melodrama has not made a large impact on post-millennial film, despite some important exceptions such as the styles of masculinity on display in Joe Wright's *Anna Karenina* (2012) and Ang Lee's *Brokeback Mountain* (2005). These works might be placed in the category of "the reimagined melodrama"—in Wright's case, the non-musical musical, in Lee's, a gay love story. In terms of melodrama and masculinity, the films of Derek Cianfrance that star Ryan Gosling—*Blue Valentine* (2010) and *The Place Beyond the Pines*

(2012)—are highly interesting meditations of melodrama, the latter being a fusion of melodrama and neo-noir.

42. Lehman, "Crying Over the Melodramatic Penis," 27. Lehman quotes from Richard Dyer's 1982 *Screen* essay "Don't Look Now."

43. Lehman, "Crying Over the Melodramatic Penis," 26–27, 39.

44. In Poe's story, the dying Valdemar has been hypnotized on the very verge of death; the men of science who stand around his bed observe his sustained state of near-deathness. When they finally release him from hypnosis, his body deliquesces into a pool of putrescence.

45. Preserving his hipster cred, Coupland's next sentence is, "I can't believe I just wrote the last sentence, but it's true: there is something psychically sparse about the present era, and artists of all stripes are responding with fresh strategies." See Coupland, "Convergences 'Gods Without Men' by Hari Kunzru," pp. 1, 10.

46. Corber, *Cold War Femme*, 75.

47. Sternberg, "Get More Action," *Reality Gendervision*, 198–99.

48. Tatum's brilliant performance in the 2014 film *Foxcatcher* is required viewing for those who would dismiss him as a mere *hunkus Americanus* and a leaden, one-note screen presence.

49. In 2014 alone, media frenzies over this topic, fueled by social media such as Twitter, Pinterest, Instagram, Facebook, and the like, swirled around debates over whether or not the outline of Afro-British actor Idris Elba's penis was visible within his trousers during a photo shoot; why the American actor Justin Theroux's endowments are made so visible on the HBO series *The Leftovers*, which premiered in 2014; and, of course, the Irish actor Michael Fassbender's penchant for full-frontal nudity.

50. For a discussion of these problems in periodicity, see Gladstone and Worden.

51. Of course, one can say that 9/11 is always already being represented even—perhaps especially—in texts that make no explicit mention of the event. Anna Froula's essay "9/11—What's That?" on the largely ignored, and quite compelling, Fox television series *The Sarah Connor Chronicles* (2008–09) makes a persuasive case for just such a view and uses Freud's theory of repetition-compulsion and trauma to make it. Froula demonstrates precisely what makes this series a significant post-9/11 text without ignoring the series' own forays into conservative re-entrenchment. "In the shadows of 9/11, the television show's flash-forwards to Los Angeles as toxic rubble under siege by an inhuman enemy eerily take on the contours of the crumbled World Trade Center." As Froula further demonstrates, the series manages to be most significant as a 9/11 text by skipping over the actual event of 9/11. This allows Froula to bring in trauma theory and the concept that one is uncannily, inescapably "possessed" by a traumatic event.

52. Examples of the interest in issues of temporality in narrative theory today include Elizabeth Freeman, *Time Binds*; Heather Love, *Feeling Backward*; Wai Chee Dimock, *Through Other Continents*. Freeman is particularly salient on the issue of the ways in which investments in political issues in distinct time periods, while being broadly related to one another (like, say, feminism and trans activism), do not always correspond neatly and undergo a rhetorical and political violence in being

homogenized. Love emphasizes the ways in which "bad feelings" from earlier and more demonstrably homophobic eras get de-emphasized in the push toward pride and other affirmational aspects of contemporary queer rhetoric. Dimock in a different literary project altogether dazzlingly traces the lineages of literary traditions over the centuries from ancient writings to the present day; in so doing she reminds us of the interconnectivity of representation. Dimock develops her concept of "deep time" as she traces these lineages.

53. Several recent studies have reexamined the depictions of masculinity in the films of the period. See Kirshner, *Hollywood's Last Golden Age* (2012); Nystrom, *Hard Hats, Rednecks, and Macho Men* (2009); and my own *Psycho-Sexual* (2012).

54. Luciano, *Looking Good*, 153. As Luciano further observes, the obsession with male body image and physical attractiveness on the part of contemporary males does not mean that men are becoming more feminized. It is, instead, part of a "quintessential male strategy whose ultimate aim is to make men more successful, competitive, and powerful" Luciano, *Looking Good*, 12.

55. Ibid, 154.

56. Appiah and Gates, *Africana*, 90.

57. Dunn, *"Baad Bitches" and Sassy Supermamas*, 24.

58. For discussions of the '80s hard body and the '90s New Man, see Susan Jeffords's now-classic study, *Hard Bodies*.

59. For a discussion of the homoerotic homophobia and sexual conservatism of *Fight Club*, see the chapter on the film in Greven, *Manhood in Hollywood from Bush to Bush*.

60. Jeanine Basinger identifies the Bliss Montage or the Happy Interlude as a signature device of the woman's film genre of classic Hollywood, the brief interlude in the heroine's life in which she can be happy, one that occurs "after she meets the man" and "before he lets her down." See Basinger, *A Woman's View*, 8.

61. For example, the first four episodes of the second season of the HBO Western series *Deadwood* (which aired for three seasons between 2004 and 2006) made the kidney-stone ailment of its major male character, Al Swearengen, the owner of the Gem Saloon, the central dramatic focus. The four-episode arc concludes with a scene in which Al's various employees, who might more accurately be called devotees, hold him up as he passes the stone out through his urethra. Al's heroic micturition is the culmination of the series' obsessive interests in his body's phallic potentialities, central to narrative even as Al is presented as aged and sallow. See my essay "The Return of the Father" on *Deadwood*.

Chapter 1

1. I generally admire both *The Sopranos* and *The Walking Dead*. What I am attempting to point out here is their perhaps inevitable complicity with a post-millennial culture of the death-drive that takes ever more pleasure in the spectacles of mayhem, joylessness, and death.

2. Conversely, a great deal of innovatively escapist fare also defines this decade: the rebirth of 3-D, the endless spate of comic-book hero movies (culminating in the reboot of the Spiderman franchise just a few years after it had already *been* rebooted), Reality TV and its endless parade of intellect-free entertainment, the renewed and rabid focus on entertainment- and celebrity-gossip, the explosion of Internet porn, and so forth.

3. Pollard, "Hollywood 9/11: Time of Crisis," *The Impact of 9/11 on the Media, Arts, and Entertainment*, 206.

4. 9/11's impact cannot be overstated, nor its calamitous domino-effect. "A rapid fire series of events—the troubled 2000 presidential election (which many considered stolen), the al-Qaeda assaults of 9/11, the resulting 'war on terror' and the Iraq War—have changed the political landscape and produced radical shifts in the daily lives and concerns of Americans," observes Charles Musser in an essay on the post-9/11 documentary form. If in the immediate aftermath of 9/11 media outlets, among other centers of knowledge, understandably wished to lend its support to President Bush, significant disturbances in the national life made this allegiance much harder to maintain. As Bush "shifted his focus from al-Qaeda and the Taliban in Afghanistan to Saddam Hussein and Iraq, underlying structural changes that hampered a questioning, independent media became more apparent" (10). See Musser, "Film Truth in the Age of George W. Bush."

5. In his 1924 essay "The Economic Problem of Masochism," a decisive shift in Freud's thinking on the subject occurs. Whereas he previously conjectured that masochism stemmed from an original sadism, in 1924 Freud takes the view of masochism as primary and erotogenic, the remnant of the human being's original death drive. What modified it, kept it from dominating, was the life-instinct, or libido, a crucial component of Freudian theory that tends to get de-emphasized, due to the cachet achieved by his theory of the death-drive presented in his later *Beyond the Pleasure Principle*, in which he argues that the chief drive of human beings, what we most ardently desire, is to move from life to inorganic lifelessness, stasis, death. See Freud, "The Economic Problem of Masochism" (1923–25), in vol. 14 of *The Standard Edition of the Complete Psychological Works of Sigmund Freud*. I discuss Freud's linkages between masochism and the death-drive at length in chapter 1 of *Manhood in Hollywood from Bush to Bush*.

6. Shaviro's *The Cinematic Body* is one of my favorite books of film criticism and has had a powerful influence on my own work, despite the fact that Shaviro is hostile to psychoanalytic theory. I dissent, however, from Shaviro's celebration of masochism and abjection as radical modes of spectatorship. As I elaborate in *Manhood in Hollywood from Bush to Bush*, masochism, while it certainly has its uses as a theoretical construct, especially in academic theory of the early- to mid-90s, too often lends itself to a vision of political cinema as political because of its foundation in ugliness and despair.

7. One has only to watch any given episode of the Fox network sitcom *New Girl* (2011–present) to see that masculinity has been opened-up while any non-normative sexual possibilities have been shut down. *New Girl*, the premise of which

lends itself to sexual speculation, stars Zooey Deschanel as Jess, a schoolteacher who lives with three roommates (eventually four) who are all heterosexual males. While her roommates and their somatic and psychic lives are not only made maximally visible but linked to regressive early stages of psychosexual development, Jess successfully leads a highly sexually un-suspect life, as do her roommates. Masculinity is rendered newly available for satirical exploration but left resolutely intact in terms of normative gender and sexual roles.

8. In *Point Break*, Keanu Reeves's undercover FBI agent Johnny Utah infiltrates the inner ranks of a male group of surfers who are also bank robbers, led by Patrick Swayze's Zen-master surfer Bodhi. Bigelow's film lingers on the beauty of male bodies, in groups and in isolation, in water, on land, and in the air. Yvonne Tasker writes of *Point Break* that it "brings together action, comedy and an exploration of the sexualized relationship between the two protagonists: all aspects familiar from the buddy movie format." I would argue that *Point Break* goes much farther in its exploration of the sexual nature of the male-male relationship than the usual buddy film, a point which Tasker's own analysis supports: "*Point Break* is also very much concerned with different images of masculinity, diverse masculine identities. . . . [it] delights in the bodies of its male protagonists. Bigelow has described the film as a 'wet western'. . . . Themes and images [of westerns of the past] . . . are intertwined with the need for contemporary films to present their heroes either nearly naked, or in the need for clinging costumes that display the body." This commodification of the male body registers, Tasker argues, 90s shifts in masculine identities and how they are defined." Tasker, *Spectacular Bodies*, 162. As I touch on in the last chapter, Tarantino's *Reservoir Dogs* evinces a similar new interest in the potentialities of representing the male body, but, as is characteristic of his sensibility, Tarantino focuses on the dismemberment and torture of this body, the varieties of violation. Mr. Blonde, or Vic Vega (Michael Madsen), one of the group of criminals behind a failed jewelry heist, ambles out, in real time, of the big hangar in which a cop, bound to a chair, awaits Mr. Blonde's return with the proper tools for torture and mutilation.

9. Tim Edwards, "Spectacular Pain," *Sex, Violence, and the Body*, 175.

10. In Deleuze's *Masochism: An Interpretation of Coldness and Cruelty*, a study of the work of Leopold von Sacher-Masoch, especially his most famous novel *Venus in Furs*, the template for masochistic male sexuality, Deleuze challenges the prevailing psychoanalytic understanding of masochism as the inversion of sadism—that, if sadism is the lust to inflict pain, masochism is simply the lust to experience inflicted pain. The most brilliant achievement of Deleuze's study is that he defamiliarizes each process to the extent that they do indeed come to seem mutually exclusive. Amongst the several crucial differences in both modes of achieving sexual gratification that Deleuze enumerates, one of the most important is that, whereas sadism "operates with the negative and pure negation, masochism operates through "disavowal and suspension." Disavowal constitutes the core of the strategy of fetishism, which seeks to disavow knowledge of the mother's missing phallus. The mother, so crucial to fetishism, crucially informs, indeed occupies the center of, masochism, hence the

chief difference between it and sadism is that whereas sadism negates the mother and inflates the father, masochism abolishes the father and makes the mother central. Deleuze, *Masochism*, 134.

11. Benjamin, *The Bonds of Love*, 55.
12. Benjamin, *The Bonds of Love*, 68–69.
13. Gerstner, *Manly Arts*, 214.
14. In many ways, I would suggest, this occurs as the result of a lack of auteurist creativity in the period. There are still auteurs whose work speaks to masculinity and/or focuses on it as a complex and onerous problem—Lars von Trier, Christopher Nolan, Quentin Tarantino, Michael Haneke—but of this grouping Haneke is the only one whose work I would be interested in thinking through as a potentially radical voice (as of this writing I am far from convinced of that). The period has had no David Cronenberg or Brian De Palma—save for Cronenberg and De Palma themselves, who continue to make brilliant movies—an idiosyncratic, daring stylist who takes issues of masculinity to the breaking point. Judd Apatow, as I will discuss in chapter 3, is certainly an auteur in the sense of being a director with a personal vision, but I will say that with rare exceptions his work, particularly in the beta male genre that he innovated, hits resolutely reactionary notes.
15. See, for example, the essays collected in *Mysterious Skin*, edited by Santiago Fouz-Hernández. I found Gary Needham's discussion in his essay "Closer than Ever" of the representation of male bodies, particularly close-ups of the penis, in contemporary French cinema to be a particularly interesting overlap with my own concerns. While noting their limitations and retrogressive aspects, Needham nevertheless finds the films he considers to be "far more compelling than their sassy American post-closet counterparts. One thing that is very striking about 'New Queer Cinema' and the films that come after is the ongoing reluctance to really invest in the male body as an aesthetic object, to show male nudity or even be close to the male body, seeing it in detail. 'Courtesy covering' is still the mainstay of many films and the flash of penis in recent queer films *Eating Out* (dir. Q. Allan Brocka, 2004) and *Testosterone* (dir. David Moreton, 2003) is often a brief split-second and thoroughly token gesture to get the mainstream gay audience hooked through clandestine images that circulate in the blogosphere. In recent US queer films, bodies are filmed at a modest distance offering an indication of something that the film cannot deliver with any intellectual or aesthetic commitment beyond the glimpse." Needham, "Closer than Ever," 130. (I would add that I found *Testosterone* to be an abysmally misconceived film.)

In general, far more daring work on the treatment of masculinity has been conducted in the international cinema of the 2000s than that being done in the United States. I have been impressed by the work of artists such as the French director Christophe Honoré. His films *Les chansons d'amour/Love Songs* (2007) and the 2006 *Dans Paris* brilliantly explore the varieties of queer desire and also their place within the family, which undergoes probing analysis in his films (the relationship between the brothers in *Dans Paris* and its homoerotic complexities, for example). The Argentine Marcelo Piñeyro made a great 2001 film *Plata quemada* (English:

Burnt Money), an action thriller written by Piñeyro and Marcelo Figueras based on a real-life case about gay bank robbers in 1960s Argentina. I have written about the film for the online publication *Bright Lights Film Journal*. The great French director Catherine Breillat's film *À ma sœur!* (2001; English title, *Fat Girl*) uses graphic, explicit depictions of tumescent male sexual organs and heterosexual sexual intercourse in her film to convey the heroine's suffering and emotional violation. The overweight teen protagonist Anaïs Pingot (Anaïs Reboux) is forced to witness her older, much more conventionally attractive sister having sex with a handsome, dark-haired young man because she happens to be in the same room as her sister and her boyfriend. Breillat's point, as I take it, is that the young couple having sex do not even notice that the "fat girl" is there and/or are indifferent to her presence. At the same time, Anaïs's sister Elena (Roxane Mesquida) clearly suffers through this experience, pressured into having sex by her boyfriend, as ruthlessly manipulative as he is handsome.

16. See Greven, "Spectral Men," *Reality Gendervision*, for a treatment of the ghost-hunter subgenre of Reality television.

17. *Donnie Darko*'s rabbit-face man grotesquely literalizes the invisible giant bunny seen only by the wealthy, amiable drunk Elwood P. Dowd (James Stewart) in *Harvey* (Henry Koster, 1950), the film version of Mary Chase's play of the same name.

18. To celebrate the resolution of the narrative problem signaled by the title, the forty-year-old virgin sings "The Age of Aquarius" and as he does so the camera focuses on Steve Carell's face. All of the other main male characters sing portions of the song as well in the extended musical sequence that follows. Catherine Keener, who plays the woman who ends the forty years of sexual solitude, is notably absent from the singing, perhaps indicating that she has little reason to celebrate herself now that her main function has been accomplished.

19. First, we think of Gloria Swanson as Norma Desmond in *Sunset Boulevard* (Billy Wilder, 1950) championing the silent era of which she was a legendary star: "We didn't need words—we had *faces*." Clearly, it is Norma Desmond's hypnotic face, in the film clips of her days as a young and lovely silent star and in her present hypnotic spectacle of theatrically defiant older age, that embodies the force of this line. Then there is the long, long close-up of Greta Garbo at the end of *Queen Christina*. One of the first film books I ever bought was called *They Had Faces Then*, a study of the classic Hollywood star. It focused exclusively on women's faces.

20. See, for example, Danielle Henderson's blog-turned-bestselling-book *Feminist Ryan Gosling*.

21. Krutnik, *In a Lonely Street*, 87.

22. In an early scene in David Cronenberg's sci-fi horror film *Scanners* (1981), about aberrant humans with tremendous psycho-kinetic abilities, a lesser Scanner's head explodes onscreen in graphic gory red during a competition with a more powerful Scanner.

23. "You cannot have Gothic without a cruel hero-villain; without a cringing victim; and without a terrible place, some locale, hidden from view, in which the

drama can unfold." He continues, "And these are also the critical elements of sadomasochism. In Freud, the hero-villain is the superego, the heroine the ego, and the terrible inaccessible place the psyche." Edmundson, *Nightmare on Main Street*, 130.

24. Lukasik, *Discerning Characters*, 10.

25. Melville, *Moby-Dick*, 139–40.

26. Interestingly, Hawthorne based the tale on the real-life story of a man known as "Strange Moody," who, in a footnote, Hawthorne describes as

> Another clergyman in New England, Mr. Joseph Moody, of York, Maine, who died about eight years since, made himself remarkable by the same eccentricity that is here related of the Reverend Mr. Hooper. In his case, however, the symbol had a different import. In early life he had accidentally killed a beloved friend; and from that day till the hour of his own death, he hid his face from men.

Hawthorne, "The Minister's Black Veil," *Nathaniel Hawthorne's Tales*, 97.

Infrequently discussed by critics, this footnote explicates that a theme central to Hawthorne's development of the story was one young man's tortured relationship to other men. Having killed a "beloved friend," he now hides his face *from* men. While "men" is used as a collective noun for all people here, to be sure, its gendered significance cannot be ignored (Hawthorne might have said "humanity" or "the world"). The veil connects Hooper to his relationships to other men and to masculinity, even as it effects a barrier between Hooper and the world. It also stands as the material emblem of what bars him from marital and sexual intimacy with women, as his failed marriage prospects—hopes for which he himself dashes by donning the veil—evince.

27. For a representative discussion of the importance of Freud's theory of the return of the repressed to horror, see Wexman, "Trauma," 34n4. Freud's essay "The Uncanny" is collected in vol. 17 of *The Standard Edition of the Complete Psychological Works of Sigmund Freud*. All quotations from Freud will be from the Standard Edition and will be noted parenthetically within the main text.

28. Worland, *Horror Film*, 15

29. See Wood's essay "The American Nightmare: Horror in the 70s," *Hollywood from Vietnam to Reagan . . . and Beyond*, 63–85.

30. Cohen, *How to Read Freud*, 17.

31. Ibid., 73.

32. Ibid., 74–75.

33. Butler, *Bodies*, 5.

34. Butler, *Bodies*, 9.

35. José Esteban Muñoz, "Photographs of Mourning: Melancholia and Ambivalence in Van Der Zee, Mapplethorpe, and *Looking for Langston*," *Disidentifications*, 64–65. Muñoz quotes from De Man's *The Rhetoric of Romanticism*, 75–76. Along similar lines, the essays on Andy Warhol in the reader *About Face* make the point that Warhol's portraits treat faces as the public masks onto which identity is

projected rather than the revealing of a "true" self. What is radical in one artist's work is less so in the mainstream practices that have colonized such sensibilities and techniques.

36. Ahab is on the side of a truth that lies beneath mesmerizing artifice, one that must be pursued no matter how violent the means. If the point of his character is that he can pursue this elusive truth while remaining utterly blind to the truth of his own obsessive insanity, the point of the male mask of the present is to *preserve* the mask, never to strike through it, to deny not only the attempt to strike through the mask but the corollary belief that something exists beneath or behind the mask in the first place.

37. Pomerance, "Introduction: Gender in Film at the End of the Twentieth Century," *Ladies and Gentlemen*, 7.

38. Deleuze and Guattari, *A Thousand Plateaus*, 176.

39. Herzog, "Suspended Gestures," 70.

40. Balázs, "The Close-Up," from *The Spirit of Film*, 109.

41. Fuss makes the case that *Silence* "labors to call up the classic psychoanalytic association of homosexuality with the morbidity, orality, and boundary confusion that define primary identification." "To do this to Jame Gumb," Fuss argues, "the camera must be at its cruelest—and its most cutting; Gumb is optically dismembered as savagely as he is known to have mutilated his victims. Only one kind of body can sustain such thorough inspection or close scrutiny from the camera: the corpse . . . [It] is impossible not to acknowledge in the end a certain insidious equation established in *The Silence of The Lambs* between homosexuality and pathology, between perversion and death." See Fuss, *Identification Papers*, 94–95.

Chapter 2

1. The slasher-horror genre has been amply discussed in criticism. See, for example, Robin Wood, *Hollywood from Vietnam to Reagan*, 198–219; Carol J. Clover, *Men, Women, and Chainsaws*; and Andrew Britton, "Blissing Out: The Politics of Reaganite Entertainment," for an argument about the predictability and ritualistic aspects of horror film. See also Adam Rockoff, *Going to Pieces: The Rise and Fall of the Slasher Film*, and Isabel Cristina Pinedo, *Recreational Terror: Women and the Pleasures of Horror Film Viewing*.

2. See Wood, *Hollywood from Vietnam to Reagan*, 108–15 for an extended discussion of *Last House on the Left* as Vietnam War allegory, and Adam Lowenstein's chapter on the film in *Shocking Representation*.

In Wood's seminal reading of 1970s horror film as the "American Nightmare," Wood discusses *Last House* as a remake of Ingmar Bergman's *The Virgin Spring* (1960), in which a roving band of louts kills a young farm woman in medieval Sweden. A revenge tale, the film concludes with the murdered woman's father (Max Von Sydow) annihilating the men who killed her when they, unbeknownst to them, take shelter with their victim's family. *Last House* ends in a similar vengeful bloodbath, as the parents of one of the two murdered young women kill off their daughters' killers, a sequence that includes the *pièce de résistance* in which the mother bites off the penis of the killer she fellates as a ruse. The allegorical critique of the film, for Wood, also includes the moment in which the killers cut open the body and examine the organs of one of their female victims, which Wood, drawing on Craven's own comments on the scene, interprets as a Vietnam War allegory.

3. See Linda Williams, "Film Bodies: Gender, Genre, and Excess."

4. *Scream* carries forward the deconstructive genre tradition that Craven had initiated with *Wes Craven's New Nightmare* (1994), about the making of a final *Nightmare on Elm Street* film. But in *Scream*, the focus has shifted from a specific concern with one franchise to the slasher-horror genre itself.

5. For a helpful summary of the transitional period of "queer's" emergence in the 1990s, see Suzanna Danuta Walters, *All the Rage: The Story of Gay Visibility in America*.

6. See B. Ruby Rich, *New Queer Cinema*.

7. That Jim's humiliation occurs before a collective gaze and that his body is made available to this gaze through technological means indicates some important shifts in male spectatorial pleasure. In the 1970s and 1980s, the consumer of pornographic films was stereotypically the solitary male who went to porn theaters or porn arcades, alone, and who then, with the transition from these venues to the home video market, rented porn videotapes for private consumption at home. Now, the sexually avid male has himself become the object of visual fascination and pleasure for an audience. *American Pie* indicates the shift from private to more public forms of male sexual performance styles, what I have called the *pornographication* of the male sexual consumer. For an analysis of the shifts in the representation male bodies in the specific period of the late '90s, see Edisol Wayne Dotson, *Behold the Man: The Hype and Selling of Male Beauty in Media and Culture*. For discussions of shifts in the consumption of pornography and its relationship to constructions of American male sexuality, see Greven, *Psycho-Sexual*, especially the discussion of the concept of "pornographication" of the male consumer of pornography, the compulsory submission to pornographic sexuality that defines our long cultural moment from the 1960s to the present; Melendez, "Video Pornography, Visual Pleasure, and the Return of the Sublime," *Porn Studies*, ed. Linda Williams, and several other essays in this reader.

8. See Greven, "Dude, Where's My Gender? Contemporary Teen Comedies and New Forms of American Masculinity," *Cineaste*, vol. 27, no. 3, June 2002.

9. Similarly, Michael Haneke, in his much-discussed Austrian film *Funny Games* (1997; Haneke remade his own film in the United States in 2008), links emergent media technologies to the murderous actions of two seemingly normal young Viennese men, Peter and Paul, who terrorize a wealthy family in their lakeside holiday home in Austria; the character of Paul breaks the fourth wall and talks directly at the camera and at one point even rewinds the primary film text itself to the killers' advantage. Peter and Paul of *Funny Games* force the family members to play various games in order to survive until 9 o'clock the next morning; by the

end of the film, Peter and Paul have killed all of the family members as well as their dog. Paul breaks the fourth wall and talks to the camera—and to the moviegoing audience; after the mother character, Anna, shoots Peter, which may lead to the family's escape from the killers, Paul actually rewinds the film, using a remote control, eliminating her heroic gesture from the narrative and along with it any chance that the victims might escape. As in *Scream*, there is much meta-discussion from the killers about horror movie conventions and, in Haneke's film, how the present film text violates them (defying genre expectations, none of the victims here survive, much less kill either of their tormentors).

10. See Clover, *Men, Women, and Chainsaws*.

11. See Creed, *The Monstrous-Feminine*.

12. While many critics have found Wood's paradigm that horror film enacts "the return of the repressed" of great use, others have also dissented from it. (And famously, Michel Foucault challenged what he called Freud's "repressive hypothesis" altogether.) But Wood himself offered a corrective to his earlier invocation of the theory in discussions of the political radicalism of '70s horror. Discussing what he viewed as the conservatism of '80s horror, he wrote,

> I suggested earlier that the theory of repression offers us a means toward a political categorization of horror movies. Such a categorization, however, can never be rigid or clear-cut. While I have stressed the genre's progressive or radical elements, its potential for subversion of bourgeois patriarchal norms, it is obvious that this potential is never free from ambiguity. The genre carries within itself the capability of reactionary inflection, and perhaps no horror film is entirely immune from its operations. It need not surprise us that a powerful reactionary tradition exists—so powerful it may under certain social conditions become the dominant one. Its characteristics are, in extreme cases, very strongly marked.

Wood, "Horror in the 80s," *Hollywood from Vietnam to Reagan . . . and Beyond*, 170.

13. Natoli, *Speeding to the Millennium*, 11–12. See also Kirsten Moana Thompson, *Apocalyptic Dread*.

14. For an extended discussion of the significance of Hitchcock's doubling of Norman and Sam in *Psycho*, see Greven, *Psycho-Sexual*.

15. See Niall Richardson, "Effeminophobia, Misogyny and Queer Friendship"; Alan Sinfield, *The Wilde Century*.

16. See Freud, *Three Essays on the Theory of Sexuality*, trans. James Strachey, vol. 7, *The Standard Edition of the Complete Psychological Works of Sigmund Freud*, 198. This work initially appeared in print in 1905, but Freud revised and added new material to it repeatedly; his final edition of it was published in 1925.

17. Freud, *Three Essays, The Standard Edition*, vol. 7, 145n1.

18. Fuss, *Identification Papers*, 95.

19. Fuss, *Identification Papers*, 89. For a critique of Fuss's reading as misrepresentative of Demme's film, see chapter 3 in Greven, *Manhood in Hollywood from Bush to Bush*.

20. Freud, *Three Essays, The Standard Edition*, vol. 7, 145n1. This footnote was added by Freud in 1910.

21. For an extended study of mimetic desire as the basis for hysteria, see Juliet Mitchell, *Mad Men and Medusas*.

22. I have argued elsewhere that Carol Clover's theory of the Final Girl needs to be updated through the perspectives of queer theory. For an elaboration of the themes in this section, see Greven, chapter 5, *Representations of Femininity in American Genre Cinema*.

23. The three plays of the trilogy—*Agamemnon, The Libation Bearers, The Eumenides*—set in motion a cycle of murder and revenge that is seemingly irresolvable (much like the killings in slasher-horror works and their sequels). In the first play, the scheming, violent, adulterous Clytemnestra, Agamemnon's wife, kills him upon his return from the Trojan War for having sacrificed their daughter, Iphigenia, for better results in the war. Seeking revenge on his mother for having killed his father, Orestes then kills Clytemnestra. His sister Electra sides with him, the inspiration for the psychoanalytic concept of the "Electra Complex" (though not a concept that Freud endorsed), the woman who sides with male power rather than the mother. The Furies—known, placatingly, as the Eumenides, or The Kindly Ones—hunt down Orestes to make him pay for his crime of matricide. These avenging deities are best understood as allegorical representations of the trauma of violence, what murder leaves ineradicably behind. Finally, Athena, the goddess of wisdom and justice, comes down and holds court. Advised by her fellow god Apollo, she decides Orestes' fate in a trial. This trial, at it has been commonly read, marks the beginnings of the modern Western justice system. Athena's declaration, influenced by Apollo's anti-woman counsel—that she prefers and always sides with the male, and that therefore Orestes is innocent—establishes patriarchal law as such.

24. *The Friday the 13th* film series, exemplary in this regard, features an undead serial killer, Jason Voorhees, who reverences his dead mother, fetishistically maintaining a spooky shrine to her decapitated head.

25. Karlyn, *Unruly Girls, Unrepentant Mothers*, 110–12.

26. The phrase "the beautiful boy as destroyer" is generally used by Camille Paglia in her chapter on Oscar Wilde's novel *The Portrait of Dorian Gray* in *Sexual Personae*.

27. Discussing another proto-bromance, *Grumpy Old Men* (Donald Petrie, 1993), in which the aged former Odd Couple Jack Lemmon and Walter Matthau, playing longtime friends who come to blows over the triangulated figure of Ann-Margaret, Hilary Radner observes, "The primacy of the males and their heterosexuality, or, more properly, their masculinity, is legitimated through their exchange and use of" the Ann-Margaret character, who "may hook up with one or the other," but in doing so will not "affect the relations between men." The woman puts the relationship between the men to the test but also effects a resolution and

a new bonding between them, especially in that each ultimately offers to give up their romantic pursuit of the woman for the sake of the other. While I completely concur with Radner about the conservative uses of the exchange of woman in such narratives, which work to resuture weakening bonds between men, I would argue that films like *Scream* expose the violence in such exchanges on multiple levels, the precarious difficulties of gendered suture. See Radner, "*Grumpy Old Men*: 'Bros Before Hos,'" *Reading the Bromance*, 70–72.

28. Modleski, "An Affair to Forget," 126.

Chapter 3

1. Kay Hymowitz, *Manning Up*; Kathleen Parker, *Save the Males*. Of special interest is that these are books written by women about the afflictions of men in a post-feminist age.

2. For a discussion of the "double-protagonist" film, see my *Manhood in Hollywood from Bush to Bush*. In that the crop of more adult-focused comedies that has flourished in the wake of the teen comedies of the late 1990s focuses on two male stars, this new comedic form evinces some of the trends that I locate in "Bush to Bush" cinema—a focus on pairs of men, rather than the hero or the male group, and, in that the themes inform the very nature of masculinity in contemporary comedy, a split between narcissistic and masochistic modes of male identity.

3. For discussions of the buddy film, see Robin Wood, "From Buddies to Lovers," *Hollywood from Vietnam to Reagan*; Robert Kolker, *A Cinema of Loneliness*.

4. DeAngelis, "Introduction," *Reading the Bromance*, 2, 3.

5. While horror has come to dominate almost all representation, ranging from the police procedurals that abound on television, with their often shockingly grisly crime scenes, to the glut of science-fiction films made by Hollywood today that eschew the cerebral in favor of blood and guts, comedy has been the chief site for explorations of beta male anxieties. Linda Williams, in her essay "Film Bodies: Gender, Genre, and Excess," referred to melodrama, horror, and pornography as the three "body genres," which share a predilection for submitting the body to extremes and provoking physical reactions in spectators' bodies. I argue that lowbrow comedy (as opposed to drawing room and manners comedy) must be counted as a body genre as well.

6. Becker writes, "Within the emerging dynamics of the bromance discourse, expressions of homosocial bonding are, it seems, no longer structured by the abjection of the gay Other, but they remain structured by the abjection of effeminacy." Becker, "Straight Men, Gay Men, and Male Bonding," *Reading the Bromance*, 252.

7. Langford, *Film Genre: Hollywood and Beyond*, 11.

8. In Freud's view, comedy emanates from the cultural repression of the "lower bodily stratum," the result of the emphasis that civilization places on our rational faculties rather than our lower bodies. In Bakhtin's, society represses the grotesque and carnivalesque aspects of bawdy humor embodied in the work of

Rabelais, opting for the "colder," more cerebral form of satire, seen as a corrective to the social order. See Paul, "Charles Chaplin and the Annals of Anality," *Comedy/Cinema/Theory*, ed. Andrew S. Horton, 113.

9. In a fascinating and very useful discussion, Ken Feil, emphasizing the crucial role of vulgarity in the bromance, delineates a history of bad male behavior dating back from 1960s "stoop" (short for stupid) to the emergence of forms of straight male camp. Crucially, "the bromance instances a culmination of hetero-male appropriations and negotiations of gay taste and, like stoop, straight camp, and metrosexuality, demonstrates the long-standing appeal of gay taste to hetero-male lifestyle—its offer of sexual and cultural liberation—and its repulsiveness due to the threatened loss of fixed hetero-male identity." See Feil, "Queer Taste, Vulgarity, and the Bromance," *Reading the Bromance*, 173.

10. While his particular sensibility as an auteur is not the main focus of this chapter, Judd Apatow's work needs special mention because it has been so crucial to the genesis and popularity of this new genre. As Steven Gaydos, executive editor of *Variety* magazine, has been quoted as saying, "Judd has had a bigger impact on the film comedy scene than anybody in a long time . . . *The 40-Year-Old Virgin* was a break-out hit, *Talladega Nights* was a break-out hit, *Knocked Up* was a break-out hit, *Superbad* was a break-out hit. *Step Brothers* was a solid hit, *Pineapple Express* was a solid hit, *Forgetting Sarah Marshall* was a solid hit. I can't think of anybody in the business who's had five years like that. His comedies have grossed well over $1bn between them." Gaydos is quoted in Tim Walker, "King of Bromance: Judd Apatow."

11. Carol J. Clover provocatively argued in 1992 that the horror film places the viewer—typically gendered male—in the masochistic position of identifying with the female victim. The Final Girl is the masculinized, virginal young woman who is the only one ultimately able to outwit, slay, and/or escape the monster—a kind of intermediary figure between the female victim and the young male spectator. See Clover, *Men, Women, and Chainsaws*, passim.

12. This topic in cinematic terms has attracted surprisingly little interest. For a definitive discussion of the homosocial, see Eve Kosofsky Sedgwick, *Between Men*. If, as I have been arguing, only a syncretic approach allows us to understand representations of gender in any given period, in this case post-millennial masculinities, the linkages between the emphasis on male homosociality in nineteenth-century American life and in the newly articulated forms of male-male relation in the beta-male comedies and bromances of the Apatow school are highly relevant.

13. See Fiedler, *Love and Death in the American Novel*. Fiedler's reading—both provocative and pathologizing—of classic American literature (James Fenimore Cooper, Melville, Twain, especially) as rife with "innocent homosexuality" has its analogue in the beta-male comedy's constant thematization of "innocent homophobia," exemplified by the "You know how I know you're gay?" exchange between the characters played by Paul Rudd and Seth Rogen in *The 40-Year-Old Virgin*.

14. Fiedler, *Love and Death in the American Novel*, 211.

15. For a discussion of the racial buddy film, see Cynthia J. Fuchs's essay "The Buddy Politic." As Fuchs observes, the '80s buddy films use the "transgressiveness

of black-white difference" to displace "homosexual anxiety," thereby sustaining "the secrecy of masculine intimacy and vulnerability." The anxieties on display in series such as the *Lethal Weapon* films fuse sex and violence, but, most "emphatically displaces homosexuality by that violence." Indeed, this violence comes to seem the deepest form of male intimacy (201–03).

16. For an excellent discussion of the social function of marriage in terms of masculinity, see Jonathan Rauch, "For Better or Worse." If, as Rauch elaborates, marriage has historically existed as an institution for the socialization of wayward men, the beta male comedies and bromances routinely depict marriage as an institution for the containment—incarceration—of men. In *Knocked Up*, Paul Rudd's character is shown to be having an affair—not, as his wife, played by Leslie Mann suspects, with another woman, but with the homosocial group of men he sneaks out to watch sports with; in *The Change-Up*, marriage (embodied once again by a neurotic, angry, unhappy, sexually deprived woman played by Apatow's wife Leslie Mann) and fatherhood are depicted as just as hollow and confining for the married male as the swinging bachelor's sexually adventurous but secretly barren existence; and so forth.

17. One is reminded as well as the stock antebellum narratives in which northern visitors to southern plantations provided an "objective" view of slavery and plantation life. Usually, such narratives were concocted for the benefit of the slavocracy.

18. As Valerie Rohy reminds us in her 2010 study *Anachronism and Its Others*, a fascination with the primitive suffuses treatments of both homosexuality and racial otherness in classical psychoanalysis especially. If blackness and homosexuality have both been framed as primitive "throwbacks," what is particularly interesting about masculinity in beta male comedies is that it is this form of white masculinity that is now being framed as such. Yet these films offer progressive developmental narratives. As Tim Walker discusses in his *Independent* article on Judd Apatow films, "Bromantic protagonists tend to be immature and ambition-free beta males, stuck in a spiral of pornography and junk food, and forced to grow up when they encounter women, children and responsibilities." The key word here is "forced," as the protagonists must inevitably climb out of their sloughs of male despond and become responsible, married, child-rearing adults.

19. Seltzer, *Serial Killers*. *Forgetting Sarah Marshall* is particularly emphatic in the equivalence it draws between the denuding of men on physical and psychic/emotional levels. Jason Segal's "shocking" full-frontal nudity early on in the film presents him as vulnerable and pitiable while heightening the excruciating emotional pain he endures when his girlfriend Sarah breaks up with him precisely in this moment. The sustained portrayal of male suffering in the film is both marked and allegorized by Segel's nudity—male body and psyche laid bare.

20. For an excellent discussion of the confluence of Gothic themes and male relationships in American literature, see Robert K. Martin's essay "Knights Errant and Gothic Seducers."

21. Brom is the template for characters such as football player and resident bully Dave Karofsky (Max Adler) on the Fox TV series *Glee* (2009–2015), who was

depicted as a bully who torments the show's openly gay teen character Kurt Hummel (Chris Colfer) in the second season. "There's this Neanderthal who's made it his mission to make my life a living hell," Kurt tearfully confesses at one point in the second season as he explains why he has had to transfer schools. Of particular interest to me is the way that *Glee* frames Karofsky's persecution of Kurt as not only menacing but erotically charged, and precisely menacing because erotically charged—Karofsky's desperate kissing of Kurt on the mouth in the second season episode "Never Been Kissed" (11/9/2010) changes the entire theme of gay bullying into the closeted homosexuality of the homophobe. In a later episode, Karofsky bullies Kurt in a way that especially terrifies him and leads him to transfer schools; the extreme of terror reached in this moment, in which Karofsky stands before Kurt, staring at him intently, and takes away one of his possessions, derives precisely from the erotic intensity of its depiction, as Karofsky presents his overpowering physical menace as a sexualized menace as well. *Glee* takes the template of "Legend of Sleepy Hollow" to a twenty-first-century extreme of explication, transforming Brom Bones's murderous fascination with loner, outsider Ichabod into a murderous erotic fascination. And, given the extraordinary plethora of fan mash-ups of the Kurt-Karofsky relationship on such sites as YouTube, this is a fascination hardly the bully's alone. Indeed, from my estimation, the number of mash-up videos celebrating the sweet anguish of this ill-fated pairing, often linked to songs such as Lady Gaga's "Bad Romance," exceeds that of homages to the much more benign relationship Kurt develops, over the course of season two, with Blaine (Darren Criss), the openly and much more confidently gay teenager at a boy's prep school who befriends the lost and frightened Kurt, leading to his transfer to Blaine's school and to his joining its glee club, The Warblers. As the seasons progressed, *Glee* transformed Karofsky into a pitiable figure hounded out of the high school for his now publicized homosexuality; Kurt ends up becoming his ally, confidante, and mentor, however uncomfortably. Indeed, Blaine and Karofsky eventually date although Blaine and Kurt get married in the final season after a long period of estrangement due to the fact that he cheated (once) on Kurt.

22. The narrator offers several competing theories as to what befell him, and the commonly accepted one in criticism is that Crane goes to New York City to pursue a law career. Yet this theory is no more textually supported than any other; one of the aspects of the tale that has been almost completely overlooked is the violence of Brom's attack against Ichabod. The blow to his head is unmistakable physical trauma; it is possible that Brom not only managed to rid Ichabod from his town but also killed him.

23. Robert D. Putnam, *Bowling Alone*. Putnam's discussion of the historical decline in American homosocial friendship and intimacy is not negated by the beta male comedies but, rather, enlarged by it. For all of the relentless foregrounding of male-male social relationships in them, very often these relationships are marked by violence and emotional inauthenticity. And when emotional connections are represented, their depiction is so overblown as to suggest a mockery of the depiction—see, for example, the "I love you" declarations at the climax of *Superbad*,

during which the Jonah Hill character proclaims that he wants to shout his love for the Michael Cera character from the rooftops.

24. See Ariel Levy, *Female Chauvinist Pigs*. Levy offers a stinging critique of the post-feminist empowerment model through which women can "take ownership" of their sexuality by emulating the very misogynistic and aggressive male attitudes that have historically oppressed women. Interestingly, she also raises this question: "A tawdry, tarty, cartoonlike version of female sexuality has become so ubiquitous, it no longer seems particular. What we once regarded as a *kind* of sexual expression we now view *as* sexuality" (5). Levy is arguing that the postfeminist female identification with pornography's views of women, embodied by Hugh Hefner and *Playboy*, indicates a failure to distinguish between "raunchy" and "liberated." One of the further questions to ask here—one raised with especially provocative force by Lena Dunham's HBO series *Girls* and her film *Tiny Furniture* (2010) and thematized, if not exactly "raised," by *Sex and the City*—is what opportunities exist for the expression of female sexual desire when that desire is relentlessly framed as both heterosexual and in service to heterosexual male desire, socially and representationally? See note 25 in this chapter for a related point. In terms of beta male comedies and bromances, women's desire is squarely situated within a domain of heterosexual male sexual need and demand.

25. Maria DiBattista, *Fast-Talking Dames*. The phrase "clever funny girls" was used by Pauline Kael to describe the women of 1930s comedies, such as Jean Arthur: "the wisecracking heroines, the clever funny girls—Jean Arthur, of course, and Claudette Colbert, and Carole Lombard, and Ginger Rogers, and Rosalind Russell, and Myra Loy, and all the others who could be counted on to be sassy and sane." Kael, *Going Steady*, 134.

26. Corliss, "Review of *Superbad*."

27. I would argue that *Bridesmaids*, while driven by the intensity of Kristen Wiig's vision of current thirtysomething femininity as a feat of sustained desperation, is also a very male-centric work, culminating in a thunderous gross-out/defecation scene that evokes *Animal House*, *Porky's*, and the late '90s teen comedies that were all male-centered. In contrast, Lena Dunham's *Tiny Furniture* is much more invested in evoking feminine experience and, especially, the modern sense of sexual disconnection *and* compulsory sexual rapaciousness. The abject scene in which the heroine and a blond, young, goateed hipster guy she desires (he is friendly to but largely indifferent toward her) have sex, on an abandoned street at night, inside a stray portion of a large pipe exquisitely embodies the contemporary sexual scene. (I will reserve judgment on the fascinating but erratic *Girls*.)

28. Wood, "From Buddies to Lovers," *Hollywood from Vietnam to Reagan*, 203.

29. The title refers to Sarah's crime sleuth-heroine's powers. In the preview, she looks at a dog, whose thoughts she can read, and her eyes as well as the dog's light up a bright blue, signifying their telekinetic link. It's like Brian De Palma's 1978 film *The Fury* without the poetry.

30. See Rosenberg, *Legacy of Rage*; Boyarin, *Unheroic Conduct*.

31. For a discussion of *Observe and Report* and Rogen's stardom, see Greven, "American Psycho Family Values: Conservative Cinema and the New Travis Bickles." *Millennial Masculinity.*

32. Fung, "Looking for My Penis." See also Eng; Locke.

33. As Ed Guerrero writes, "we hear her [the Mammy's] echo today as she smiles at us (in a less caricatured version) from pancake boxes or contemporary films like *Clara's Heart*." Guerrero, *Framing Blackness*, 16. I assume Guerrero is referencing the corporate makeover of Aunt Jemima, pancake-batter-goddess, who has transformed from kerchief-wearing slave mammy to businesswoman.

34. For further discussion of this scene in the context of Spike Lee's film *25th Hour*, see the next chapter, note 6.

35. Leslie Mann played, for example, Paul Rudd's obnoxious wife in *Knocked Up*. Mann has only been able to reveal the range of her talent in different kinds of vehicles, such as *I Love You, Philip Morris*, directed by Glenn Ficarra and John Requa, and released in 2010, starring Jim Carrey and Ewan McGregor as lovers who meet in prison, and based on a real-life case.

36. Both *The Change-Up* and the 2011 beta male comedy *Jeff, Who Lives at Home*, directed by Jay Duplass and Mark Duplass (the latter co-starred in *Humpday*), reflect a current preoccupation with returning men to the bathroom-as-womb. In a key shot in the latter film, the brothers Pat (Ed Helms), playing a sadsack with a failing marriage, and his brother, the titular, hapless Jeff (Jason Segel), compare notes about their respective levels of despair while sitting together in a hotel bathtub. Regression, a return to infancy/childhood in the scenes of the two brothers "bathing" together, in a film heavily focused on the family leads to renewal. The relationship between the brothers, initially contentious, is ultimately renewed in a loving manner; their relationship to their office-worker mother Sharon (Susan Sarandon) is also key. (Sharon finds herself embarking on a surprising, most likely platonic lesbian affair with Carol, a coworker played by Rae Dawn Chong, who is present at the restorative birthday party scene near the close of the film.) By the end, the wayward beta male Jeff has saved his brother's life (after he attempted to save someone who had fallen off of a bridge), learned how to do the household chores properly that his frustrated mother commanded him to do, and seems headed for change and progress. So, too, is his more "normal" but unhappy brother, now reunited with his despondent, neglected wife Linda (Judy Greer) after he discovered she was having an affair (what led the brothers to the hotel room). The early hints of queerness in the Segel character are interesting—he spots a young African-American male from a distance, gets off his bus to follow the young man around, infiltrates his basketball game, and then, in a scene with a cruisy ambiance, is initially drawn into intimate conversation with the young man, who then leads Jeff into an ambush in which the other guys who had been playing basketball rob Jeff. But the film represents, along with *Funny People*, an intensely misguided attempt to sentimentalize the beta male genre, though it does contain the poignant image of the sad brothers sitting in an empty bathtub.

Chapter 4

1. While further development of the valences between our arguments exceeds the space I have here, Rey Chow's discussion of the fate of Orientalism in contemporary cultural practices—mediatized, digitized, altogether technologized—has striking overlaps with my findings as well as critical language in this study. Discussing Foucault and Ang Lee's sublime 2007 film adaptation of *Lust, Caution*, based on the novella of the same name published in 1979 by Chinese author Eileen Chang, Chow observes,

> ethnic sex or erotic art is now presented in the form of an aggressively spectacular, technologically impeccable production-cum-exposé. Sensational details, from the characters' genitalia to their contorted facial expressions and their torturous manners of seizure, penetration, copulation, climaxing, and release, are shown with methodical finesse and screen polish. In terms of visibility, there seems to be no (more) repression, only skillful professional manipulation (of camera angles): nothing is withheld; everything is rendered in and as plain sight. If these lurid images have outdone the most fanciful orientalist depictions of a debauched Orient, it is because the Orient is no longer a veiled mystery but an infinitely visualizable surface, one that embodies the potency—and promise—of being stripped naked, of being opened up in the most unmentionable of perspectives.

See Chow, *Entanglements*, 178. I do not want to appropriate Chow's analysis in a different political and cultural context for my own (despite overlaps in our aims, I would imagine). Nevertheless, what could unite this colonized, endlessly available Orient and the straight white masculinity on display in mainstream films that I have been discussing, which share the status of being "infinitely visualizable"? I believe the key term here is "veiled mystery." If straight white masculinity was, even though rarely understood as such and in an even more recalcitrant manner than that which characterized the history of screen femininity, the great veiled mystery of the cinema (and television), in recent years that mystery's unveiling has itself constituted a central drama in representation, and as this central drama, mediated through "aggressively spectacular, technologically impeccable" methods, it has stimulated a desire for further unveiling. Certainly, the idea that repression no longer holds sway in a post-queer moment is a factor here as well. And as films such as Steve McQueen's *Shame* (2011) and the film adaptation of *Fifty Shades of Grey* (2015) evince, there is a gathering interest in depicting the male body in states of sexual excitation in mainstream film. This chapter understands the deployment of the psychoanalytic mode in contemporary representations of masculinity as a reactionary technologization of anxieties regarding the current state of American manhood.

2. In the fictions of James Fenimore Cooper, Hawthorne, Melville, and Henry James, the sexual blankness of male characters signify, as I argued in *Men*

Beyond Desire, a resistance to regimes of sexual containment and functionality that were equally rife in the nineteenth century. The sexually inviolate male of nineteenth-century American fiction is a response to the demands to control and to exhibit sexuality that coterminously informed cultural understandings of masculinity in the century, beginning with the Jacksonian period.

3. Castle, *The Apparitional Lesbian*, 45.

4. For an acute reading of futurity in the bromance, see Michael DeAngelis, "Queerness and Futurity in *Superbad*," *Reading the Bromance*, 213–32.

5. See, for example, Mark Edmundson's *Nightmare on Main Street*, in which he likens Freudian theory to the horror film.

6. In chapter 4 of *Manhood in Hollywood from Bush to Bush*, a discussion of the double-protagonist in contemporary film, I reference this scene as exemplary of what I call *the masochistic gaze*.

7. On anamorphic desire, see Žižek (1992); Rohy.

8. In looking back to see if Tom is looking at him, Dickie establishes himself, despite all of his galvanizing erotic power, as a flawed, fragile Narcissus in need of the affirmation of the desiring gaze, in need of registering that he *is* desired. He is therefore the antithesis of Theodore Reik's pure narcissist who needs nothing and no one else.

9. Indeed, Ripley becomes the fall guy for Dickie's own tormented misrecognition in the mirror; we can say that Dickie misrecognizes himself *as* the mirror, looking back at Ripley for affirmation that Dickie can function as Ripley's mirror, Ripley's fantasy image of wholeness and attained desire. The mirror of Narcissus becomes the mirror of psychoanalysis becomes the mirror of cinema becomes the mirror of contemporary conflicts over gender identity, sexual desire, and class anxiety, even as the 1950s serve, in terms of the retrospective impulse, as a perverse mirror for the imminently millennial moment of the film's making.

10. Linderman, "Cinematic Abreaction: Tourneur's *Cat People*," 73.

11. Jacques Lacan, "The Mirror-Stage as Formative of the Function of the I," in *Ecrits: A Selection*, trans. Alan Sheridan (New York: Norton, 1977), pp. 1–7. For a lengthy discussion of the mirror stage as it applies to film, see chapter three, "Identification, Mirror," in Christian Metz, *The Imaginary Signifier: Psychoanalysis and the Cinema* (Bloomington: Indiana University Press, 1982), 42–57. For a discussion of Metz's limitations, see Rodowick, who observes that, despite the brilliance of his arguments and his efforts to revise Saussureanism by comparing image to signifier, sentence, and so forth, "Metz maintained a concept of discourse that could not break with its linguistic foundations." Rodowick, *Reading the Figural*, 4–5.

12. Metz, *The Imaginary Signifier*, 6.

13. This is Todd McGowan's point in *The Real Gaze*:

> Early Lacanian film theory's conception of desire actually has more in common with Nietzsche and Foucault than it does with Lacan, which is one reason why Joan Copjec claims that "film theory operated a kind of 'Foucauldinization' of Lacanian theory."

The Real Gaze, 8; Copjec's *Read My Desire*, 22.

McGowan, following Copjec, argues that the Foucauldianized Lacan of theorists like Laura Mulvey led early Lacanian film theory to equate the gaze with the desire for mastery, which then led to the theorization of this desire for mastery as indicative of patriarchal heterosexual male desire, i.e., the "male gaze." While a complex series of unpackings of Lacanian theory that cannot be easily summarized here, McGowan's response is to point out that something closer to masochism than sadistic mastery is inherent in Lacan's theory of the gaze—our masochistic enjoyment of our submission to the mysterious power of the object.

14. Benjamin argued that "the audience's identification with the actor is really an identification with the camera. Consequently, the audience takes the position of the camera." Benjamin, *Illuminations*, 228.

15. Metz, *The Imaginary Signifier*, 48 (emphasis in the original).

16. Metz, *The Imaginary Signifier*, 49 (emphasis in the original).

17. Film theory practice today has made psychoanalytic theory its antithesis. As exemplified by the reader *Post-Theory* that they edited, David Bordwell and Noël Carroll have led a movement towards the appreciation of film aesthetics that rejects the psychoanalytic methodologies so central to film theory in the 1970s and '80s. Instead of revising and reimagining the uses of psychoanalytic theory—despite its inherent limitations the most insightful methodology available for the study of gendered identity, desire, and the emotional experiences of sexual subjectivity—the post-theory position dispenses with it altogether. With this dismissal of psychoanalysis has come a de-emphasization of issues of gender and sexuality in Film Studies from the establishment wing occupied by critics like Bordwell and Carroll. But what critical practice eschews does not go off somewhere to die a quiet, hidden death. The psychoanalytic reading of film that defined the 1970s and '80s (Metz, Mulvey, Doane, Silverman, et al.) may be avoided in Film Studies of today, but continues to inform filmmaking practice.

18. Though it remains a frustrating interpretation, full of blind spots, especially of classical Hollywood, Mulvey's model of the male gaze remains an important early intervention in the heterosexual visual economy of gender in mainstream film. See Laura Mulvey, "Visual Pleasure and Narrative Cinema" (1975). I am not going to delve into the absolutely vast bibliography of responses to Mulvey's essay here, including those by Mulvey herself.

19. See Kibbey, *Theory of the Image*, 40.

20. In their 2005 essay "Hegemonic Masculinity: Rethinking the Concept," R. W. Connell and James Messerschmidt broaden the concept of hegemonic masculinity, offering a model of divergent masculinities related to temporal and geographic spaces. While I believe that these critics are right to offer a more complex portrait of hegemonic masculinity, I also believe that post-millennial texts make it vividly apparent that a broadly powerful and intelligible set of concerns cohere in terms of maintaining a troubled yet stable and resilient white heterosexual male identity able to weather all challenges.

21. Baker, *Masculinity in Fiction and Film : Representing Men in Popular Genres 1945–2000* (London: Continuum, 2006), 68. I do not share Baker's Foucauldian perspective here, seeing this development as a feature of the Freudian death-drive.

22. As Sara Salih clarifies in her study of Judith Butler's work, "Crucially, Butler is not suggesting that gender identity is a performance, since that would presuppose the existence of a subject or actor who is *doing* that performance. Butler refutes this notion by claiming that the performance preexists the performer, and this counterintuitive, apparently impossible argument has led many readers to confuse performativity with performance. She herself admits that, when she first formulated the idea, she did not differentiate clearly enough between performativity—a concept which has specific linguistic and philosophical underpinnings—and straightforward theater." Salih, *Judith Butler*, 11. So, for Butler, gender is performative, not a performance.

23. Indeed, one critic, writing in the context of Robin Wood's fusion of Marxism and psychoanalysis and the slasher-horror film, describes this explication of theoretical interpretation in primary cinematic texts themselves as a kind of vomiting up: "critical methodologies drawn, however broadly from cultural studies and psychoanalysis . . . continue to be employed. It is not surprising that movies have begun to regurgitate this theory to the point that the kinds of meanings arrived at through criticism of the original slasher movies are now explicitly built into their remakes." See Nelson, "Traumatic Childhood Now Included: Todorov's Fantastic and the Uncanny Slasher Remake," 115.

24. José Esteban Muñoz, "Photographs of Mourning: Melancholia and Ambivalence in Van Der Zee, Mapplethorpe, and *Looking for Langston*," *Disidentifications*, 64–65. Muñoz quotes from De Man's *The Rhetoric of Romanticism*, 75–76.

25. Kelly did make two short films before *Donnie Darko*: *The Goodbye Place* (1996) and *Visceral Matter* (1997).

26. For an extended analysis of the development of the film from a curiosity to a bona-fide cult phenomenon, see Geoff King, *Donnie Darko* (New York: Wallflower Press, 2007).

27. Hoberman, *Film After Film*, 56n3.

28. Linda Ruth Williams, "Movies, Smart Films, and Dumb Stories," 55. My analysis focuses on the 2005 Director's Cut edition of *Donnie Darko*.

29. Smith, *Hideous Progeny*, 158. Smith references Kracauer's *From Caligari to Hitler*, 63–67.

30. Elsaesser, *Weimar Cinema and After*, 231–32. Elsaesser is discussing F. W. Murnau's silent film classic *The Last Laugh* (1924), in which Emil Jannings plays a doorman for a luxury hotel who loses everything—his position, the love of his community—until the redemptive ending.

31. Hayward, *Cinema Studies: The Key Concepts*, 189–90.

32. Žižek, "'I Hear You with My Eyes'; or, The Invisible Master," 94.

33. Rank, *The Double: A Psychoanalytic Study*, 74; 85.

34. Bruhm, *Reflecting Narcissus: A Queer Aesthetic*, 44.

35. Freud, "Some Neurotic Mechanisms," *The Standard Edition*, vol. 18, 223.

36. *Gods and Monsters* suggested that Karloff's version of Frankenstein's Monster, or the Creature as he is called in Mary Shelley's novel, was an apt symbol for postwar American masculinity. In Condon's film (one of the great works of the late '90s), this is specifically a masculinity in the Cold War 1950s context informed by a new sexual explicitness that signaled, on the one hand, an awareness of, and possible interest in, homosexuality, and, on the other hand, a newly virulent homophobia. Condon's film is set in 1957 and explores the last days of James Whale (played by Ian McKellan), the British director of the Universal Studios horror classics *Frankenstein* (1931), with Boris Karloff legendary as the titular scientist's Monster, *Bride of Frankenstein* (1935), and *The Invisible Man* (1933), as well as a film not customarily discussed as his own project, the film adaptation of the musical *Show Boat* (1936). Based on Christopher Bram's novel *Father of Frankenstein*, Condon's film explores the fictional relationship between the old and increasingly debilitated Whale, who retired from Hollywood in the late 1930s, no longer lives with his lover, and is suffering from recurrent strokes, and Clay Boone (Brendan Fraser), a twenty-six-year-old ex-Marine and the Whale property's gardener. After having coming close to submitting to the aged director sexually when Boone poses naked for him one thunderstorm-swept night, Boone then comes close to murdering the aged Whale when he makes explicit advances toward him. Boone moves from gay panic to clarity about the situation, crying out poignantly, "I am not your monster!" He has realized that Whale's endless erotic goading of him has had a dark agenda—prodding Boone to murder Whale. The maddened and suicidal Whale, finally realizing the truth of Boone's statement, takes matters into his own hands instead, drowning himself in his pool, once the site of glittering parties with beautiful young men. McKellan is utterly superb in this film, and is ably matched by Fraser and Lynn Redgrave as Whale's comic, long-suffering German housekeeper.

37. Their relationship recalls those in 1950s films such as *Peyton Place* (Mark Robson, 1957), based on Grace Metalious's scandalously sexual novel, between sensitive teenagers who transcend the conformity of their repressive worlds (I am referring to the tender bond between the characters played by Diana Varsi and Russ Tamblyn).

38. In Lacan's theory of the subject, subjectivity emerges through language, the acquisition of which splits off the human being from whatever he or she was prior to language and that subject remade in the phallic image of language. The subject is therefore a fundamentally split being. Michel Foucault's work, critical of psychoanalysis, argues that the subject is the person who confesses his or her desires, in earlier periods to the priest, in the modern era to the psychiatrist. Donnie certainly seems like the confessional subject, especially in that he adheres to a larger program of sexual normalization in his psychiatric "confessions."

39. Sedgwick, *Between Men*, 21–28. Sedgwick drew on the work of René Girard and his theories of desire and rivalry in literature and on Gayle Rubin's theories of the patriarchal "traffic in women."

40. As an example, in Book 12 of *Paradise Lost*, Milton has Eve sleep through the decisive conversation between Adam and the archangel Michael, who produces a

series of prophetic visions of the future events that await mankind for Adam before he and Eve are evicted from paradise.

41. A similar bloody-male-eye Oedipus motif informs *One Hour Photo*, (Mark Romanek, 2002), another film obsessed with the plight of a lone troubled man who wants to save the family. For a discussion of this film, see Greven, "American Psycho Family Values," *Millennial Masculinity*.

42. See Dixon, *It Looks at You: The Returned Gaze of Cinema*, 81–82.

43. See Wood's essay "The American Nightmare: Horror in the 70s," *Hollywood from Vietnam to Reagan . . . and Beyond*, 63–85.

44. It is interesting to compare Redford's first film to Kelly's. Sundance Film Festival innovator and actor Redford's sensitive (and long forgotten, despite its Best Picture and Director Oscar wins) film focuses on similar subjects, but Kelly adds an entire dream-like framework to his work. There is nothing especially queer about *Ordinary People* (or is there?); a queer sensibility animates certain aspects of *Donnie Darko*. At one point in *Ordinary*, Conrad discusses masturbation with his tough, kind, pushy, nurturing Jewish psychiatrist (a rather astonishingly clichéd character nevertheless played with tenacious commitment by Hirsch). Telling his psychiatrist that he masturbates, Conrad then responds, to his psychiatrist's question "Does it help?" with a somewhat lyrical-sounding, "For a minute." It's hard to imagine a similar scene, played so utterly straight, taking place in a film of the present; a knowingness about potential homoerotic tension between even this unlikely pairing of men would, most likely, demand a much jokier tone. Like *Donnie Darko*, *Ordinary People* presents its troubled teen protagonist as someone whose dark wit carries him through emotional travails that stem squarely from familial conflicts. But *Ordinary People* is squarely situated within the tradition of the 1950s-style Freudian domestic-family-in-crisis drama; so is *Donnie Darko*, but it furiously cross-fertilizes this tradition with the Gothic (Frank) and the science-fiction (time travel and apocalyptic fear) genres.

The most homoerotic dimension of *Ordinary People* is the idealization of Buck, Conrad's older, blond, sportsman brother, who died in a boating accident. Conrad's steely mother (Mary Tyler Moore) passionately loved Buck, presented in a flashback as a hunky, humorous blond Adonis who could make his mother laugh raucously and sensually. In contrast, the Beth of the present is a closed-off, tightly wound, bitter, repressed, repressive woman who deeply resents her surviving son's emotional difficulties and cannot express any affection toward him. Calvin (Donald Sutherland) is the hapless father. The film ends with Conrad's emotional breakthrough in an emergency session with his psychiatrist (his "crime," he realizes, is that he survived the accident: "I held on"), Calvin's rejection of cold, held-in Beth ("I realize that I don't know if I love you anymore, and I don't know how I am going to live without that."), Beth's long-deferred emotional breakdown as she prepares to move out of the house, and a fraught embrace between the father and his recovering, now more stable son. What has enabled this transcendent connection between father and son has been not only Calvin's rejection of Beth, but also the burgeoning romance between Conrad and Jeannine Pratt (Elizabeth McGovern), a teenage girl who sings in Conrad's choir as well.

Donnie does not simply discuss masturbation during a therapy session but actually comes close to performing the act for his female (and WASP-typed) therapist when she puts him under hypnosis. Casting Katharine Ross as the therapist is probably Kelly's nod to her role as Benjamin Braddock's (Dustin Hoffman) beloved Elaine Robinson in Mike Nichols 1967 *The Graduate* and its ode to youthful white male ennui. ("Elaine—*Elaine*!" Benjamin cries out from a high window as his beloved is about to be married in a church. Elaine escapes her wedding and runs away with Benjamin, but their blank, bewildered looks as they ride off on a bus, she still in her wedding gown, augur confusing times for this tortured couple.) In contrast to Nichols's and Redford's youthful male protagonists, squarely positioned within a heterosexual context, Donnie Darko's sexuality is polymorphous-perverse, suggestive of a range of sexual pleasures and typings—which is not to suggest, of course, that he is not also squarely situated within heterosexual masculinity.

The impact of queer visibility on *Donnie Darko* lies in the sexualization of the *hero*, as opposed to the sexualization of the women whom he desires: not only Elaine Robinson but also Mrs. Robinson (Anne Bancroft), Elaine's mother, who amply succeeds in seducing Benjamin in *The Graduate*; the sweetly goofy, pretty, unconventional Jeannine Pratt in *Ordinary People*.

45. See Greven, "American Psycho Family Values," for a discussion of the demonization of the child molester in films made in an era in which homophobia is no longer countenanced on the level of manifest content.

46. The equally suspect *American Beauty* (Sam Mendes, 1999) similarly conceals its conservatism within displays of subversive hedonism. The film is a misogynistic fantasy of male freedom from a termagant wife (here played by Annette Benning) that evokes "Rip Van Winkle." Scenes such as the one in which the former corporate honcho and sadsack husband (Kevin Spacey) smokes a joint with his teenage daughter's rebel boyfriend, who makes "lyrical" camcorder movies about suburban malaise, once again exemplify Leslie Fiedler's thesis that American masculinity wants nothing so much as the escape from women, family, and the domestic sphere through transgressive male bonding, as we discussed in the previous chapter. The wife remains strictly constrained to her shrewish and shallow role in *American Beauty*; it is the husband's quest for freedom from stifling conformity that entirely concerns the film.

47. Hoberman, *Film After Film*, 56. "The events of September 11 rendered most movies inconsequential; the heartbreaking *Donnie Darko*, by contrast, felt weirdly consoling. . . . A splendid debut under any circumstances, as released for Halloween 2001, it had an uncanny gravitas." I agree with Hoberman that *Donnie Darko* is an impressive debut film, galvanized by Gyllenhaal's breathtakingly deft and wide-ranging performance, but I don't find it a consoling film at all.

48. McGowan, *Out of Time*, 77.

49. After the night he has spent with Jack, Ennis briefly comes back inside his family's apartment in Riverton. Ennis's inability to recognize his wife Alma's (Michelle Williams) sufferings is a key indication of his narcissistic solipsism, as is his stoic reserve in the face of Jack's fervent need. Quickly packing up stuff for

his weekend getaway with newly returned Jack, Ennis stops for a moment in the bathroom. Ennis opens the medicine cabinet; the mirrored surface captures his image. Lee contrasts this image against the parallel one of Ennis's actual body, so that we can his face *and* its reflection. Yet uncannily, the mirror reflection, because of the angle at which it hangs, appears to have a different expression from Ennis's own. I discuss this scene in my chapter on *Brokeback Mountain* in *Manhood in Hollywood from Bush to Bush*.

50. Moreover, it bears continued evidence of Lee's unquestioned investment in heterosexual male privilege, the chief corollary of which is an essentialist, indeed, misogynistic, view of women. This subject requires a discrete treatment.

51. Deleuze and Guattari, *A Thousand Plateaus*, 176.

52. Monty's speech is an example of a cinematic apostrophe. According to the OED, the rhetorical term apostrophe is "A figure of speech, by which a speaker or writer suddenly stops in his discourse, and turns to address pointedly some person or thing, either present or absent; an exclamatory address." This moment in *25th Hour* allows us to consider the distinction between the apostrophe and prosopopoeia (the latter concept, I have argued, is embedded in "ghost faces"). These terms suggest differing positions on the giving of face. The apostrophe presents *to* the faceless, while prosopopoeia attempts to represent the faceless. This scene is an apostrophe offered by one man to a series of unseen persons and ultimately to his own mirror image, as the final address, "No, fuck you, Monty Brogan," reveals. If prosopopoeia dominates this period's filmmaking, men wearing the masks of masculinity and impersonating the male figure, here, the man addresses, apostrophizes, himself *as* image. The apostrophe and prosopopoeia are, in some ways, inverses of each other. Both are faceless in some kind of way—the apostrophe in that one is rhetorically addressing a faceless individual, the prosopopoeia in that one is speaking as someone else (and thus has neither one's own face nor the other person's).

53. In *Looking Good*, Lynne Luciano notes that "Most men admire the muscular, athletic bodies typified by ancient Greek statues, but for ideal facial images they turn to twentieth-century icons, including comic-book heroes like Superman and Dick Tracy. . . . [conforming to these looks carries] an aura of respectability because they are intended not so much to beautify as to project strength and ruggedness." See Luciano, *Looking Good*, 182. If this is the case, it is interesting that the straight Monty is linked to Montgomery Clift, whose particular handsomeness evokes the feminine male rather than Superman or Dick Tracy.

54. See Sedgwick, chapter 3, "Some Binarisms (II): Wilde, Nietzsche, and the Sentimental Relations of the Male Body," *Epistemology of the Closet*, 131–82, in particular the discussion of male self-pity, pp. 149–51.

55. On the subject of prison rape: by calling it mythologized, I in no way mean to suggest that prison rape is not a real phenomenon, only to call our attention to how the open secret of homosexuality functions socially. The mythology of prison rape homosexuality is deployed as the ultimate violation of the straight men who are sent to prison, in a cautionary manner that depends on homophobia no less than it does on the related fears of effeminacy, racism, and class bias, a complex

welter of issues that demand a discrete analysis. Demonstrating the resilience of the fear of prison rape as a defining male trope, but also one that, as such, works to establish heterosexual male self-awareness of male sexuality as attractive to other men, consider the highly odd, no doubt intended-for-laughs rivalry between Jason Sudeikis and Jason Bateman over who would be more "rapeable" in prison in *Horrible Bosses*. Adding to the homoerotics of this form of homophobic irony, the men enlist their other beta male friend, played by Charlie Day, to arbitrate (he picks Bateman as the more rapeable, and when forced to give an explanation observes that Bateman is "weaker and more vulnerable," and therefore precisely what the prison rapists will be looking for. As a prime example of the way in which the reality of prison rape of men is almost immediately treated as fodder for obnoxious humor, see the comments section of Mary Elizabeth Williams's article for Salon.com, "Reminder: Men get raped too," posted on May 6, 2013, 04:13. <http://www.salon.com/2013/05/06/reminder_men_get_raped_too/>

56. As Clarice finally reveals to the incarcerated (though not for long) cannibal-psychiatrist Hannibal Lecter, when she was a girl adopted by her farmer uncle and his wife, she walked in on an early morning scene of slaughter, as her uncle killed the farm's lambs. The girl Clarice runs away and tries to save one of the lambs, but she cannot ("he was too heavy"); she is punished, sent away to an orphanage. Lecter correctly deduces that it is this familial/childhood backstory that is the emotional foundation for Clarice's desire to save young women from the serial killer Buffalo Bill/Jame Gumb (Ted Levine).

57. For important insights into the issues of the cultural silencing of prison rape and its male and female victims, see David Kaiser and Lovisa Stannow's essay "Prison Rape and the Government."

58. See Morrison, *The Explanation for Everything*.

59. Melnick, *9/11 Culture*, 12. Melnick takes a much more sympathetic view of this film than I do, seeing *25th Hour* as a bracingly critical treatment of the "complexity of post-9/11 grief and mourning" (9). Whereas he reads everything about the description of Monty as complex in this manner—from the opening scene in which Monty rescues the beaten-up dog he names Doyle (recalling Popeye Doyle from the '70s crime classic *The French Connection*, more retrospectiveness, I would add) to the "incredibly powerful" (10) fantasy of Monty's escape to the desert and the West offered by James Brogan to Monty at the end—I view all of these details as part and parcel of the conservative, elegiac, sentimental nostalgia that characterizes the re-entrenchment of heteromasculinity in the post-millennial era. For example, what could be more reassuring and normalizing than showing us that Monty is an essentially good person by having him *adopt an injured dog* at the start of the film? Similarly, Lori Harrison-Kahan argues that *25th Hour* is a film about Monty discovering responsibility and accountability, and being affirmed—as the benevolent final montage of lyrical faces saying goodbye to Monty symbolizes—for having finally done so, clearly a corrective to post-9/11 American foreign policy. I am not in agreement with her about the political merits of Lee's films, finding

them, as I do, both heterosexist and devoted to a regime of the heteromasculine. See Harrison-Kahan, "Inside *Inside Man*: Spike Lee and Post-9/11 Entertainment."

60. Gilbey, "*25th Hour*," 58.

61. Spike Lee is one of the least queer-minded directors working in the industry, and I wouldn't be entirely surprised if the gay resonances of the Montgomery Clift motif were lost on the filmmaker, his films from the 1986 *She's Gotta Have It* (despite its female protagonist, her lesbian friend who encourages the heroine to have sex with her instead of the frustrating men in her life, and its ostensibly feminine narrative of a woman's juggling of numerous potential male suitors) to *Mo' Better Blues* (1990) to *Jungle Fever* (1991) to *Summer of Sam* (1999) to *25th Hour* and beyond being consistently devoted to male heterosexual privilege.

62. For an analysis of noir masculinity, see Krutnik's *In a Lonely Street: Film Noir, Genre, Masculinity*; for an analysis of Clift's queer star masculinity, see Brett Farmer, *Spectacular Passions: Cinema, Fantasy, Gay Male Spectatorships*.

63. Benioff, *The 25th Hour*, 179.

64. The ending of *The Odyssey* is itself deeply ambiguous, with a halt to the fighting inorganically imposed by Athena, rather than a victory straightforwardly achieved by the three generations of men. Then, of course, there are the hints of what's to come *after* the Odyssey's narrative, for example the journey that Odysseus will have to make far inland to sacrifice to Poseidon, and (in some versions) his death at the hands of his son by the goddess Calypso, who kept Odysseus in amorous captivity for several years, and with Calypso marrying Telemachus, and Penelope marrying Odysseus's and Calypso's son. (*The Odyssey* would make for a great soapy cable television mini-series.) My thanks to Alexander J. Beecroft for his insights into Homer's text.

Chapter 5

1. The films of Quentin Tarantino exemplify this goad to the audience to find mayhem funny. Nolan's *Dark Knight* films may contain an overarching "moral" discourse tied to its tormented crime-fighting hero's muddled but earnest efforts to clean up Gotham, the endlessly excremental city, but their preponderant tone enshrines ugliness and brutality to such a degree that the only response available is to revel in these modes.

2. Kawin, *How Movies Work*, 94.

3. I would argue that Nispel's reboot of *Friday the 13th* has its moments. Particularly impressive is the scene in which the hockey-mask-wearing killer Jason Voorhees first discovers and dons his mask, which Nispel stages as a variation on the Lacanian mirror stage.

4. I will be discussing the Unrated Director's Cut of Zombie's film, released on DVD in 2007. Before the film's theatrical release, a "workprint" was leaked online, representing, for many, Zombie's original vision, which was then altered to

match marketplace and studio demands in the theatrical version. In any event, the Unrated Director's Cut is, in my view, much richer and more interesting than the theatrical release, hence my discussion of it.

5. The historical themes of the contemporary horror remake situate the genre within a larger cultural fascination with revising American history *through* horror, a tendency that also defines the "ghost-hunter" subgenre of Reality TV shows, such as *Ghost Hunters* (2004–); *Paranormal State* (2007–), *Ghost Hunters International* (2009–), *A Haunting* (2005–2007), and especially the Travel Channel series *Ghost Adventures* (2008–). The ghost-hunter subgenre, along with Wes Craven's *Scream* films and their recurrent killer, "Ghostface," has inspired this book's title. The eerie green-lit, white-eyed night vision faces of the male investigators during their self incarceration at night in the haunted houses they "explore," male faces captured in green-hued night-vision photography, in the denatured light of the supernatural feminine zone, signal horror's new investments in the denaturing and haunting of conventional, heterosexual masculinity—of this typing of masculinity in particular.

6. I touch on *Halloween II* in chapter 5 of *Representations of Femininity in American Genre Cinema*, 143–45.

7. Sanjek, "Same as It Ever Was: Innovation and Exhaustion in the Horror and Science Fiction Films of the 1990s," 111.

8. Roth, "Twice Two: *The Fly* and *Invasion of the Body Snatchers*," 226. Roth discusses the original-remake relationship in terms of film "cycles." Further emphasizing the linkages between classic American literature and horror remakes, Roth's essay ends with a tantalizing, though underdeveloped, reference to the chapter "The Emptiness of Picture-Galleries" in Hawthorne's 1860 novel *The Marble Faun*, about young artists in Rome, murder (with overtones of a prior incestuous involvement), the stain of blood guilt, and the history of Western art. Roth links the remake to the novel's thematization of the weariness that ensues from the endless replication of the same few subjects in art (237).

9. Leitch, "Twice-Told Tales: Disavowal and the Rhetoric of the Remake," 54.

10. Ibid.

11. Ibid., 49.

12. Sipos, *Horror Film Aesthetics*, 94.

13. In her work on the Japanese horror cinema, Colette Balmain, while noting the distinctions between Japanese and American slasher films, establishes that significant overlaps between national versions of the genre exist in their shared evocation of a destabilization in masculine identity, "a crisis in hegemonic constructions of masculinity"; masculinity emerges as a series of masks that reflect "patriarchal anxiety over the shifting of masculinity as a stable sign." Balmain, *Introduction to Japanese Horror Film*, 157.

14. Lane, Review of *Halloween: H20*.

15. Some cultures use masks to denote the passage from adolescence to adulthood—for example, the "Hemba Mask" worn by the young boys of The Suku, who live in the Democratic Republic of Congo and the Republic of Congo, during

initiation ceremonies. The mask is believed to protect the boys during these ceremonies, which mark their transition from boyhood to adulthood; later the masks symbolize that they have become adult members of their society. But horror film turns everything upside down and into dust—Michael's passage here is a passage into nullity, not knowledge; oblivion, not life.

16. Chasseguet-Smirgel, *Creativity and Perversion*, 91.

17. Chasseguet-Smirgel, *Creativity and Perversion*, 91.

18. For a discussion of the gendering of interior spaces such as the home, see Rafael E López Corvo's clinical analysis of a patient, from the perspective of W. E. Bion's theories, in *Wild Thoughts Searching for a Thinker: A Clinical Application of W. R. Bion's Theories*, 80–82, in which the front of the house is associated with frontal genitality, the back of the house the anus.

19. Dumas, *Un-American Psycho*, 46.

20. For a discussion of differences between Carpenter's and Zombie's film that makes use of Tzevetan Todorov's theory of the fantastic, see Andrew Patrick Nelson, "Traumatic Childhood Now Included: Todorov's Fantastic and the Uncanny Slasher Remake." Nelson emphasizes that Carpenter's film emblematizes Todorov's view that the fantastic crucially depends on a level of interpretive "uncertainty." Nelson argues, "what Todorov's model ultimately provides is an indication of how a study attuned to structure—that is, concerned with describing themes and configurations rather than naming meanings—has the potential to shed new light on one of the darker, more blood-splattered corners of the schoolhouse of horror" (117). In the course of his discussion, Nelson argues that psychoanalytic interpretation, among other approaches to genre film, "rely on extremely broad readings that neglect the formal and thematic specificities of the films in question" (117). My hope is that I have demonstrated that this need not be the case. I would also object to the flippant tone of the position Nelson takes: "psychoanalysis has yet to tire of delineating the myriad ways in which we are all so gosh darned repressed, which means that the cultural engine that drives slasher films' masked maniacs is fed by a bottomless barrel of fuel" (116–17). Such a usage of psychoanalytic theory could only be characteristic of psychoanalytic criticism at its most jejune. For all of his insights, Nelson misses out on what is significant in Zombie's work because of Nelson's insistence on maintaining Todorov's paradigm of uncertainty—and anti-interpretation—as the horror standard.

21. Hawthorne, "The Gentle Boy," *Nathaniel Hawthorne's Tales*, 47–48.

22. Lee, "True Believer," 50. This essay is an analysis of Zombie's 2012 *Lords of Salem*.

23. Linnie Blake has also linked Zombie's films to the literature of the early republic, discussing them within the context of J. Hector St. John de Crèvecoeur's 1782 work *Letters from an American Farmer*, in which, as Blake parses, the author "stresses the enormous disjunction between the backwoodsmen and those good country people whose adherence to the Protestant values of sobriety" and like virtues helped to transform the "unknowable" American wilderness into a utopian society. For Blake, Zombie's films such as *House of 1000 Corpses* (2003) and *The Devil's*

Rejects (2005) represent the height of the related film subgenre of "hillbilly horror." See Blake, "I am the Devil and I'm Here to Do the Devil's Work," 187.

24. See Stockton, *The Queer Child,* especially the chapter "Feeling Like Killing? Murderous Motives of the Queer Child," which includes a moving treatment of Van Sant's Columbine-evoking *Elephant,* for a related discussion.

25. Lowenstein, *Shocking Representation,* 127; Benjamin quoted from "Theses on the Philosophy of History," 255.

26. Lowenstein, *Shocking Representation,* 2–3.

Chapter 6

1. Pollard, "Hollywood 9/11: Time of Crisis," 203.

2. While a discrete analysis of his body of work is needed, James Franco's films, both those in which he stars and has directed, demand attention for their self-conscious staging of the very conflict between a straight masculinity under siege and an increasingly visible queer sexuality that defines the films of the later 1990s and the '00s in terms of male sexuality. Franco, as I adumbrated in my remarks about *The Interview* in chapter 3, is a highly problematic figure in that his films and his public personae (interviews, selfies, tweets, publicity, Oscar-hosting, celebrity grad student-enrollment, et al.) actively foreground a homo-affiliation while they also resolutely establish and maintain his stature as unimpeachably heterosexual. The gay-baiting that characterizes the beta male and bromance subgenres applies no less to Franco-focused films such as *This is the End* and *The Interview,* even though it takes a different form in his films—an obsessive demonstration of "in-the-know" awareness of homosexual possibility that supports, rather than undermines, the heterosexual structure of bromance in that this homosexual possibility is always presented as an extreme, unthinkable event. The film that James Franco and Travis Matthews directed, *Interior. Leather Bar.* (2014) and in which Franco plays himself indexes the problematic aspects of Franco's public homo-affiliation. The 1980 film, *Cruising,* starring Al Pacino and directed by William Friedkin, is set in the gay leather/SM underworld of New York City; according to film lore, 40 minutes of sexually explicit material was deleted from the film due to censorship. Franco and Mathews film a "reconstruction" of this lost footage and conduct a casting call for the shoot, eventually assembling a mix of gay and straight men. Franco himself does not perform in the newly made lost footage-film; rather, he periodically gives interviews exploring his own mixed feelings about homosexuality and homophobia, his journey towards gay tolerance. In one scene, a real-life gay male couple, actors cast in the mock-*Cruising* film, make love on a sofa as Franco films them with a handheld camera (and the rest of the set watches). This scene is a set-piece of heterosexual white male privilege even as it purports to film authentic gay sex and gay men in their element. The zoological dimensions of this enterprise seem lost on the co-director Franco. Franco holds up a non-resistant, exploitative counter-mirror here to the relentless efforts of films of the '00s to lay straight, white masculinity

bare. The complexity of Franco's screen personae, however, makes further analysis of his work necessary; for example, his exquisitely tender performance as the gay poet Allen Ginsberg in the fine film *Howl* (Rob Epstein and Jeffrey Friedman, 2011) represents not just a triumph over an obvious miscasting but also an affecting affiliation with a gay visionary.

3. "However, even as patriotism immediately after September 11 was inextricably tied to a reinvigoration of heterosexual norms for Americans, progressive sexuality was championed as a hallmark of U.S. modernity," with the United States portrayed as feminist in relation to the Taliban's treatment of Afghani women, "gay-safe" in comparison to the Middle East. Puar, *Terrorist Assemblages*, 40–41.

4. See Halberstam, *Skin Shows*; Muñoz, *Cruising Utopia*; Susan White, "*Vertigo* and Problems of Knowledge in Feminist Film Theory," *Alfred Hitchcock: Centenary Essays*, eds. Richard Allen and Sam Ishii-Gonzalès (London: British Film Institute, 1999), 279–307.

5. The term "torture porn" apparently originates with Edelstein in his article "Now Playing at Your Local Multiplex: Torture Porn. Why has America gone nuts for blood, guts, and sadism?" *New York Magazine*, Jan. 28, 2006.

6. See Lowenstein, "Spectacle Horror and *Hostel*: Why 'Torture Porn' Does Not Exist."

7. See the section in Waugh's *Hard to Imagine* called "Stag Films," 309–22.

8. Zimmer, "Caught on Tape?" *Horror After 9/11*, 84.

9. Williams makes this point frequently throughout *Hard Core*.

10. Ibid., 84.

11. These attitudes manifest themselves through what, in the paradigm Linda Williams provided, have come to be known as the "body genres": melodrama, horror, and pornography, and, I would add, lowbrow comedy. See Williams, "Film Bodies: Gender, Genre, and Excess."

12. See Irigaray, *Speculum of the Other Woman*. For a very helpful reexamination of Irigaray's thought, see Judith Butler, "Desire."

13. From the outset, I want to make clear that the patterns I am tracing out in these diverse forms of representation are often haphazard, not forming a completely coherent and tangible pattern. Indeed, much as in dreams, condensation and displacement organize the available symbols. This chapter is an attempt to think through the dream-life of conservatism and reaction, no less oneiric and "imaginary" then that of the creative, visionary, and daring filmmaker if this filmmaker's politics are leftist. That having been said, genre films also make these patterns remarkably explicit.

14. Wilhelm Reich described "phallic-narcissistic" men as misogynistic and driven by a "strong phallic aggression." Such men view their own penises as instruments of deadly violence. Reich, *Character Analysis*, 219–20.

15. In one striking scene in *American Pie*, the wild, anarchic Stifler (Seann William Scott) accidentally drinks another man's semen (emitted into a glass of beer). "Hey, how'd you like that pale ale!" jeers another guy in his circle of friends. This period's spate of teen comedies evince their indebtedness to the gross-out

aesthetic that was popularized by the Farrelly Brothers (*Shallow Hal* [2001], *There's Something About Mary* [1998], *Dumb & Dumber* [1994]). Recalling the scene between the protagonists in the "man-cave" in *I Love You, Man* (2009) in which one friend discusses his use of the man-cave as place in which to masturbate, we can establish that the tropes of masturbation and semen have come to define the new openness about males and their bodies, moving from the gross-out shock of the late '90s teen comedies to something indicative of male-bonding in *I Love You, Man*. Unlike the pornographic film, defined by its famous "money-shot," no narrative mainstream work would show a man literally ejaculating onscreen, although the act might be strongly suggested. Yet, at the same time, this unrepresentable phenomenon has been making an all-but-explicit impact.

 16. The spectral blues, reds, and whites recall the dazzling expressionistic color schemes of the Italian horror movie director Dario Argento (the "garlic Hitchcock"). Roth proceeds from a metatextual cinematic basis much like Tarantino before him, and Brian De Palma before Tarantino. De Palma's sensibility is in no other manner similar to that of the later filmmakers; unlike Tarantino and Roth, De Palma is a genuinely leftist filmmaker and creative visionary.

 17. This entire scene recalls one that occurs in the Merchant-Ivory film adaptation of E. M. Forster's gay classic *Maurice* (1987), in which the closeted titular character reacts with equal violence from an older man's advances on a train.

 18. Bernard, "*Hostel*-ity Toward Whiteness."

 19. "He comes at us in sections, scaring us a little at a time," writes Vito Russo of the cinematic Sebastian, "like a movie monster too horrible to be shown at once." See Russo, *The Celluloid Closet*, 117.

 20. Sebastian has very mysteriously died while they were on holiday in Europe; his wealthy, Southern-gorgon mother, Violet Venable (Katharine Hepburn), is the one demanding that Catherine be lobotomized. A psychiatrist (played, bizarrely, by the closeted gay actor Montgomery Clift), attempting to get to the bottom of this mystery, discovers that Sebastian was a homosexual who used the women—first his mother, before she got too old, then his young and beautiful cousin Catherine—to "procure" young men he could then himself use for sex. In Catherine's extraordinary climactic monologue at the end of the film, she reveals to the psychiatrist, much to Violet Venable's protests, what actually happened. She and Sebastian used to travel to the Spanish town of Cabeza de Lobo, where they spent their days on the beach. Eventually, Catherine realizes that Sebastian is using her as bait to reel in the young impoverished men who are constantly gaping at her sexual spectacle on the beach. Their poverty makes them susceptible to Sebastian's sexual stratagems. But, after glutting himself on these dark young men, Sebastian announces that he is "famished for blondes" and makes plans to take Catherine along with him to the northern countries. Before leaving, though, Sebastian and Catherine are besieged by the once-victimized boys, furiously playing music on makeshift, scrap-metal instruments. When Sebastian rejects their demands for money, they hound him, surround him, and finally trap him. Finally, the desperate Catherine catches up with them, only to watch in horror as the boys of Cabeza de Lobo literally tear

Sebastian apart and devour his flesh. She cries out for help, which never comes, and can do nothing to stop this murder through mass-cannibalism.

21. Lowenstein, "Spectacle Horror and *Hostel*," 52.
22. Ibid., 52–53.
23. See Gunning, "The Cinema of Attractions."
24. A Senator from Idaho, Larry Craig was arrested on June 11, 2007, in a restroom sting operation at the Minneapolis-St. Paul International Airport. Charged with lewd behavior—soliciting gay sex in the restroom—it was widely reported that Craig disputed the charges by claiming that, rather than moving his foot into another man's toilet stall and tapping it to signal sexual interest, he had innocently taken "an unusually wide stance." The phrase has now thoroughly infiltrated the popular lexicon.
25. *Billy Budd, Sailor* (1891), Melville's famous novella, famously homoerotic, offers in its titular figure a young sailor whose outward physical beauty extrudes the essence of his moral beauty, specifically his lack of knowledge of evil. Claggart, the Master-at-Arms on the man-o'-war the *Bellipotent*, seethes with a homoerotically charged envy of Billy so intense that it drives him to frame Billy for mutiny. Claggart may be said to perform an elaborate initiation rite, in which Billy is made to confront evil in the form of Claggart and his false accusations. Famously, Billy, who stutters when anxious, cannot speak in this moment, cannot articulate his own innocence—he can only strike, and he does so, striking Claggart dead on the spot. In *Epistemology of the Closet*, Eve Kosofsky Sedgwick interprets Claggart as the first homosexual (in the full discursive, juridical sense of the term) character in literature (94, 96). For Sedgwick, what Melville depicts in this work is a life imagined "after the homosexual": "*Billy Budd* is a document from the very moment of the emergence of homosexual identity. But already described in that emergent identity . . . [is] the fantasy trajectory toward a life after the homosexual" (127). *Hostel* vigorously pursues much the same fantasy.
26. Any progressive attempt to "deterritorialize" queer subjectivities, hailed here as a community of consumers, is made much more difficult by the specific atmosphere created by the Internet. "It is hard to deterritorialize neat categorical distinctions when the interface demands a choice between a limited number of categories of being, and when sexual orientation (among other culturally charged variables) is foregrounded as a primary and distinct asset in menu-driven interaction. See Freedman, *Transient Images*, 131.
27. Franklin Melendez discusses this film in the Linda Williams-edited *Porn Studies*. "Structurally and thematically, *Shock* preoccupies itself with the persistent problem of representing and conveying sex through seemingly constricting technological avenues. In an effort to convey sexual ecstasy, *Shock* experiments with not only with extravagant content details like costumes and mise-en-scène, but more radically with the workings of the video medium." The question Melendez extracts from his reading of more creative earlier porn works is a pertinent one: "Is the screen as important as the body it makes visible?" Today, the making visible of the straight male body of gay porn is the clearly the important aspect, a project

tied to the almost Naturalist "realism" of the raw, reality-TV production values of the contemporary gay porn film, which eschews the earlier forms' stylizations, intertextuality, and metatextuality (Melendez likens *Shock* to Cecil B. De Mille films). See Melendez, "Video Pornography, Visual Pleasure, and the Return of the Sublime," 406.

28. For further discussion of Jacksonian masculinism, see Greven, Introduction, *Men Beyond Desire*.

29. Purcell, *Pornography and Violence*, 116.

30. Cante and Restivo, "All-Male Moving Image Pornography," 153, 159.

31. For discussions of shifts in the consumption of pornography and its relationship to constructions of American male sexuality, see Greven, *Psycho-Sexual*.

32. Chion, *The Voice in Cinema*, 122.

33. Cowie writes,

> The concept of fantasy . . . allows us to understand cinema as an institution of desire and as a scenario for identification which avoids the models of the cinematic apparatus arising in the work of Christian Metz and Jean-Louis Baudry so aptly dubbed "the bachelor machines" by Constance Penley, insofar as they posit a centered and unitary subject of desire, a masculine subject. The linear progression of narrative is disturbed and re-ordered by the drive of fantasy, disrupting the possibility of a coherent or unified enunciating position.

See Cowie, *Representing the Woman*, 164. Cowie refers to Penley's book *The Future of an Illusion*. While I certainly concur with Penley about the potentially liberatory uses of fantasy (which she also qualifies, hardly celebrating as a subversive alternative to the strictures of conventional moviemaking and spectatorial practices), my reading of the works under scrutiny in this chapter seeks to draw out not only their reactionary aspects but also what, in a comparative context, they collectively reveal about enduringly phobic understandings of queer male sexuality and the enduring privilege in fantasies of straight masculinity.

34. Waugh, *Hard to Imagine*, 26–27.

Coda

1. Kyle Stevens has treated Ford's film with finesse and sensitivity in a fine 2013 *Cinema Journal* article.

Bibliography

Alberti, John. *Masculinity in the Contemporary Romantic Comedy: Gender as Genre.* New York: Routledge, 2013.

Altman, Rick, and British Film Institute. *Film/Genre.* London: BFI Publishing, 1999.

Appiah, Kwame Anthony, and Henry Louis Gates, eds. *Africana: Arts and Letters: an A-to-Z Reference of Writers, Musicians, and Artists of the African American Experience.* Philadelphia: Running Press, 2005.

Baker, Brian. *Masculinity in Fiction and Film : Representing Men in Popular Genres 1945–2000.* Continuum Literary Studies. London: Continuum, 2006.

Balmain, Colette. *Introduction to Japanese Horror Film.* Edinburgh: Edinburgh University Press, 2008.

Balázs, Béla. *Béla Balázs: Early Film Theory: Visible Man and The Spirit of Film.* Edited by Erica Carter. Translated by Rodney Livingstone. New York: Berghahn Books, 2010.

Barker-Benfield, G. J. *The Horrors of the Half-Known Life: Male Attitudes towards Women and Sexuality in Nineteenth-Century America.* New York: Routledge, 1999.

Barthes, Roland. *Mythologies.* New York: Macmillan, 1972.

Basinger, Jeanine. *A Woman's View: How Hollywood Spoke to Women, 1930–1960.* Wesleyan University Press, 1995.

Baume, Nicholas, Douglas Crimp, Richard Meyer, and Andy Warhol. *About Face: Andy Warhol Portraits.* Hartford, Pittsburgh, Cambridge, MA: Wadsworth Atheneum; Andy Warhol Museum. Cambridge, MA: MIT Press, 1999.

Beam, Dorri. *Style, Gender, and Fantasy in Nineteenth-Century American Women's Writing.* New York: Cambridge University Press, 2010.

Becker, Ron. "Straight Men, Gay Men, and Male Bonding on U.S. TV." *Reading the Bromance.* Edited by Michael DeAngelis. 233–54.

Beltrán, Mary C. "The New Hollywood Racelessness: Only the Fast, Furious, (and Multiracial) Will Survive." *Cinema Journal* 44.2 (2005): 50–67.

———. "Fast and Bilingual: *Fast & Furious* and the Latinization of Racelessness." *Cinema Journal* 53:1 (Fall 2013): 75–96.

Benjamin, Jessica. *The Bonds of Love: Psychoanalysis, Feminism, and the Problem of Domination.* New York: Pantheon, 1998.

Benjamin, Walter. *Illuminations*. Edited by Hannah Arendt. Translated by Harry Zohn. New York: Schocken Books, 1978.

———. "Theses on the Philosophy of History." *Illuminations*. 253–64.

Benshoff, Harry. *Monsters in the Closet: Homosexuality and the Horror Film*. Manchester, UK: Manchester University Press, 1997.

Benshoff, Harry M., and Sean Griffin. *Queer Images: A History of Gay and Lesbian Film in America*. Lanham, MD: Rowman & Littlefield, 2006.

Berger, John. *Ways of Seeing* (1972). London: London; New York, NY: British Broadcasting Corp.; Penguin Books, 1990.

Bergland, Renée L. *The National Uncanny : Indian Ghosts and American Subjects*. Hanover, NH: Dartmouth College, University Press of New England, 2000.

Bergson, Henri. *Laughter: An Essay on the Meaning of the Comic*. København; Los Angeles: Green Integer; St. Paul, MN, 1999.

Bernard, Mark. "*Hostel*-ity Toward Whiteness: The Subtext of Eli Roth's *Hostel* and *Hostel: Part II*." *The ECCCS* (December 2008). http://www.the-ecccso.org/issue-0-0.

Bernardi, Daniel. *The Persistence of Whiteness: Race and Contemporary Hollywood Cinema*. New York: Routledge, 2008.

Bersani, Leo. *Homos*. Cambridge, MA: Harvard University Press, 1995.

Blake, Linnie. "'I am the devil and I'm here to do the devil's work': Rob Zombie, George W. Bush, and the limits of American freedom." *Horror after 9/11: World of Fear, Cinema of Terror*. Edited by Aviva Briefel and Sam J. Miller. 186–200.

———. *The Wounds of Nations: Horror Cinema, Historical Trauma and National Identity*. Manchester, UK; New York, NY: Manchester University Press. Distributed exclusively in the USA by Palgrave, 2008.

Bishop, Kyle William. *American Zombie Gothic: The Rise and Fall (and Rise) of the Walking Dead in Popular Culture*. Jefferson, NC: McFarland & Co., 2010.

Bordwell, David, and Noël Carroll. *Post-Theory: Reconstructing Film Studies*. Madison, WI: Wisconsin University Press, 1996.

Boyarin, Daniel. *Unheroic Conduct: The Rise of Heterosexuality and the Invention of the Jewish Man*. Vol. 8. *Contraversions*; 8. Berkeley: University of California Press, 1997.

Bradshaw, Peter. "Observe and Report," *The Guardian*, April 24, 2009. Accessed on February 24, 2011. http://www.guardian.co.uk/film/2009/apr/23/observe-and-report-film-review.

Briefel, Aviva, and Sam J. Miller. *Horror after 9/11: World of Fear, Cinema of Terror*. 1st ed. Austin: University of Texas Press, 2011.

Britton, Andrew. "Blissing Out: The Politics of Reaganite Entertainment." *Movie* 31/32 (1986).

———. "Blissing Out: The Politics of Reaganite Entertainment." *Britton on Film: The Complete Film Criticism of Andrew Britton*. Edited by Barry Keith Grant. Detroit, MI: Wayne State University Press, 2009.

Brown, Norman O. *Life Against Death: The Psychoanalytical Meaning of History.* New York: Vintage, 1959.

Bruhm, Steven. *Reflecting Narcissus: A Queer Aesthetic.* Minneapolis: Minnesota University Press, 2001.

Buchanan, Ian, and Patricia MacCormack. *Deleuze and the Schizoanalysis of Cinema.* London; New York: Continuum, 2008.

Butler, Judith. *Bodies That Matter.* New York: Routledge, 1993.

———. "Desire." *Critical Terms for Literary Study.* Edited by Frank Lentricchia and Thomas McLaughlin. Chicago: Chicago University Press, 1995.

———. *The Psychic Life of Power: Theories in Subjection.* Stanford University Press, 1997.

Butters, Gerald, Jr. "Masculinity in Film: The Emergence of a New Literature." *CHOICE: Current Reviews for Academic Libraries.* February 2014, 955–63.

Calvert, Ben et al. *Television Studies: The Key Concepts.* 2nd ed. New York: Routledge, 2007.

Capper, Charles. *Margaret Fuller: An American Romantic Life. Vol. 1. The Private Years; Vol. 2. The Public Years.* New York: Oxford University Press, 1992.

Cante, Rich, and Angelo Restivo. "The cultural-aesthetic specificities of all-male moving-image pornography." *Porn Studies.* Edited by Linda Williams. 142–66.

Castle, Terry. *The Apparitional Lesbian: Female Homosexuality and Modern Culture.* Gender and Culture. New York: Columbia University Press, 1993.

Castronovo, Russ. *Necro Citizenship: Death, Eroticism, and the Public Sphere in the Nineteenth-Century United States.* Durham, NC: Duke University Press Books, 2001.

Chasseguet-Smirgel, Janine. *Creativity and Perversion.* 1st British ed. London: Free Association Books, 1985.

Chow, Rey. *Entanglements: Or Transmedial Thinking about Capture.* John Hope Franklin Center Book. Durham, NC, and London: Duke University Press, 2012.

Cixous, Hélène. "Castration or Decapitation?" (1976). *Contemporary Literary Criticism.* Edited by Robert Con Davis and Robert Scheifler. Repr. New York: Longman, 1989.

Clark-Flory, Tracy. "The Twisted World of 'Ex-girlfriend Porn.'" Salon.Com, Monday, Feb 28, 2011. Accessed on March 1, 2011. http://www.salon.com/life/feature/2011/02/28/exgirlfriend_porn/index.html.

Clayton, Alex. *The Body in Hollywood Slapstick.* Jefferson, NC: McFarland & Co, 2007.

Cohan, Steven. *Masked Men: Masculinity and the Movies in the Fifties.* Bloomington: Indiana University Press, 1997.

Cohan, Steven, and Ina Rae Hark, eds. *Screening the Male: Exploring Masculinities in the Hollywood Cinema.* New York: Routledge, 1993.

Cohen, Josh. *How to Read Freud.* New York: Norton, 2005.

Connell, R. W. *Masculinities*. 2nd ed. Berkeley, CA: University of California Press, 2005.
Clover, Carol J. *Men, Women, and Chainsaws: Gender in the Modern Horror Film*. Princeton, NJ: Princeton University Press, 1992.
Connell, R. W., and James Messerschmidt "Hegemonic Masculinity: Rethinking the Concept." *Gender & Society.* December 2005 19: 829–59.
Corliss, Richard. "Review of Superbad." *Time*, August 2007.
Corber, Robert J. *Cold War Femme : Lesbianism, National Identity, and Hollywood Cinema*. Durham, NC: Duke University Press, 2011.
———. *In the Name of National Security: Hitchcock, Homophobia, and the Political Construction of Gender in Postwar America*. Durham, NC: Duke University Press, 1993.
Corrigan, Timothy. *American Cinema of the '00s: Themes and Variations*. Screen Decades : American culture/American Cinema. New Brunswick, NJ: Rutgers University Press, 2012.
Corvo, Rafael E. López. *Wild Thoughts Searching for a Thinker: A Clinical Application of W. R. Bion's Theories*. London: Karnac, 2006.
Cott, Nancy F. "On Men's History and Women's History." *Meanings for Manhood: Constructions of Masculinity in Victorian America*. Edited by Mark Christopher Carnes and Clyde Griffen. Chicago: University of Chicago Press, 1990: 209–13.
Coupland, Douglas. "Convergences: 'Gods Without Men,' by Hari Kunzru." *New York Times Book Review*, March 8, 2012.
Cowie, Elizabeth. *Representing the Woman: Cinema and Psychoanalysis*. Minneapolis, MN: University of Minnesota Press, 1997.
Crain, Caleb. "Lovers of Human Flesh: Homosexuality and Cannibalism in Melville's Novels." *American Literature*, 66, 1 (1994), pp. 25–53. 12.
Creed, Barbara. *The Monstrous-Feminine: Film, Feminism, Psychoanalysis*. New York: Routledge, 1993.
DeAngelis, Michael, ed. *Reading the Bromance: Homosocial Relationships in Film and Television*. Contemporary Approaches to Film and Media Series. Detroit, MI: Wayne State University Press, 2014.
———. "Introduction." *Reading the Bromance*. Edited by Michael DeAngelis, 2014. 1–28.
———. "Queerness and Futurity in *Superbad*." *Reading the Bromance*. Edited by Michael DeAngelis, 2014. 213–32.
Deleuze, Gilles, and Leopold von Sacher-Masoch. *Masochism, an Interpretation of Coldness and Cruelty: Together with the Entire Text of Venus in Furs*. New York: Braziller, 1971.
Deleuze, Gilles, and Félix Guattari. *A Thousand Plateaus: Capitalism and Schizophrenia*. Minneapolis: University of Minnesota Press, 1987.
De Man, Paul. "Autobiography as De-Facement." *The Rhetoric of Romanticism*. New York: Columbia University Press, 1984. 67–81.

Demory, Pamela, and Christopher Pullen. *Queer Love in Film and Television: Critical Essays*. 1st ed. New York: Palgrave Macmillan, 2013.
DiBattista, Maria. *Fast-Talking Dames*. New Haven, CT: Yale University Press, 2003.
DiPiero, Thomas. *White Men Aren't*. Durham, NC: Duke University Press, 2002.
Dimock, Wai Chee. *Through Other Continents: American Literature Across Deep Time*. Princeton, NJ: Princeton University Press, 2008.
Dixon, Wheeler Winston. *It Looks at You: The Returned Gaze of Cinema*. New York: SUNY Press, 1995.
Dotson, Edisol W. *Behold the Man: The Hype and Selling of Male Beauty in Media and Culture*. Haworth Gay & Lesbian Studies. New York: Haworth Press, 1999.
Doty, Alexander. *Making Things Perfectly Queer: Interpreting Mass Culture*. Minneapolis, MN: University of Minnesota Press, 1993.
Dunn, Stephane. *"Baad Bitches" and Sassy Supermamas: Black Power Action Films*. Champaign, IL: University of Illinois Press, 2008.
Dyer, Richard. 1982. "Don't Look Now." *Screen* 23, no. 3/4: 61–73.
———. "The White Man's Muscles." *Race and the Subject of Masculinities*. Edited by Michael Uebel and Harry Stecopoulos. Durham, NC: Duke University Press Books, 1997. 286–314.
———. *White*. New York: Routledge, 1997.
Edelman, Lee. *No Future: Queer Theory and the Death Drive*. Durham, NC: Duke University Press, 2005.
Edelstein, David. "Now Playing at Your Local Multiplex: Torture Porn. Why Has America Gone Nuts for Blood, Guts, and Sadism?" *New York Magazine*, Jan. 28, 2006.
Edmundson, Mark. *Nightmare on Main Street: Angels, Sadomasochism, and the Culture of Gothic*. Cambridge, MA: Harvard University Press, 1997.
Edwards, Tim. "Spectacular Pain: Masculinity, Masochism and Men in the Movies." *Sex, Violence and the Body: The Erotics of Wounding*. Edited by Vivien Burr and Jeff Hearn. Basingstoke [England]; New York: Palgrave Macmillan, 2008. 157–76.
Elsaesser, Thomas. *Weimar Cinema and After: Germany's Historical Imaginary*. New York: Routledge, 2000.
Eng, David L. *Racial Castration: Managing Masculinity in Asian America*. Durham, NC: Duke University Press, 2001.
Farmer, Brett. *Spectacular Passions: Cinema, Fantasy, Gay Male Spectatorships*. Durham, NC: Duke University Press, 2000.
Feil, Ken. Queer Taste, Vulgarity, and the Bromance as Sensibility and Film Genre." *Reading the Bromance*. Edited by Michael DeAngelis. 165–90.
Fiedler, Leslie. *Love and Death in the American Novel*. 1960; New York: Dell, 1966.
Forrest, Jennifer, and Leonard R. Koos. *Dead Ringers: The Remake in Theory and Practice*. SUNY Series, Cultural Studies in Cinema/video. Albany, NY: SUNY Press, 2002.

Forster, Peter. "Rad Bromance (or *I Love You, Man*, But We Won't Be Humping on *Humpday*)." *Reading the Bromance*. Edited by Michael DeAngelis. 191–212.

Fouz-Hernández, Santiago. *Mysterious Skin: Male Bodies in Contemporary Cinema*. London; New York, NY: I. B. Tauris, 2009.

Freeman, Elizabeth. *Time Binds: Queer Temporalities, Queer Histories*. Durham. NC: Duke University Press Books, 2010.

Freud, Sigmund. 1993. *Beyond the Pleasure Principle, Group Psychology, and Other Works. The Standard Edition of the Complete Psychological Works of Sigmund Freud*, vol. 18. Translated by James Strachey, in collaboration with Anna Freud, assisted by Alix Strachey and Alan Tyson, 24 vols. London: Hogarth Press and the Institute of Psychoanalysis. (Orig. pub. London: Hogarth Press, 1953–74.)

———. "Fetishism." *The Future of an Illusion, Civilization and its Discontents and Other Works. The Standard Edition*, 21:149–59.

———. "Medusa's Head." *The Standard Edition*, 18: 273–74; ([1922]; published in 1940).

———. "The Uncanny." *An Infantile Neurosis and Other Works. The Standard Edition of the Complete Psychological Works of Sigmund Freud*. 17:217–56.

Frost, Laura. "Black Screens, Lost Bodies: The Cinematic Apparatus of 9/11 Horror." *Horror After 9/11*. Edited by Aviva Briefel and Sam J. Miller. 13–39.

Froula, Anna. "9/11—What's That?": Trauma, Temporality, and *Terminator: The Sarah Connor Chronicles*." *Cinema Journal*, vol. 51, no. 1, Fall 2011.

Fuchs, Cynthia J. "The Buddy Politic." *Screening the Male: Exploring Masculinities in Hollywood Cinema*. Edited by. Steven Cohan and Ina Rae Hark. New York: Routledge, 1993.

Fung, Richard. "Looking for My Penis: The Eroticized Asian in Gay Video Porn." *How Do I Look?: Queer Film and Video*. Edited by Cindy Patton, et al. Seattle, WA: Bay Press, 1991. 145–61.

Fuss, Diana. "Oral Incorporations: *The Silence of the Lambs*." *Identification Papers*. New York: Routledge, 1996. 83–107.

Garber, Marjorie. *Shakespeare's Ghost Writers: Literature as Uncanny Causality*. New York: Methuen, 1987.

Gardener, Lee. "*Restrepo* and *The Oath* Show Different Perspectives on the War on Terror." *Metro Pulse*, December 15, 2010. Accessed September 23, 2011. http://www.metropulse.com/news/2010/dec/15/restrepo-and-oath-show-different-perspectives-war/.

Gerstner, David A. *Manly Arts: Masculinity and Nation in Early American Cinema*. Durham, NC: Duke University Press, 2006.

Gilbey, Ryan, "*25th Hour*," *Sight & Sound*. March 2003, vol. 13, issue 3.

Girard, René. *Deceit, Desire, and the Novel: Self and Other in Literary Structure*. Baltimore, MD: Johns Hopkins University Press, 1961.

Gladstone, Jason, and Daniel Worden. "Introduction: Postmodernism, Then." *Twentieth-Century Literature* 57.3/4 (Fall/Winter 2011): 291–308.

Gledhill, Christine. "Introduction." *Gender Meets Genre in Postwar Cinemas*. Edited by Christine Gledhill. Urbana: University of Illinois Press, 2012. 1–11.

Grant, Barry Keith *Film Genre: From Iconography to Ideology*. Vol. 33. London; New York: Wallflower Press, 2007.

———. *Shadows of Doubt: Negotiations of Masculinity in American Genre Films*. Contemporary Approaches to Film and Television Series. Detroit, MI: Wayne State University Press, 2011.

Greven, David. "American Psycho Family Values: Conservative Cinema and the New Travis Bickles." *Millennial Masculinity: Men in Contemporary American Cinema*. Edited by Timothy Shary. Detroit, MI: Wayne State University Press, 2012. 143–62.

———. "*Dexter*, Straight Homosexuality, and the Normalization of the Psycho." *Flow*. http://flowtv.org/2013/05/dexter-straight-homosexuality/.

———. "Dude, Where's My Gender? Contemporary Teen Comedies and New Forms of American Masculinity." *Cineaste*. vol. 27 no. 3, June 2002.

———. "Making Love While the Bullets Fly: *Plata Quemada* (*Burnt Money*), Representation, and Queer Masculinity." *Bright Lights Film Journal*. http://brightlightsfilm.com/80/80-burnt-money-plata-quemada-queer-cinema-masculinity-greven.php#.U0Knc_ldXwg.

———. *Manhood in Hollywood from Bush to Bush*. Austin: University of Texas Press, 2009.

———. *Men Beyond Desire: Manhood, Sex, and Violation in American Literature*. New York: Palgrave Macmillan, 2005.

———. *Psycho-Sexual: Male Desire in Hitchcock, De Palma, Scorsese, and Friedkin*. Austin: University of Texas Press, 2013.

———. *Representations of Femininity in American Genre Cinema: The Woman's Film, Film Noir, and Modern Horror*. New York: Palgrave Macmillan, 2011.

———. "The Return of the Father: *Deadwood* and the Contemporary Gender Politics of Complexity." *The Last Western: Deadwood and the End of American Empire*. Edited by Jennifer Greiman and Paul Stasi. New York: Continuum, 2012. 194–214.

———. "Spectral Men: Femininity, Race, and Traumatic Manhood in the RTV Ghost-Hunter Genre." *Reality Gendervision: Sexuality and Gender on Transatlantic Reality Television*. Edited by Brenda R. Weber. Durham, NC: Duke University Press, 2014. 316–39.

———. "Strike Through the Mask: Male Faces, Masculinity, and Allegorical Queerness in *Breaking Bad*." *Flow*. http://flowtv.org/2013/03/strike-through-the-mask/.

———. "The Walking Straight: Queer Representation in *The Walking Dead*." *Flow*. http://flowtv.org/2012/11/the-walking-straight/.

Guerrero, Ed. *Framing Blackness: The African-American Image in Film*. Philadelphia: Temple University Press, 1993.

Gunning, Tom. "The Cinema of Attractions: Early Film, Its Spectator and the Avant-Garde." *Wide Angle*, vol. 8, nos. 3 & 4 Fall, 1986.

Halberstam, Judith. *In a Queer Time and Place: Transgender Bodies, Subcultural Lives*. New York: NYU Press, 2005.

———. *Skin Shows: Gothic Horror and the Technology of Monsters*. Durham, NC: Duke University Press, 2000.

Hantke, Steffen. *American Horror Film: The Genre at the Turn of the Millennium*. Jackson: University Press of Mississippi, 2010.

———. "Historicizing the Bush years: politics, horror film, and Francis Lawrence's *I am Legend*." *Horror after 9/11: World of Fear, Cinema of Terror*. Edited by Aviva Briefel and Sam J. Miller. 165–85.

Harrison-Kahan, Lori. "Inside *Inside Man*: Spike Lee and Post-9/11 Entertainment." *Cinema Journal* 50, no. 1, Fall 2010, pp. 39–58.

Hart, Kylo-Patrick R. *Queer Males in Contemporary Cinema: Becoming Visible*. Lanham, MD: The Scarecrow Press, 2013. Print.

Hawthorne, Nathaniel. "The Minister's Black Veil." *Nathaniel Hawthorne's Tales*. Edited by James McIntosh. New York: Norton Critical Editions, 1987.

Hayward, Susan. *Cinema Studies: The Key Concepts*. 4th ed. Routledge Key Guides. Abingdon, Oxon; New York: Routledge, 2013.

Henderson, Danielle. *Feminist Ryan Gosling: Feminist Theory (as Imagined) from Your Favorite Sensitive Movie Dude*. Philadelphia: Running Press, 2012.

Herzog, Amy. "Suspended Gestures: Schizoanalysis, Affect, and the Face in Cinema." *Deleuze and the Schizoanalysis of Cinema*. Edited by Ian Buchanan and Patricia MacCormack. 63–74.

Hirshman, Linda R. *Victory: The Triumphant Gay Revolution*. New York: Harper, 2012.

Hoberman, J. *Film After Film : or, What Became of 21st-century Cinema?* Brooklyn, NY: Verso, 2012.

Holland, Sharon Patricia. *Raising the Dead: Readings of Death and (Black) Subjectivity*. Durham, NC: Duke University Press, 2000.

Holmlund, Chris. *Impossible Bodies: Femininity and Masculinity at the Movies*. London; New York: Routledge, 2002.

Horton, Andrew. *Comedy/cinema/theory*. Berkeley: University of California Press, 1991.

Hymowitz, Kay. *Manning Up: How the Rise of Women Has Turned Men into Boys*. New York: Basic Books, 2011.

Irigaray. Luce. *Speculum of the Other Woman*. Trans. Gillian C. Gill. Ithaca, NY: Cornell University Press, 1985.

Jackson, Richard. "The 9/11 Attacks and the Social Construction of a National Narrative." *The Impact of 9/11 on the Media, Arts, and Entertainment: The Day That Changed Everything*. Edited by Matthew J. Morgan. New York: Palgrave Macmillan, 2009. 25–35.

Jeffords, Susan. *Hard Bodies: Hollywood Masculinity in the Reagan Era*. New Brunswick, NJ: Rutgers University Press, 1994.

———. *The Remasculinization of America: Gender and the Vietnam War*. Vol. 10. Theories of Contemporary Culture. Bloomington: Indiana University Press, 1989.

Johnson, Jr., Michael. "Queer Negotiations Between Love and Work: A Critical Ethnographic Case Study of a Gay Porn." *Queer Love in Film and Television: Critical Essays.* Edited by Pamela Demory and Christopher Pullen. 219–31.

Kael, Pauline. *Going Steady.* Boston: Little, Brown, 1970.

Kaiser, David, and Lovisa Stannow. "Prison Rape and the Government." *New York Review of Books*, March 24, 2011. Accessed September 1, 2012. http://www.nybooks.com/articles/archives/2011/mar/24/prison-rape-and-government/.

Kaplan, E. Ann, ed. *Psychoanalysis and Cinema.* London: Routledge, 1990.

Karlyn, Kathleen Rowe. "Comedy, Melodrama, and Gender: Theorizing the Genres of Laughter," *Screening Genders.* Edited by Krin Gabbard and William Luhr. New Brunswick, NJ: Rutgers University Press, 2008, 155–67.

———. *Unruly Girls, Unrepentant Mothers: Redefining Feminism on Screen.* Austin: Texas Press, 2011.

Kawin, Bruce. *How Movies Work.* Berkeley, CA: University of California Press, 1992.

Kibbey, Ann M. *Theory of the Image: Capitalism, Contemporary Film, and Women.* Bloomington: Indiana University Press, 2004.

King, Geoff. *Donnie Darko.* New York: Wallflower Press, 2007.

Kimmel, Michael. *Guyland: The Perilous World Where Boys Become Men.* New York: Harper Paperbacks, 2009.

Kipnis, Laura. *Bound and Gagged: Pornography and the Politics of Fantasy in America.* New York: Grove Press, 1996.

Kirshner, Jonathan. *Hollywood's Last Golden Age : Politics, Society, and the Seventies Film in America.* Ithaca, NY: Cornell University Press, 2012.

Kolker, Robert. *A Cinema of Loneliness: Penn, Stone, Kubrick, Scorsese, Spielberg, Altman.* 4th ed. New York: Oxford University Press, 2011.

Kord, Susanne, and Elisabeth Krimmer. *Contemporary Hollywood Masculinities: Gender, Genre, and Politics.* New York: Palgrave Macmillan, 2011.

Kracauer, Siegfried. *From Caligari to Hitler: a Psychological History of the German Film.* Princeton, NJ: Princeton University Press, 1947.

———. *Theory of Film; the Redemption of Physical Reality.* New York: Oxford University Press, 1960.

Lacan, Jacques. "The Mirror Stage as Formative of the Function of the I as Revealed in Psychoanalytic Experience." *Écrits: A Selection.* Translated by Bruce Fink. New York: W. W. Norton, 2002, 3–9.

———. "The Signification of the Phallus." *Écrits: A Selection.* 271–80.

Krutnik, Frank. *In a Lonely Street: Film Noir, Genre, Masculinity.* New York: Routledge, 1991.

Lane, Anthony. Review of *Halloween: H20* (Steve Miner; 1998). *The New Yorker*, August 17, 1998.

Lang, Robert. *Masculine Interests: Homoerotics in Hollywood Films.* New York: Columbia University Press, 2002.

Langford, Barry. *Film Genre: Hollywood and beyond.* Edinburgh: Edinburgh University Press, 2005.

Lee, Nathan. "Rob Zombie: True Believer." *Film Comment* (May/June 2013), 48–50.

Lehman, Peter. "Crying over the Melodramatic Penis: Melodrama and Male Nudity in the Films of the 90s." *Masculinity: Bodies, Movies, Culture*. Edited by Peter Lehman. New York: Routledge, 2001. 25–42.

———. *Running Scared: Masculinity and the Representation of the Male Body*. Culture and the Moving Image. Philadelphia: Temple University Press, 1993.

———. *Running Scared: Masculinity and the Representation of the Male Body*. New ed. Detroit, MI: Wayne State University Press, 2007.

Lehman, Peter, and Susan Hunt. "The Naked and the Dead: The Jewish Male Body and Masculinity in *Sunshine* and *Enemy at the Gates*." *The Persistence of Whiteness: Race and Contemporary Hollywood Cinema*. Edited by Daniel Bernardi. New York: Routledge, 2008. 157–64.

Leitch, Thomas. "Twice-Told Tales: Disavowal and the Rhetoric of the Remake." *Dead Ringers*. Edited by Jennifer Forrest and Leonard R. Koos, pp. 37–62.

Levy, Ariel. *Female Chauvinist Pigs: Women and the Rise of Raunch Culture*. New York: Free Press, 2006.

Linderman, Deborah. "Cinematic Abreaction: Tourneur's *Cat People*." *Psychoanalysis and Cinema*. Edited by E. Ann Kaplan. London: Routledge, 1990, pp. 73–97.

Locke, Brian. " 'The White Man's Bruce Lee': Race and the Construction of White Masculinity in David Fincher's *Fight Club* (1999)." *Journal of Asian American Studies*, vol. 17, no. 1, February 2014, pp. 61–89.

Lotz, Amanda D. *Cable Guys : Television and Masculinities in the Twenty-First Century*. New York: New York University Press, 2014.

Love, Heather. *Feeling Backward: Loss and the Politics of Queer History*. Cambridge, MA: Harvard University Press, 2007.

Lowenstein, Adam. *Shocking Representation: Historical Trauma, National Cinema, and the Modern Horror Film*. Film and Culture. New York: Columbia University Press, 2005.

———. "Spectacle Horror and *Hostel*: Why 'Torture Porn' Does Not Exist." *Critical Quarterly*, vol. 53, no. 1, pp. 42–60.

Luciano, Lynne. *Looking Good: Male Body Image in Modern America*. New York: Hill and Wang, 2002.

Lugowski, David. "Ginger Rogers and Gay Men?: Queer Film Studies, Richard Dwyer, and Diva Worship." *Screening Genders*. Edited by Krin Gabbard and William Luhr. New Brunswick, NJ: Rutgers University Press, 2008. 95–110.

Lukasik, Christopher J. *Discerning Characters: The Culture of Appearance in Early America*. Early American Studies. Philadelphia: University of Pennsylvania Press, 2011.

Martin, Robert K. "Knights Errant and Gothic Seducers: The Representation of Male Friendship in Mid-Nineteenth-Century America." *Hidden from History: Reclaiming the Gay and Lesbian Past*. Edited by Martin Duberman, Martha Vicinus, and George Chauncey. New York: Plume, 1990.

McGowan, Todd. *Out of Time: Desire in Atemporal Cinema*. Minneapolis: University of Minnesota Press, 2011.

———. *The Real Gaze: Film Theory After Lacan*. Albany, NY: SUNY Press, 2007.

Melendez, Frank. 'Video Pornography, Visual Pleasure, and the Return of the Sublime." *Porn Studies*. Edited by Linda Williams. Durham, NC: Duke University Press, 2004. 401–31.

Melnick, Jeffrey. *9/11 Culture*. Malden, MA: John Wiley & Sons, 2011.

Melville, Herman, Harrison Hayford, and Hershel Parker. *Moby-Dick: or, The Whale* (1851). 2nd ed., 150th anniversary. A Norton Critical Edition. New York: Norton, 2002.

———. "To Nathaniel Hawthorne, [1 June?] 1851, Pittsfield." *Correspondence. The Writings of Herman Melville*. Vol. 14. Edited by Lynne Horth. Evanston, IL: Northwestern University Press and Newberry Library, 1993. 188–94.

Mercer, Kobena. *Welcome to the Jungle*. New York: Routledge, 1994.

Metz, Christian. *The Imaginary Signifier : Psychoanalysis and the Cinema*. Bloomington: Indiana University Press, 1982.

Mitchell, Juliet. *Mad Men and Medusas: Reclaiming Hysteria*. New York: Basic Books, 2000.

Morgan, Matthew J. *The Impact of 9/11 on the Media, Arts, and Entertainment: The Day That Changed Everything?* New York: Palgrave Macmillan, 2009.

Morrison, Paul. *The Explanation for Everything : Essays on Sexual Subjectivity*. Sexual Cultures. New York: New York University Press, 2001.

Musser, Charles. "Film Truth in the Age of George W. Bush." *Framework: The Journal of Cinema and Media*, vol. 48, no. 2, Fall 2007, pp. 9–35.

Mulvey, Laura. "Visual Pleasure and Narrative Cinema" (1975). *Screen* 16 (3): 6–18.

———. "Afterthoughts on 'Visual Pleasure and Narrative Cinema' inspired by *Duel in the Sun*" [1981], *Framework* 15/16/17 (1981): 12–15.

Muñoz, José Esteban. *Cruising Utopia: The Then and There of Queer Futurity*. New York: NYU Press, 2009.

———. "Photographies of Mourning: Melancholia and Ambivalence in Van Der Zee, Mapplethorpe, and *Looking for Langston*." *Disidentifications: Queers of Color and the Performance of Politics*. Vol. 2. Cultural Studies of the Americas. Minneapolis, MN: University of Minnesota Press, 1999. 57–74.

Natoli, Joseph. *Speeding to the Millennium: Film & Culture, 1993–1995*. Albany, NY: SUNY Press, 1998.

Neale, Steve. "Masculinity as Spectacle." *The Sexual Subject: A Screen Reader in Sexuality*. New York: Routledge, 1992.

Neale, Stephen, ed. *Genre and Contemporary Hollywood*. London: British Film Institute, 2002. Print.

Neale, Stephen, and Frank Krutnik. *Popular Film and Television Comedy*. London; New York: Routledge, 1990.

Needham, Gary. "Closer than Ever: French Cinema and the Male Body in Close-Up." *Mysterious Skin: The Male Body in Global Cinema*. Edited by Santiago Fouz-Hernandez. London, I. B. Tauris, 2008. 127–41.

Nelson, Andrew Patrick. "Traumatic Childhood Now Included: Todorov's Fantastic and the Uncanny Slasher Remake." *American Horror Film: The Genre at the Turn of the Millennium*. Edited by Hantke. 103–18.

Nystrom, Derek. *Hard Hats, Rednecks, and Macho Men : Class in 1970s American Cinema*. Oxford ; New York: Oxford University Press, 2009.

Paglia, Camille. *Sexual Personae: Art & Decadence from Nefertiti to Emily Dickinson* New York: Random House

Parker, Kathleen. *Save the Males: Why Men Matter, Why Women Should Care*. New York: Random House Trade Paperbacks, 2010.

Paul, William. "Charles Chaplin and the Annals of Anality." *Comedy/Cinema/Theory*. Edited by Andrew S. Horton

———. *Laughing, Screaming: Modern Hollywood Horror and Comedy*. New York: Columbia University Press, 1994.

Penley, Constance. "The Future of an Illusion : Film, Feminism, and Psychoanalysis." *Media & Society* 2. Minneapolis, MN: University of Minnesota Press, 1989.

Penley, Constance, and Sharon Willis, eds. *Male Trouble*. Minneapolis, MN: University of Minnesota Press, 1993. Print.

Pinedo, Isabel Cristina. *Recreational Terror: Women and the Pleasures of Horror Film Viewing*. Albany, NY: SUNY Press, 1997.

Phillips, John. *Transgender on Screen*. New York: Palgrave Macmillan, 2006.

Pollard, Thomas. "Hollywood 9/11: Time of Crisis." *The Impact of 9/11 on the Media, Arts, and Entertainment: The Day That Changed Everything?*. Edited by Matthew J. Morgan, New York: Palgrave Macmillan, 2009. 195–207.

Pomerance, Murray. "Introduction: Gender in Film at the End of the Twentieth Century." *Ladies and Gentlemen, Boys and Girls: Gender in Film at the End of the Twentieth Century*. Edited by Murray Pomerance. New York: State University of New York Press, 2001. 1–15.

Puar, Jasbir K. *Terrorist Assemblages : Homonationalism in Queer Times*. Next Wave. Durham, NC: Duke University Press, 2007.

Putnam, Robert D. *Bowling Alone: The Collapse and Revival of American Community*. New York: Touchstone Books, 2001.

Radner, Hilary. "Grumpy Old Men: 'Bros Before Hos.' " *Reading the Bromance*. Edited by Michael DeAngelis. 52–78.

Rauch, Jonathan. "For Better or Worse." *Same-Sex Marriage: Pro and Con: A Reader*. Edited by Andrew Sullivan. New York: Vintage, 1997.

Rank, Otto. *The Double: A Psychoanalytic Study*. Translated by Harry Tucker, Jr. Chapel Hill, NC: University of North Carolina Press, 1971.

Ray, Robert B. *A Certain Tendency of the Hollywood Cinema, 1930–1980*. Princeton, NJ: Princeton University Press, 1985.

Reich. Wilhelm. *Character Analysis*. Translated by Victor Carfagno. 1945; New York: Noonday Press, 1991.

Reik, Theodor. *Masochism in Sex and Society*. 1941; New York: Pyramid Books, 1976.

Rich, B. Ruby. *New Queer Cinema: The Director's Cut*. Durham, NC: Duke University Press, 2013.

Riegert, Kristina and Anders Johansson. "The Struggle for Credibility during the Iraq War." *The Iraq War: European Perspectives on Politics, Strategy and Opera-

tions. Edited by Jan Hallenberg and Håkan Karlsson. New York: Routledge, 2005: 178–194.

Richardson, Niall. "Effeminophobia, Misogyny and Queer Friendship: The Cultural Themes of Channel 4's Playing It Straight." *Sexualities*, vol. 12, no. 4, 525–544 (2009).

Rockoff, Adam. *Going to Pieces: The Rise and Fall of the Slasher Film, 1978–1986*. Jefferson, NC: McFarland & Co., 2002.

Rodowick, D. N. "The Difficulty of Difference." *Wide Angle*, 1982, vol. 5, no. 1.

———. *Reading the Figural, or, Philosophy after the New Media*. Post-contemporary Interventions. Durham, NC: Duke University Press, 2001.

Rohy, Valerie. *Anachronism and Its Others: Sexuality, Race, Temporality*. Albany, NY: SUNY Press, 2009.

Rosenberg, Warren. *Legacy of Rage: Jewish Masculinity, Violence, and Culture*. Amherst, MA: University of Massachusetts Press, 2001.

Roth, Marty. "Twice Two: The Fly and Invasion of the Body Snatchers." *Dead Ringers,*. Edited by Jennifer Forrest and Leonard R. Koos, pp. 225–242.

Rubin, Gayle. "The Traffic in Women: Notes on the 'Political Economy' of Sex." *Toward an Anthropology of Women*. Edited by Rayna R. Reiter. New York: Monthly Review Press, 1975: 157–210.

Russo, Vito. *The Celluloid Closet: Homosexuality in the Movies*. 1981; New York: Harper and Row, rev. ed., 1987.

Ryall, Tom. "Teaching through Genre" (1975). *Screen Education*, 17: 27–33.

Sanjek, David. "Same as It Ever Was: Innovation and Exhaustion in the Horror and Science Fiction Films of the 1990s." *Film Genres 2000: New Critical Essays*. Albany, NY: SUNY Press, 2000. 111–123.

Salih, Sara. *Judith Butler*. London; New York: Routledge, 2002.

Schiesari, Juliana. *The Gendering of Melancholia : Feminism, Psychoanalysis, and the Symbolics of Loss in Renaissance Literature*. Ithaca, NY: Cornell University Press, 1992.

Sedgwick, Eve Kosofsky. "Gender Asymmetry and Erotic Triangles." *Between Men: English Literature and Male Homosocial Desire*. New York: Columbia University Press, 1985: 21–27.

———. *Epistemology of the Closet*. Berkeley, CA: University of California Press, 1990.

Seltzer, Mark. *Serial Killers: Death and Life in America's Wound Culture*. New York: Routledge, 1998.

Shary, Timothy, ed. *Millennial Masculinity: Men in Contemporary American Cinema*. Detroit, MI: Wayne State University Press, 2012.

———. "Introduction." *Millennial Masculinity*. 1–18.

Shaviro, Steven. *The Cinematic Body*. Minneapolis, MN: University of Minnesota Press, 1993.

———. *Connected, or What It Means to Live in the Network Society*. Minneapolis, MN: University of Minnesota Press, 2003.

Silverman, Kaja. *Male Subjectivity at the Margins*. New York: Routledge, 1992.

Sinfield, Alan. *The Wilde Century: Effeminacy, Oscar Wilde, and the Queer Moment.* New York: Columbia University Press, 1994.

Sipos, Thomas M. *Horror Film Aesthetics: Creating The Visual Language of Fear.* Jefferson, NC: McFarland & Co., 2010, 94.

Smith, Angela M. *Hideous Progeny: Disability, Eugenics, and Classic Horror Cinema.* Film and Culture. New York: Columbia University Press, 2011.

Sternberg, Lindsay. " 'Get More Action' on Gladiatorial Television." *Reality Gendervision.* Edited by Brenda Weber. 192–210.

Stevens, Kyle. "Dying to Love: Gay Identity, Suicide, and Aesthetics in *A Single Man*." *Cinema Journal*, 52.4 (2013): 99–120.

Stockton, Kathryn Bond. *The Queer Child, or Growing Sideways in the Twentieth Century.* Series Q. Durham, NC: Duke University Press, 2009.

Stoller, Robert J. *Presentations of Gender.* New Haven, CT: Yale University Press, 1985.

Studlar, Gaylyn. *In the Realm of Pleasure: Von Sternberg, Dietrich, and the Masochistic Aesthetic.* New York: Columbia University Press, 1993.

Stratton, Jon. *The Desirable Body: Cultural Fetishism and the Erotics of Consumption.* 1st Illinois paperback. Urbana: University of Illinois Press, 2001.

Tasker, Yvonne. *Spectacular Bodies: Gender, Genre and the Action Cinema.* New York: Routledge, 1996.

Thompson, Kirsten Moana. *Apocalyptic Dread: American Film at the Turn of the Millennium.* Albany, NY: SUNY Press, 2007.

Todorov, Tzvetan, and Richard Howard. *The Fantastic: a Structural Approach to a Literary Genre.* Cornell Paperbacks. Ithaca, NY: Cornell University Press, 1975.

Walker, Tim. "King of Bromance: Judd Apatow." *The Independent*, August 19, 2009.

Walters, Suzanna Danuta. *All the Rage: The Story of Gay Visibility in America.* Chicago: University of Chicago Press, 2001.

Warner, Michael. *The Trouble with Normal: Sex, Politics and the Ethics of Queer Life.* New York: Free Press, 1999.

Waugh, Thomas. *Hard to Imagine: Gay Male Eroticism in Photography and Film from Their Beginnings to Stonewall.* New York: Columbia University Press, 1996.

———. "Homosociality in the Classical American Stag Film: Off-Screen, On-Screen." *Porn Studies.* Edited by Linda Williams. 127–141.

Weber, Brenda R., ed. *Reality Gendervision: Sexuality and Gender on Transatlantic Reality Television.* Durham, NC: Duke University Press, 2014.

White, Susan. "*Vertigo* and Problems of Knowledge in Feminist Film Theory." *Alfred Hitchcock: Centenary Essays.* Edited by Richard Allen and Sam Ishii-Gonzalès. London: British Film Institute, 1999. 279–307.

Wiegman, Robyn. *American Anatomies: Theorizing Race and Gender.* Durham, NC: Duke University Press, 1995.

Williams, Linda. "Film Bodies: Gender, Genre, and Excess." *Film Quarterly*, vol. 44:4 (Summer 1991), pp. 2–13.

———. *Hard Core: Power, Pleasure, and the "Frenzy of the Visible."* Expanded pbk. Berkeley: University of California Press, 1999.

———. *Porn Studies*. Edited by Linda Williams. Durham, NC: Duke University Press, 2004. 401–31.

Williams, Linda Ruth. "Movies, Smart Films, and Dumb Stories." *American Cinema of the '00s*. Edited by Timothy Corrigan. 40–60.

Willeman, Paul. "Anthony Mann: Looking at the Male," *Framework*, no. 15–17, Summer 1981, pp. 16–20.

Williams, Tony. *Larry Cohen: The Radical Allegories of an Independent Filmmaker* (Jefferson, NC: McFarland & Company, 1996).

Wood, Robin. *Hollywood from Vietnam to Reagan . . . and Beyond*. 1986; New York: Columbia University Press, 2003.

———. *Sexual Politics and Narrative Film: Hollywood and Beyond*. New York: Columbia University Press, 1998.

Worland, Rick. *The Horror Film: An Introduction*. Malden, MA: Wiley-Blackwell, 2006.

Zimmer, Catherine. "Caught on tape? The politics of video in the new torture film." *Horror after 9/11*. Edited by Aviva Briefel and Sam J. Miller. 83–106.

Žižek, Slavoj. *Looking Awry: An Introduction to Jacques Lacan Through Popular Culture*. Cambridge, MA: The MIT Press, 1992, 79.

———. "'I Hear You with My Eyes'; or, The Invisible Master." *Gaze and Voice as Love Objects*. Edited by Renata Salecl and Žižek. Durham, NC: Duke University Press, 1996.

Index

1970s: buddy films, 123; film theory, 140, 264; grindhouse, 223; horror, 94, 170, 243, 252; masculinities, 6, 16, 18, 32, 37, 38, 39; teen comedies, 212, 244, 253

1980s: action movies, 32, 36, 74; buddy films, 112; cultural preoccupation with, 32; 39, 94; *Donnie Darko*, 22, 144; gay consumer, 244; genre film, 14, 32; horror remakes, 16, 71, 170, 204; masculinities, 5, 32, 47, 74, 78; night-time soap operas, 74; pornography, 253; queer visibility (emergence of), 7, 73; teen comedies, 134

1990s: gender shifts, 65, 82, 199, 209; genre film, 14; masculinities, 39, 142; millennial fears, 40; queer films, 47, 241; queer visibility (emergence of), 2, 6, 39, 72, 274; teen comedies, 134; violence in films, 45

25th Hour (2002), 152–68

40-Year-Old Virgin, The, 27, 51, 52, 55, 105, 120, 127, 128, 131, 136, 257

À ma soeur! (English title, *Fat Girl*), 124, 250

Abu Ghraib, 198, 224

action movies, 32, 242

adaptation, film, 155, 158, 163

AIDS, 16, 64, 73, 143, 174, 242

alibi: of heterosexuality, 97, 237

All-American Heroes, 200, 231–36

Altman, Rick, 14

American Beauty, 40, 268

American Pie, 34, 40, 73, 74, 75, 116, 151, 209, 211, 253, 275

American Psycho, 148

anality, 185–90

anal father, 186

antebellum American literature, 2, 27, 59, 64, 111, 113, 152, 170, 171, 172, 176, 190, 258; Gothic: 27, 33, 59–63, 94, 111, 115–20, 137, 138, 170–75, 185, 190, 192

anti-Asian prejudice, 221

anti-social thesis, 3

Apatow, Judd, 15, 34, 43, 73, 101, 105, 115, 129, 134, 135, 136, 171, 249, 257, 258

apostrophe, 63, 64, 158, 269

Argento, Dario, 276

Bagans, Zak, 54

Baker, Brian, 142

Ball, Alan, 40

Balázs, Béla, 67

Barbarella, 214

Basic Instinct, 19

Batman and Robin, 40

Baudry, Jean-Louis, 140

Becker, Ron, 108
Bernard, Mark, 213
beautiful boy as destroyer, 99, 104
Behind the Candelabra, 10, 243
Beltrán, Mary C., 14
Benioff, David: see *25th Hour*
Benjamin, Jessica, 49–51
Benshoff, Harry M., 12, 226
Bersani, Leo, 3
beta male comedies, 105–34; 2, 9, 15, 20, 22, 34, 43, 47, 51, 54, 59, 72, 73, 75, 80, 99, 171, 192, 205, 206, 209, 210, 225
Blake, Linnie, 273
Blaxploitation, 38
Blood of a Poet, The, 143, 146
body genres, 5, 17, 20, 21, 22, 72, 199, 205, 244
Boogie Nights, 25, 243
Brando, Marlon, 111
Breillat, Catherine, 250
Bridesmaids, 260
Brokeback Mountain, 117, 152, 239
bromance, 77, 99–104; 105–34; melancholia in, 102–103; woman's threat to, 100
Bruhm, Steven, 147
buddy films, 77, 112, 123
bullies and bullying, 190
Buñuel, Luis, 192
Bush, George H., 33, 73, 144
Bush, George W., 231
Butler, Judith, 6, 64, 102, 143, 218

Cabin Fever, 202
Carell, Steve, 27, 28, 29, 111, 120, 128, 131, 250
Carpenter, John, 16, 44, 72, 79, 93, 94, 95, 148, 170, 171, 172, 174, 175, 187, 193
Carrie, 88
Casino Royale: representative of sadomasochism, 48, 56–57
Castle, Terry, 6, 137

Casualties of War, 194, 222
Change-Up, The, 15, 23–24, 129–30, 258
Chasseguet-Smirgel, Janine, 184–90
child as killer, the, 182, 184–90
Chow, Rey, 135
chora, the, 150
Christian iconography of Christ on the Cross, 96
Chronicle, 17
Cianfrance, Derek, 244
cinema of attractions, 224
Clinton, Bill, 39
class, 178–79
classicism, 58, 93, 165–67
Clift, Montgomery, 162–64
close-up, the, 55, 67–69
Clover, Carol J., 78
Cocteau, Jean, 143
Cohan, Steven, 13
Cohen, Josh, 62
Coldness and Cruelty (Deleuze), 52
Columbine High School shootings (1999), 72, 82
comedy, 21, 25, 110; carnivalesque, 256; highbrow versus lowbrow, 21; and horror, 115, 169
Condon, Bill: see *Gods and Monsters*
Connell, R. W., 5, 264
Corber, Robert J., 19, 35
Corvo, Rafael E. López, 273
Coupland, Douglas, 31
Cowie, Elizabeth, 237
Craig, Daniel: eroticism of star image, 56
Craven, Wes: see *Scream*
Crazy, Stupid, Love, 27–29
Creed, Barbara, 78
Cronenberg, David, 98, 249
cruising, 146
Cruising, 38
Crying Game, The, 25

Dances with Wolves, 3, 39

danger porn, 41
Dawn of the Dead (2004), 16
De Angelis, Michael, 106
de Lauretis, Teresa, 6
De Palma, Brian, 194, 222, 223, 249, 260, 276
Deadwood, 33, 36, 246
death drive, 3, 45, 46, 246, 247
Deep Throat, 38
Dean James: in *Rebel without a Cause*, 86, 88
Deleuze, Gilles, 43, 49, 52, 55, 56, 66, 67, 156, 248
de Man, Paul, 63; see also *prosopopoeia*
desire, 61
"Dick in a Box," 118
dismantling: defined, 20; 47, 104, 223; gay porn, 42, 228–38; horror, 223–28
disrecognition: defined, 30
Dixon, Wheeler Winston, 150
Django Unchained, 33, 222
Doane, Mary Ann, 13, 264
Dog Day Afternoon, 38
Dora (Freud case study), 149
double, the, 146–47
Dovzhenko, Alexander, 67
Donnie Darko (2001), 144–52; 22, 32–33, 169, 222
Dornan, Jamie, 36
double-protagonist films, 256
Drive, 55–58
Duck Dynasty, 7
Dude, Where's My Car?, 40
Dunas, Chris, 185
Dukakis, Michael, 33
Dunham, Lena, 9, 120, 260
Dunn, Stephanie, 38
Dyer, Richard, 25
dystopia girls, 8

Edelman, Lee, 3, 6
effeminophobia, 88, 107, 108
Eisenstein, Sergei, 67

Edmundson, Mark, 49–51, 171
effeminacy, 8, 88, 92, 107, 108, 112, 140, 226
Elsaesser, Thomas, 146
Enlightened, 118
ethnic masculinities, 38, 39

faciality (Deleuze and Guattari concept), 1, 66, 67, 156
"Facts in the Case of M. Valdemar, The" (Poe story), 27
Farrelly Brothers, The, 25, 73, 276
Fat Girl, 124, 250
fanboys, 87; see also geek-culture
fatal woman, 222
father, the, 98
Feil, Ken, 110
fellatio, 24, 234, 253
female bodies, 16, 19, 135
female bonds, 97
female ethnographic observer, 114
femininity, 6, 13, 18, 22, 26, 52, 57, 93, 99, 114, 135, 139, 205, 240; pornography, 235
female voices and pornography, 235
fetishism, 17, 43, 52, 56, 66, 67, 103, 248
Fiedler, Leslie, 112
Fifty Shades of Grey, 9, 36, 50
Fight Club, 40, 41, 115
film noir, 55–56
film theory: 1970s, 140, 264
Final Girl, 79; 92; see also Finalizing Woman
Finalizing Woman, 97
Forgetting Sarah Marshall, 123–26; 34, 105, 133, 135
Foxcatcher, 245
Franco, James, 7, 101, 107, 108, 121, 126, 129, 198, 274
Frankenstein (1931), 148
Freud, Sigmund, 3, 40, 43, 46, 49, 56, 59, 61, 62, 88, 89, 90, 91, 102, 110, 114, 146, 147, 163, 185, 226

Friday the 13th, 104
Friedkin, William, 174
Froula, Anna, 245
full-frontal nudity: *see* male bodies; penis
Funny Games, 253
Funny People, 101
Fuss, Diana, 68, 90, 252

gamer media, 50
gay male Internet pornography, 228–38; 2, 41, 44, 114, 202; bliss montage, 42; dismantling of male bodies, 41; danger porn, 41; Reality porn, 41; *see also* racism
gay male sexuality, 3, 226
gay marriage, 6, 242
gaze theory, 17–20, 113; *see also* masochistic gaze, the; the psychoanalytic scene
geek-culture, 52
genre film, 12–17, 55
"Gentle Boy, The" (Hawthorne story), 171, 188–89
German Expressionism, 33, 78, 145
Gerstner, David, 53
Ghost Adventures, 272
Ghost Faces: defined: 45–70; *see also* faciality
"ghost-hunter" TV shows, 272
Girls, 9, 120
Gledhill, Christine, 13
Glee, 7, 258–59
God Told Me To, 38
Gods and Monsters, 148, 266
Godzilla vs. the Smog Monster, 223
Gosling, Ryan, 28, 29, 30, 55, 56, 57, 181, 239, 244
Gothic, the: 49–51, 238; antebellum American literature, 27, 33, 59–63, 94, 111, 115–20, 137, 138, 170–75, 185, 190, 192; masculinity, 35; fatal woman, 222; female Gothics of the 1940s, 35

Graduate, The, 268
Grant, Barry Keith, 13, 15
Grant, Beth, 151
Griffin, Sean, 12
Griffith, D. W., 188
Guattari, Félix, 49

Halberstam, Jack [Judith], 18, 113, 199
Halloween (1978), 93–99, 172
Halloween (2007), 135, 169–96
Halloween II (1981), 178
Halloween II (2009), 16, 172, 178, 272
Halperin, David, 6
Hangover, The 15, 34, 105, 127
Hark, Ina Rae, 13
Hart, Kylo-Patrick, 13
Harvey, 250
Hawthorne, Nathaniel, 33, 34, 35, 61, 94, 137, 171, 172, 173, 176, 188, 189, 190, 211, 251
Hellbent, 206–207
Hayward, Susan, 146
Heroes, 17
hillbilly horror, 274
Hispanic-American as the Ugly American, 216
historical masculinity: defined, 31; 37, 43, 57–63; genre, 93–99; horror, 190–91
Hitchcock, Alfred, 85
Hoberman, J., 268
Holmlund, Chris, 19
homophobia, 197–238; 2, 30, 42, 68, 72, 79, 88, 92, 103, 108, 110, 130, 150, 179, 194
homosexual rape, 110, 129, 153, 160, 161, 194, 214, 223; prison rape, 129, 161, 269; *see also* Horrible Bosses; This is the End; 25th Hour
homosexuality: Freud's theory of male: *see* negative Oedipus complex
homosociality, male, 27, 37, 40, 51, 53, 69, 74, 87, 103, 112, 114, 120,

131, 133, 161, 173, 189, 190, 194, 200, 205, 210; homoerotic violence, 87, 96; pornographic viewing, 205; race, 112; torture of nonnormative male, 51, 188–89, 218; violence, 101, 102, 107; woman's relation to, 101, 114
Honoré, Christophe, 249
"Hop-Frog" (Poe story), 182
Horrible Bosses, 15, 128, 160, 161, 270
horror: Gothic, 35, 137; merging with comedy, 76, 115; historical masculinity, 93, 190; Ghost Faces, 169; German Expressionism, 170; masks, 176, 181, 193; remakes, 173–75
Hostel (2005), 197–238
Humpday, 15, 34, 99, 106, 261
Hunger Games, The, 8
hysteria, 92

I-camera, 224
I Love You, Man, 15, 75, 99–101, 106, 113, 116–19, 120, 122, 123, 131–32
Inglorious Basterds, 203
innocents abroad theme, 210
Insidious, 16
Insidious, 16
Intimacy, 123
Interior. Leather Bar., 274
Interview, The, 107–109, 274
Irigaray, Luce, 205
Irving, Washington, 34, 60

Jade, 18
Japanese horror cinema, 272
Jeff, Who Lives at Home, 15, 261
Jeffords, Susan, 6
Jewish masculinity, 126–27

Kael, Pauline, 260
Kaplan, E. Ann, 13
Karlyn, Kathleen Rowe, 93
Kelly, Richard: see *Donnie Darko*

Kibbey, Ann, 142
Kimmel, Michael, 8, 125, 210
Knocked Up, 34, 101, 102, 114, 119, 121, 135
knowing sexual nod and wink, 49
Kord, Susanne, 13
Kracauer, Siegfried, 145
Krimmer, Elisabeth, 13
Kristeva, Julia: theory of the "chora," 150
Krutnik, Frank, 13, 55
Kunzru, Hari, 31

Lacan, Jacques, 18, 25, 61, 90, 129, 139, 140, 145, 152, 185, 186, 263; *see also the* psychoanalytic scene
Lang, Robert, 13
Langford, Barry, 109
Last House on the Left, The, 71
"Legend of Sleepy Hollow, The" (Irving story), 60, 115–20, 134
Le Sang d'un poète (English title, *The Blood of a Poet*), 143, 146
Lee, Spike: see *25th Hour*
Lehman, Peter, 13, 25
Leitch, Thomas, 174
Leopold and Loeb case, 83
Lesbian sexuality, 7, 19, 137, 151
Lethal Weapon series, 112
life drive, 3, 46
Lillard, Matthew, 86, 92
Los Olvidados, 192
loss, 46
Lotz, Amanda, 9
Love, Heather, 6–7
Love and Death in the American Novel (Fiedler), 112
Lovecraft, H. P., 58
Lowenstein, Adam, 192, 200, 224
Luciano, Lynne, 38
Lukasik, Christopher, 60
Lust, Caution, 262

Magic Mike, 8–12

male bodies: 21, 24–25, 133; Ben Stiller comedies, 25; hypermasculine, 195; male body genres, 20, 30; melodramatic penis, 25; penis/full-frontal male nudity, 25, 28–30; screen objectification, 17, 19; wounding, 31; *see also* homosexual rape; torture
male body genres, 20, 30
male face, 5, 19, 43, 49, 52, 57, 63, 103, 136, 148, 155, 157, 198; *see also* Ghost Faces
male weepies, 102
mammy figure, 127
Man of Steel, 241
Manhood in Hollywood from Bush to Bush (Greven), 2, 4, 30, 68, 78, 159, 199
masculine autogenesis, 205
masculinity: crisis, 8; disaffection, 111; ethnic, 38, 39; Gothic, 35; horror of, 16; hypermasculine, 6; James Bond's, 56; military, 198; millennial, 40; 9/11 nostalgia, 156–57; opening-up theme, 10, 47, 114; parallels between constructions of straight and Orientalism, 262; passivity, sexual appeal of, 81; perceived threats to, 35; reverential attitudes toward, 115; straight, 17, 42; traditional, 4; 36; working-class, 11, 155, 232; *see also* historical masculinity; homosociality
mask, the, 54, 60, 65, 135, 170, 184; "Hemba Mask" of the Suku, 272; *see also* Ghost Faces; horror; *prosopopoeia*
masochism; 2, 3, 4, 18, 45, 49, 52, 67, 111, 126, 159, 160, 187, 200; Freud's theory, 247; *see also* sadomasochism
masochistic gaze, 30
master-slave relationship, 50
McFarlane, Seth, 135

McGowan, Todd, 18, 152, 263
Medusa, 222
Meek's Cutoff, 33, 240
Meet the Parents, 25, 73
melancholia, 102
Melnick, Jeffrey, 162
melodrama: 25–26, 117, 126, 244; melodramatic penis, 25–26
Melville, Herman, 34, 35, 60, 61, 99, 128, 137, 169, 175, 190
Men of a Certain Age, 112
Metz, Christian, 140–43
millennial fears, 80, 99
Miller, D. A., 6
mimetic desire, 92
"The Minister's Black Veil" (Hawthorne story), 62, 94, 171
misogyny, 84, 88, 94, 103, 125, 160, 184, 206, 221
Moby-Dick, 60, 112, 128, 169, 176
Modleski, Tania, iv, 13, 102
Moon, Michael, 6
Morrison, Paul, 162
mothers and maternal figures, 18, 34, 78, 85, 88–93, 154, 163, 175, 179-80, 184–85, 189, 193, 205, 235, 239, 248, 254; maternal kitchen, 90
Mulvey, Laura, 13, 17, 56, 103
Munch Edvard, 77
Muñoz, José Esteban, 30, 143

narcissism, 2, 3, 24, 44, 85, 91, 92, 96, 126, 130, 140, 143, 146, 156, 158, 160, 205, 209, 221
Natoli, Joseph, 80
Neale, Steve, 13, 18, 19
Needham, Gary, 249
negation, 168
negative Oedipus complex, 88–92
New Girl (TV series), 247
New Man, 6
New Queer Cinema, 6, 73, 83, 111, 249
Night at the Adonis, 236

Nightmare on Elm Street 3: Dream Warriors, 223

Odyssey, The, 165–67
Oedipus, 33, 155
Oedipus complex, the: negative, 88–92; perverse child and, 185
oral stage, 90
Ordinary People, 151, 267
Oresteia, The, 93
orgy: queer potential of, 12
Orphée (English title: *Orpheus*), 143
overcoding, 67

Paglia, Camille, 99
Parker, Kathleen, 8, 32
Paul, William, 110
penis: fecal penis, 185; full-frontal male nudity, 25, 28–30, 133, 135; male stars' penises, 245
melodramatic penis, 25–26; *see also* male bodies
Penley, Constance, 13
perverse child, 184–90
Peyton Place, 266
phallic narcissism, 209
Pineapple Express, 15, 80, 101, 102, 105, 121, 126, 127
Place in the Sun, A, 163
Plata quemada (English title: *Burnt Money*), 149
Point Break, 248
Poe, Edgar Allan, 27, 34, 59, 171, 182
Pollard, Thomas, 197
Pomerance, Murray, 65
pornography: *see* gay male Internet pornography; danger porn; pornovoice; Reality porn; women's sexual cries
pornovoice, 235
postfeminism, 9, 34, 66, 134; spectatorship, 9–11
Post-Theory (Bordwell and Carroll), 264
Prometheus, 58–59

prosopoeia, 63–66
Psycho, 16, 79, 85, 104
psychoanalytic scene, the: defined, 139–44
Puar, Jasbir K., 7, 198
Purcell, Natalie, 235
Putnam, Robert B., 190

queer: heterosexuality, 4; visibility (emergence of), 2, 6, 36. 39, 72, 274

race, 14, 66, 112, 126–30, 198, 231, 232
racism, 108, 156, 158, 198, 221; gay male Internet pornography, 232
Rambo, 3, 32, 38, 107
Rank, Otto, 147
rape: 194, 222; *see also* homosexual rape; misogyny
Reagan, Ronald, 3, 6, 16, 32, 39, 73, 78, 94, 144
Reality porn, 40
Reality television, 35, 40
Reichardt, Kelly: see *Meek's Cutoff*
Reik, Theodore, 263
remakes, 173–75; allegory of, 183
Reservoir Dogs, 203–205
retrospective impulse, the: defined, 32
return of the repressed, 80
"Rip Van Winkle" (Irving story), 34, 268
Risky Business: male sexuality displayed, 74
Rocky, 38
Rodowick, D. N., 18
Rogen, Seth, 7, 27, 34, 43, 51, 75, 102, 107, 109, 110, 114, 119, 121, 124, 126, 128, 129, 134, 147, 160, 205, 261
Rohy, Valerie, 52
Romero, George A., 16
Rope, 85, 89
Roth, Eli: see *Hostel*

Rudd, Paul, 27, 43, 51, 75, 99, 109, 116, 117, 121, 122, 123, 124, 128, 132, 136, 192

Sachs, Ira, 239
sadism, 49, 209
sadomasochism, 49–54, 209
Sanjek, David, 173
Santorum, Rick, 7
Sarah Connor Chronicles, The, 245
satire, 110
Saw, 78
Schiesari, Juliana, 102
Schwarzenegger, Arnold, 6, 32
Scream, 71–104
Scream 2, 93
Scream, The (Edvard Munch painting), 77–78
Seancody.com, 36, 41, 114, 200, 231
Sedgwick, Eve Kosofsky, 6, 103, 112, 147, 149, 160
Segel, Jason, 117, 126
Seltzer, Mark, 31
sentimentalism: male, 159–60
September 11, 2001, 31, 45, 46, 81, 153, 162, 167, 173, 197, 198
serial killer, figure of the, 22, 31, 44, 45, 48, 68, 148, 172, 174, 176, 179, 186, 205, 221
Seven, 221
Sex and the City, 9
Sexual Revolution, the, 32, 37
Shadow of a Doubt, 186
Shame, 135
Shary, Timothy, 8
Shaun of the Dead, 16
Shaviro, Steven, 247
Shock (Michael Ninn), 232
Silence of the Lambs, The, 68, 72, 85, 90
Silverman, Kaja, 3
Six Feet Under, 40
Smith, Angela, 145
Smith, Will, 14

Soderbergh, Steven, 10, 114, 135, 190
"Some Neurotic Mechanisms in Jealousy, Paranoia and Homosexuality" (Freud essay), 147
Source Code, 54
Spirit of the Beehive, The (El espiritu de la colmena), 193
Stallone, Sylvester, 6
Star Trek (2009), 35
Stiller, Ben, 25
Story of O, The, 50
Straight College Men, 41
straight masculinity: cruising, 11; new gendered uncanny, 138; sentimentalism, 159–60; *see also* masculinity
Studlar, Gaylyn, 18
Suddenly, Last Summer, 219
Superbad, 15, 34, 101, 102, 105, 106, 119, 120, 121

Talented Mr. Ripley, The (film), 40, 138
Tarantino, Quentin, 203
Tasker, Yvonne, 13, 19
Tatum, Channing, 12, 245
Taxi Driver, 38, 117, 158
teen comedies of the late '90s, 33, 41, 72–75, 101, 109, 110–13
television, 2, 9, 14, 16, 17, 32, 50, 59, 74, 76, 113, 133, 141, 169, 171, 235, 239, 241; Reality
temporality, 31, 36–42, 68, 186; *see also* historical masculinity
Terminator: Genisys, 32
Texas Chainsaw Massacre, The, 16
There's Something About Mary, 25, 74
This Is the End, 110
Thousand Plateaus, A, 49
Three Essays on the Theory of Sexuality, 89
Tiny Furniture, 260
Tony Manero, 38
torture, 46, 205; torture of nonnormative male, 51, 188–89, 218

torture/porn: defined, 201
Town, The, 57
transgender identity, 4, 6, 30, 68, 114
Traffic, 165
Trejo, Danny, 176
12 Years a Slave, 39, 240

Ulrich, Skeet, 86
"Uncanny, The" (Freud essay), 62

Vertigo, 18
victim-monster, the: defined, 219–23
Videodrome, 98
voice, cinematic (Chion's theory), 237
voyeurism, 17–19, 30, 43, 52, 53, 74, 103, 113, 201, 225, 226
vulgarity, 110

Walking Dead, The (AMC TV series), 14, 16, 45, 239
Warhol, Andy, 251
Washington, Denzel, 14
Waugh, Thomas, 200, 237
We Need to Talk about Kevin, 16
Weeks, Jeffrey, 6

White, Edmund, 163
White, Susan, 18
whiteness, 63, 66, 156
Wild One, The, 111
Williams, Linda, 21, 72
Williamson, Kevin, 93
Willis, Sharon, 13
women: faces, 55; female ethnographic observer, 114; heteronormative standards, enforcing, 123; sexual cries in pornography, 235; triangulated desire and, 149
Wood, Robin, 3, 62, 71, 80, 94, 123, 150, 243, 265
Wordsworth, William, 63
World War Z, 16

"Young Goodman Brown" (Hawthorne story), 33

Zimmer, Catherine, 201
Žižek, Slavoj, 146
Zombie, Rob: see *Halloween* (2007)
Zombieland, 16
Zoolander, 25

Made in the USA
Columbia, SC
23 October 2017